D1555131

OUR MAN IN MEXICO

Our Man
in
Mexico

Winston Scott and the
Hidden History of the CIA

JEFFERSON MORLEY

Foreword by
MICHAEL SCOTT

 University Press of Kansas

A version of chapter 21 first appeared in the October 1, 2006, issue of *Proceso*, the Mexican newsmagazine.

Portions of this book have appeared in different form in the *Washington Post, Salon, Washington Monthly,* and *Miami New Times.*

All photographs from Michael Scott's archive, except where noted

Published by the University Press of Kansas (Lawrence, Kansas 66045), which was organized by the Kansas Board of Regents and is operated and funded by Emporia State University, Fort Hays State University, Kansas State University, Pittsburg State University, the University of Kansas, and Wichita State University

Library of Congress Cataloging-in-Publication Data

Morley, Jefferson.
  Our man in Mexico : Winston Scott and the hidden history of the CIA /
Jefferson Morley ; foreword by Michael Scott.
     p.   cm.
  Includes bibliographical references and index.
  ISBN 978-0-7006-1571-1 (cloth : alk. paper)
  1. Scott, Winston, 1909–1971. 2. United States. Central Intelligence Agency—Biography.
3. Intelligence officers—United States—Biography. 4. Intelligence officers—Mexico—
Biography. 5. Spies—United States—Biography. 6. Spies—Mexico—Biography. 7. United
States—Foreign relations—Mexico. 8. Mexico—Foreign relations—United
States.   I. Title.
  JK468.I6S376 2008
  327.1273072092—dc22
  [B]

British Library Cataloguing-in-Publication Data is available.

Printed in the United States of America
10 9 8 7 6 5 4 3 2 1

The paper used in this publication is recycled and contains 50 percent postconsumer waste. It is acid free and meets the minimum requirements of the American National Standard for Permanence of Paper for Printed Library Materials z39.48-1992.

Covert operations are important, illegal manipulations of society done secretly.—*John Whitten, CIA official*

Now I was sitting in the middle of it, in the best position to sniff the breezes of office politics and well placed to discover the personalities behind the faces that passed me in the corridors.—Kim Philby, British intelligence official and Soviet spy

If the United States is to survive, long-standing American concepts of "fair play" must be reconsidered. We must develop effective espionage and counterespionage services and must learn to subvert, sabotage and destroy our enemies by more clever, more sophisticated and more effective methods than those used against us.—General Jimmy Doolittle, U.S. Air Force

Ye looked for much, and lo, it came to little.—Haggai 1:9

Contents

Two photograph sections appear following pages 96 and 246.

Foreword

For those who know the history of American espionage, Winston Scott was a legendary figure, one of our best intelligence warriors during the long Cold War with the Soviet Union. For those who worked closely with him, he was a hardworking, talented, and congenial colleague, who had climbed the ladder of success by dint of his own sweat and smarts to become a station chief in one of the CIA's most important postings—Mexico City. But, for me, he was simply my father, my dad.

Given the nature of his work and how often it kept him away from our home life, it took a while before the two of us could connect. Eventually, however, I got to know my dad in my early teens, and I remember those years with a great deal of affection because of his determined efforts to take me under his wing and develop a real father-son relationship with me. All that began in 1968, around the time I turned thirteen. I remember him supervising my first driving lesson and frequently inviting me to accompany him to the office when he worked on weekends, even though it was never quite clear to me what that work actually was. It seemed to be very important, I assumed, given the important people he knew and dealt with, including the Mexican president and other government dignitaries.

During that period, the last few years of his life, we spent most of our time and had our best times together on the golf course, with me only driving the golf cart at first, and later graduating to become his partner in a foursome. Gradually, our relationship deepened, especially during the summer of 1970 when I worked for him as an office assistant. Later that fall I left home to attend boarding school, where I endured many moments of homesickness because of how close we'd become. While there, I received letters from him every week without fail. Then, the following spring, he died.

Despite my best efforts to be stoic in the face of his death, it hit me very hard. The sudden absence of such a larger-than-life and reassuring figure from my life, right after we'd begun to grow quite close, was devastating at some level, even if I didn't let on at the time. But as the years passed and as I found out more about my own life and a little bit about his, whatever sorrow I felt was replaced by a strong desire to better understand who my father was and what his own life and work were all about. His presence in my life was still intense, but the essential nature of that presence seemed shrouded in mystery, made all the more intriguing by my discovery that Dad had written a memoir that the CIA refused to release to our family, let alone the public at large. That revelation drew me back to my father and sent me on a very personal quest that has now taken more than three decades, led to my collaboration with Jefferson Morley, and produced the book that you are about to read.

My quest often took on a life of its own, fueled by an urgency to document recollections of his friends and associates before they passed on. At the same time, that quest was infused with a lot of anxiety about what I would likely find by digging so deeply into the past. I knew enough about the darker side of the CIA to have reason to worry that my exploration would unearth some fairly unseemly aspects to my father's life. So, I was definitely concerned that any such discovery might undermine my own idealistic view of him. I also wondered if I had the right to expose secrets that he had intended to take to the grave. But my longing to understand him, to get to know him better, was so great that ending my quest prematurely was never an option.

As a son, I'm still not sure that I have done the right thing. Only time and the reactions of others will tell. Dad himself might be less than thrilled with this book, since it delves into his personal affairs and exposes agency operations that he may have chosen to keep secret. But it's the product of my sincere effort to reconnect, to build upon and extend the close relationship we'd forged just before his death, even though he's no longer with us. It was something I had to do and, by doing so, I have finally gained some long-awaited and much-needed closure. For that, I am grateful.

Michael Scott
October 2007

Acknowledgments

Michael Scott's persistence, creativity, and candor in pursuing the story of his father's life made this book possible. He did an awesome amount of research before we ever met. I am grateful to him for trusting me with the story. Any errors of reporting are mine alone.

The original idea of writing an article about Michael's efforts to obtain his father's memoir came from his attorney Mark Zaid more than a decade ago. Mark also played a key role in bringing about the publication of this book and has been generous in sharing his files on Michael's lawsuit against the CIA.

I am grateful to all the people who took the time to talk to me, especially Anne Goodpasture, Helen Philips, Tony Lanuza, and the late Peter Jessup, whose stories and humor are missed. My aunt, Lorna Morley, encouraged me early with tales of her days at the CIA.

I am indebted to the National Security Archive in Washington, D.C., for my education in how the national security system really works. Scott Armstrong, Tom Blanton, and Peter Kornbluh are my professors. Kate Doyle gave succinct guidance on Mexico and arranged for the publication of a version of chapter 21 in the Mexican newsweekly *Proceso* in October 2006.

Francesa Jessup's interest and encouragement helped sustain me over the long haul. The confidence shown by David Talbot inspired me. Tony Summers provided a key suggestion and much more. Jorge Casteneda's enthusiasm and suggestions were a blessing, as was Gerald Posner's spontaneous support. Steve Mufson and Ken Silverstein never doubted the mission. Nesti Arene kept the computer going. Elias Demetracopoulous gave wise counsel.

Paul Hoch, the dean of the JFK researchers, commented on drafts with droll economy. Peter Dale Scott offered provocative interpretations that challenged my thinking. Frank Snepp and Michael Kurtz offered thoughtful comments that made the second draft a big improvement over the first. While writing this book, I was lucky to make the acquaintance of the aptly named Malcolm Blunt, whose hobby of perusing JFK assassination records provided me with countless documents that I never would have found otherwise. Rex Bradford, the genius behind MaryFerrell.org, the definitive online archive for JFK documents, commented on early drafts of these chapters and answered many obscure questions without hesitation or error.

Margot Williams, researcher extraordinaire, assisted in finding long-lost people and documents. Dick Russell provided me with several interviews of people who had died. Jan Earwood, Michael's cousin, shared photos of Win's early days. The chapters involving British intelligence benefited from e-mail comments by Nigel West. Larry Keenan shared his recollections and a chapter from his own manuscript. Larry Hancock shared thoughts and documents on David Phillips. Gus Russo tipped me off to a key document.

I want to thank the archivists who helped me navigate complex document collections to find the material I was looking for. At the National Archives in College Park, Larry McDonald guided me through the records of the Office of Strategic Services. Esperanza de Varona facilitated my research in the Cuban Heritage Collection at the University of Miami's Richter Library. Jennifer Cuddeback made my short visit to the LBJ Library in Austin a productive one. Leigh Golden helped me with the Norman Holmes Pearson Collection in Beinecke Library at Yale. David Linke did a gratis search of the Allen Dulles Papers in the Seely Mudd Library at Princeton.

My sons, Diego and Anthony, showed heroic patience with my various excuses for spending too much time at the keyboard. My wife, Teresa, made this book possible by never letting me lose sight of the big picture: that Michael Scott's story about his father had to be told.

Prologue: April 28, 1971

The day after she buried her husband in Mexico City, Janet Scott opened the front door of her house to find herself looking into the face of a man she loathed. James Jesus Angleton doffed his homburg and entered. He wore a black suit and a white shirt. Another man in a suit trailed him.

Janet Scott had known Jim Angleton for many years and rarely liked him. He had been a longtime friend of Scottie, as she called her late husband. Like Scottie, Angleton was a big deal in the CIA, the chief of the agency's Counterintelligence Staff. Janet knew why Angleton had come. He wanted something. Scottie had served for thirteen years as chief of the CIA's station in Mexico City, the largest office of U.S. intelligence operations in the Western Hemisphere and a frontline post in the Cold War against the Soviet Union. He wanted Win's secrets. Angleton's admirers thought him brilliant. Others shared Janet's keen distaste. Win's assistant, Anne Goodpasture, who had also worked at Angleton's side for several years, said Angleton was "weird, loosely put together," and she was not just talking about his gangly frame. Janet Scott's opinion was harsher. She told one of her sons that Angleton was a "drunken idiot." She underestimated him.

"Why did it take so long for you to come?" she asked sarcastically.

Angleton mumbled words of regret that Janet did not believe. He said the director, Richard Helms himself, sent his condolences, his regrets . . . that all of Win's friends . . . his service to his country . . . you know how sorry . . . the benefits to which you are entitled. . . . Angleton's hands were expressive. His aquiline face, made sallow by the years, featured brown eyes glinting of a morning martini and much more.

Janet Scott was a handsome woman, forty years old, with olive skin, dark hair, and an air of bemused impatience. She wanted to be alone with the shock of her husband's sudden passing, and now she had to deal with this man.

"Of course our current information is tentative," Angleton coughed. He was talking about her benefits. Angleton was a master of arcane subjects, including CIA regulations. He wanted to refer her to competent staff from the legal counsel's office—"to ensure every advantage for your self and your children."

Janet had been around the CIA long enough—twenty-plus years—to recognize the sheathed blade of a polite threat: do what we say or we will cut off Win's pension. We have our ways of getting things.

"Did Win have a will?" Angleton asked.

"I don't know," she said. "I don't even know who Scottie's lawyer or executor is."

"Could you find out," he nodded at the man trailing him, "and let John know?"

God, how she hated him. It would have killed Scottie to see Jim Angleton in his house, in his living room, calling with his condolences.

"I have an unpleasant task," Angleton went on. "There were some papers."

Janet did not respond.

"Were you aware that Win was coming to Washington to see the director about his book?" Angleton asked.

"I knew he had written something," Janet countered. She was surprised Angleton knew about the book. "I haven't seen it," she said.

"You didn't read it?"

"He asked me to type it," Janet sneered. "I told him to go hire a girl."

"Janet, you do *not* want to read what Win wrote," Angleton said, as if doing a favor.

"Why not?"

"It discusses, in an open way, intimate matters of his first marriage."

Janet had thought the book a bad idea from the start, but Win considered himself a writer so. . . .

"The information in there would, if it was made public, violate two different secrecy agreements that he signed. Damn it, Janet, this is important. It would do great harm, grave harm, to our relationships with other governments, with some of our closest allies. Win wouldn't want that. It would disturb his friends."

Janet feared this bureaucratic ghoul. He looked like a man whose ectoplasm had run out.

"It would harm his reputation and his memory."

"I knew something was wrong when he told me he was going to see Helms," she said. "Why do you think he wrote it?"

"We want the manuscript," Angleton said. "All the carbons and any other papers he might have brought home. Where is his office?"

He must have talked to Anne Goodpasture, Janet thought. She must have told them about the stuff Win had squirreled away.

"Over there."

Janet nodded at the door that led to a side garden beyond which stood the converted garage that served as Win's private study.

"It's locked. No one goes in there. Not even to dust."

"Do you have the key?"

"It's somewhere," she said. "You can have everything."

She didn't want problems. She had bigger things to think about. Angleton did not force his advantage.

"Perhaps when John here comes back tomorrow, you could . . ."

Angleton nodded at his sidekick, John Horton, the chief of the Mexico City station whom Janet knew and rather liked.

"We want the manuscript and any classified material he kept."

Janet could take no more. They could have their damn papers. Angleton bit off some more condolences. She showed him the door. The awful man was gone but not soon enough.

Thirty-five years on, Win Scott's son, Michael Scott, had elusive memories of the day his father died.

"I think it was a Monday, a Monday afternoon." It was indeed Monday, April 26, 1971. Michael was fifteen years old. He was a "mid," meaning a tenth grader, at the Taft School, a comfortably white Anglo-Saxon Protestant institution of red brick and ivy in the stately countryside of western Connecticut. His father, Win, short for Winston, was back in Mexico City. After serving for thirteen years as the first secretary in the U.S. embassy there, Win had retired to run a consulting business, where Michael worked in the summer.

"Everybody at Taft had to have an extracurricular activity, so I worked at the Jigger Shop, a little student-run cafeteria thing, off on the other side of campus," Michael went on. "I made hamburgers and milkshakes. Between three and six P.M. if you weren't doing sports, that's where you'd go. Or after sports, that's where you'd go, to hang out. Somebody came in and said you're wanted in the dean of students office."

Michael set off on the long walk across campus. When he arrived at the dean's office, who should join him but his long-haired stepbrother, George Leddy, also fifteen years old and a "mid."

In middle age George Leddy would have a different file of memories of what all agreed was a miserable day. Michael, a filmmaker, remembered events and images. George, a political activist, remembered feelings and situations. They had enrolled at Taft the previous September. For both, the exclusive boarding school marked a huge change from Greengates School, the unpretentious British day school that they had attended in Mexico City.

"Until I got to Connecticut, I didn't know that rich people lived in wooden houses," George quipped. Dark-haired, observant, and easygoing, Michael had no trouble making friends. He joined the hockey team. George broke an ankle and became the projectionist in the campus film society.

Michael could not remember exactly what the dean said, but it was something like, "'We got a call from Mexico and we have some bad news. Your father died.'"

Michael remembered a moment of denial.

"I remember thinking, I didn't really hear it that way. I didn't quite hear it as he had died. I thought he was probably in the hospital or something, you know. And I guess they clarified it. He was dead. I don't remember asking any questions. I think George and I just kind of listened."

Michael was the only son of a loving man. His mother had died when he was seven years old. His father had remarried and, for that time, remained an attentive dad. Win had given him his first horse, his first camera. He taught him how to golf. He gave him his first job as a messenger boy at Diversified Corporate Services, the consulting business that Win had set up after his retirement. Now that Michael was away at school, Win wrote a letter every few days without fail, full of family news, advice, and encouragement. If Michael did not feel emotional about the news of his father's death, it was because he could not imagine life without him.

George's feelings for his deceased stepfather were more complex. His mother, Janet Graham Leddy Scott, had divorced his father when he was six years old. He rarely saw his real father. For a long time he felt like Win was the ideal stepfather, strong-willed but caring and sensitive. He and his mother occasionally waged loud arguments punctuated by slamming doors, but that was it. Win tutored him patiently in math and taught his sister, Suzanne, how to ride horses. But he missed his real father, who lived back in the States in Carlisle, Pennsylvania.

"I had emotional issues around not knowing my dad," George Leddy said. "I remember thinking, 'What would it be like if I lived with my dad?'

My mom didn't talk him up as an interesting or nice person. If she got mad at me, she liked to say, 'I'm going to send you to live with your father.' My dad at that time was working for the United Nations and the U.S. Army War College in Carlisle, Pennsylvania. She portrayed Carlisle, where he lived, as stifling, and she was probably right. She was critical of middle-class American life. She wanted us to have a more cosmopolitan, international upbringing."

In the dean's office, Win's death did not make much sense.

"We sat there shell-shocked," George said. "I was very anxious. I remember thinking, 'This isn't supposed to happen.'"

Michael only recalled the dean saying, "'OK, you're dismissed now.'"

George's brother John, attending Fairfield University in Connecticut, was supposed to come pick them up and drive them to the airport. "Amazingly, we did not get it together in time," George said. Michael thought they took a wrong turn on the highway to New York. George thought they never left Connecticut. In any case, they missed their flight to Mexico City. They arrived at the house a few hours after Jim Angleton had left.

Gregory Leddy, Michael and George's oldest brother, had been first to hear the news. He was twenty-two years old, fresh out of college, and teaching English in Mexico City. He had gotten the call at work from his aunt. "It's about Scottie," she said. "Is he dead?" Gregory asked, already knowing the answer. Gregory went straight home to the two-story American-style ranch house at Rio Escondido 16, a gated roundabout in the Lomas Chapultepec section of western Mexico City. His mother was in a daze. His stepfather's body lay behind closed doors in his bedroom. Gregory listened to Bink Goodrich, a family friend who served as Win's lawyer, tell the world that Scottie was dead. Goodrich was on the phone with a reporter, saying, "Winston Scott died of a massive heart attack."

Gregory already knew that Win was not the First Political Officer at the embassy, as he sometimes said. He knew that his stepfather actually worked for the CIA, that he was, in fact, "station chief," a very important person in the Mexican scheme of things.

"I thought, 'massive heart attack?' Where did he get massive?" Gregory recalled years later. "He had no way to know. In fact, where did he get that it was a heart attack?"

Gregory's mother, Janet, did not say much. Scottie had keeled over as they talked at the breakfast table, she said. She had gone into the kitchen to check on the eggs when her mother, the *abuelita,* sitting at the table with Win, suddenly shouted. Janet came back into the room to see Win's head slumped forward.

"I knew he was gone," was all she could say. "As soon as I looked, I knew."

Michael, George, and John arrived the next day from Connecticut. They had missed Win's funeral. Mexican law required burial within twenty-four hours of death. Win had been laid to rest that morning among the hedges of the narrow central pedestrian boulevard of the Panteon Americano. Michael barely remembered going to the cemetery that afternoon. George recalled it well. Seeing the grave was no comfort. "I remember how crowded the cemetery was, how close together the gravestones were," he said. Win's stone was not complete. George did not like the scene. The smoky steel apparatus of a Pemex oil refinery looming over the north wall of the cemetery somehow discouraged contemplation. George was worried about Michael—would he stay with the family now that his father was dead? Were they going to be able to stay at Taft? He wanted to talk to his mother, but Janet Scott had other things on her mind. Like what was in Win's study that the CIA wanted so bad?

In his later years, John Horton would swear it had all been Janet Scott's idea. In April 1971, Horton was relatively new to the station chief job. He said that Win Scott's widow had voluntarily given the agency everything that her late husband possessed in the way of agency records, that Jim Angleton did not have to pry anything out of her hands. In Horton's account, freely shared with colleagues in later years, it was Win's wife who had called him. She told him that Win had died. He came immediately to express regrets and help her in any way possible. "Janet had one urgent request," Horton wrote in a cable to headquarters, "and that was that I retrieve the files in Win's study." He admitted that some might say the agency had "pulled a fast one" in taking away Win's personal papers. He feared people might conclude that Angleton sought to hide "some vile knowledge on the part of the agency," perhaps "damning evidence" about the assassination of President John F. Kennedy eight years earlier.

It wasn't so, Horton insisted.

After Angleton's departure, Horton returned the next day to the Scott home on Rio Escondido and spent several hours behind the locked door of Win's study. Janet shooed away various people who had come calling. Her children came and went with no inkling that there was a visitor in the study, much less one from the CIA. Horton was "amazed" at what he found though he didn't specify why. The haul included a plethora of secret files, including tapes and photos of accused presidential assassin Lee Harvey Oswald visiting communist embassies, and the unpublished memoir of a CIA man whose career spanned the era from the Blitz of London to the Tet Offensive. When no one was looking, Horton lugged three large cartons and four suitcases to an unmarked truck parked at the curb. The contents of Win's home office were shipped by plane back to CIA headquarters in Langley, Virginia.

The agency had taken possession of Win Scott's personal correspondence, including letters about his children's schooling; travel itineraries; medical claims; credit union correspondence; financial records; appointment books for the years 1967, 1968, and 1969; assorted pages from his appointment books for the years 1957, 1961, and 1963; and at least one short story, entitled "A Time to Kill." There were extraordinarily sensitive tape recordings. From Win's safe, Horton obtained a stack of eight-square-inch reel-to-reel tape boxes. One tape was marked "Black Panthers." Another was labeled "Lesbians." The biggest batch, a stack of tapes three or four inches thick, was marked "Oswald."

The treasure in the trove was a 221-page manuscript entitled "It Came to Little." The story that Win Scott told in those pages displeased and disturbed his longtime friends in CIA headquarters, including Angleton and the director of Central Intelligence himself, Richard Helms. Helms and Angleton were the two most powerful men in the American clandestine service. Both had known Win for more than twenty-five years. By snatching up the only two copies of the manuscript, Horton thought the agency had dodged a proverbial bullet.

"Think worst has been avoided through Angleton's persuasiveness and Mrs. Scott's good cheer," he cabled Washington that day.

When Michael and George and the other children returned from down the street, Janet said nothing about the visit of the CIA man. They did not need to know. A week later, Janet told family and friends, she found a handwritten note from Win to Helms in the unlikely location of her late husband's sock drawer. The note read, "Dear Dick I will completely follow your wishes about publication." Janet was relieved and gave the note to John Horton to show that Win was not intending to do anything behind the agency's back.

George was worried about Michael, and he could not figure out how to talk to his mother. He was worried his stepbrother would be cast adrift.

Janet was too devastated to talk to her son.

"She wasn't as reachable or accessible as I hoped," George recalled. "I had my emotional needs, a lot of confusion, a lot of guilt."

Janet was focused on Michael. The weekend after his father's death, she summoned her sixteen-year-old stepson to her bedroom. Her brother Alec

Graham, who lived in Mexico City was there. He was now Michael's legal guardian. Janet had to break some difficult news to Michael that Win had always avoided.

"You need to be aware of something," Janet said. "Your father never told you, but you should know that you were adopted."

Uncle Alec took up the story.

"Your father had another son from a previous marriage, and there's some concern that he may claim part of the estate, and if he does so, we want you to know that he exists out there," he said.

Michael was stoic. He had seen a picture of a boy up on a shelf in Win's office. He had heard mention of someone named Beau. He wasn't surprised. Adoption seemed to be the bigger deal to his stepmother and uncle. They seemed to be worried that he would be disturbed by the news that he was adopted. Michael was not fazed.

"I played it completely like 'Yeah, so?'"

Michael laughed at his teenage bravado, but it was true. He was the son of an intelligence officer, after all. He had figured out the secret of his adoption years before Janet's disclosure.

"I had had hunches about being adopted," he said. "There was always talk among the Leddy kids about them knowing something about me that I didn't know. I didn't really care. I think everybody else made it a much bigger issue than I did. I was already in boarding school, I was entrenched on my path."

Michael went on to attend Occidental College in Los Angeles, majoring in film with a minor in Latin American studies. He realized "the outfit" his father had worked for was the CIA. He learned about how the agency had overthrown the government of Jacobo Arbenz in Guatemala in 1954. He heard his stepmother tell the story of Jim Angleton's strange visit and the disappearance of Win's unpublished life story.

What Michael did not know about his father, he would eventually learn, would fill a book. He did not know that his father had been present at the creation of the CIA, served as the first chief of station in London, and became one of the agency's top officers worldwide; that he had been friendly with Kim Philby, the genial British diplomat and closet communist who was among the most audacious and effective spies in the annals of espionage; that his father had overseen the surveillance of accused presidential assassin Lee Harvey Oswald just weeks before the assassination of President Kennedy; that he had recruited a generation of Mexican politicians, including three presidents, as his paid agents; and that he had received one of the agency's highest honors upon retirement. His father, he came to understand, embodied as well as anyone the rise of America's Central Intelligence Agency as a force in the world.

Michael did not know much of this because Jim Angleton had purloined the only copies of his father's life story as Win himself wanted to present it. As Michael's quest to recover his father's story deepened and expanded, he began in effect to write the book that his father never published. Michael was fascinated by his father's story, and he knew that he did not know the half of it.

Act I

London

I

Up from Escatawpa

The Central Intelligence Agency, it is said, was built by two kinds of Americans: men of the Ivy League and men who were one generation from the plow. Allen Dulles and Win Scott embodied the epigram. They first met in London a few weeks after the end of the war against European fascism in May 1945. They warmed to each other's style and remained close friends for the next twenty-five years as the CIA grew into a worldwide empire of violence, propaganda, influence, and power.

Dulles was the pipe-smoking epitome of the American spy. He came from the educated elite, which was not quite the same as the American aristocracy of money. He had grown up in Watertown, New York, the son of a very middle-class Presbyterian minister in a family imbued with the ideals of public service. His grandfather had served as secretary of state for President Grover Cleveland. His uncle held the same job for President Woodrow Wilson.

Win Scott was the charming personification of the provincial striver. He grew up in a house made out of discarded railroad boxcars near the border of Alabama and Mississippi. His grandfather knew the handle of the cotton plow the way Allen Dulles's grandfather knew a diplomatic pouch. Win was not one of "the very best men," those CIA officers from the East Coast who lived in the leafier neighborhoods of metropolitan Washington and, later in life, gave interviews to selected reporters and historians about the glory days of U.S. intelligence. He was not a son of privilege, nor did he ultimately land in Washington's more posh precincts. He lacked the superior humanistic education and subtle social advantages that delivered Dulles and other well-bred friends into positions of power unreachable by men of more humble circumstance. But Win Scott proved that there was another path to power.

Michael Scott only began to understand the full dimensions of his father's story fifteen years after his death. By then Michael was a documentary filmmaker in Los Angeles with steady work on *Unsolved Mysteries* and other popular TV shows. But as he dug deep into other people's histories, he started to have the feeling that he was avoiding his own unsolved mysteries. Now a father, he felt the loss of his own father more keenly. He could barely remember his mother, Paula, and there was so much he did not know about his family. Who was his mother? What did his father really do in "the outfit"? How did his parents come to adopt him? Why had the agency seized Win's manuscript? What did it say that was so secret? And what did the manuscript say about Win himself? Michael's wife, Barbara, from a large, loving midwestern family, encouraged him. "You have a right to know where you came from," she told him.

Michael decided he would seek to recover his father's unpublished memoir. His stepmother, Janet Scott, hated the idea and discouraged him, but Barbara supported him. He wrote a letter to the CIA, describing what he knew of his father's career and expressing an interest in getting a copy of the manuscript. He was rewarded with an invitation to come to CIA headquarters in Langley, Virginia. On a work trip to Washington, Michael took time out to go to the massive marble building hidden by trees. He passed the injunction "The Truth Will Set You Free" in the lobby, and was escorted to a higher floor. In a conference room, he found himself in an amiable chat with two men, an agency spokesman named Lee Strickland and a "senior" agent who did not share his last name. They spoke highly of Win, of his great reputation and his many contributions to the agency. They said they were glad to share with Michael what they could of his father's story. They pushed a fat envelope across the table. Of course, one of the suits said, some portions had to be withheld on grounds of national security.

"Like what?" Michael asked.

"Well, there was the Lee Harvey Oswald business," one of them said. "Oswald visited Mexico City a few weeks before President Kennedy was killed. That's very sensitive. There are sources and methods which have to be protected. By statute."

Oswald? Michael's imagination was tickled. He thanked them profusely. He was looking forward to finally reading the story, and did not really care if a few secrets had been left out. The senior suit said he would escort him to his car. Outside in the parking lot, the man took a confidential tone. Michael had been expecting a pitch to join the agency. The man said he was retiring soon and had a story to tell. Did Michael have any Hollywood contacts who might be interested in his screenplay?

Michael drove away laughing. Curiosity instantly got the better of him, and he pulled the car to the side of road and ripped open the envelope. He flipped through the papers. Many had whole paragraphs blacked out. Some pages were almost entirely blank, with only a single sentence left uncensored. In between were white sheets for different chapters that said "[Deleted in entirety]." Out of the 220 pages that his father had written, the CIA had given him barely 90. They told the story of the first thirty-five years of Win's life, from his birth to the day he put himself in harm's way for his country. The rest had been blanked out. His search for the real story of his father's life, he realized, was not going to be easy.

Winston MacKinley Scott was born on March 30, 1909, in Jemison, Alabama, a small town in the piney woods northwest of Mobile. His father, Morgan Scott, was a teetotaling Baptist, jolly at times, fond of playing guitar and retelling his favorite jokes. His mother, Betty Scott, the daughter of a preacher, was a strong-willed disciplinarian. Morgan had started out as a tenant farmer working bottomland acreage along Escatawpa River and its tributaries. In 1915, he got a job with the Louisville and Nashville railroad company, working as a section hand on a gang that maintained the L&N tracks. In time he became the foreman of the gang, which included both black and white workers. The Scotts lived right next to the tracks where Morgan worked. Passenger trains sped by a dozen times a day, churning up the sound of a metallic tornado that they learned not to notice. Occasionally, Win and his brothers and sisters would see Special Excursion trains go by with well-dressed people headed for the University of Alabama football games. During the week, they walked three miles to school in the nearby town of Brookwood. On Sundays, attendance at the local church was mandatory.

Win later wrote a fictional first-person memoir that described a different, more romantic childhood, in which the narrator grew up in rural Alabama, raised by a single father who entrusted his care to an African American nanny named Amy. This Alabama boy came of age with his nanny's twin sons, MacGee and MacGill, who were his best friends. In Win's happy tale, they were a carefree trio of mischief makers, clever and adventurous, who ran rampant among the houses, churches, schools, and nearby Escatawpa Swamp. They stole watermelons, tormented stray cats and schoolteachers, harassed drunks, devised schemes to make money, suffered innumerable whuppings, sneaked into church revival meetings, pondered the difference between boys and girls, and generally had themselves a good old time. At every chance Win's fictional alter ego escaped the tedium of school and church to pursue the pleasures and possibilities of the less regimented Negro world. The only hint in Win's tale that he might be destined for a life of international intrigue came at age thirteen. In a bout of boredom, the three boys decided to run away and join the French Foreign Legion so they might go off to fight pirates and the like. The trio hitchhiked to New Orleans, where they planned to get on a ship that went to France. They did not get very far before they were stopped by a kindly policeman. There was a phone call, and they were sent home. A few months later, the boys turned fourteen. The iron tradition of Jim Crow was applied. Black and white boys could not associate as they approached manhood. They could never be friends again.

Janet Scott thought her husband's childhood stories exaggerated and wishful, depicting a life of carefree, color-blind camaraderie that he wished he had, not the strict and conventional childhood he actually had. "I think things were a lot tougher in his childhood than he let on," she told Michael once. In Win's fictional story, his grandmother, appalled by his friendship with the black boys, insisted he be sent to Virginia for preparatory school. In reality, Win's family had educational aspirations but not the means for a prep school. The local high school in Brookwood was not accredited, so in his junior year, Win had to go live with an aunt and uncle in Bessemer, the sooty steel factory town southeast of Birmingham. There he excelled in math and sports and won a scholarship to attend Livingston Teacher's College in Birmingham. He applied himself to algebra in the classroom and devoted his free time to sports. He dated a classmate, Besse Tate, who was studying education. One Thanksgiving, they took the train home, and Win told his father to fetch the justice of the peace. They wanted to get married. His father said that sounded like a right fine idea to him, and he would attend to it. No, Win said, now.

"Winston insisted that my father walk over to Brookwood to get the justice of the peace," Win's younger sister Ruth recalled decades later. Then just a little girl, Ruth watched the domestic drama in awe. "My mother used to laugh about that. She wanted them to wait until the morning. She said, 'We have plenty of space for you to stay.' But they insisted. So my father walked over to Judge Murray's house and brought him back to marry them. Mama woke us kids up to see them get married at four o'clock in the morning. I loved Win. I was this little girl and he was my giant big brother who could do anything, go anywhere. I thought he could paint the moon."

Win found a happy routine of sports and numbers. He and Besse would teach in the winter, then come home in the summer. He took more classes in mathematics at the University of Alabama at Tuscaloosa and played semi-professional softball in his free time. With two incomes, they lived comfortably in the hard times of the Great Depression. In his later years Win dropped occasional hints of his baseball prowess, and with his physical grace they were believable. But he rarely let on that his game was softball. He preferred to give the impression of rougher pursuits.

Win had a knack for numbers. He earned a master's degree in math with a thesis on "roulettes" and became a math instructor at the University of Alabama. He played more softball and unraveled more equations. Starting in 1938, he traveled north every summer to the University of Michigan to pursue a Ph.D. in algebra. His impatient father increasingly thought him a "fancy pants" who was avoiding a real job. As he approached the age of thirty, Win could not avoid the question of what he was going to do when he grew up.

Fortune and the FBI found him. One of his mathematical papers, which concerned the use of matrices in coded communication, was published in the *Annals of Mathematics*. Win argued that one coded message could be based on two different matrices, better to thwart any potential code breakers. The publication came to the attention of J. Edgar Hoover, the director of the Federal Bureau of Investigation in Washington. Hoover knew that America's enemies might be trafficking in coded communications. Although having only the dimmest comprehension of Win's algebraic artistry, Hoover's aides sent word into the field. An FBI agent contacted Win and asked him if he might be interested in applying for a job.

Would he? Win regarded Hoover as the greatest living American. He quit his baseball team and got ready to move. But the FBI never got back to him. There was no job. Win got over his disappointment by taking a fellowship to study matrix theory in Scotland. He sailed across the Atlantic and quickly fell in love with the charms of ancient Edinburgh and one of his fellow students, a tiny, shapely, and beautiful Jewish mathematician from Germany named Anita. She touched him so deeply that he decided to leave his wife.

"She had the brightest eyes, which were very black and almost always very shiny," Win recalled in the uncensored portions of his unpublished memoir. "Most of the time, her eyes looked as if she had just washed them with something which gave them a special glossiness. . . . Anyone who looked carefully into her eyes knew immediately that she was brilliant, lively and profound. . . . At times, I saw fear, felt she was still haunted by some deep-seated feeling that all around her was not right. She probably feared that a Nazi would appear, grab her and torture her, treat her as so many of her people were then being treated."

Win had a romantic streak that he would never lose, an impulse to love in spite of social conventions and marital vows.

"Perhaps it was a deeply imbedded fear which I thought I saw in her eyes which made me want so much to love her," he wrote, "and perhaps this fear made it possible for her to make love with me. For she said several times that life was too short and pleasures too infrequent and fleeting for her to worry about whether it was right or not for us to make love."

Win wanted to divorce Besse and marry Anita. But Anita's parents, while fond of him, could not approve of a marriage to a gentile, he recalled. The spread of war across Europe imposed travel restrictions on Americans living overseas, and Win had to return to the States. Back in Alabama he moped for a couple of months. His marriage was stale, his softball career kaput. His career prospects were limited to teaching math, and he had no desire to do that. He felt like an "overeducated failure" who had failed his father.

"Perhaps, I thought, I should just stay home, be satisfied with being a farmer and forget all those years, wasted years of hard and continual study," he would later write. "I knew that I would have to kill many things inside me, destroy memories, forget things learned and remake myself internally to be able to become even an apparent farmer. I knew that I would never be happy; but, I was certainly not a contented man in my present rudderless and confused state."

"So I decided after some additional thinking . . . I would tell my father that I had given up any hopes of teaching and give up any additional study and become a farmer. I thought I would tell him that I wanted to help him make some improvements, some I had heard him dream of making on the farm—and I believed he would be happy with this decision."

Win was rehearsing the doleful speech when a telegram arrived from FBI headquarters in Washington. He had belatedly been accepted as a Special Agent. He was expected to report to the Department of Justice on March 17, 1941. He sped out of Alabama. On his arrival in the nation's capital, Win and his twenty-five fellow trainees had the privilege of seeing J. Edgar Hoover in the flesh. Decades later, Win could still recall the details of Hoover's passion for order and hierarchy.

"We were asked to align our chairs carefully, sit as if at attention, look straight ahead and wait quietly," he said. "Meanwhile, all the shades were adjusted to the same height—and some three young men examined the lines of the chairs, had corrections made in these alignments and saw to it that everything was clean and shipshape."

"Mr. Hoover appeared and we rose as one man, applauded loudly until he had reached the lectern and signaled us to stop. He then welcomed us to the finest organization in the world, told us that he would get to know each and every one of us and expressed his great appreciation for our spontaneous applause." Hoover told his new charges that they would be on duty twenty-four hours daily, each and every day of the year. The work would be hard and trying. For Win, it was a formative moment. "It was so obvious that Mr. Hoover himself was willing to work as hard as any one of us; that he was so proud of the Bureau and its achievements; that he was giving his entire life to this essential work for our country; that every man in the group was touched, deeply moved."

After his training course, Win asked not to be assigned to the Cryptography Section. He wanted to be a Special Agent, he said, not "spend my time trying to break anagrams on the Post Toasties Box Tops," which, he noted, was about as sophisticated as FBI cryptography got at that time. Hoover, he was told, "heartily approved" of this rather cheeky request. Win was sent to Pittsburgh, where he kept an eye on the local German population for Nazi sympathizers.

With the Japanese attack on Pearl Harbor in December 1941, America went to war. The FBI, with its network of offices throughout the Caribbean and South America, had the job of keeping track of Germans in Latin America as well. In February 1943 he was loaned out on "Special Confidential Assignment" to the U.S. embassy in Cuba, an unusually rapid promotion. Win loved wartime Havana at first. He served as assistant to the embassy's legal attaché, an FBI man named Raymond Leddy, and liked him immediately. Leddy was a trim, correct man, a native of New York City and a product of the finest Jesuit schools: Xavier High School, Holy Cross College, and Fordham Law School. Astute about FBI office politics, Leddy spoke fluent Spanish and moved with ease both in the world of the embassy and among the Cubans. He took Win to the jai alai arena and introduced him to the famous writer Ernest Hemingway whose leftist political sympathies made Leddy suspicious. The bearded novelist's alcohol-fueled reports of German submarines in Havana Bay had become the gag of the office. Win rented a room in Leddy's tidy seaside house in the Miramar section of Havana, and their friendship grew. "He was well-educated, had good, even if accented, Spanish—and he had a car. He has proved to be one of my best friends; and we have kept in contact," Win wrote, though there was much, much more to the story than that.

With Americans fighting in Europe, Win started to worry. "I felt that I was not doing all that I could," he recalled. "I was young, strong and healthy;

and I felt Americans in Cuba looking at me, wondering why I was allowed to walk around Habana in civilian clothes when I was not even in the Embassy." One day, while playing baseball with some embassy employees, he heard spectators saying he must be a draft dodger. Against Leddy's advice, he wrote to Hoover requesting a leave of absence from the FBI to enlist in the marines. In November 1943, the answer came back with good news and bad news. Yes, he could take leave, but first he was being transferred to Cleveland.

Win traveled to wintry Cleveland and told his superiors he was going to war. He stopped in Alabama for a last passionate reunion with Besse, then took a train to Washington to enlist. He was rejected because of an injury from his days on the softball diamond. He then enlisted in the navy—and was immediately assigned to a desk job in a radar research laboratory. In his first day on the job, his supervisor told him he would be there for the rest of the war. Win had jettisoned the FBI but wound up as far from the frontlines as ever.

He retreated to the bar of the Wardman Park Hotel on Connecticut Avenue. He bought himself a drink, and who should show up but a friend from FBI training school who was already in the navy. Win complained about his assignment. His friend said he had just been posted to England, thanks to a man named Jimmy Murphy in something called the Office of Strategic Services, or OSS. Win should talk to them. Win said why not. The friend telephoned Murphy, who was still working at his desk at nine in the evening. Murphy—a wise, low-key Irishman from New York City—stopped by the bar on his way home.

An athletic former FBI man who knew something about cryptography? Murphy liked the cut of Win's jib. He asked him to apply to the OSS and bought another round. The next day Win went down the Mall and filled out the application. He had no doubt he could handle high-level responsibilities. "My scientific training and university background make it possible for me to mingle with University leaders who, in Latin American and European countries, play important roles in political affairs," he wrote.

If J. Edgar Hoover had rescued Win from farm life, Washington's wartime meritocracy delivered him into the OSS, the embryo of what would become the Central Intelligence Agency. At the time, the OSS was a small outfit with a big reputation as an enterprise dominated by liberal Ivy Leaguers. (OSS stood for "oh so swish," some joked, or "oh so socialist," said others.) OSS had been formed just two years earlier, the brainchild of William Donovan, a hero of World War I who went on to work in the Justice Department and then to establish a lucrative law practice on Wall Street. Headstrong and politically ambitious, Donovan became convinced in the 1930s that the rising power of Nazi Germany would sooner or later force the United States to go to war in Europe. Donovan had the ear of President Franklin Roosevelt. FDR thought much the same thing but did not dare say so publicly. A solid majority of Americans wanted no part of another European war. Even as Hitler annexed Czechoslovakia and attacked Poland, the Congress and most Americans held themselves aloof from Europe's problems. FDR did what he could to aid the British war effort. Pushed by Donovan, he started to create a foreign intelligence service.

FDR arranged funds for Donovan to open an office called the Coordinator of Intelligence. By 1940, the Nazis had rolled into France, unmolested by French martial valor, such as it was. The British had suddenly lost their intelligence networks in Europe's central capital and soon faced a daily barrage of Hitler's V-1 rockets. Roosevelt saw the good sense of Donovan's ambition to create an American intelligence service that would serve as the eyes and ears of the military forces needed to roll back Hitler's ambitions to dominate Europe. Donovan, in turn, visited the best universities, starting with Yale, recruiting professors who knew how to collect and organize information. Then he arranged for those scholars to learn from the British, who had been playing the intelligence game for centuries.

The British connection was key to the formation of Donovan's operation. London's Secret Intelligence Service, known as SIS, had been founded in 1909, but the kingdom's tradition of covert organizations that collected information and acted in a clandestine manner to advance political ends went back at least as far as the royal court intrigues of King Henry VIII. Over the centuries, British police forces in the far-flung British Empire built their own tradition of intelligence collection. In India, the Caribbean, and the Far East, British officers practiced the black arts of clandestine politics, necessary to anticipate political subversion and sustain their domination of much larger native populations. In time, the British embraced imperialism as a national trait and right. In the twentieth century, they developed the SIS and local constabularies as institutions and instruments of power.

The Americans, of course, were not uninitiated in the projection of power. The young republic, led by a brash young general named Winfield Scott, had annexed half of Mexico in 1846. Fifty years later, the United States had ousted Spain from Cuba and the Philippines and went on to subordinate the Central American republics from afar throughout the first half of the twentieth century. But the military, political, and commercial forces that propelled these adventures disdained colonialism and avoided the chores of administering what Americans increasingly called their "backyard." The United States did not seek to rule directly like a traditional empire. Instead, Washington ceded local control to strongmen, brutal with their own people but compliant with Washington.

Congress provided Donovan with $10 million in "emergency" funding in 1941 and then $35 million in 1942. Over the objections of J. Edgar Hoover and the War Department, Donovan was granted the right to siphon off men and women willy-nilly from the other armed services, eventually taking on some 13,000 people who were stationed around the world. The Office of Strategic Services, as Donovan dubbed his enterprise, was launched in London, where a series of offices collected and analyzed information, organized secret operations against the Germans and countered their espionage efforts. From the Brits, Donovan knew enough to know that this last function —counterespionage or counterintelligence—was essential. He chose Jimmy Murphy, a slim, quiet lawyer who had worked for him at the Justice Department, as his counterintelligence chief.

From the moment they met in the bar of the Wardman Park Hotel, Jimmy Murphy thought Win's mathematics background might contribute to code-breaking efforts in England. He sent Win for three months of training in the Virginia countryside. While he was there, his wife, Besse, wrote to say she was pregnant. In June 1944, Win was off to war. As the Allied forces landed at Normandy to take back Europe, he arrived in London to join the burgeoning OSS operation. He was assigned to work at Bletchley Park, an ugly mansion on an estate in north London that the British secret service had taken over a few years earlier.

In temporary huts thrown up around the grounds, Win listened to British and American lectures on the nature of espionage. Espionage was directed toward compromising the enemy's security of communications. Counterespionage (or counterintelligence) was devoted to penetrating the enemy's intelligence service. He learned that their Secret Intelligence Service, known as SIS or MI6, had a domestic counterpart, the Security Service, or MI5, the equivalent of the FBI. The former collected intelligence in countries that did not belong to the British Empire and conducted counterespionage to prevent other powers from learning about its secret operations. The latter conducted counterespionage, countersabotage, and countersubversion operations within the empire.

After hours of indoctrination, Win quaffed warm beer with the Brits. He marveled at their stoic good humor, urbanity, and effortless generosity amid conditions of widespread scarcity and more than a few moments of naked fear. As he wrote years later, the British "took the American neophytes . . .

into their own offices and shared almost everything they got in the way of intelligence and counterintelligence with us."

Win thrilled to spend a few weeks at another makeshift intelligence office headquartered in Blenheim Palace, the ancestral home of the Dukes of Marlborough and the family of Prime Minister Winston Churchill. Although the Tenth Duke of Marlborough remained in residence, the rest of the premises were all but taken over by MI5. Win was sent there to learn the art of honorable treachery from His Majesty's finest. On one occasion his British mentors drafted what they thought was a brilliant project and received permission to present it to Churchill himself. They let Win tag along.

Win and his British colleague, Tommy Robertson, took the train to London and a taxi to the prime minister's residence. Robertson dressed in his handsome Scottish Black Watch colonel's uniform, complete with Highland troos, as such trousers were called. He "was very nervous," Win recalled, "and I was even more shaky, as we walked through the halls, past the guards at 10 Downing Street. We were finally admitted into the Great Man's private office; and he received us with a grunted welcome."

Churchill was a prodigious worker in wartime, reading hundreds of pages of material a day, before going home to drink and write his own books. He did not suffer fools gladly or otherwise. Win's colleague made a brief speech and handed over a one-page summary of the proposed operation. "Mr. Churchill read it, slowly; and I thought, with great interest," Win recalled. "Then, without a word, he reached for his pen—and I thought he was ready to sign it without a question. . . . Mr. Churchill then drew a line diagonally across the entire sheet of paper, wrote the word 'Balls.' " Churchill handed the paper back to the interlopers and returned to the more serious matters on his desk. Win and Robertson hastily retired to a local pub for a drink and a quick decision not to tell anybody.

Within a few weeks, Win's training was deemed complete. He was sent to London to work in the counterintelligence office of the OSS, known as X-2, a sly reference to its secret agenda of double-crossing the enemy. The X-2 was located in a drafty office block off St. James Square in central London. Hitler's rockets had decimated scores of buildings in the neighborhood. Buckingham Palace, the London seat of the king of England and still standing amid the Nazi barrage, was a ten-minute walk to the west. Ten Downing Street was a similar jaunt to the east. The headquarters of MI5 were right across St. James Street. Win had finally arrived where he wanted to be: in the thick of the war effort. He had come a long way from the house made of boxcars and the Escatawpa Swamp.

2

The Apprentice Puppet Masters

They made a handsome couple, the American serviceman and the Irish model strolling down Park Lane on the evening of September 4, 1944. At thirty-four years of age, Winston Scott, a junior grade navy lieutenant, stood six feet tall, weighed 185 pounds, and had blue eyes, brown hair, and a ruddy complexion. By his side was Paula Maeve Murray, a dark-haired twenty-four-year-old former track star from Northern Ireland. They had first met at the flat in Berkeley Square that Win shared with John Hadley, a gregarious Californian who served as his assistant at the Office of Strategic Services where they worked. Hadley introduced Win to Paula. For him, at least, it was a case of proverbial love at first sight. "I shall never recover, believe me," he told her a year later, "and am sure that it is not now possible for me to ever be the same."

It was a propitious moment for Anglo-American romance. The Allied armies' return to continental Europe on D-Day had proved a smashing success. As General Dwight D. Eisenhower drove his legions eastward across France, in Westminster, Prime Minister Churchill felt increasingly confident that the insolent Nazis were doomed. The invasion had routed Germany's rocket launching pads in Belgium, apparently ending the siege of the deadly V-1 missiles on the British capital. Many dared to hope the war would be over soon, within weeks. In the night sky over Hyde Park, Win and Paula saw a shooting star. Despite the fact that he already had a wife and infant son back in the States, Win took the streak of heavenly light as a portent of true love. Paula did not.

Win fell in love that day and became a spy the next. The following day, on September 5, 1944, he took over as chief of the Germany section, the largest section of the X-2 office on Ryder Street. He shared quarters with British colleagues in Section V of MI5, the British intelligence office in charge of thwarting the German spies. As an entry-level job in the intelligence profession, Win's new post was hard to beat. In his British colleagues, he had the ablest intelligence mentors in the world. Their cleverness astounded. They had figured out how to intercept the communications of the Germans and Japanese armies. Win began to learn about the supersecret ULTRA program, which monitored and deciphered the communications of Germany's various military intelligence services. Using ULTRA intercepts, the British had captured literally every German agent in the United Kingdom. Instead of imprisoning them, they "doubled" them—forced them to send a steady flow of plausible but bogus reports back to Berlin. For example, the Abwehr, the German military intelligence, was told by its British-controlled agents that their missiles were consistently overshooting their targets in London. The Germans naturally programmed their rockets to fly a bit a shorter—and thus fell short of London, doing less damage. In this and a myriad of other ways, the British used ULTRA to covertly control the Germans' perception of battlefield realities. ULTRA was one of the most sensitive operations of the entire war, and Win was let in on it early. "He was trained by MI-5 and worked with [Kim] Philby in the early days. He had the ULTRA clearance, I'm sure," said Cleveland Cram, a colleague of Win's.

Win saw right away the difference between the American and British styles. Back in Washington, the tradition-bound U.S. Army and Navy had refused to give the OSS a role in procuring or analyzing enemy signals. The Joint Chiefs of Staff decreed that the Office of Naval Intelligence and the Military Intelligence Section would do the intelligence gathering. Thanks to Bill Donovan, the OSS secured a seemingly minor role in the war effort. The British would share "counterintelligence"—what they knew about the enemy's intelligence services—with selected Americans in the OSS's X-2 office. On this narrow patch of bureaucratic territory, the OSS took root. As a CIA historian put it, "Here was a field in which OSS would have otherwise been unable to participate effectively at all. The British provided files, sources of information, operating techniques, training, and facilities, which proved indispensable. It would have taken OSS perhaps decades to gain by itself the experience reached in only two years of British tutelage, and to build up the extensive files it was able to copy from British sources. X-2 swiftly became an elite within an elite."

Win thrived in this select company. The first assignment to land on his desk came from Bill Donovan himself. The OSS chief wanted to know about the Werewolf, an underground German fighting force thought to constitute the nucleus of a resistance movement that the retreating Nazis were going to set up to harass the advancing Allied forces. Win organized and passed along material collated from different battlefield sources. He titled his memo "Present and Future Prospects of Clandestine Resistance Movements in Germany" and downplayed Allied fears. Based on twenty-five penetration cases that counterintelligence units in the battlefield had reported over the summer of 1944, Win said that the Werewolf was not a postwar resistance scheme, merely an irregular force that had only sporadically engaged in sabotage, terrorism, and harassment. The Werewolf had no bite, Win wrote. It was, he said, "a failure."

A few days later, a new type of German missile, dubbed the V-2, smashed into a crowded London market, killing scores of people. The war, alas, was not going to end soon. Win and the gang on Ryder Street soldiered on. Besides John Hadley, Win had two secretaries to help. They were Bette Balliet and Barbara Freeman, known as the Gold Dust Twins for their blonde coiffures and complementary taste in clothes. Working conditions were wretched. "Due to sickness and sore throats due to crowded conditions we constantly have a large number of personnel on sick leave and persons staying away from their jobs who have slight colds for fear of spreading sickness throughout the whole office," Win's friend and boss Jimmy Murphy wrote to Washington. Top officers worked in rooms with six or eight typists or clerks banging typewriters and working on index files. "We must conduct our Indoctrination courses and our language brush-up courses in rooms which were constructed for storage space and which do not have any windows," he complained.

Win and his staff all worked in one large room with a fireplace. As winter approached, they were allotted exactly one bucket of soft coal per day to heat their work space. They dressed in long johns and overcoats, wore gloves inside, and still shivered throughout the workday, except when Hadley—"a miraculous scavenger," according to Win—could swipe something to burn. One day Hadley appeared carrying ten wooden toilet seats. Risking censure for looting, he lugged them back to the Ryder Street office, where he set them ablaze in the fireplace. "We warmed our hands and enjoyed a cup of tea while the salty seats burned with green, red, and yellow flames," Win said.

Win's job was central to the rear guard of the Allies' drive toward Berlin. He kept track of developments in Germany, Austria, Switzerland, Czechoslovakia, Poland, and Scandinavia. He absorbed and processed information from all these countries, as well as from "special sources," meaning the top-secret British intercepts of German communications. He and his staff prepared lists of German intelligence operatives, complete with capsule biographies and addresses, for all areas into which the Allies were entering. As the advancing Allied forces took German territory, they also captured German spies. They sent documents and interrogation reports back to Ryder Street for quick translation, synthesis, and analysis. Win then relayed the information back to the appropriate units in the field, and the whole process was repeated. From the start, Win's superiors recognized how smoothly he kept things running.

Win, however, was not the mostly highly regarded American in London / X-2. That distinction fell to the chief of the Italy desk, James Jesus Angleton, working in Room 23-B of the Ryder Street office. He was a Yale man, a bit odd but undeniably brilliant. He was younger than Win, a mere twenty-six years old, but canny beyond his years. His grandfather had founded the National Cash Register Company, whose machines rang up the surpluses of the American Dream. His father, Hugh Angleton, built NCR into a multinational corporation. Jim had grown up in Italy, went to boarding school in England, and matriculated at Yale, where he studied indifferently and poured his energies into producing a world-class poetry magazine. Upon graduation he spent a year at Harvard Law School but dropped out. With the help of one of his Yale professors, he dropped into the OSS and quickly discovered its peculiar demands suited his voracious curiosity and intellectual personality. His section was smaller than Win's. He had only one secretary, a young woman named Perdita Doolittle. Their office, clouded with smoke from Angleton's ever-present cigarette, consisted of two desks, two chairs, and two green filing cabinets. Jim's work was much the same as Win's. He identified and targeted fascist intelligence assets and reviewed interrogation reports. He was more intellectual than Win. He had, in the words of CIA historian Burton Hersh, "an aesthete's suspicion that everything he encountered could ultimately be interpreted in a variety of ways, few innocent." His superiors appreciated his "passionate meticulousness, the instinct to chew something twice and taste it three times."

Rubbing shoulders in the hallways of Ryder Street, Win and Jim soon became friends. They had a lot in common. They both had wives back home whom, truth be told, they did not always miss. Cicely Angleton, a vivacious Vassar graduate, was in Arizona taking care of their son, James Jr., and wondering if their marriage would survive Jim's episodic disinterest. Besse Scott, a schoolteacher, was back in Alabama with their newborn son, Winston Jr. Like Angleton, Win had never laid eyes on his namesake. Both men had restless, well-trained, and acquisitive minds that were grasping the challenge of intelligence work, feeling its power and importance, and recognizing their own attraction to it. But their most important bond was their unlikely mentor, a short, slightly stooped Yale professor named Norman Holmes Pearson.

Pearson was Jimmy Murphy's deputy, one of those Ivy Leaguers recruited to learn and teach the arts of intelligence. He came from a comfortable Massachusetts clan that prized book learning. He had been an honors student at Yale, earned a couple of graduate degrees at Oxford University in England in the 1930s, and then returned to Yale to get his doctorate for his dissertation on the Italian notebooks of Nathaniel Hawthorne, the American transcendental novelist and short-story writer. Norm, as his pals called him, had just moved into a junior professorship at Yale when the war came. A colleague invited Pearson to join the OSS. He was assigned to the newly formed X-2 office in 1943 on the justified guess that his bookish erudition would make him sympathetic to the sometimes snobbish Brits. Pearson became Murphy's liaison to the British intelligence agencies. As Pearson absorbed the British way of organizing intelligence operations, he applied the analytical skills previously devoted to American fiction to the no less profound nuances of spying. He distilled what he learned into a series of concise lectures on the intelligence profession, which he then delivered to successive classes of OSS recruits. As Win and Jim heard these lectures during their training days, Pearson's precepts became part of their professional DNA and would influence their actions for decades.

Professor Pearson thought the potential of counterintelligence was underestimated. "It is my opinion that counter-intelligence unfortunately has been viewed with respect to its objective as having what I shall describe as a negative or passive character, and as a result activities carried on within this field are inclined to be defensive rather than offensive in purpose," he declared, the words underlined in his lecture notes. That was a mistake, Pearson said. As a tactic, counterintelligence was no more inherently defensive than, say, the counterattack in military action. It could have an offensive character if assigned that goal. The key was the double agent.

"It is the use of the double agent that gives to counter-intelligence activity this ultimately offensive character," he said. The job was not deception as much as perception. "The suborning of an agent in the employ of another country, for example, requires imagination, a thorough knowledge of the racial and individual psychology of such a person, and the ability to plan a strategic battle of individual personalities," Pearson said.

One must exploit human frailty, he said. "The counter-intelligence officer must find the 'controlling point of vulnerability' of his potential contact.

This 'Achilles heel' of a potential contact must of necessity be psychological and therefore the search to uncover and understand it must proceed on a psychological basis." Pearson admitted the task was not easy. "The predominant motivation becomes more complex and abstract [as one grows up]. Undoubtedly the predominant motivation may change periodically during adulthood but at any given point in time there is always the more powerful, the more important, the controlling incentive, the satisfaction of which results in a particular course of conduct."

The exploitation of the double agent's ambiguous motivation was the key to successful use of the "hidden hand" that would invisibly manipulate events in the global Anglo-American empire of influence. Once the counterintelligence officer properly manipulated the "controlling point of vulnerability," Pearson insisted, he (or she) could control the future actions of an individual "as effectively as a marionette handler controls his puppets." Norm Pearson knew how to pull strings. He was the brainy professor who doubled as a puppet master of espionage. Win Scott and Jim Angleton would prove to be his most able apprentices.

Win's and Jim's lives outside the office were minimal. Angleton had a bleak flat in Paddington Station but often slept on an army cot in the office when he was not traveling to the X-2 offices in Paris and Rome. Win was not as single-minded. In his off-hours he continued to court Paula Murray with mixed success. Paula came from an accomplished family. Her father ran a successful business and served as judge near Belfast. He arranged the best possible education for all his seven children. Paula had been sent to the Loreto Convent in County Bray at a time when it was quite unusual for a girl to go to boarding school. She went on to Queens University in Belfast, where her brothers studied law. An honors student throughout, she also excelled at sports. Her teammates dubbed her "Legs" because her shapely extremities gave her speed afoot. Health problems forced her to abandon her pursuit of a social science degree: an operation in her late teens for tuberculosis had left her debilitated. When she recovered, she came to London and enrolled as a student at a well-known fashion school, the Lucy Clayton Model Agency. She lived with her sister Deirdre on Hill Street, off Park Lane.

Win started visiting the apartment frequently and she sometimes chafed at his attentiveness. In November 1944, Paula shunned him because of what Win described as "one of our little misunderstandings." Perhaps inspired by the poetic bent of his new friends Pearson and Angleton, he took to writing verse about his unrequited passion.

I walk alone. Slowly. No hurry.
Nobody's waiting. My love, who loved me (she said), is gone.
My love is gone.

Jim Angleton was not detained by love. In November 1944, he was sent to Italy. The youngest OSS man to run a station, he proved adept at translating Pearson's teachings about offensive counterintelligence into action. The concept, again, came from the British: a small team of counterintelligence officers would take highly classified information into the field and act on it. But the British ran what they called Special Counterintelligence (SCI) units conservatively, noted one OSS study of the subject. They believed that "these units should fill a narrow and specialized role and merely interpret and make available to the military 'Most Secret' material." British soldiers would actually do the arresting and the interrogating.

"The American SCI units, by contrast, have had to prove their usefulness and in the process have often been called upon to do general security work," the memo noted. In Rome, Angleton was soon running double agents and overseeing interrogations of captured German intelligence officers. Angleton's intellectualism honed a practical operational style. He organized a team of operatives to mount a leafleting campaign to deter Italians from cooperating with German intelligence. "These leaflets contained the pictures of executed agents with the description of their treatment and were distributed with a very noticeable effect," said one admiring colleague. Angleton's unit, known as SCI/z, launched a series of raids and captured all sixteen known Italian intelligence assets known to be working in Florence.

If Jim excelled in the field, Win excelled in the office. He got along better with the British officers of MI5 and MI6, even better than Pearson. Although respected by his British counterparts, Pearson was a scholar at heart. He liked nothing better than to talk poetry over tea with Hilda Doolittle, the mother of Angleton's secretary and a highly respected poet known by her initials, H.D. Hobbled by chronic back ailments, he could scarcely ride a bike. To the bluff former colonial policemen who manned the upper ranks of SIS, Win proved a rather more sympathetic bloke. By day, he was a courteous gentleman with just a whiff of the genteel American South. At night he gravitated to the pubs, loved his mild and bitters, and, as some embarrassing passages of his memoir disclosed, indulged in his share of drinking and whoring and brawling on the darkened streets of wartime London. The combination endeared him to his British counterparts, most notably Tommy Robertson, the huge MI5 officer of Scottish extraction. Pearson soon ceded more liaison duties to Win.

The winter of 1945 turned snowy and bitter cold. Bottled milk froze on the stoops of London. The V-2s continued to lay waste to people and property. The task at hand for X-2 was huge: merging the OSS and MI5 counterintelligence operations into the Supreme Headquarters of the American Europe Forces in Paris. The idea was to incorporate the collection and analysis of German intelligence services directly into Eisenhower's battlefield command structure, the better to kill or capture Abwehr officers as the Allied forces rolled east toward Berlin. In January 1945, Eisenhower asked the heads of OSS, MI5, and MI6 to establish a joint Counter Intelligence Bureau in London to furnish information and advice to the Counterintelligence Staffs on the war front. The director would report to Eisenhower's assistant chief of staff heading the G-2 intelligence section. The operation, dubbed the War Room, was turned over to Tommy Robertson, who took on Win as his deputy.

The collaboration of the British and American counterintelligence services was growing ever tighter. The mission, as Win outlined it in a memo, was to "provide a central clearing house, registry and point of co-ordination for information passed to it by CI staffs and the 'Special Agencies,'" meaning OSS and MI5 and MI6. The job was to produce "personality cards." These were colored index cards with names, addresses, and biographies of German intelligence officers, which would be used to create personality reports. The War Room would furnish the battlefield counterintelligence units "all information likely to assist them in seeking out and arresting wanted individuals" and "commentary and advice on interrogation reports."

Win's bosses praised his "skillful personal negotiations with the highest officers in American and British intelligence." He displayed "an unusual combination of intelligence, imagination and tact" as he "maintained the most cordial relationships with the German Section and Double Agent Section of British Counter Intelligence" and ensured "a constant flow of information from them for the benefit of the American Armies." In a letter of commendation, his superiors said, "The high degree of cooperation between the American and British Counter Intelligence Services has perhaps never been equaled in the history of collaboration between Allied services." In career terms, though, Win remained a half step behind Angleton. Jim was chief of X-2 for all Italy. Win was effectively the number two man in London / X-2, the largest of all the OSS offices.

The question Win had addressed in his report on the Werewolf recurred: How would the Germans respond to defeat? Would the Allies have to fight a guerrilla war? Or would the Germans surrender? As British and American forces rolled toward the Rhine and the Red Army advanced from the east, the world was about to find out. From Switzerland, Allen Dulles, the avuncular chief of the OSS office in Bern, played up the possibility of a Nazi retreat to mountainous southern Germany. There, he swore, die-hard partisans of National Socialism would wage a war of resistance from an Alpine redoubt, which he invariably described with the Swiss word *reduit*. Given his excellent sources in the upper reaches of German society and government, the *reduit* scenario had a lot of credibility. It also reflected Dulles's own political predilections. As a corporate lawyer on Wall Street, Dulles had represented many important clients in the German business world whom he knew as decent men uncomfortable with the Nazis' vicious anti-Semitism. In the cozy OSS office in Bern he had met other ordinary Germans who risked their lives to help the Allies defeat the Nazis. All along, he had thought that President Roosevelt's demand that Germany surrender unconditionally was misguided. Throughout the war, Dulles hoped for "separate peace" with the "good Germans" who disliked Hitler.

When emissaries of top German field commanders in the Italian theater approached Dulles in February 1945 with an offer of a separate surrender, he seized the opportunity. While careful not to act against U.S. policy, he made every effort to let the military high command in Washington know that he regarded the offer as genuine and worthy. He dubbed the secret negotiations to effect the surrender Operation Sunrise. He told anyone who would listen that it could help bring the war to a speedy conclusion. Otherwise, Germans would fight to the bitter end, resulting in a guerrilla war that promised to be as bloody as it was pointless.

The issue landed on Win's desk in the form of a draft report from the Research Analysis branch with the inevitable title, "The Alpine Reduit." Win circulated it to all the desks in his section for comment. On the one hand, the report was full of convincing details, like where the Nazis would actually retreat. Most of the reporting agreed "on the general area of the central reduit in South Germany and Austria. With Berchtesgaden as the HQ, the reduit would extend [northeast] to the mountains of the Salzkammergut, south to the Brenner pass, west to Voralberg." The research branch, however, saw no evidence that the Nazis' talk about the reduit was being accompanied by actual preparation. "The Nazis' effort to create a people's war have been unsuccessful," the report concluded. Win's reporting on the Werewolf from the previous September had not been significantly contradicted. But thanks to Dulles's persuasiveness, the "reduit" had taken root in the bureaucratic imagination.

The report concluded that "the concept of war to the end, and the area chosen for it, are both completely in line with the attitude of Nazi party leaders. . . . The combination of military defensibility, homeland love, and melodramatic setting that appears in the fight from a reduit in the Bavarian Austrian Alps is exactly what would appeal to the Wagnerian sense of Hitler and his closest advisers."

In fact, what might appeal to Germans and what they were actually doing in the face of defeat were two very different things. It turned out that there was no organization in southern Germany that possessed weapons, communications, and personnel to fight the Allied onslaught, only a few desperate officers who talked of such things. Some say the deployment of Allied troops southward discouraged such a coalescing. With the benefit of hindsight, "the Alpine *reduit*" seems less a reality than an instance of what sociologists would later dub "groupthink." Not for the last time, U.S. intelligence operatives had talked themselves into believing that what they thought *ought* to be true of their foes *had* to be true.

The collapse of German resistance swiftly rendered Operation Sunrise irrelevant. The end of the war came with a giddy rush in London in April 1945. The V-2 rockets finally ceased, and the weather turned warm. Whiskey was becoming more plentiful. Victory was nigh, and Americans in London sensed their dreams of home might soon be realized. Then came the sudden death of President Roosevelt. Two weeks after that, Hitler committed suicide.

Win was happy personally and professionally. On April 13, he jotted a note about his unseen son in his pocket calendar, "Winston 9 Months Old!!" On May 7, Win was formally promoted to assistant to the chief of the London/X-2 office. The big news of the day was in the banner headline in the *Times* of London: "End of War in Europe in Hand." The streets around the Ryder Street headquarters were thronged. Just a few blocks away, Piccadilly was decked with red and white and blue ribbons. The next day, Win dutifully attended two interrogation sessions. But by midafternoon the church bells were pealing, and the men of X-2 headed to Trafalgar Square.

Win's hero, Winston Churchill, appeared on a distant balcony. "God bless you all," the prime minister shouted. "This is your victory! It is the victory of the cause of freedom in every land. In all our long history we have never seen a greater day than this. Everyone, man or woman, has done their best. Everyone has tried. Neither the long years, nor the dangers, nor the fierce attacks of the enemy, have in any way weakened the independent resolve of the British nation."

The crowd roared back its approval. The gimpy Norman Holmes Pearson clambered up on a stone lion to get a better look.

"I rejoice we can all take a night off today and another day tomorrow," Churchill went on. "Tomorrow our great Russian allies will also be celebrating victory and after that we must begin the task of rebuilding our health and homes, doing our utmost to make this country a land in which all have a chance, in which all have a duty, and we must turn ourselves to fulfill our duty to our own countrymen, and to our gallant allies of the United States who were so foully and treacherously attacked by Japan. We will go hand in hand with them. Even if it is a hard struggle we will not be the ones who will fail."

Win Scott cheered. In the morning, he was back at his desk.

3

His Friend Philby

In middle age Michael Scott's search for his father became something more than a hobby, more like therapy but less expensive. The satisfaction and the insights came from the accumulation of details, from finding the tangible stuff of family bonds, and from discovering himself in his father's life. It was almost as if he was a spy, tracking down elusive leads and connecting dots of seemingly unrelated data. It took him many years, but in the late 1990s he finally followed up on something his mother had once mentioned to him: that Win had entrusted her sister with a trunk full of his old navy uniforms. In 1997, Michael asked his aunt if he could come take a look at the trunk. She said he was welcome to it. All he had to do was retrieve it from a storage facility in Pasadena, Maryland. Michael picked up the trunk on a beautiful summer evening and decided to open it on the spot. With a screwdriver, he popped open the lock on the trunk and lifted the lid, expecting to see a musty white sailor suit.

He found himself looking at paper, lots and lots of paper. There were letters, calendars, notebooks, file folders. He pulled out a fat envelope and looked inside. It was filled with neatly bundled letters. He slipped one out. "Dear Puggy," it began. It was a love letter from his father to his mother, Paula. His first mother. His first-known mother. He started to read and he was transported back more than a half century in time to bombed-out postwar London. In his father's and mother's handwriting came the story of a spy in love.

It was August 1945, and Win was miserable. Late one night he sat in his Berkeley Square flat composing a letter on the typewriter while listening to his favorite record on the phonograph. It was a wistful popular hit called "I Wish I Knew."

> I wish I knew someone like you could love me
> I wish I knew you place no one above me
> Did I mistake this for a real romance?
> I wish I knew, but only you can answer.
> If you don't care, why let me hope and pray so
> Don't lead me on, if I'm a fool just say so,
> Should I keep dreaming on, or just forget you?
> What shall I do, I wish I knew

The summer of 1945 that had started so full of peaceful promise had ended in desolation. The problem was not work. Win's standing at the office had never been higher. He had won a Bronze Star for his work in the War Room. His superiors described the London station as "the professional equal of its British counterpart" with "the organization and the trained personnel to carry on independently when the association with the British is terminated." When General Donovan came from Washington, he and Win dined at Claridge's, one of the poshest restaurants in London.

No, Win's problem—his personal crisis, really—was the lovely elusive Irish girl who welcomed and spurned his affection with equal ease. In early July, Paula Murray told him she was going home to see her family in Ballynahinch, a small town near Belfast. In the taxi to the train station, Win professed his love. She felt divided, saying she wanted to "ponder" things. He sent her off, filled with ardor. "You have, you know, the very bad habit of looking your most beautiful when you are most inaccessible—and at the station you were running true to form," he wrote a few days later.

He posted letters to Ballynahinch almost daily, giving her the pet name of "Puggy," in honor of her nose. He soared when she called and moped when she didn't. He told her he had to travel to the Continent for work and what he would be thinking about when he did: "Constantly, I'll wonder what your decision is: whether you are coming back to London and on what condition." The reality was that he was insisting she be his girlfriend while he was still married. A practicing Catholic, she balked. His efforts to be understanding only highlighted her conflict. "I do fully appreciate the necessity for you having your battle with yourself and deciding which side is the victor," he wrote.

When she stopped writing and calling, life grew lonelier. John Hadley had gone back to the States, and so had the Gold Dust Twins and most of the other Americans. Norm Pearson remained and invited Win to his house for dinner but the lovelorn spy was not consoled for long. The professor, with his zest for office politics and teasing meaning out of texts, loved to speculate about the emerging postwar story: What was going to happen to OSS now that the war was over? What would happen to its network of offices? Was the Soviet Union a worthy ally or an emerging threat? Win's mathematical mind, trained for precision, not conversation, was not aroused by such speculation.

Besides, Pearson could afford to talk. He could count on returning to Yale. Dulles had a high-paying position waiting at the white shoe Wall Street law firm of Sullivan Cromwell. Win's option was Alabama, where he would find a wife he did not love and would have to choose between the spiritual death of his father's farm, which he had barely escaped four years earlier, or the less than enthralling future of teaching the quadratic equation to teenagers. In Win's mental state, Paula Murray was not merely fetching, lively, popular, and challenging. She embodied what his life might be. Then Paula wrote that she would not return to London. She had decided to take a job at Supreme Headquarters of the American and European Forces, General Eisenhower's command post, in Paris. Win felt betrayed.

"Dear Puggy, you must remember how very many times we've taken vows to each other and how much I trust you and believe in you now. How could you, then, make a decision so important without waiting to discuss it? . . . I, of course, think now that there must be someone else."

She said she would write. She didn't. She said she would call. She didn't. Win watched a silent telephone until he fell asleep. "Never have I felt so completely whipped, beaten and utterly impotent," he wrote to her the next day. "Finally, I'm beginning to realize how thoroughly I've been fooling myself all these past months." And still he sought to win her over, promising to send along his weekly ration of cigarettes.

Without Paula's affections, London held little charm. He told her he had decided to turn in his application for immediate return to the States. He was pathetic, and he knew it. "I have a feeling I'm writing too often too much and know the letters are no good," he wrote. Still he could not stop himself. "Do you think me a 'whiner?'" he asked redundantly a few days later. "I'm sure you never realized I was so lacking in independence." He enclosed another poem:

A little thin moon scars the sky
Then I slept. . . . my arm around the emptiness of you beside me.

On September 4, the first anniversary of their meeting, he returned to Park Lane and shuffled about looking for the spot where they had seen the shooting star. Call it heavenly portent or hormonal understanding, but within ten days, Win and Paula were reunited. He wrangled his way onto a weekend military flight to Paris, and she agreed to see him. He took a train out to Versailles, where she was billeted with a bunch of unfriendly girls. She stayed home from work one morning and pounced on him. When he returned to London, he was still ecstatic at what had transpired.

"The time with you was wonderful, Darling," he wrote as soon as he arrived. "You are by far the most wonderful, sweetest person I have ever met." At the office, his desk was piled high with work and three letters from her. They were, he said, "wonderful letters, beautiful letters now that I've seen, talked to and been convinced that you do love me! . . . And to have you say you love me with all your heart is the most exciting reading I could have."

Win and Paula's volatile love had taken root.

At the same time, Win was falling under the personal and professional spell of his British colleague Kim Philby, who has been described without exaggeration as "the most remarkable spy in the history of espionage."

The story began, as so many would, in Win's in-box. Among the papers piled high on Win's desk upon his return from Paris was the unsettling news that the OSS would shortly be abolished. Back in Washington, the White House had drafted plans to liquidate OSS and other war agencies during the summer. In late August, President Truman rejected the lobbying efforts of tireless Bill Donovan and suddenly ordered that OSS be closed as soon as possible. Win trudged over to MI5 headquarters on St. James Street to attend a large meeting where the War Room was formally dissolved. The Brits discussed the repossession of their precious files from the OSS and their own reorganization efforts. The MI6 Reorganization Committee was headed by a senior civil servant whom Win knew casually through Norm Pearson: Harold Adrian Philby, known to all as Kim.

Philby served as chief of what was known as Section V, the office within SIS that was concerned with collection of counterespionage information from foreign countries. Win and Kim had first met when Philby lectured Win and other OSS novices in the summer of 1944. Philby was not impressed. The Americans "were a notably bewildered group," he later wrote, "and they lost no opportunity to tell us they had come to school."

What the Americans did not know was that Philby was working as an agent of the Soviet intelligence service. Some of Philby's colleagues in SIS knew that he had fallen in with the campus communists during his days at Cambridge in the early 1930s, but that youthful indiscretion was long forgotten. In 1945, Philby seemed to embody dowdy civil service competence. He dressed in perennial corduroy trousers and an old tweed jacket. Sometimes he wore an army bomber jacket, eccentric by British standards. He wrote incisive memoranda, drove his staff hard, and defended them loyally. He smoked a well-worn Dunhill pipe and drank martinis by the pitcher without visible misbehavior. He kept up a presentable family life with a brood of four children. His conversation, sparkling with a sharp but genial wit, was leavened by the humanity of an occasional stammer. Americans especially gravitated to his understated style, and he did little to discourage them. Philby thought Norm Pearson was "terribly funny" about the foibles of the notoriously slapdash OSS, whose initials, he joked, stood for "oh so sexy." Philby occasionally wandered into the OSS office on Ryder Street to share a laugh with Pearson or a word with Jim Angleton, to whom he took a shine.

This artfully constructed image of a conventional man on the rise concealed Philby's true political convictions. He had never abandoned his undergraduate belief that bourgeois democracy was but a facade for rule by the rich. He saw the Soviet Union as a better model for mankind than the United Kingdom or the United States, and saw that he could serve the cause of socialism by infiltrating the SIS. On the side, he met secretly with Russian intelligence officers assigned as diplomats to the Soviet embassy in London and passed along virtually everything he knew. His Soviet handlers referred to him in their communications with the Soviet intelligence headquarters, Moscow Center, by the code names SONCHEN and later STANLEY. With the end of the war, Philby turned his sights on the U.S. intelligence service. His first step was to cultivate Win.

Win was looking to move on. With the disbanding of OSS, the much-diminished staff of the London X-2 office vacated the Ryder Street building and moved to quarters closer to the so-called Broadway Buildings, where British secret service was headquartered. The remnants of the OSS were renamed the Strategic Services Unit (SSU). When Norm Pearson announced his intention to return to Yale in the spring of 1946, Win stood in line to succeed him as chief of U.S. intelligence in London. He foresaw a life lived around the world. He told Paula he wanted to take her away to sunny Latin America. "We will not always stay here, you know, and just now I am looking into the possibilities of our going to some place like Havana or Buenos Aires for a year or two at first; then probably we can head to the States forever—except for the very few days, in scattered years, which I'll give you in Ireland," he wrote. This fantasy was presumptuous. Paula did not dignify it with a reply. Still, she was the reason he remained. "He was so infatuated with Paula that he couldn't leave," said Cleveland Cram, an aide.

Jim Angleton, now OSS station chief in Italy, had worse woman problems. Recalled to Washington for a two-week consultation, he made a two-day layover in New York, where he attempted a reunion with his wife, Cicely. It was a disaster. "We just didn't know each other anymore," Cicely later recalled. "Jim was wishing we were not married, but he was too nice to say it. He thought the situation was hopeless. He was all caught up in his career. We had both changed. It was typical of a war marriage." Cicely was not unhappy to see him return to Europe.

One bit of good news for Win was that Kim Philby had come out on top in the postwar reorganization of British intelligence. The offices dealing with counterespionage and the Soviet Union were going to be combined into a new section run by Philby. Norm Pearson approvingly reported to Washington that Philby's office would "play a much larger role than before." And so the U.S. government first learned of one of the most astonishing coups in the history of espionage without understanding that what it thought was a welcome development was actually an astonishing betrayal. It would be more than four years before Win and Jim began to grasp the true implications of Philby's promotion. *Philby, a secret agent of the Soviet intelligence service, had taken charge of British operations against his employer.* And his best American friend was Win Scott.

Win and Kim spent the next few months preparing for their new assignments: Win was taking over as chief of the London station; Kim was becoming one of the top section chiefs in the British spy organization. On New Year's Day 1946, Kim was made an officer of the Order of the British Empire, just one rank below knighthood. Then he set off on a tour of MI6 stations in France, Germany, Sweden, Italy, and Greece to brief his new subordinates. Win worked a more leisurely schedule, waiting for Washington to sort out its intelligence priorities. He already had the air of a man on the rise. Tom Polgar, who went on to a long career in the agency, was a young OSS officer passing through London at the time, and Win loomed large. As he recalled in an interview, "Win Scott was, when I knew him, how shall I put it, a demigod, a navy captain, an FBI man with a Ph.D. in mathematics, one of the pillars of the original communications intelligence effort, very handsome, very much of a womanizer. We thought this was a real hero. I was, what twenty-three, twenty-four years old. I didn't know anybody more important."

Win organized the station along British lines. He had about a dozen employees working out of an office at 71 Grosvenor Street. A mattress store occupied the first floor and provided cover for the people coming and going.

The top floor was the MI5's "watcher service," which monitored radio communications. Win's station included an office that checked the background of people seeking entry to the United States. "A lot of them were refugees from Eastern Europe," recalled Cleveland Cram. "The office became the pipeline or channel by which we did a check with MI5 for security and Scotland Yard for criminal. A lot of people got turned down." There was a four-person Foreign Intelligence section which processed the raw intelligence flowing into the office and sent it back to Washington where reports were actually written. The finished reports were then sent back by cable and delivered to the British secret services. And finally there was a counterintelligence section, known as X-2, which sought to prevent penetration of U.S. intelligence activities.

When Philby returned from his tour in spring of 1946, he made his move on Win. He was under strict orders not to communicate with U.S. intelligence offices, so he had to convey his preferences privately. Over lunch, he asked Win if he might clarify the plans of the U.S. government. He had heard Americans saying that the SSU, the new name for OSS, would soon be history and its role would be taken over by the Office of Naval Intelligence or a domestic law enforcement agency like the FBI. Kim said he wanted to work with the OSS network on all counterintelligence matters of common interest. Philby much preferred the cosmopolitan OSS/SSU men over the uniformed military officers in ONI or, God forbid, the starchy, conservative G-men from Hoover's FBI.

Philby had his own private reasons for preferring to develop a relationship with Win. The SSU, if it followed the path blazed by the OSS, would be dedicated to secret intelligence and covert operations. It was sure to have more secrets of interest to the Soviet Union than a "ships and sailors" outfit like the ONI or a police agency like the FBI. Knowing the best way to get information was to offer it, Kim told Win that if Washington would establish SSU as the permanent lead U.S. intelligence agency in London, he would make sure that "certain materials," denied to SSU under the current bureaucratic dispensation, would be made available.

Win thought the request reasonable and wrote to Washington. In a long memo, entitled "London Station Status," he emphasized his friend Philby wanted "immediate clarification of our status; delineation of our jurisdiction. . . . In all conversations with British Intelligence personnel they have repeatedly stressed the need for more coordination of our intelligence services."

As politely as possible, Win said Washington's dithering about the organization of the intelligence effort had to end, lest he lose access to Philby.

"For the good of the American government the question of the status of our organization must soon be settled one way or the other; relations which are of extreme importance to American intelligence are not going to be possible to maintain unless we have definite status soon."

The question was settled within the year. The SSU was rechristened the Central Intelligence Agency and assumed the lead in relations with the British secret service. Win's relationship with Philby smoothed the way.

After Win finished his memo to Washington, he tried to call Paula without success. Dawn came and there was still no answer. He wrote her a note with no salutation, no pet names, just a wounded plea: "How can you be so cruel? Why not give me some word?"

As Win's romantic agonies deepened in the spring of 1946, so did his friendship with Philby. These developments were probably not entirely coincidental. Win needed a friend. He did not owe his rapid progress in the insular world of U.S. intelligence activities to superb contacts and political breeding, à la Allen Dulles, or to penetrating intelligence and intricate intrigue, à la Jim Angleton. He excelled at that most benign of the espionage arts, the art of making friends with people with different loyalties. His specialty was "liaison." He bonded with the British, knowing how to elicit their cooperation and secrets, despite the fact that they were self-interested and sometimes snobbish. He abstained from politics while smoothing over the inevitable conflicts and soothing the insufferable egos associated with the organized undertaking of secret and illegal activities on behalf of two very different sovereign states. At the same time, his American friends were slipping away. Jimmy Murphy, the man who hired him on first sight two years earlier, had been forced out of his job by the infighting of Washington. Norm Pearson, the ebullient egghead, had returned to the Yale English department. His wise counsel on office politics was now available only via the occasional gossipy letter. Ray Leddy had returned to the States to launch his own business, the North American Transatlantic Corporation, seeking to tap into the resumption of international trade. On the British side, Win's friend Tommy Robertson had resigned from MI5 to take the job as chief of security for the code breakers at the General Communications Headquarters (GCHQ). By default, Philby became one of the most familiar faces in Win's life at the very moment his life was getting more complicated.

If his girlfriend was elusive, his wife was not. Now that Win had accepted the job as head of U.S. intelligence in London, Besse Tate Scott decided she would join him. On July 10, 1946, she and Winston Jr. arrived on a flight from the United States. Win was delighted to see his son, now two years old. He was perhaps less delighted to learn that Besse called him "Beau," not "Winston Jr." as he desired. Win arranged to show the boy movies of Donald Duck and Mickey Mouse, which sent him chattering with delight. As his correspondence showed, Win still yearned for Paula daily, but she told him, in no uncertain terms, that she did not want him calling her. She left again to visit her family in Ireland. He wrote her a letter anyway. "My Darling Pug," he began. "This huge, sprawling, ugly place seems habitable when you're in it, near and 'reachable'—so barren, empty and lonely when it isn't possible to get in touch with you." When she returned to London, they started seeing each other again.

At the office, Win's lunches and meetings with Philby grew more frequent and friendly. They talked about how the American and British intelligence services might foment rebellion inside the Soviet Union. The Ukraine, where the Nazi invaders had found many willing collaborators, was thought to be especially ripe for intervention. They talked about how best to support the nationalist groups operating there. In the evening he and Besse occasionally had cocktails at Philby's house at 18 Carlyle Square in Chelsea. One afternoon, he took Beau to Philby's house to play with Kim's children of the same age.

Win and Kim each lived the private dance of a double life. Each understood that the other served the useful purpose of sustaining his own architecture of dissembling. Kim knew that Win's fellowship ratified his standing as the British intelligence official most congenial to the Americans. Win knew that Kim's hospitality sustained the so-called special relationship between England and America, not to mention his image as husband and devoted father. Yet for both men, the reality of their secret lives—Kim as Soviet spy and Win as Paula's sometime lover—commanded their every step.

Philby understood his posting as an SIS section chief could not last indefinitely, not if he wanted a promotion. He knew his track record needed filling out. "As all my work for SIS had been concerned with counterespionage at headquarters, I was obviously due for an early change of scenery," he later wrote. His time with Win had been well spent because he believed that the Americans, not the British, loomed as the Soviet Union's only serious rival. But if he wanted to get to Washington, he would have to accept the detour of a foreign assignment. At a morning meeting in December 1946, Kim told Win that he would soon depart to run the SIS station in Istanbul, Turkey.

Win, too, had a secret goal. He was living with wife, Besse, but constantly seeing Paula with the goal of making her his new wife. A few weeks later he paid a visit to Paula's flat, intending to ask her to marry him. Hoping to deliver a surprise, he received one of his own. There was a man in her bedroom. Win got mad, and Paula grew hysterical. She insisted the man was but "a distant admirer" who had burst into her room uninvited. Win later wished he had punched the man but did not. He excused himself, feeling defeated. The next day, Christmas Eve, he typed out another letter to Paula, coming to terms with his cluelessness. "Now that I stop and think, too, there are many things which were without explanation which seem now to be slightly more clear. For instance, the times when, on two different Saturdays, you arrived late and could not eat at lunch—I, stupidly, did not realize you had already lunched."

The mental clouds were parting, and he did not like what he saw.

"Also, the time you told me that I did not care whether you had coats and other clothes or not and even intimated that there were others who did care—and I, dumbly, failed to get the significance of the remark and had no idea there were others who had already proved they cared that much!"

It was almost painful for Michael to read about his father's ingenuousness. One can see how easily Philby duped him. If Win could not even pick up the most obvious hints dropped by a disenchanted girlfriend, he had no ability to guess, much less see through, the effortless deceptions of a man who risked a trip to the gallows just by showing up for another day of work. Philby was a creature of supernatural cunning, while Win's bright personality shielded no small measure of naïveté.

All the same, Win was alert to Philby as well. He had once attended a party at Philby's and found himself listening to a red-haired woman who freely expressed anti-American and pro-Soviet politics. He was surprised to learn she was Helena Philby, Kim's sister, who was also an SIS officer. Win was taken aback. He later mentioned the incident, verbally and in writing, to Cleveland Cram. "This encounter may have been the point at which, in the American secret circle, doubts began to form about Philby's own politics," wrote one of Philby's biographers. Cram always said that Win claimed his doubts about Philby dated back to meeting his sister in 1946. But whatever Win's qualms about Kim, they did not prevent him from seeing him often before his departure. One day they lunched at the American Club. On the weekend, they went to see an American-style football game. They bid good-bye at a martini-sodden farewell bash, and Kim left for Turkey.

Win started moping again. The weather was foul. Besse drank too much and embarrassed him on social occasions. Paula had gone off to New York on a modeling job and was not responding to his letters. About the only good news was a letter from Ray Leddy, a friendly punch on the arm from his old buddy from their days in Havana sending congratulations for his latest promotion.

"Dear Scotty," wrote Ray. "First let me salom three times, draw in the breath with a slight Japanese hiss and purr 'My Commander!' Delighted it came through for you Scotty, and would like to see how well that extra half stripe looks on the rugged arm of the former Slugger of Sock of Tuscaloosa."

Act II

Washington

4

Spies on the Rise

The friendship that grew up between Win Scott and Jim Angleton is evoked in an undated, scratched black-and-white photograph that Michael found among his father's personal effects. It shows the two men lounging in a garden in Rome, probably taken in 1946 or 1947. Angleton was the chief of the Rome station of the newly created CIA. Win was the chief of the London station. In the photograph, Angleton, lanky and broad-shouldered, sits cross-legged, arms draped across his long legs while leaning a confidential elbow on his friend's chair. He is penetrating, professorial, coiled, detached, and slightly askew. Win is more upright, open, and ingenuous. His round face, full cheeks, blondish hair, and little ears suggest the scion of a prosperous family. A handkerchief flaring from his breast pocket bespeaks attention to detail and appearances. He sits, slightly slouched, knees apart, hands splayed, a smile playing on his lips as if he has just given a command to the photographer to capture him at his best.

They were reunited in Washington in late 1949. Angleton returned from Italy to take the job of chief of Staff A, the foreign intelligence branch of the CIA's Office of Policy Coordination. OPC handled "special operations"—the euphemism of the day for sabotage, subversion, psychological warfare, and all manner of dirty tricks. Win worked in the Office of Special Operations (OSO), which had responsibility for secretly gathering information, that is, espionage. Some of the Ivy League types in OSO, living in a world of cables, dossiers, and index cards, resented the rise of the more swashbuckling operatives in OPC, who reveled in a world of guns, fake IDs, and unmarked cash. Not Win. He had helped Allen Dulles, now a practicing corporate lawyer but still angling to get back into government service, write two influential reports about how the new CIA should operate. Dulles, like Win, felt strongly that it was imperative for the new agency not just to collect information via espionage but to also mount secret operations against communist forces everywhere. Win had good friends on both sides of the OPC-OSO rivalry. For example, Ray Leddy had returned to intelligence work, abandoning his fledgling import-export business to take up the fight against communism in the OPC's burgeoning operations in Venezuela. "He was very smooth, polished, and a good man to work for," recalled one subordinate. Before long Leddy was the chief of OPC operations for the whole hemisphere.

Win was a spy on the rise, but he was also a mess. His life throbbed with conflicts. Things had not worked out with Besse, mainly because he had never lost his ardor for Paula. Besse had left him in the spring of 1948 and returned to Alabama with their son, Beau, now four years old. Win wanted to marry Paula and take a job in Washington, but she wanted to live in New York, where she could work as a model. Back in Alabama, his father was dying of diabetes. When Win arrived in Washington in December 1949, he was frightened and lonely. "Please tell me you still love me," he beseeched Paula in one letter. In another, he asked, "You haven't felt 'liberated' and 'free' since I left, have you?"

Maybe he was just plain frightened by the world he lived in. He had gone away to war against the Germans five years earlier and stayed on for the Cold War against the Russians. He was still on the front lines. As one British official described the mood in London and Washington at that time, "The Soviet menace was everywhere; the dream of a cooperative postwar world was long dead; the iron curtain was solid. The Berlin blockade was a recent and instructive memory; the captive nations were not a slogan but a vivid reality. Soviet hostility and duplicity were taken for granted."

Headlines about the arrest of nuclear scientist Klaus Fuchs, who had passed atomic secrets to the Soviet Union, served as a reminder that there might be traitors in his midst. Win knew the cost of failure. The Ukrainian anticommunist forces that he and Philby had helped organize had been decimated by arrests. More recently, Albanian commando squads, sponsored by the U.S. and British intelligence services, had been ambushed as they landed in the Balkans. Some were killed, the rest captured. The Albanian government announced they would be put on trial.

Win visited the agency's main office at 2430 E Street in Washington, which consisted of four masonry buildings on top of a hill across the street from the rather grander State Department. He called on friends in two temporary structures located on either side of the Reflecting Pool in front of the Lincoln Memorial, known as the K and L Buildings. He was reunited with Bill Harvey, a former FBI man turned counterintelligence specialist, who had become a frequent lunch companion on visits to London. Like Win, Harvey hailed from the American heartland, not the East Coast elite. He was, as one intelligence historian has noted, "one hell of a case," a hard-drinking, pistol-packing cop who walked like a duck, talked like a frog, and thought like a detective. But Win appreciated his keen mind and strong anticommunist politics.

Win remained in touch with Dulles, who was still in New York, and the network of OSS veterans who manned the new agency. There was Frank Wisner, a fellow southerner from a wealthy Mississippi family who had served with the OSS in Romania. There was Tom Karamessines, a plainspoken former cop and prosecutor from New York City who had overseen the transformation of the OSS into the CIA in Greece. Most of all, he saw a lot of Richard Helms, a well-bred navy lieutenant who had served as an assistant to Dulles during the war and who brought a crisp administrative style to the sometimes chaotic K and L Buildings.

Win's job, for a while, was to do nothing more than to circulate between the staffs and answer questions: about the British services, secret operations to roll back communism, techniques of counterespionage, the trustworthiness of the French. In the hallways between appointments, Win mouthed greetings to old acquaintances from the war whose names and very existence he had forgotten. At age thirty-seven, he was a veteran in a young organization that was struggling to establish its routines and its missions.

In the gap between Win's professional stature and his personal insecurity lay the consolation of Paula. Back at his hotel, he was reassured and thrilled to get a couple of passionate letters from London whose contents were so revealing Paula put no return address on them. She seemed to be resolving her own doubts in his favor.

"You are, as ever, enormously attractive and appreciated since you went away," she told him. "I'm being a very good girl, my darling, belonging to you completely in every way. I just know we were meant to be together. I too want no more separations."

Win was ready to get on with his life. He caught a train to Alabama. First, he visited his father, who turned out to be much more ill than Win had known. Morgan Scott had lost so much weight that Win barely recognized him. He had never felt close to his father, and rarely got an encouraging word from him. Still, the son could not be faulted if he faltered at the sight of the man wasting away before his eyes, the man who had built their house with his own hands and demanded that Win make something of himself beyond the foolishness of softball and school teaching. Win had done all that, and now the source of his will in the world was fading.

As a father himself, Win yearned to see Beau for the first time in ten months, but Besse had turned hostile. She told him he could only see the boy at the office of her attorney, William Vance, who had previously handled legal matters for the two of them. When Win arrived, the lawyer presented him with a divorce decree. Besse threatened to go to his superiors if he did not start delivering previously agreed upon child support payments. Win, to his everlasting regret, signed the divorce papers on the spot.

Only the prospect of remarriage consoled him. As he wrote Paula, a little nervously, from his hotel room in Birmingham, "You haven't much time left now in which to back out; not very much time in which to decide upon this lifetime arrangement 'for better or for worse!'" Paula wrote back to say her parents opposed her plans, thought she was "rushing off" to come to America. As observant and traditional Catholics, they opposed marriage to a divorced man. To assuage their fears, Win talked of converting to Catholicism and visited a priest. He shopped for a ring, seeking a diamond set with two emeralds. He went on a diet, stopped drinking, and lost eighteen pounds. He wrote to tell Paula he had done an "awful thing": he rented an apartment on R Street in Dupont Circle in Washington. "There were sixteen (16)! people ahead of me who wanted it but I outtalked them for I thought you'd love it so much," he told her.

Paula finally relented. Putting her parents' wishes aside, she made plans to come to Washington. Then, on January 19, Win got the phone call from the secretary of his younger brother, Morgan, a doctor in Georgia. "Pop had just died," he wrote to Paula the next day. "Although I knew he was seriously ill and saw that he looked a shadow of his former self. I was really shocked." He was sixty-one years old. After begging Paula to come, Win had to ask her to postpone her trip for one week. He went home by train and buried his father in Jemison, not far from the stretch of railroad tracks that had been the center of his life.

And so Win's future was forged. The ordeal of indecision was over. The agony of divided love was coming to an end. Win's wish on the shooting star in the sky above battered London in 1944 came to fulfillment on February 15, 1950, in the unlikely venue of the District of Columbia courthouse in downtown Washington. Win and Paula applied for and received a wedding license. There was no ceremony. They celebrated with a few friends in a private room at the Golden Parrot restaurant down the street. Joining Mr. and Mrs. Scott in toasting their new life were Cicely and Jim Angleton.

Win ascended to a new job, chief of the Western European division of the Office of Special Operations. He oversaw all espionage operations collecting intelligence in the friendly nations of West Germany, France, and Great Britain. "He was the chief of the most important division in the agency," recalled Cleveland Cram, a career officer who served under him. "He really had things going his own way. He was a big deal in the Agency."

Jim Angleton was something more: a legend in the making. Perhaps more than any of his colleagues he combined a practical mastery of espionage techniques with a theoretical understanding of their logical implications. In the words of one admirer, Angleton "brooded longest, and perhaps with the greatest penetration, over the specialized methodology of counterintelligence. . . . He was ends-oriented and could remember his own lies, surely a necessary brace of qualities for a successful spy. He also had the professional's necessary interest in ambiguity: an intense commitment to the elimination of ambiguity where sources conflict (rather than the amateur's tendency to attempt to reconcile conflicting statements, as though both might be true, rather than both being false)."

He was also attractive, a trait that would often be forgotten in his notorious later years. "He was tall, lanky in the much admired Marlboro cowboy style, tailored by Brooks Brother, and wore a gold fob watch, New and Lingwood shirts, and the official Homburg," wrote British historian Anthony Cave Brown. "His mode of transport was less grand; his official vehicle was a battered Studebaker. His hair was going steely gray already, his facial bones were good and his skin was light brown velvet. But he was not quite a WASP. He was different. Apart from all else, he was Anglo-Mexican in origin."

What made Win and Jim friends was not only the memories of the OSS office on Ryder Street, that soldierly bond forged working in cold offices under the threat of the V-2s, but also the odd meshing of temperament. Jim, with his wealthy parents and Yale education, was hardly an outsider among the Ivy Leaguers of the CIA. But he was not quite of them either. His Mexican mother, his hybrid childhood in Ohio, Italy, and England, and his love of avant-garde poetry had blessed him with an analytical detachment and passion for truth that made him a uniquely independent and effective intelligence operative. Win, with his homely roots in rural Alabama, had arrived in the world of U.S. intelligence as an outsider to its East Coast ethos. He effaced his past, suppressed his fears (save to Paula), and transformed himself into the CIA's ambassador to the British secret services. They shared a fondness of poetry and a friendship with Kim Philby, recently called from Istanbul to serve in Washington at the British embassy on Wisconsin

Avenue. Win had jotted down both men's phone numbers and addresses in his pocket calendar: Philby, at EM-4117, 4100 Nebraska Avenue in Washington, Angleton, VA-8-8234, at 4814 Thirty-third Road in Arlington.

But time and circumstances had altered the shape of their triangular relationship. Four years earlier, when Win served as the highest-ranking U.S. intelligence official in the United Kingdom and Angleton was off in Italy, Win was probably Kim's closest American acquaintance. Now Philby was in Washington, having been named chief of the British intelligence station in the American capital. He had his choice of interesting and knowledgeable Americans from both the CIA and the FBI. He chose Jim over Win, and not just for professional reasons. Win, who loved British manners and married an Irish woman, might have been exactly the kind of Yankee Anglophile whose pretensions amused Philby. Angleton, by contrast, impressed him with his open rejection of "Anglomania."

In 1950 and 1951, Philby and Angleton met at least once a week for lunch. "There were few restaurants in central Washington in that period," says one Philby biographer, "and the circle tended to gather at the same one or two each day. Harvey's or the Occidental on Pennsylvania Avenue. Several days a week . . . Angleton, Philby and their group were found to be lunching together while [FBI director] J. Edgar Hoover and [assistant] Clyde Tolson munched lobster in another corner." Jim and Kim also spoke on the phone "three or four times a week," in Philby's estimation. Angleton even invited Philby to his house for Thanksgiving in 1950.

"Our close association was, I am sure, inspired by genuine friendliness on both sides," Philby wrote later. "But we both had ulterior motives. Angleton wanted to place the burden of exchanges between CIA and SIS on the CIA office in London—which was about ten times as big as mine. By doing so, he could exert the maximum pressure on SIS's headquarters while minimizing SIS intrusions on his own. Who gained the most from this complex game I cannot say. But I had one big advantage. I knew what he was doing for CIA and he knew what I was doing for SIS. But the real nature of my interests he did not know."

Win was not so close to Philby. His appointment book from 1950 disclosed only one meal with the British spy. Win was advancing on a different front. In the fall of 1950, President Truman appointed General Walter Bedell Smith to replace Admiral Roscoe Hillenkoetter as director of the CIA. Hillenkoetter, a genial but ineffectual manager, had been eased out because he failed to anticipate North Korea's invasion of South Korea earlier that year. Win benefited because Beetle Smith, as his friends called him, had served as Eisenhower's chief of staff when Win worked in the War Room in the final months of the war. He and Smith also had a very good friend in common, General Kenneth Strong, the chief of British military intelligence whom Win still saw on trips to London. Perhaps best of all for Win, Smith brought his old friend Allen Dulles back into the agency, first as a consultant and then as a deputy. It was in this job, wrote one colleague, that Dulles began to perfect "the image of the genial bluff avuncular figure with a Midas touch in affairs clandestine." And Win, as a longtime friend of Dulles, began to perfect his reputation as an effective, indispensable troubleshooter for the spymaster.

One of the programs Win kept up with, via British friends, was a cryptography operation known as VENONA. Its origins were improbable. Polish agents had found a Russian codebook during the war and turned it over to the U.S. and British intelligence services. Through painstaking analysis of its contents, American cryptographers had managed to decipher some wartime cables, which showed the Soviets had a spy working in the British embassy in Washington in 1944 who was known by the code name HOMER. Philby also followed these developments. On a visit to the American cryptography center in Arlington, Virginia, he learned about the hunt for HOMER and deduced immediately that the still-unidentified target was his old friend Donald Maclean, whom he had recruited as a Soviet spy during their college years at Cambridge. Maclean was also rising in the British ranks. In 1944, he had been posted to the First Secretary's job in the British embassy in Washington. He had served on a sensitive committee that oversaw the development of America's atomic bomb. Philby realized that the Americans were not far from identifying his friend as a spy. "They will succeed in the next twelve months," he wrote his Soviet handler. "The situation is serious."

Philby had another reason to worry. He was renting a room in his house on Nebraska Avenue in northwest Washington to another friend from Cambridge days, Guy Burgess, who was also spying for the Soviets. He also had to protect Burgess, whose outrageous drinking habits and insatiable taste for young men constantly put him in compromising situations. One warm winter's evening in January 1951, the facade around Philby's secret life began to crack when he threw an alcohol-fueled party. Win missed this most famous get-together because he had gone to London on a work trip, but many of his friends from the CIA, the FBI, and the British embassy were there, including Bill Harvey. The party was in full swing when Burgess came in. Harvey's wife, Libby, never terribly comfortable in the cosmopolitan world of the diplomats and intelligence officers, had heard of Burgess's skill as an artist. She pestered him to do a drawing. Burgess, drunk and outrageous as ever, responded by drawing a caricature of Mrs. Harvey that either gave unflattering emphasis to her rather larger jawbone or showed her with legs splayed in an obscene pose. Whatever the image, it provoked the portly Harvey to jump on Burgess with fists flying, and the two men had to be pulled apart. The party was ruined, and the guests fled into the night, leaving behind the disconsolate Philby sitting in his kitchen, his head in his hands. "How could you?" he moaned to the unrepentant Burgess. "How could you?" Philby took Harvey to lunch the next day to apologize, but the CIA man was not mollified. The incident shattered the hail-fellow-well-met style of Anglo-American intelligence cooperation. Such hostility was unusual, if not unprecedented. It bespoke hidden tensions and would not be forgotten.

Win was present for the second sign of emerging catastrophe in April 1951, when an old British friend named Geoffrey Patterson, a senior official at MI5, came to visit Washington. Patterson was monitoring the progress of the VENONA cryptographers seeking to identify HOMER, the Soviet spy who had served in the British embassy during the war. The list of suspects had narrowed to nine and then to one when a deciphered telegram finally yielded a distinctive detail about HOMER. In June 1944, his wife was living in New York City with her mother and expecting a baby—information that described Donald Maclean and no other suspect.

Patterson ate dinner with Win on the night of Friday, April 13. In London on the following Monday, top MI5 officials met to review the Maclean case. Patterson's meeting with Win might have been a way of giving Washington an informal heads-up about what MI5 was about to formally tell the FBI: that Donald Maclean was suspected of being a Soviet spy and the British were going to put him under surveillance. Win was certainly current with the investigation. He met on April 24, 1951, with deputy FBI director Mickey Ladd, who knew that Americans had a Soviet spy under surveillance. On May 2, he had cocktails at the home of Brigadier General John H. Tiltman, who served as the British liaison to the American code breakers working on the VENONA program and was an experienced cryptographer, specializing in Soviet communications.

Philby was now in real danger. If Maclean was interrogated about spying, he might well reveal Philby's collaboration with the Soviets. Philby arranged to meet Burgess at a Chinese restaurant in northwest Washington that had a jukebox at each table, the better to drown out their voices to potential eavesdroppers. He still felt confident he could evade detection. "For nearly two years I had been intimately linked to the American services, and had been in desultory relationship with them for another eight," he later recalled. "I felt that I knew the enemy well enough to foresee in general terms the moves he was likely to make."

He dispatched Burgess to London to tell the Soviets that Maclean was about to be arrested and should be, in the lingo of spies, "exfiltrated" to the Soviet Union lest Philby himself be compromised. Moscow Center, as the headquarters of Russian intelligence was known, agreed to evacuate Maclean from Britain. Unbeknownst to Philby, the Soviets also instructed Burgess to accompany Maclean to Moscow. Burgess picked up Maclean at his home outside of London. They drove to Southampton, the port town on the English Channel, where they caught a pleasure boat to Saint-Malo, France. They boarded a train to Paris. They switched to a train to Zurich, where they bought tickets to fly to Stockholm via Prague. They deplaned in Prague and were embraced on the tarmac by Soviet intelligence officers. When Maclean did not show up for work in London the following Monday, British authorities swiftly figured out what had happened.

MI5 sent a "Most Immediate" cable to the British embassy on Wisconsin Avenue, where Geoffrey Patterson decoded it. Philby was hovering outside his office, anxious to learn its contents. Patterson, Kim thought, "looked gray" as he relayed the bad news.

"Kim," he said in a half-whisper, "the bird has flown."

Philby, who already knew that Maclean had fled, pretended to be surprised. "What bird? Not Maclean?" he asked disingenuously.

Patterson had a real surprise for him. "Yes, but there's worse than that," he said. "Guy Burgess has gone with him."

"At that," Philby later recalled, "my consternation was no pretense."

The unexpected flight of Burgess had put Philby in even greater danger. By fleeing, Maclean had confirmed his guilt as a Soviet spy. Burgess, by vanishing at the same time, had implicated himself. The question flaring in American minds was, who had tipped them off? Was there a "third man" who had tipped off the first two? The most plausible suspect was Philby. Indeed, two CIA men said from the very start that he was the only suspect: Bill Harvey and Win Scott.

Win joined in the phone calls flying back and forth between the FBI and CIA officials who recalled the now notorious cocktail party six months earlier where Burgess had outraged Bill Harvey and implicitly insulted all the American guests. "We speculated on the link between Burgess and Maclean, and worried about the more sinister implications of Burgess's having lived in Philby's home in Washington," one FBI man wrote. Win had more to contribute than most to such discussions. He had known Philby longer and had closer personal dealings with him than anyone in the CIA, except for Jim Angleton. He could recall his encounter with Philby's socialistic sister five years earlier. It was not difficult now to gauge its disturbing implications.

The ever-cool Philby offered an explanation, and his friends at the FBI initially accepted it. Maclean, said Philby, had detected the MI5 surveillance in London, and the Soviets had decided to withdraw both him and Burgess. On June 7, the *Daily Express* in London headlined the news that two British diplomats, Burgess and Maclean, were missing. The next day the *Washington Post* reported that Secretary of State Dean Acheson thought their disappearance was a serious matter. The *Post* story noted that Burgess had lived at 4100 Wisconsin Avenue. The story did not mention that Philby also lived at that address, but Win, Jim Angleton, and Bill Harvey already knew that.

Beetle Smith ordered Harvey to review what was known about Philby. He consulted with Win about Philby, according to Cleveland Cram. "Whatever Harvey wrote about Philby, it was with Win's help," said Cram. The usually perceptive Angleton seemed clueless, as if in denial about the growing possibility that he had been duped by his British friend. Philby was ordered back to London. He met Angleton for a farewell drink and passed what Philby called a "pleasant hour in a bar." Angleton, Philby noted, "did not seem to appreciate the gravity of my personal situation."

On June 11, Philby left for London. That same day Win met with Angleton and General Willard Wyman, the chief of the Office of Special Operations, and his deputy, General Charles Thayer. American suspicions of Philby were hardening into certainty. Sir Percy Sillitoe, the chief of MI5, came to Washington to tell J. Edgar Hoover that the British secret service now believed that Burgess, Maclean, and Philby were all Soviet spies. Bill Harvey submitted a five-page memorandum to Wyman stating categorically that Philby was a Soviet agent. Angleton submitted his own thoughts, but few were impressed. Clare Petty, an officer who later worked for and admired Angleton, described Harvey's assessment as "lucid and full of hard facts." Angleton's, he said, was "fuzzy, strange and irrelevant from an intelligence point of view." Cram said Angleton's memo was a "rather shallow" document.

The mandarins of British intelligence spurned the Americans' suspicions. The notion that genial hardworking Kim Philby, a good Cambridge man near knighthood, was a secret Bolshevik seemed preposterous. They accepted Philby's explanation that Maclean and Burgess had acted on their own and that the Americans, in their anticommunist fervor, were unfairly implicating him. Sir Stewart Menzies, the legendary chief of SIS who was known to most people only as "C," sent a deputy, Jack Easton, to Washington to hear the Americans' case. Win, who knew Menzies and Easton well from his London days, played the host. He took Easton to see Beetle Smith. Easton said that Philby was guilty of nothing worse than boarding Burgess at his house. Smith turned frosty and cut the meeting short. Win escorted Easton to lunches with Frank Wisner, the chief of the OPC, and Dick Helms, now a top assistant in OSO. Easton said the meetings were cordial, and that no one had presented any evidence Philby was a Soviet spy, "although it was clear that this is what they suspected." Within a few weeks Menzies dismissed Philby from MI6 because of the shadow cast by the flight of Burgess and Maclean. Not charged with any crime, Philby became a journalist and continued to proclaim his innocence. He would not admit his ultimate loyalties until January 1963, when, sensing his arrest was imminent, he fled to Moscow.

Philby's impact on world history, the CIA, and his American associates was profound. By the summer of 1951, he had been a Soviet spy for seventeen years. His superiors in the Soviet intelligence headquarters later calculated that he, Burgess, and Maclean had provided more than 20,000 pages of valuable classified documents and agent reports over the years. Philby had kept Moscow apprised of British and U.S. intelligence reorganization efforts after the war. He had short-circuited the Anglo-American campaign to promote anticommunist rebellion in Albania, the Balkans, and Ukraine (although several CIA hands came to believe those secret uprisings probably would have failed anyway due to their own shortcomings). He had warned the Soviets that scientist Klaus Fuchs was under investigation, enabling other agents in that atomic spying network to avoid detection and escape prosecution.

General Douglas MacArthur charged that Philby had betrayed the U.S. order of battle in Korea, resulting in the deaths of tens of thousands of American servicemen. The numbers may be debatable, but it seems likely that the Soviet premier Joseph Stalin did know, via Philby's reporting, that President Truman was not willing to use nuclear weapons in the Korean War. Armed with this knowledge, Stalin was able to persuade Chinese leader Mao Tse-tung to send his troops across the Yalu River into the war. The Chinese forces repulsed MacArthur's invasion, with deep casualties on the American side, and the war eventually ended in stalemate. Whether Stalin and Mao would have acted the same way without the information obtained by the British spies is impossible to know. Certainly Philby's espionage fortified the cause of communism worldwide and rattled the once-solid alliance of the American and British intelligence services.

Jim Angleton was personally traumatized by Philby's treachery. "It was a bitter blow he never forgot," his wife, Cicely, told journalist Tom Mangold. "Jim was obsessed by Kim's betrayal," said Peter Wright, a British official who shared Angleton's politics and worked closely with him in later years. Another CIA associate, John Gittinger, said, "It absolutely shattered Angleton's life in terms of his ability to be objective about other people." Jerrold Post, an academic psychologist who worked with the agency, said, "He must have wondered if he could ever trust anyone again. Psychologically, it would have been a major event." Dick Helms, a friend and patron to Angleton for his entire career, agreed. "The exposure of Kim Philby," said Helms, "was lodged in the deepest recess of Jim's being."

Win too was affected. He had trusted Philby as a friend. He had taken little Beau to Philby's house in Carlyle Square to play with Kim's kids. He and Besse had dined with Kim and his wife. So had he and Paula. They had drunk and laughed, plotted and planned, even watched American football. Win trusted Kim as he trusted all his British friends, and now had to live with his shadow on all that they had accomplished. At the end of his life he wrote that Philby's treachery could not "destroy the marvelous record of the loyal and hard-working Englishmen who worked in their intelligence services during and after World War II." Angleton, for his part, could not bring himself to say anything about Philby.

Win Scott and Jim Angleton were certainly the two CIA officers closest to Kim Philby during his years of maximum effectiveness as a communist spy. Win may have had his suspicions, but, almost to the end, they had both failed to see through his affable, alcoholic charm. They had looked the communist in the face and seen a friend. They shared in a historic mistake. But if they felt shame, guilt, or remorse, they hid it from the world and from each other. Their friendship had taken root in poisoned soil.

5

Operation Success

If you had to pick a moment when it all began to rot—when the clandestine life led his father and the country astray—Michael thought, one such moment might be Guatemala 1954. They called it Operation Success at the CIA, an optimistic code name that belied the cynical nature of a venture that brought down a democratically elected government of a small country said to pose a threat to the national security of the United States. The CIA's covert operation propelled a growing democracy into decades of civil war that cost some 200,000 people their lives. Win, Michael was relieved to learn, did not play much of a role in Operation Success. But Win's good friend Ray Leddy did. And so did his future good friend David Phillips, a failed actor turned psychological warfare artist. It all began at lunch.

According to one of Win's pocket calendars, Win had lunch with Ray on November 11, 1951. They likely went to the Army-Navy Club on Farragut Square, where glasses clinked louder than at the more pretentious restaurants frequented by Jim Angleton and other top CIA men. Ray was back in Washington for good. As the merger of the OPC and the OSO took effect, Leddy's position had become redundant. Allen Dulles arranged with his brother, John Foster Dulles, now the secretary of state for President Eisenhower, to bring Ray into the State Department. There he became a deputy assistant secretary of state and a strong advocate of CIA policies.

Ray thought it a perfect fit. He had soldiered during the war, seen the world, worked the import-export trade on Wall Street, and then learned the arts of secret operations in Caracas and other Latin capitals. He knew war, politics, and the ways of U.S. foreign policy. Foggy

Bottom was a natural. His wife, Janet Graham, a woman of American and Peruvian descent whom he met at a job interview, had brought their kids up from Venezuela. They had bought a beautiful old colonial house in a leafy enclave deep in Montgomery County.

Win felt flush, too. With Beetle Smith as director, Allen Dulles his top deputy, and Dick Helms as assistant director of covert action, all of the CIA's top men were close personal friends. He had almost daily meetings with Helms, with whom he got along just fine. The two men shared a passion for orderly work and detail. Win's mathematical mind impressed Helms, as did his ability to drink and chat up the ladies. Win and Paula lived in a grand brick home on Princess Street in Alexandria, Virginia, a genteel, slightly shabby enclave south of Washington. Located within sight of the Potomac River, the house had ten rooms and was "furnished in perfect taste," according to one visitor. There was a small brick patio and enclosed garden in the back. Paula was an exemplary wife, "very sweet and very pretty," in Cleveland Cram's estimation. They hosted large dinner parties for the regular parade of visitors from London, including Sir Stewart Menzies, the legendary "C," now finishing up his tenure as head of the British service. By day, the visitors and their hosts carved up a signal intelligence empire that spanned the globe, the British supplying locations across their former empire, the Americans supplying the money and the technology. Kim Philby, dismissed from the British service, faded as a bad memory.

The friendship of Ray Leddy and Win Scott deepened. The high-stakes secretive work, the lush Washington summers, the lights flickering on the Potomac gave their lives the feel of elegant adventure. They had dinner at each other's houses, took in the occasional play at Arena Stage. The Seaport Inn, a pricey restaurant in Alexandria, became a favorite evening destination. Win and Paula often attended parties or late dinners at the Dulles's house on Twenty-ninth Street in Georgetown. Bill Harvey was a pal. When Janet needed help getting U.S. citizenship, the rotund genius used his legendary connections to solve the problem.

Jim Angleton remained a good friend with whom Win lunched and occasionally played poker. Angleton's intellectual superiority fostered a brazen gambling style, said one of the card players. "Angleton would sit there and he would use his money to browbeat everybody. If I raised ten dollars, he would raise a hundred, and there wasn't anything I could do about it. I never liked him. He wasn't near as good an officer as he seemed to think he was."

Women and children found Angleton delightful. "He had more depth than any man I'd ever met," said a child of his friend Tony Bradlee, wife of future *Washington Post* editor Ben Bradlee, then an up-and-coming journalist in the capital city. "He had extraordinary sensitivity and an interest in people." Another friend loved his "very fascinating romantic Bohemian side. . . . His tastes ran to poetry and romance in general." A solitary genius, he would dance solo to songs by Elvis Presley at boisterous pool parties.

These were "the halcyon days of the Central Intelligence Agency," said Dulles biographer Peter Grose. "The service was young and adventurous; the men and women accepting its call were smart, dedicated, and with no reason to doubt their own integrity and that of their new organization. The enemy was clearly identifiable and vicious. Public enthusiasm for the Cold War effort was high, with a corresponding readiness to sanction whatever seemed necessary to defeat the evils of Sino-Soviet communism. . . . working for the CIA was the highest public service imaginable."

But all was not well for Win. The office politics at the CIA were cutthroat, the social climbing ferocious. Win was a charming man with a capacious intellect but not a lot of political sophistication. He was also a generous entertainer living on a civil servant's salary. He always felt short of money, especially due to the onerous conditions in the divorce decree. Paula was pregnant but then had a miscarriage, according to Win's brother, Morgan Scott. "Paula was never happy because she wanted children, and until she had you, she was very frustrated," Uncle Morgan told Michael, who could only imagine Paula's predicament. At that time in middle-class America, wives were not supposed to work. Even if Paula wanted to work, there were no modeling jobs for a woman past thirty, especially in Washington, a company town that specialized in drab dresses, dark suits, and deferential mothers. London might have been dreary, but it was not a one-company town. Win was no longer wooing her and was spending longer hours at the office. To amuse herself, she played a lot of golf—she remained an excellent athlete—and she drank.

In the daily round of meetings in the K and L Buildings, Win understood what everyone could see. The agency's agenda of aggressive secret operations against the Soviet Union and its Eastern European allies, which Allen Dulles had been pushing since at least 1948, had collided with at least two hard realities. First, the British and French secret services did not have a lot of patience for rhetoric about "rolling back" communism in Eastern Europe. The European allies thought "rollback" to be a pipe dream, if not a script for war. They felt the communists in power in Warsaw, Prague, Budapest, and Bucharest were there to stay. Fantasies of overthrowing them via cliques of financially dependent exiles in distant capitals were American romance, not serious politics. In the words of one British historian, "The British and American secret services now found themselves increasingly at odds on the ground."

Second, the American crusade in Eastern Europe was hindered by fraudulent friends. Win knew that better than anyone. An agency audit revealed that most of the anticommunist émigré organizations funded by the agency were nothing more than "paper mills" whose fabricated reports and exaggerated activities were, in the words of one insider, "useless." That harsh but accurate assessment did not sit well with Dulles. He ordered the report, initially classified as secret, to be stamped "top secret" and withdrawn from circulation around CIA headquarters. Only a few officers read what one historian described as "its devastating judgment on the agency's intelligence collection capabilities."

The free ride that the agency had gotten from Capitol Hill was ending. Black budgets once approved with a nod were suddenly being scrutinized. Certain barons from the House of Representatives presumptuously asked whether the American taxpayers were getting their dollars' worth at the CIA. They squinted at Dulles's soothing assurances that communism would soon be rolled back and balked at passing along a blank check at appropriations time. To head off demands for more accountability, Beetle Smith created a new job, inspector general, and turned it over to Win. It might have sounded like a promotion, but it took him away from the central tasks of espionage and into the secondary business of covering the agency's increasingly exposed posterior. Truth be told, he had been kicked sideways into a job that required managing bureaucratic failure, not achieving espionage success.

As inspector general, Win had to deal with the realities of the agency, and they could be publicly humiliating. In December 1952, the Soviets made the CIA spooks look especially silly. Since the end of the war, the Americans and the British had been funding and advising an anticommunist Polish émigré group known by its initials, WIN. The Soviets had controlled the WIN for many years, using the group in classic counterintelligence fashion. They fed disinformation back to the CIA. Stories that the Urals were aswarm with anticommunist rebels ready to rise up had usually been well received in Washington. As for any WIN partisans who actually tried to do something, the Soviets could arrest them and ship them to prison camp without exertion. Adding propaganda insult to operational injury, the Soviets called a press conference and described in extravagant detail to attentive reporters how they had controlled the Polish anticommunists and duped the agency.

Beetle Smith had had enough. Never as enthusiastic about secret operations as Dulles, he resigned as CIA director to move to the number two job at the State Department. Dulles took over the top job and promptly sent Win to London to write a postmortem on the WIN fiasco. Win prodded the chiefs of Eastern Europe operations to cable London on the same subject. He knew firsthand what others had a hard time admitting: the failure of joint American-British operations in the Soviet bloc countries could not be blamed on the treachery of Kim Philby or Donald Maclean. It was due to political weakness and isolation of the pro-American forces and the naïveté of their CIA patrons.

The Central American republic of Guatemala, by contrast, offered prospects for a quick win for the United States. The problem was not a communist regime beholden to Moscow and hostile to U.S. interests but the democratically elected government of President Jacobo Arbenz, which included a small but influential group of communist advisers. The government prepared a land reform program to mitigate the vast gap between the rich and poor. Win was not involved in Latin American operations, but Dulles and most other top CIA men saw Arbenz as an incipient communist threat—and an opportunity to redeem the agency's name. Most officials at the State Department counseled restraint. Guatemalan reform, if done legally, was not a threat to U.S. interests, they said. The most vocal dissenter was Ray Leddy. After four years of running OPC operations in Latin America, the former FBI man favored covert action over diplomacy.

When Arbenz's government announced in August 1953 that it was expropriating 174,000 acres of land owned by United Fruit, the CIA found the pretext it was looking for. Within hours, the agency's Psychological Strategy Board called a meeting. The board, responsible for reviewing and approving all plans for covert action, authorized Dulles to give "extremely high operational priority" to overthrowing the Guatemalan government. In light of previous State Department objections, CIA operatives unilaterally decided that Foggy Bottom would be cut out of the action. Beetle Smith helped out by recommending that CIA personnel "have no direct dealings" with the State Department officials because virtually all of them opposed covert intervention in Guatemala.

The CIA's plans, noted some State Department veterans, bore more than a passing resemblance to communist trickery. "Our secret stimulation and material support of the overthrow of the Arbenz Government would subject us to serious hazards," declared a State Department policy paper submitted to the NSC a few days later. "Experience has shown that no such operation could be carried on secretly without great risk of its leadership and backers being fully known. Were it to become evident that the United States has tried a Czechoslovakia in reverse in Guatemala, the effects on our relations in this hemisphere, and probably in the world at large, could be as disastrous as those produced by open intervention."

In 1948, the Soviets had engineered a coup in Czechoslovakia in which a liberal democratic government with widespread popular support was overthrown by a small communist faction. The communists immediately imposed their rule and routed the bourgeoisie and its representatives. The diplomats of the State Department saw a secret coup of a pro-American minority against a democratically elected government in Guatemala as morally equivalent. A poll of twenty-three staff members working on Central America found only one who supported the idea of CIA intervention: Ray Leddy. Unbeknownst to his colleagues, he was doing what he could to advance the CIA's agenda. He was, noted a colleague, "a man who could clam up."

Excluding the State Department enabled the agency to tailor its intelligence findings to promote its covert action agenda. The State Department's review of Latin America in late 1952 found it "improbable that the Communists will gain direct control over the policy of any Latin American state, at least during the next several years." The Soviet Union had no presence in Guatemala. Communist diplomats in neighboring Mexico rarely visited. On the clandestine side, the prevailing CIA view was different: any communist influence was a sign of incipient Soviet control, no matter what Guatemalan democracy decided. The challenge, said covert operations chief Frank Wisner, was to overcome Arbenz's "substantial popular support." The United States had to undermine the "loyalty of the army high command and most of the army" to his government. It would require a cutoff of military assistance to the government; promises to aid anyone who overthrew Arbenz; critical public statements from Washington; and, most important, the insertion of psychological warfare specialists into Guatemala to shape the perceptions of the Guatemalan public and political elite in advance of the decisive blow.

Operation Success lasted eight months and cost about $3 million. Allen Dulles saw a chance to recoup his embarrassing losses in the Eastern European theater. "This is a top priority operation for the whole agency and is the most important thing we are doing," he explained at a staff meeting. He assigned a favorite protégé, Tracey Barnes, to serve as deputy and troubleshooter. Dulles arranged for Colonel Albert Haney of the U.S. Army to help organize a shadow insurrectionary force.

Among the CIA field operatives assembled for Operation Success was David Atlee Phillips, a tall Texan whom colleague Howard Hunt described as "theatrically handsome." A trust fund kid from Fort Worth whose parents shipped him east for college, Phillips had dropped out of Williams in an alcoholic haze. He returned home to get his degree from Texas Christian University and marry disastrously. Divorced at twenty-one, he spotted a beautiful blonde named Helen Hausch poolside at a Fort Worth country club, swiped her from the military man she was dating, and found himself in a passionate romance. David and Helen wed. Sharing a taste for adventure, they picked a country at random and caught a boat to Santiago, Chile. He sold his late father's oil stocks to finance an agreeable lifestyle of acting and writing the Great American Novel. In an unpublished memoir of the time, Phillips cheerfully recounted one film role in which he played a man who took three sisters as his lovers. But one thing did not lead to another in his acting career. So when the opportunity arose, Phillips bought the local English-language expatriate newspaper, the *South Pacific Mail*. It was in the role of failing newspaper publisher that he came to the CIA's attention. Phillips had three children and as many rejected book manuscripts, so he sent his résumé to the CIA. Hunt, formerly the deputy chief of OPC in Mexico City brought him into the operation for his fluent Spanish, liked him and made the pitch. The United States was going to launch a "psychological warfare" program to help assist in the liberation of Guatemala from communist tyranny. Was he interested? Phillips did not hesitate.

Win's friend and former boss, Dick Helms, now the assistant director of clandestine operations, was skeptical of the whole enterprise. Helms had risen steadily from his OSS days in Berlin. More disciplined than Dulles and savvier than Win, Richard McGarragh Helms was a sleek, alert man who struck some more superficial social butterflies of Georgetown as stodgy. He was certainly careful. With his slicked-back hair, just beginning to be streaked with gray, and an emerging widow's peak, he had the poise of a bird of prey and the manners of a gentleman. In the ramshackle temporary buildings along the Reflecting Pool, he kept one of the neatest desks. Helms pointed out various weak spots in the Operation Success planning. The favored Guatemalan client, a certain Lieutenant Castillo Armas, did not have a particularly inspiring personality. He claimed a following in the officer corps, but the agency had no way to discern his motivation or gauge the extent of his popularity. He clearly did not have the experience to organize the military side of the operation. Arbenz already knew the CIA was recruiting allies in the top ranks of his armed forces. He purged the officer corps of disgruntled conservatives. In his weekly radio speeches, he warned the

Guatemalan people that foreign forces were stirring up trouble, and his aides were shopping for weapons in Eastern Europe to arm his supporters in the countryside. Helms thought the terrain unpromising.

Win kept up with Operation Success in regular meetings with Tracey Barnes, Dulles's favorite; Frank Wisner, an increasingly manic advocate of secret operations; and the more mellow J. C. King, another former FBI man who served as chief of secret operations in the Western Hemisphere. Win also talked frequently on the phone with Ray Leddy, who was quietly heading up the effort within the State Department without letting his colleagues know that he was sitting in on the CIA's weekly meeting on Operation Success. In March Leddy and another State Department hand expressed concern that Operation Success might not be sufficient and indicated more deadly plans might need development. "It may be necessary to take more calculated risks than before," they said, according to a CIA memo. When asked what that meant, Leddy replied, "The best way to bring about the fall of the Arbenz government would be to eliminate 15–20 of its leaders with [Dominican Republic dictator] Trujillo's trained pistoleros." Leddy did not blanch at the prospect but worried that U.S. sponsorship of the rebellion was in danger of being exposed. "High level State thinking is that an act which can be pinned on the United States will set us back in our relations with Latin American countries by fifty years," he said. The CIA took up Leddy's idea of slaughtering the leftist leaders of Guatemala. Three weeks later, a top agency official solicited staff officers to help compile an "eliminate list," of "proven Communist leaders," other officials "irrevocably implicated in Communist doctrine and policy," and "individuals in key government and military positions of tactical importance whose removal for psychological, organizational or other reasons is mandatory for the success of military action."

Win helped out where he could. When the Success operatives suspected in April 1954 that Arbenz was importing arms from a Czech supplier shipping through West Germany, they asked Win to use his contacts with the Germans to intercept the ship. He asked the German government to instruct the vessel's owners to dock in Jamaica for inspection on suspicion of a false manifest entry for its cargo. British authorities could inspect the boat. Win thought it was "a perfectly workable idea" and arranged for it to happen. The British searched the ship but found no weapons.

Dulles's operatives plunged ahead, nervous that conditions seemed less than optimal. Castillo Armas never had much success at rousing support in the Guatemalan military or among the population. By May 1954, when the uprising was supposed to begin, he had only a few hundred men in arms and less than a dozen aircraft. The Guatemalan armed forces had thousands of soldiers. The dwindling odds only energized Ray Leddy. "There is a one hundred percent determination, from the top down, to get rid of this stinker," he said of Arbenz, "and not to stop until that is done."

In learning the story of the CIA's campaign against Guatemalan democracy, Michael was relieved to find out that his father was on the sidelines. But the roles of his father's once and future friends, Ray Leddy and David Phillips, were less reassuring. Operation Success helped make both men's reputations in the U.S. government. Leddy helped ramrod into reality a policy of what would in another era be called "regime change," a policy that destroyed an incipient democratic tradition in favor of clientelism and chaos. Phillips, with the support of an admiring Howard Hunt, wrote large the fictional scenario that would convince Arbenz and the Guatemalan government to surrender sovereign power to the allies of North American interests. Phillips could not sell a novel in New York or a play to Broadway, but he did sell a phantom pro-American uprising to the Guatemalan public, the bourgeois government of Guatemala, and its supporters. Arbenz panicked, and Washington struck a resounding blow against "world communism" from which the people of Guatemala would still be reeling a half century later.

Phillips's instrument was the Voice of Liberation, a commercial radio station based in Honduras that played music and reported on developments in the Guatemalan countryside. The format was upbeat and lively. His scripts included news reports, largely fictional, about antigovernment guerrillas purportedly gathering support in the mountains. Rebel forces were advancing here. Government soldiers had thrown down their guns there. Phillips excelled at adding seemingly unrelated bits of news that raised uncertainty, if not dread. No, it was not true, Voice of Liberation reported, that the waters of Lake Atitlan, the country's biggest body of fresh water, had been poisoned. "Unrest turned to hysteria among the populace as the rebel station sent out shortwave reports of imaginary uprisings and defections and plots to poison wells and conscript children," notes one recent history of the agency. Phillips's superiors were more than impressed.

When Arbenz declared martial law to head off the U.S.-sponsored subversion in May 1954, the State Department turned the screws, calling Guatemala a communist beachhead in the Western Hemisphere. President Eisenhower authorized a diplomatic offensive. Ray Leddy coordinated U.S.

demands for the inspection of all Guatemala-bound ships for weapons coming from Soviet bloc countries. He demanded ambassadors from other Latin American countries sign a diplomatic resolution condemning "communist aggression" in Guatemala. Having achieved political and diplomatic confrontation, all that remained was the application of force. The uprising was planned for June 17. In what would be presented as a spontaneous uprising, the pro-American rebels, led by Castillo Armas, would take over a military garrison. A small squadron of U.S.-supplied planes would bomb key military installations in the city. That would soften up Arbenz and encourage the military to overthrow him. That was the plan.

On the appointed day, Win and Ray met for lunch at the Roger Smith Hotel, just a few blocks west of the White House. There is no record of what they talked about, but Guatemala was surely discussed. Leddy had been working on Guatemalan issues for the past fifteen months and on Operation Success for the last nine. Win knew the agency's plans. As friends, they had shared hopes and dreams of U.S. success in Latin America since their days in Havana during World War II. As covert operatives, they believed in the justice of the hidden hand of American power. They must have looked forward to its exercise.

Operation Success went public with a bang. Castillo Armas launched his attack on Guatemala City. Reading from a Dave Phillips script, he told a nationwide radio audience, "At this moment, armed groups of our liberation movement are advancing everywhere throughout the country. . . . The hour of decision has struck." His message stressed the indigenous nature of the uprising made in Washington: "This is not a foreign intervention but an uprising of the honest, Christian, freedom-loving people of Guatemala to liberate our homeland from the foreign intervention which has already taken place, from control by the Soviet Union which has made Guatemala an advanced outpost of international commie aggression, from rule by Soviet puppets."

For a couple of days, the rebels seemed on the verge of defeat. The armed forces did not turn on Arbenz as expected. There was no popular uprising. But Castillo Armas's few planes managed to knock out all the country's radio stations, leaving the CIA station as the only source of information. Phillips's broadcasts fostered the impression of a massive uprising sowing fear among an urban population that trusted the news reporting of the broadcast media. The chief of CIA operations at the time, Frank Wisner, did not recoil from the use of force. Like Win, Wisner was a son of the South, deeply conservative in his politics. He had seen communist treachery up close while serving the OSS in Romania. When CIA men in the field begged for Washington to authorize more air strikes, Dulles and Wisner persuaded Eisenhower to authorize them, admitting the chances of success were slipping. Castillo Armas's air force, kept aloft by the CIA, strafed oil storage tanks and airfields.

In the end, improbably, victory emerged from the combination of Arbenz's weakness, the aerial attacks, and Dave Phillips's cleverness. Phillips's propaganda had created the "completely notional situation" in which the Guatemalan government felt far more threatened than it actually was. As American secret operatives desperately sought to persuade senior military officers to move against their president and the constitutional government, the tiny rebel force managed to repulse a Guatemalan army assault in a remote area. On the slightest evidence amplified by Phillips's media blitz, the CIA's case became more persuasive. The bombings continued. Some of the generals pleaded with Arbenz to quit. On June 27, he finally capitulated. He resigned from the presidency, said one historian, "crushed by what his limited imagination perceived as a revolt of his own military."

The Guatemala military named one of its own as his successor, Colonel Carlos Enrique Diaz, who pledged to fight Castillo Armas's forces. His succession to the presidency infuriated U.S. officials who thought him too sympathetic to Arbenz's left-wing policies. To Leddy's then wife, Janet, it seemed like Operation Success was being run out of the basement of their house in Spring Valley, Maryland. She remembered the late nights with strange men coming and going. She remembered the cheers for victory and then her husband bellowing on the phone, "No, Diaz is not OK. It has to be Castillo Armas." Pause. "No, Diaz is not acceptable. We will not recognize his government. Castillo Armas, or else."

And so power flowed from Montgomery County to Guatemala City, 4,000 miles away. Diaz's presidency lasted less than twenty-four hours. Castillo Armas was brought forward as the new leader of Guatemala. The United States had won a Cold War victory. Communism had been "rolled back" in the Americas. David Phillips would win one of the agency's highest honors, a Distinguished Intelligence Medal, for this media trickery. In the very first covert operation Phillips ever participated in, his bosses said he had "developed and sustained a completely notional situation which was without parallel in the history of psychological warfare. The medium he created became the inspiration of the people and the nemesis of the enemy."

Win celebrated over lunch with Jim Angleton. It was a great day for the agency.

Win may not have figured in Operation Success, Michael concluded, but Operation Success had certainly inscribed itself in his family. Michael had minored in Latin American history. He knew the story of the CIA's coup and how Guatemala was wracked with bloody civil war for decades afterward. He knew it was a difficult subject for his siblings. For his stepbrother George, his father's moment of glory embodied his personal connection to the Latin American societies that he wrote about in his academic research. Operation Success, it was no exaggeration to say, made Ray Leddy's son a committed Marxist and opponent of U.S. policy in Latin America. Years later when George met Guatemalan Nobel Prize winner Rigoberta Menchú at a conference, he found himself crying. "I said, 'I'm so sorry, I'm so sorry,'" George recalled. "I just couldn't help myself. She didn't know what my problem was, and I couldn't really explain the complicated story of who my father was. All I could think was, they had thirty years of war after what my father and his colleagues did there. Thirty years." George wasn't self-righteous or self-pitying about it. "Somebody should cry about thirty years of war, right?" he asked brightly.

In George's question, something about the world of their fathers hit home for Michael: the menace of success.

6

A New Life

Serendipity played no small part in Michael's search for his father. In 1988 he was working as an associate producer on the TV show *Unsolved Mysteries*. He was thirty-three years old, had married his girlfriend, Barbara Fisher of Shaker Heights, Ohio, and was contemplating having children of his own. He walked into work one morning, and the receptionist said he had a letter from a relative in the South.

"I don't have any relatives in the South," he laughed as he made his way to the editing room. Probably some nut. He stopped and went back to the receptionist.

"Let me see that."

It was a note from his aunt, Ruth Grammar, Win's youngest sister, who was living, as always, in southern Alabama. It had been twenty-three years since Michael had seen or had contact with anyone in his father's family. He had seen Aunt Ruth only twice, as a young boy on summer vacations. But she never forgot her big brother's son. She knew somehow that he had gone into the movie business. Years later, when Ruth saw the name "Michael Scott" in the rolling credits after an episode of *Unsolved Mysteries*, she guessed correctly that it was her long-lost nephew. She wrote to NBC, which referred her to his production company. Michael called her right back. He was touched, and she was delighted to talk to him. When he said he was interested in finding out more about his dad, Ruth said he should really talk to Morgan, Win's youngest brother, who was the closest of all the siblings to Win. Michael remembered Uncle Morgan from a visit to Mexico City in the mid-1960s. Thanks to Aunt Ruth's persistence, Michael met Dr. Morgan Scott a few months later at an airport motel in Roanoke, Virginia. When they shook hands, Michael was inwardly jolted. Morgan Scott Jr. had been born fourteen years after Win. At the time of their first meeting, Morgan was sixty-five years old—not much older than Win the last time Michael had seen him. The sound of his uncle's voice and the pattern of his speech echoed Win. "It was chilling," Michael said. "I really felt for a second that I was speaking to my father."

With Morgan, Michael wanted to uncover a family secret that had nothing to do with the CIA: the story of his adoption, that is, how he came to be Win and Paula Scott's only son. His birth certificate said that he was born in St. Petersburg, Florida. How, he wondered, had he gone from Florida to Washington as a newborn? Uncle Morgan knew the story—at least a version of it—and he told it to Michael in the airport motel.

In the early 1950s, Morgan had just graduated from medical school and taken a job working as the only doctor in Thomaston, Georgia, a small town dominated by the local textile mill. He often traveled up the highway to Washington to see his big brother. Paula, he recalled, was close to despair. She kept getting pregnant and kept having miscarriages.

"She had about six of them in a row," Morgan said. "She felt really guilty because she could never have a baby. She talked to me about it. [She said] 'A woman is supposed to have children.' The Irish Catholic people have tremendous amounts of guilt if you don't produce children. Women are supposed to produce children. They're not supposed to engage in sex without the possibility of children. She had a lot of guilt about that."

Michael did not have many memories of his mother, and Uncle Morgan's story would color them. Paula became his mother because she could bear no children of her own. Initially, she did not want to adopt, he said. Win and Morgan had to talk her into it.

"Your father and I discussed this many times," Morgan recalled. "He felt that maybe if she had an adopted child, she could feel better about it. Win asked me if I would be on the lookout for a child that they could adopt." Warming to the memory of his big brother, Morgan explained that he had a patient who was a nurse in Atlanta who had become pregnant by one of the interns in the hospital where she worked. The intern, already engaged to another woman, had no intention of marrying the impregnated woman. "She came to me because she didn't want to go to an Atlanta doctor and have her nursing career ended," Morgan recalled. "So, I arranged for her to be in contact with Win."

But why would a nurse in Atlanta go to St. Petersburg to have her child? Michael wanted to know. Morgan said it was for legal reasons; that was where the paperwork could be processed more easily. Michael was not convinced. Only years later, after Uncle Morgan had died, did Michael learn the true story, which emerged from adoption records he obtained from the State of Virginia. His biological parents were not a doctor and nurse of "good stock," as Morgan insisted, but rather a pretty seventeen-year-old high school dropout and a philandering TV anchorman.

In the paperwork, Michael found the real story. He had been born of a woman named Martha Scruggs. She was the middle daughter of five children raised by a single mother who worked at the textile mill in Thomaston, where Morgan Scott was the company doctor. At age sixteen, Martha met a man with whom she fell in love and married. One year and many fights later, they knew it was impossible and got divorced. Martha's mother encouraged her to get out of Thomaston and go visit an aunt in Greenville, South Carolina. Martha obeyed. She went to Greenville and took a job as a cashier at the S&S Cafeteria, where she caught the eye of a local television personality named Reggie who hosted a fifteen-minute-long newscast. He succumbed to her charms, and she to his. On at least one occasion, Reggie promised Martha that he would leave his wife to marry her. But then he reconciled with his wife, and Martha moped her way back to Thomaston, where she discovered she was pregnant. Her mother was sympathetic but already had two sons living at home and no child support. As the only one of four adults in the house with a job, she could not contemplate a pregnant daughter hanging around town with a visible bellyful of a child whose father was unknown. It would shame the family. Martha's mother explained her daughter's predicament to Dr. Scott at the textile mill. He said he knew an elderly couple in St. Petersburg, Florida, who could take in a pregnant young woman. Martha's mother put her expectant daughter on a bus to St. Petersburg. All the while Morgan was thinking of Win and Paula's desire to adopt a child.

As the winter of 1954 turned into the spring of 1955, Win had secured a position of trust in the commanding councils of the CIA, not as a policy maker but as a troubleshooter. He was handling not one but two onerous chores for Allen Dulles, whose reputation for avoiding hard work—Kim Philby noted it—was deserved. It was a measure of Dulles's confidence in Win that he gave him responsibility for two matters of personal interest to President Eisenhower himself that Dulles preferred to sidestep. Eisenhower, a military man, had some skepticism about the efficacy of secret operations by civilians. And, a thrifty midwesterner at heart, Ike wanted to know if the clandestine service really deserved all the taxpayers' dollars it was getting. Citing pressure from congressional leaders, Eisenhower had informed Dulles in mid-1954 that he was forming two committees to investigate the CIA. One, headed by General Jimmy Doolittle, a famed air commander, would assess the agency's competence in clandestine work. The other, headed by retired general Mark Clark, an effective field commander in World War II, would look at the agency's performance in all other areas. Dulles dared not object to Eisenhower's wishes. The failure of rollback, the WIN fiasco in Poland, and accusations of communist influence had all taken their toll on the agency's reputation. Operationally, the CIA director conceded the need to be more cautious, to compartmentalize. Bill Harvey, Jim Angleton, and the counterintelligence people had been saying so all along. Politically, Dulles needed to build bridges to Congress and the White House. He assigned Win to serve as his point man with both the Doolittle and the Clark committees.

Win started briefing Doolittle in July 1954, before the committee had even been publicly announced, whispering Dulles's view that the CIA was in danger of losing its secret war against the KGB. In the months that followed, Doolittle came to agree. He thought the agency was a mess, "a vast and sprawling organization manned by a large number of people, some of whom were of doubtful competence." But he also thought that it had to become more ruthless in its clandestine activities. "Because the United States is relatively new at this game," Doolittle wrote, "and because we are opposed by a police-state enemy whose social discipline and whose security measures have been built up and maintained at a high level for many years, the usable information we are obtaining is still far short of our needs."

Nothing less than national existence was at stake, Doolittle said. In self-defense, CIA personnel would have to learn to betray their values without compunction. "If the United States is to survive, long-standing American concepts of 'fair play' must be reconsidered," he argued. "We must develop effective espionage and counterespionage services and must learn to subvert, sabotage and destroy our enemies by more clever, more sophisticated and more effective methods than those used against us."

Operation Success proved that Americans could subvert, sabotage, and destroy their perceived enemies and feel good about it. Doolittle ratified the moral consensus in Washington that fair play was passé. Win had no doubts about the CIA's mission, but others in Washington were not so sure. To effect the changes called for by Doolittle and Clark, Eisenhower eventually named a board of distinguished but discreet private citizens to monitor intelligence operations. In 1956, two of its members, Robert Lovett and David K. Bruce, would take yet another look at the agency's covert action programs. Both men embodied the East Coast elite. Lovett was a partner in a Wall Street investment banking firm. Bruce was an independently wealthy State Department man who happened to be one of Allen Dulles's oldest and closest friends. The reality of CIA secret operations disturbed them, and they said so in a top-secret report to Eisenhower.

"We felt some alarm that here was an extremely high-powered machine, well endowed with money, . . . the idea of these young, enthusiastic fellows possessed of great funds being sent out in some country, getting themselves involved in local politics, and then backing some local man. . . . [It] scared the hell out of us," Lovett and Bruce wrote. There was no independent review of secret operations to gauge their effectiveness, they noted. "No one, other than those in the CIA immediately concerned with their day-to-day operation, has any detailed knowledge of what is going on." Psychological warfare and paramilitary operations were the province of "bright, highly graded young men who must be doing something all the time to justify their reason for being . . . a horde of CIA representatives many of whom, by the very nature of the personnel situation are politically immature."

Lovett and Bruce did not mention Guatemala by name, but their tone suggested that they did not see Operation Success as such a great model for advancing the interests of the U.S. government. In fact, they delivered a devastating indictment of the agency's secret operations under Dulles: "The CIA, busy, moneyed and privileged, likes its 'king making' responsibility. The intrigue is fascinating—considerable self-satisfaction, sometimes with applause, derives from 'successes'—no charge is made for 'failures'—and the whole business is very much simpler than collective covert intelligence on the USSR through the usual CIA methods! . . . There are always, of course, on record the twin, well-born purposes of 'frustrating the Soviets' and keeping others 'pro-Western' oriented. Under these, almost any [psychological and political] action can be, and is being, justified."

It scared the hell out of us. Lovett and Bruce recommended pruning back covert operations and putting one person in charge of looking at their overall impact. But they had no way to create such a position. Eisenhower felt he could not fire Dulles. He also knew he could ignore Lovett and Bruce's moralistic stance, by keeping their report highly classified. The hidden hand of the CIA remained unbound.

Win had never been one to take vacations, but in the summer of 1954 he took two, going to the Atlantic seashore town of Rehoboth Beach not once but twice. He was a man in search of wider horizons. That winter, he found himself alone in the big house in Alexandria. Paula had returned to Ireland to see family and brood about her inability to have a child. In his pocket calendar Win made a note to send her flowers. Paula's sister, Deirdre, came to Washington. Win met with her and with Paula's priest, a Father Moffat, and agreed he would convert to Catholicism. He had drinks and dinner and still more drinks with Bill Harvey, who moved on to become the chief of the CIA base in Berlin. Harvey, with his swaggering girth and agile mind, served on the front lines of the war against Soviet communism. Located a hundred miles inside communist East Germany, Berlin was perhaps the most important agency outpost in the world.

Jim Angleton had also landed a promotion. General Doolittle had recommended the "intensification of the CIA's counterintelligence efforts to prevent or detect and eliminate penetrations of the CIA." So Dulles decided to create a Counterintelligence Staff and put Angleton in charge. "Harvey was heeding the call to glory," said one journalist. "Angleton was following the path to power."

Win could have been forgiven for feeling he was on the path to nowhere. He had been sidelined from the operational work of the agency. He and Paula had no children, and if he cared to face the truth (which he did not), he was losing touch with Beau, his son back in Alabama. The last time he would see him was in the summer of 1954 when Besse brought him for a three-week trip. Paula was depressed. Win's desk calendar showed that she was seeing a psychiatrist, a Dr. Wallace, twice a week in the spring of 1955. At the same time, she and Win were keeping up their social schedule. In late April they had dinner with Ray and Janet Leddy. But the company of old friends might not have been entirely comforting to Paula in her barren state. Ray and Janet Leddy now had four children: Gregory, who was six; John, who was five; Suzanne, who was two; and George, who had just been born.

Michael, sifting through the evidence, sensed his father must have been dissatisfied at this time of his life. During World War II, Win had run from V-2 missiles over Ryder Street and courted a beautiful young woman while drinking the nights away with witty Brits. Now he attended a lot of meetings, many of them unrelated to the intelligence-gathering work he loved. In the office hierarchy, his friend Dick Helms was ensconced ahead of him by dint of hard work and Ivy League grooming. Win commuted six miles daily, leaving Alexandria and driving up the parkway to Washington, where he went to work in the buildings by the Reflecting Pool. He saw the cherry blossoms come and go. He saw Jim Angleton for lunch regularly, and he and Paula sometimes went to the Angletons' house in Arlington for dinner. But Angleton and Harvey had moved onward and upward while he still was giving lectures on the organization of the British secret services to the young men who would go out to do the real job.

In September 1955, Win became a father again. On September 1, 1955, seventeen-year-old Martha Scruggs went into labor in a St. Petersburg hospital and delivered a healthy baby boy. Twelve days after that, Morgan brought the infant to Washington and delivered him into the loving arms of Paula and Win. Paula delighted in taking snapshots of Win and his new son with her Kodak Brownie camera. They decided to name the baby Michael. Decades later, Michael could only marvel at the sheer randomness of it all. He was born of a working-class single mother with limited prospects in life and could have, would have, and probably should have been adopted by any random couple in rural Georgia. Sheer luck had dropped him into the arms of a former model turned beautiful mom and a handsome dad who happened to be a spy.

Win and Paula were making plans. She arranged for an Irish girl named Rose to help take care of the baby. Win finally arranged for surgery to treat a thyroid condition that had sometimes left him tired or depressed. In February 1956, they celebrated their sixth anniversary. The next morning Win walked into Dulles's office to ask for a new job. He wanted out. He wanted something in Latin America. He had fond memories of Cuba, living with Ray Leddy in Havana, and playing baseball in the hot sun. He had once promised Paula he would take her to Rio or Havana, and now he wanted to make good on it. Life was going to be just fine, just as soon as he could get the hell out of Washington. Dulles responded with a deserved prize. Win would be the chief of the CIA's station in Mexico City.

Act III

Mexico City

7

The American Proconsul

Anne Goodpasture, as much as anyone, would tell the tale of Win Scott's glory days in Mexico. She wrote the definitive history of the CIA's Mexico City station during his tenure as station chief. Her masterpiece—a meticulously typed and footnoted 500-page tome—remains, a half century after the events it describes, mostly a state secret. It always impressed Michael how sensitive his father's life story was. Somehow his long-forgotten deeds still mattered enough to the U.S. government to be kept secret well into the twenty-first century.

Michael remembered Anne Goodpasture—"Miss Goodpasture" to him. She had bestowed many kindnesses upon him when he was a boy. Little did he know that the serene lady who showed him around his father's office excelled in the clandestine arts. She looked like a librarian but had the skills of a burglar. In the science of "flaps and seals"—opening other people's mail, reading it, copying it, and figuring out what they were up to without anyone being the wiser—Miss Goodpasture was unsurpassed. So, too, in the art of keeping a secret. When she and Michael spoke at her south Dallas condominium many years later, Goodpasture recalled Win with critical precision and dry humor. Her spy stories sparkled most often when she executed an impeccable defensive maneuver around a bit of classified information that was at least forty years old. "I don't talk about operations," she said. Decades on, she still knew how to parry.

Anne Goodpasture understood Win more than most because she had risen in the outfit in much the same way he had. She was from the South, the daughter of Tennessee schoolteachers, and lived up to the state's reputation for producing shrewd people. She had landed in the OSS during the war, served in Burma, and excelled far more than her colleague Julia McWilliams, who married and went on to fame as a cookbook author, Julia Child. Anne Goodpasture went on to a desk job in CIA headquarters, where she came to the attention of Jim Angleton.

Angleton, as chief of the new Counterintelligence Staff, was building an empire. He was just a bit stooped now. The good looks of the brilliant young comer had hardened into the glacial glare of the seasoned bureaucratic warrior. He had a larger corner office in the L Building with venetian blinds in the windows that blocked a view of the Lincoln Memorial. He employed no fewer than six secretaries. Office lore had it that he had cracked the Philby case, which was far from true. He was, said David Phillips, the "CIA's answer to the Delphic Oracle: seldom seen, but with an awesome reputation nurtured over the years by word of mouth and intermediaries padding out of his office with pronouncements which we seldom professed to understand fully." One awestruck FBI man saw Angleton as a wraith: "His hair was slicked back from a pale forehead, a bony blade of nose, sunken cheeks, and an elegantly pointed chin—a chiseled, cadaverous face." His intellectually sweeping defense against the Soviet KGB's efforts to penetrate America's secret operations required eternal vigilance. He had secured big budget increases from Dulles. His staff included ninety-six professionals, seventy-five clerical workers, four staff agents, and one contract agent. He drank to the point of inebriation daily. He also functioned brilliantly.

In 1957 Angleton needed someone to help run down leads on a suspected Soviet spy living in Mexico City. He sent Goodpasture. She outperformed the station officer who was supposedly working the case, and Angleton noticed. When that officer left Mexico, Angleton arranged with Win for her to stay.

As station chief in the Mexican capital Win needed—no, demanded—help. "Shortly after I arrived," Goodpasture recalled, "someone who was a woman, who was a reports officer, was standing just outside the door of the office where I was sitting and Mr. Scott walked by and said to this lady, 'Type this up,' and she said, 'I'm not a typist, I'm a reports officer, that's not my job.' And he said, 'I'm chief of station here, your job is to mop the floor if I tell you to.'" A loyal and laconic woman, Goodpasture adapted to her new boss. "I caught on real quick that when he told me to do something, even if it was someone else's area, if he wanted me to type something, I would type it, and then I would take it to the person and say Mr. Scott told me to write this." Win came to rely on her. Goodpasture's memory was phenomenal. So was her efficiency.

Win and Paula moved into a comfortable colonial-style house at 316 Avila Comacho, just off Reforma, the central boulevard of Mexico City, near Chapultepec Park, the capital's grandest green oasis. He had a black Lincoln and a chauffeur named Raul. He and Paula often gravitated to the golf course at the Chapultepec Country Club, where she surprised at least one CIA man by outshooting her husband. They had plenty of friends, new and old. Ray and Janet Leddy had just arrived from Buenos Aires with their brood of children. Ray took over as the embassy's top political officer. Win was officially part of the State Department too. For public consumption, his job title was First Secretary of the U.S. Embassy.

At home, Win and Paula were smitten with their one-year-old baby, Michael. A visiting social worker sent by adoption officials back in Washington to report on Michael's well-being informed her superiors that the Scotts "are over-protective and solicitous of his welfare. Mr. Scott believes there should be little discipline during the first years and even though Mrs. Scott does not agree, she follows this plan." The demanding spy was an indulgent dad.

The politics of Win's assignment in Mexico were not simple. The United States was not popular in a country that it had alternately bullied and ignored for a century. The relatively new CIA station was less of a presence than the FBI, which had maintained an office in the Mexican capital since 1939. The station was located in the U.S. embassy, which occupied the upper floors of a nondescript eighteen-story office building on Reforma. Below the diplomatic offices were the bustling crowd in Sanborn's coffee shop. At Win's insistence, the CIA station moved from a middle floor to take over the very top floor.

The debut of the CIA in Mexico had not been auspicious. One of the first CIA operatives in Mexico was E. Howard Hunt, a graduate of Brown University and a novelist with a gift for clichés. He came in 1951 as chief of the OPC station. A brash man of outspoken conservative convictions, Hunt inevitably offended the finer sensibilities of some at the embassy and more than a few Mexicans, who mistrusted his Yanqui style. When he moved on to join Operation Success in Guatemala in late 1953, he was not missed by many. To say that Win Scott surpassed Howard Hunt in Mexico City is an understatement. Win wasted no time in stepping up the scope and power of CIA operations. With the leaders of the Mexican government he could be his natural self, an easygoing man, equally at home in male or female company. He had tasted the Latin life in Havana as a young man and never forgotten its charms. He seduced Mexicans just as he had enchanted the British after the war: with a sly, confident, soft-spoken American charm.

Michael could well imagine how Win felt liberated by his escape from the Anglo-Saxon Washington to Mexico's less emotionally constricted ambience. Imbued with a bit of machismo himself, Win seems to have intuited the Latin male style, complete with all its ambitions and insecurities. His Spanish was only average, and he remained a deep Anglophile, but his sincerity compensated. He did not condescend to the low-level resentment that many Mexicans harbored toward the United States, nor did he ignore it. Win had a small library of books on Mexico and its history. He knew full well that "Win Scott" was not a popular name among Mexican officials. One hundred ten years earlier, another Win Scott from Washington—General Winfield Scott of the U.S. Army—had arrived in Mexico City, at the head of a column of U.S. soldiers. They occupied the city for nine months in 1848. By the time the first Win Scott departed, Texas had become part of the United States, and Mexico was half as large as it had been before he arrived. The second coming of Win Scott to Mexico City had the potential to be awkward, if not unpleasant. Win had enough sense to fib about his name. Sometimes he said that Winfield Scott was a distant relative. Other times he claimed to have been named after the American conqueror. In fact, neither was true, but such stories helped him live down the legacy of Winfield Scott. He spoke to powerful Mexicans as a warm and reliable friend from the modern empire to the north. The first Win Scott took Mexico with weaponry, troops, and disdain. The second Win Scott came with technology, cash, and friendship.

His task, as defined in a yearly mission statement from headquarters, was to combat communism. Mexicans shared a real interest in this agenda. The ruling party, the Partido Revolucionario Institucional, defied ideological labels. In its foreign policy, the PRI governments were anticommunist, but public opinion and the party line demanded distance from the United States. Domestically, the government allowed alliances with North American capital but depended on protective tariffs, local industrial barons, and nationwide unions. When Win arrived in the Mexican capital, it was a city of 6 million people, with a growing middle class. The government enjoyed broad, if sometimes thin, popular support. Intellectuals liked the government's public works projects, ranging from highways to housing projects, and the nationalistic heritage, which offered an alternative to Yanqui capitalism and foreign communism. The technical classes enjoyed growing universities and factories. Mexicans noted with pride that the inventor of the color television, Guillermo Gonzalez Camarena, was a native son. The official story was that Mexico was revolutionary enough not to need a revolution.

In fact, modern Mexico did not extend far beyond the federal district and a few other big cities. In the countryside was a vast land of caciques (local chieftains) and campesinos. Technology was primitive. Attitudes were xenophobic. The memory of the 1910 Revolution vindicated calls for communal action and the rebuke of the rich. Unlike in many Latin American countries, the prosperous did not enjoy the public blessing of religion because the Catholic Church had been hobbled and harassed since 1910. But as the presidents and the leaders of Mexico's security agencies spoke the rhetoric of revolution, they increasingly feared the reality of the society they ruled—and therein lay Win's opportunity. The Mexican power elite had to be anti-American in public discourse. In private, they wanted to protect their privileges. Win was only too glad to keep an eye on communists. In Mexico City he kept files on the multinational cast of rebels fleeing from the cruelties of South America's many despots. He quickly learned that Mexico's Defensa Federal de Seguridad (DFS), the police force of the president, had things under control.

Fidel Castro's brief stay in Mexico was proof of that. Shortly before Win arrived in August 1956, the DFS had arrested Castro and twenty-three *companeros* at a farm outside of Mexico City. Castro was an exile from Cuba, a tall, gawky twenty-nine-year-old lawyer who led something called the 26 of July movement, which had taken up arms against the government of Fulgencio Batista on the island. Batista had put Castro in jail for two years, then banished him to Mexico. Castro was reorganizing his forces and pondering his next move when he was arrested. A cache of weapons was seized from the farm. In Castro's pocket, police found the card of a Soviet journalist, Nikolai Leonov. Castro rejected the charge that he was a communist and declared his arrest the work of Batista and the U.S. embassy. Castro spent a month in jail until the chief of immigration enforcement for the DFS, a twenty-eight-year-old lieutenant named Fernando Gutiérrez Barrios, decided to let him go.

In time, Win would come to appreciate Gutiérrez Barrios's way of handling things. *El Pollo* (The Chicken), as he was known for his prominent beak, was smart and practical and would in time reign as the most powerful law enforcement official in Mexico. When Castro promised that his band of men would soon set sail for Cuba, Gutiérrez Barrios shook his hand and bade him farewell. Leaving aside the question of whether any money changed hands, Mexico's security forces had one less cause to worry. Win would get to know *El Pollo* much better in the years to come.

In Washington, Mexico was viewed as a battlefield. For the Soviet KGB, Mexico offered a foothold in the Western Hemisphere. The Mexican government let the communists open embassies with large staffs of whom at least half were intelligence professionals of one sort or another. Castro's friend Nikolai Leonov, the incoming Third Secretary at the embassy, was a cagey young journalist who had grown up in Moscow and came to study literature and philosophy at the Universidad Nacional Autonoma de Mexico (UNAM). He spoke fluent Spanish and had an ever-widening circle of acquaintances thanks to his love of Mexico, its people, and its distinctive cultural traditions. If Win's mission to Mexico was driven by Washington's bipartisan imperative of turning back communism, the espionage of his Soviet counterparts was driven by their Marxist-Leninist understanding of the historical fate of Mexico. Like Win, Leonov was well read in the history and politics of Mexico, beginning with the conquering expedition of Hernán Cortés and ending with the revolution of 1910–1918. As a Russian, Leonov could identify with a country that endured many foreign efforts to enslave its people. He knew that the Spanish, the French, the English, and the Americans had invaded Mexico in recent centuries. He admired how the long-lasting fight for independence had forged the psychology of the Mexican people. "This friendly nation had the most militant-sounding national anthem," he noted in his memoir. "Each note of it calls for combat."

And so Mexico City became a labyrinth of espionage, a city of intrigue like Vienna or Casablanca with the spies of at least four powers angling for advantage: the United States, the Soviet Union, Cuba, and Mexico. For the partisans of counterintelligence like Jim Angleton, the KGB and Cuban presence in Mexico City required a response and not just a defensive one. As Norman Holmes Pearson had emphasized in his lectures, the essence of counterintelligence was its offensive character. Dulles wanted a "stepped up program" for Latin America. Angleton was looking for opportunities, and Win was the tip of the spear.

Win clashed right off with Ambassador Robert Hill, an engaging if fusty man who did not even speak Spanish. Win insisted the embassy give more job slots to CIA personnel. Hill, an earthy man, had little patience for spooks and no tolerance of the subtleties of intelligence work. He agreed only on the condition that the embassy would have no responsibility for CIA actions. Soon Win's station was performing tasks that had not occurred to Hill, like tracing the names of visa applicants and persons on the guest lists for embassy functions. Win spoke up at the ambassador's daily staff meeting. He briefed reporters and visiting U.S. congressmen. When he noticed there was a row of four townhouses overlooking the garden of the Soviet embassy on

Avenida de la Revolucion, he arranged for a lawyer friend, code-named LIMOUSINE, to buy them all. He had plans.

He brought all the lessons of his years as London station chief to bear on the Mexico City station. At night everybody had to take all their papers and put them into safes in a central room protected by security alarms. He overhauled the station's file room. He instituted a new filing system, producing new index cards, new personality files, and new subject files. He vastly expanded the photographic files. File cabinets began filling up with arcane but necessary documents such as the manifests of the flights of every airline coming or going from Mexico City. He was ambitious and exacting.

"Win wrote constantly," Anne Goodpasture told Michael. "Pages and pages and pages. He read everything that other people wrote and he had a pen. He corrected their grammar. He corrected their spelling. He put file numbers on things. He made notations of where things should be filed, how many copies should be made. On transcripts of intercepted conversations, he wrote notes in longhand. He typically put in dates—'28 September, 10:32 hours,'—even when that [information] was already in the transcript. If a dispatch had a file number on it and indication of where all the copies went, he might write—on each page—in big style, handwritten style, the same file number that was typed there."

"You could tell from his office that he was a professional man," said a now retired Washington man who worked with Win "He had a standard government-issue executive desk. He was very organized, had his papers stacked neatly, and he was always working on something. This was not the work space of some prima donna."

When necessary, Win ran operations himself. At a diplomatic party he recruited a man who boasted, quietly and accurately, that he had access to all outgoing communications of certain Soviet bloc countries. A price was agreed upon. Once a month Win would meet the man in a parked car at a random location and escort him to a safe house. Win and the man would chat amiably in the living room of the safe house while Anne Goodpasture busily copied the purloined documents with a high-speed Recordak camera in a maid's room off the kitchen. Win then returned the documents to his spy, and he and Anne returned to the office, communist secrets in hand.

Back at headquarters, Win's shop was extolled as a model. "Our Mexico station was the most elaborately equipped and effective in the counterintelligence field of any we had in the world," said John Whitten, who played a big role in the CIA's Mexican and Central American operations for close to five years. Win had already eclipsed Ambassador Hill as a power in the Mexican scheme of things. "Hill never learned two words of Spanish," said one aide who did all his translating. Hill was obsessed with American domestic politics, not Mexican politics. His circle of friends included the other American ambassadors to the Central American republics—some of them Sun Belt entrepreneurs who owed their ambassadorships to generous donations to the Republican Party, not diplomatic experience. They had rejoiced in the overthrow of Arbenz in Guatemala, and they worried about Cuba. The dictator Batista, once useful to the Americans, now seemed more obtuse than shrewd.

Win had the advantage of secrecy. "There was a tremendous amount going on which we didn't know about," said another State Department hand in Mexico at that time. "As Win worked his contacts and built his nets, he became the go-to guy. The Mexicans called the CIA station, 'the real embassy.'"

Not surprisingly, the ascendancy of the "real embassy" in the CIA station on the top floor of the U.S. embassy on Reforma did not always sit well with the diplomats on lower floors. Ray Leddy, as first political officer, felt particularly overshadowed, says one of his colleagues. Ray had to go to Win to learn what was really happening in Mexican political circles. "I had the feeling—and it grew as I became aware of the relationship between the embassy and the station—that he was overshadowed and he was uncomfortable about it," said one foreign service officer who knew them both. "That's why I was surprised at the friendly relations with Win. Ray was formal and more anxious than Win, who was such an amiable fellow, always so relaxed and confident. When it came to work, Win probably ate his lunch."

The exact moment that Win arrived at the commanding heights of Mexican power can be pinpointed with some precision. Anne Goodpasture, of course, nailed the details. It happened on a Sunday morning in August 1958. Ambassador Hill escorted Win to a Sunday morning breakfast with a Mexican friend. The host was a confidant of the soon-to-retire president Miguel Aleman and of the incoming president Adolfo Lopez Mateos. The latter, scheduled to take office in December 1958, was curious to meet the man whom Ambassador Hill introduced as his "expert on communism." Win spoke with authority. "He was a distinguished-looking man with almost white hair," recalled an aide to Hill. "He was well-built but not taut. He had a ruddy complexion. He carried himself well. He commanded respect."

From that summertime breakfast would emerge the operation known as LITEMPO, a network of paid agents and collaborators in and around the Mexican president's office that proved to be one of Win's greatest professional accomplishments. The code name betrayed little of the operation's importance. "LI" was a diagraph used to refer to operations based in Mexico. "TEMPO" suggested notions of structure and pace that were not inappropriate to the orchestration of a political friendship and national alliance. The program originated as "a productive and effective relationship between CIA and select top officials in Mexico," Goodpasture wrote in her history of the station. It soon blossomed into political understanding par excellence. Win's LITEMPO agents, she said, provided "an unofficial channel for the exchange of selected sensitive political information which each government wanted the other to receive but not through public protocol exchanges."

The new president, Adolfo Lopez Mateos, did not need a LITEMPO moniker because he was already an agent, known as LITENSOR. He was a handsome, industrious politician who had made his mark as a minister of labor. He was patient, most comfortable with the consensus and order that the one-party Mexican political system prized. "Liberty is fruitful only when it is accompanied by order," he declared in his inaugural address. He described his government as one of the "extreme left within the constitution," a carefully calibrated formulation that deeply offended Allen Dulles. He espoused the egalitarian ideals of the Mexican Revolution, if only rhetorically. He enjoyed the perquisites of office with widely admired amorous exploits that involved extended foreign travel. When he was out of the country, he assigned Gustavo Díaz Ordaz, his minister of government, to run things.

By the spring of 1960, Win had formalized his arrangements with Lopez Mateos and Díaz Ordaz. Win chose one of his best friends, a reliable FBI man in the embassy legal staff named George Munro, to handle the details of their secret relationship. Munro was a brash Californian with the brains of an engineer and the cojones of a burglar. He had graduated from Pomona College at age sixteen and Stanford Law School by age twenty-one. Thanks to his millionaire father, he was independently wealthy. Like Win he had joined the FBI before the war, wound up in Latin America, and taken leave to work for the OSS. After the war, he returned to the bureau. He served as assistant legal attaché in the embassy for more than a decade, so he knew his way around the Mexican capital from the finest salons to the thieves' market where crooks fenced their goods. Facing the prospect of reassignment to San Francisco, Munro resigned from the FBI on a Friday. Win hired him on the following Monday.

On the Mexican side, Díaz Ordaz, a homely lawyer with an impressive work ethic, chose one of his nephews, a car dealer named Emilio Bolanos, to serve as his contact with the Americans. Munro and Bolanos became buddies. In CIA communications Munro was identified as "Jeremy K.

Benadum" and Bolanos as LITEMPO-1. At that point, the annual LITEMPO budget of $55,353 supported four employees, a five-man surveillance team, "walking around" money for Munro, and stipends for agents. Anne Goodpasture scoffed at Munro and Bolanos, thinking they did not have a clue about how to obtain useful positive intelligence, meaning specific information about the Mexican or Cuban government's plans and policies. But her very professional view did not matter. Win liked Munro's cowboy style and the practical results.

Win's closeness to Lopez Mateos and Díaz Ordaz became the stuff of agency legend. Philip Agee, the future CIA defector who was then an officer in the Western Hemisphere division, heard that Win bought a car for a girlfriend of Díaz Ordaz's. When Lopez Mateos heard, he insisted that Win buy a car for his girlfriend, too. And so he did. How much money Win gave to Lopez Mateos and Díaz Ordaz is not known. At least one top CIA official thought it was too much. In a review of the LITEMPO program a few years later, John Whitten, the chief of the Mexico desk, complained, "the agents are paid too much and their activities are not adequately reported."

Anne Goodpasture thought Lopez Mateos was greedy. She objected to Win's arrangement in which he gave the president $400 a month in the expectation that he would pass it on to another LITEMPO agent. The money "may well have gone into the presidential pocket," she wrote in a classified agency report, adding that the payment "was in addition to [dollar figure deleted] per month paid to LITEMPO-1 as station support asset."

But whatever LITEMPO cost, Win considered the expense worthwhile. Win certainly needed LITEMPO if he was going to fulfill Washington's expectations about using Mexico to combat the new threat in Cuba. On January 1, 1959, the once inconsequential Fidel Castro had trounced the military-organized crime alliance that controlled the government in Havana. Castro had shrewdly forged alliances with both the nationalistic but anticommunist rebels of the Revolutionary Directorate and the orthodox communists of the Cuban Communist Party, as well as with more conventional politicians without compromising his own freedom of maneuver. In the countryside his armed guerrillas had exhausted Batista's forces. In December 1958, Castro's top commander, a former Argentine doctor named Ernesto "Che" Guevara, led a guerrilla force into the regional capital of Santa Clara and routed Batista's troops. As Castro's forces prepared to move on Havana, the dictator loaded up a plane with gold bars and other ill-gotten gains and flew to Miami. Castro took power by acclaim.

Cuba suddenly was a huge political problem for the United States in Mexico. Castro's victory inspired admiration on the streets of Mexico and unsettled Win's friends at the top of the government. The overthrow of a corrupt autocrat by a young revolutionary vanguard was almost a religious revelation for many Mexicans. The newsreel footage of bearded young rebels forging a new political order on the island, said one historian, "made Mexicans of the same age feel uncomfortable with their old and moldering revolution." Mexico seemed energized by Castro's example.

With leftists challenging the government-dominated "charro" unions, U.S. officialdom in Mexico worried about "instability." Win and others did not flinch when President Lopez Mateos responded forcefully to a nationwide railroad strike. It happened during *semana santa,* Easter week 1959, when millions of Mexicans traveled to visit relatives. Fourteen thousand workers walked off the job in one day seeking higher wages. Lopez Mateos declared the strike "non-existent" and ordered troops to occupy the train yards. Other workers rallied to the strikers' cause. Longshoremen walked off in Vera Cruz. Around the country, thirty-eight other sympathy strikes took place. Then Díaz Ordaz, the minister of government, pounced. In a lightning strike throughout the country on the day before Easter, the police, the army, and squads of special agents, wielding clubs and bayonets, arrested 10,000 workers. The strike was broken in a day. Thirty-four leaders of the union movement received long prison terms. The very real threat that communist-led forces might push the Mexican Revolution to the left had been put down. "The severity of the challenge explains the harsh punishment," observed one historian.

In his brisk way, Win recruited agents for the LITEMPO program by showing that there were practical advantages for Mexicans who privately cooperated with the Americans. In 1960, he proposed to his Mexican friends that the wiretapping of the Soviet embassy on Avenida de la Revolucion be vastly expanded. How? they asked. A special aircraft arrived from Washington to disgorge a bounty of technology: ten Ampex tape recorders, thirty machines to record the numbers called, and eleven Wollensak and eleven Revere playback machines. Engineers from the CIA's Technical Services Division installed the equipment in a gleaming new office in the central part of the capital. The Americans and the Mexicans had been tapping six phones in the embassy. Now thirty telephone lines could be tapped, and not just the communist diplomatic offices. Win also arranged for taps on the phone lines used by domestic political rivals of Lopez Mateos and Díaz Ordaz such as Vicente Lombardo Toledano, a leftist labor leader, and former president Lazaro Cardenas, who thought Castro's example offered a way to renovate Mexico's revolution. Win also wiretapped David Alfaro Siqueros, a famous sculptor arrested for his support of striking railroad workers. Soon teams of Mexican and English transcribers worked around the clock listening to tapes of the calls and generating reams of transcripts. Win assigned Anne Goodpasture to pick up the most interesting transcripts every morning and deliver them to his desk by nine o'clock. At lunch, Win could offer his Mexican friends a cornucopia of intelligence on communists and other enemies. How could the Mexicans not be impressed with the soft-spoken First Secretary of the U.S. embassy?

Lopez Mateos placated the more nationalistic sectors of the ruling party with slogans of independence. Before a crowd, he would speak of revolution knowing all the while that he was one step ahead of those who wanted to push his government to the left. Díaz Ordaz, a desk jockey with stomach pains, was content to play the heavy and tend to his paperwork. He too accepted money from Win. He became known in Win's cables to Washington as LITEMPO-2. He also became personal friends with Win.

Díaz Ordaz was canny enough to deploy his unfortunate face as political cover. "I'm ugly enough so that people can be afraid of me," he liked to say. He had no problem confronting the increasingly militant unions and other challengers to PRI power. He knew how to use the information generated by Win's surveillance operations to protect the power of the ruling elite. "When there was union, peasant, student or electoral repression," observed historian Enrique Krauze, "it was ultimately directed from Díaz Ordaz's office on Avenida Bucareli" in downtown Mexico City.

The Mexican apparatus of repression and LITEMPO grew together. Fernando Gutiérrez Barrios, an up-and-coming power in DFS, became LITEMPO-4. An ambitious aide to Díaz Ordaz named Luis Echeverria was LITEMPO-8. When Gutiérrez Barrios sent one of his minions—a young policeman named Miguel Nazar Haro—to deliver a message to the U.S. embassy, Win took an immediate shine to the messenger. Win sent him back to his boss with a message: "I like this guy. Send him again." Nazar Haro too would become a friend of Win's and a CIA collaborator. To say that Win had the ruling class of Mexico in his pocket was little exaggeration. He was America's proconsul.

At this point in the chronology of his father's life, Michael Scott sometimes paused for personal reasons, to take a proverbial breath and reconsider his quest to know his father. How far did he really want to go with this? The question was not really about CIA dirty tricks. Family espionage was more a matter of the heart. His few memories of his first mother, Paula, came from around the time when Fidel Castro came to power, John F. Kennedy had proclaimed a New Frontier, and John Glenn had orbited the earth in a

Mercury spacecraft. These memories could move him to tears or to quasi-scientific objectivity, but he was usually content to leave them alone. But as he pursued the story of his father's life, he could not help but uncover his mother's story as well. It was like spying on her, and he was not sure that he wanted to do it.

But he did anyway. The women who were Paula's friends in those days told him about the American embassy crowd in Mexico, how they lived a good life in a sprawling modern city. She was, everyone agreed, a gallant woman, not prone to self-pity. Like the men in her life, she drank her share and more. She did not flourish on the diplomatic party circuit, although she tolerated it for Win's sake. She was more comfortable at the Chapultepec Country Club, where she liked to read novels in her lawn chair by the side of the pool while the kids frolicked. She especially impressed young girls with her combination of blonde beauty and athletic grace. She was a fine golfer, perhaps the best woman player in the club. "She had such a great manner, great wit, always something enjoyable to say," recalled Eugenia Francis, whose parents were good friends of Win and Paula. "She had such a darling figure, so gracious, so pretty. She was popular with men but not threatening to women."

But Paula was sad while Win was busy and important. That was the long and the short of it. She was sad, she told her best female friends, because Win's love for her had died. Who could say why? If Uncle Morgan was to be believed—and he often was not—Paula's sadness was rooted in her not being able to bear a child. She was a good mother. She loved little Michael enough to discipline him, which was more than Win could claim. But if Paula ever told female friends that infertility made her sad, none betrayed her confidence to Michael. He thought it must have.

One of Michael's few memories of early childhood captured the day when he was about five years old and playing driver in the front seat of his father's black Lincoln as it was parked in the driveway of their house. The emergency brake may not have been on when he got into the car. It certainly was not on when the car rolled backward toward Avila Camacho. Michael sensed danger and spun the wheel. The car demolished a neighbor's wall but not the car. Michael could not exactly recall the consequences, but they did not come from his father.

Win's driver at the time, a young man named Raul Alonso, became something of a babysitter for Michael. Sometimes Michael would go with his father on his daily rounds. Win often visited the home of a smart young lawyer and son of a prominent Mexican banker, who had been helpful on various matters. Raul would drive him to the house. Outside Raul would play with Michael, correct his Spanish, and talk with him about *futbol*. Win would emerge, and they would ride back to the embassy. Amid fleeting memories of Raul and Paula, Michael had an enduring recollection of the bank vault–style door, with its impressively engineered stainless steel contours, that led to his father's office. He remembered how he had to step over the lip of the vault to get into this place of work. All he knew when he was a kid was that his dad had an important job. As he uncovered his father's story as an adult, he found Win as not just an audacious spy but also a sensitive man seeking emotional fulfillment, a man of secret action and hidden needs.

Parents: Morgan Winston Scott and Betty Gothard Scott with their infant son Winston MacKinley Scott in Alabama around 1909.

Family: The Scotts around 1921. Front row, from left: China, Winston, Ruth, and Ora; back row: Grandmother Scott, Betty Scott, Morgan Scott with Morgan Jr. in his arms. (Jan Earwood)

Athlete: Win as depicted in his yearbook photo from Bessemer High School in Bessemer, Alabama, 1925.

Agent: Win learned to handle a gun while in training for the Federal Bureau of Investigation, probably in 1942.

Abroad: Win at ease in Havana in March 1943.

Honored: Admiral William Halsey awards Win a Bronze Star in January for his OSS work.

Romance: Win dines with his future wife Paula Murray at Jack Dempsey's bar and restaurant in New York City in December 1947.

Betrayed: Kim Philby, an affable senior British intelligence official, befriended Win Scott in 1946. Scott was among the first to identify Philby as a Soviet spy. (Getty Images)

8

AMCIGAR

The great AMCIGAR fiasco of 1960 demonstrated that, even after four years as station chief, Win still had a few things to learn about the ways of Mexico. AMCIGAR was the CIA's code name for the executive committee of the Frente Revolucionario Democratico, a loose coalition of Cuban political parties and civic organizations opposed to Castro that had decamped to Miami. They were not welcome in revolutionary Cuba. Castro's security forces, with the able advice of the KGB and other Eastern bloc comrades, were tracking, harassing, and arresting anyone who was even thinking about mounting armed or unarmed opposition to Cuba's revolution. The AMCIGAR cryptonym belied the official story that agency operations were named at random by a computer. Sometimes they were. But only a computer with a droll sense of humor could have dubbed a collection of Cuban politicians, the CIGARs. It was an apt moniker for a group whose ambitions to replace Castro were about to go up in smoke.

Win, like most everybody at headquarters, was worried about the runaway popularity of Castro's revolution in Mexico and the United States. In the spring of 1960 the Cuban leader went to Washington to tell the Senate Foreign Relations Committee that good relations between the United States and Cuba depended on full equality. He met with Vice President Richard Nixon, who asked for his opinion of dictatorship and democracy. "Dictatorships are a shameful blot on America, and democracy is more than just a word," Castro responded. When the Cuban communist spoke at Columbia, Harvard, and Princeton, young Americans applauded.

By March 1960, Allen Dulles had seen enough. He went to the White House with a plan to overthrow Castro. Eisenhower approved it in principle but wanted to hear the details of the plan as they were developed. Win was briefed on the concept at a conference of Western Hemisphere station chiefs in Panama in May. The model was Guatemala 1954, Operation Success. The scale would be much larger, and Cuba, unlike Guatemala, was surrounded by water, not undeveloped countryside where Americans could operate freely. Otherwise, Operation Zapata, as the plan was dubbed, would follow much the same course of action used to oust Jacobo Arbenz six years earlier. It would culminate, six months later, in the invasion at the Bay of Pigs.

Few doubted the formula would work. The United States, using overt and covert means, would isolate the anti-American regime diplomatically while fomenting internal rebellion. Propaganda and paramilitary action would reinforce each other. As an invasion force would be assembled and trained by the CIA in a neighboring country, psychological warfare operations would amplify its manpower, weaponry, and feats of arms through disguised newspaper, radio, and television assets. In an atmosphere of mounting uncertainty, the communist leadership clique would be delegitimized and confused. Amid hope generated by the incipient arrival of U.S. force, the proxy army would strike. A new leadership, under CIA tutelage, could reliably promise all local power groups that they would enjoy the financial and political benefits of Washington's support if they abandoned the leftists and the communists. Faced with the application of America's overwhelming military might, the sensible and the naive alike would understand the choice facing Cuba and act accordingly. Castro and his minions would be captured, or killed or would go the way of Arbenz (who, as Win's phone taps showed, was living in Mexico City and drinking heavily).

Many of the veterans of Operation Success returned to reprise their roles from six years earlier. Dulles welcomed the idea but, as usual, did not ride herd on the details. Tracey Barnes, who had done so well in 1954, returned to oversee political and psychological warfare. Jake Esterline, who ran the Washington war room for Operation Success, was named chief of a new Cuba task force. Howard Hunt, the snappy-dressing spy novelist who handled the political agenda of the Guatemalan rebels, was recalled from Uruguay to organize the AMCIGARs. Hunt's good friend Dave Phillips, who had organized the clandestine radio and propaganda operation in 1954, took on the same duties for the Cuban exile cause. At the State Department, Ray Leddy took the lead coordinating a report from "the intelligence community" declaring that Castro was "pro-Communist and his advisers either communist or pro-Communist," an assessment that was more accurate than the agency's description of Arbenz. Leddy also testified to the Senate Internal Security Subcommittee about the threat of Castro.

This time, Win had a significant role: to secure the Mexican rear guard. At first, the plan called for the AMCIGARs to set up shop in San José, Costa Rica, because the State Department wanted less taint of U.S. involvement with an effort to overthrow a sovereign government. When the Costa Ricans balked, the Americans decided their Cuban friends should settle in Mexico City. Win checked with Lopez Mateos and Díaz Ordaz, who said they had no objections as long as the Cubans did not violate any Mexican laws. Win relayed the word to Washington, and the plan proceeded. Howard Hunt felt that Win had promised "a welcome mat" in the Mexican capital. In fact, the Cuban exiles became a doormat.

Ordering the relocation of the AMCIGARs to Mexico City in the summer of 1960 embodied the Americans' arrogance. In Washington, Cubans and Mexicans might have been politically interchangeable. In Mexico City, they were far from simpatico. The exiles favored by the agency were typically from Cuba's Catholic elite, the backbone of the country's middle class. They were nationalist and anticommunist. They were island cosmopolitans trying to wage war from Mexico, a vast foreign nation whose identity was forged in the anticlerical revolution of 1910. The Americans had persuaded their Cuban clients to publicly demonstrate their independence by submitting to Washington's whim.

While historians would later dissect the military and intelligence mistakes that doomed Operation Zapata, cultural chauvinism and ideological arrogance played a role too. Few of the operatives working to violently overthrow Castro's new government knew much about the country or the people they sought to liberate.

Phillips was the most experienced of the bunch, having spent eighteen months there beginning in April 1955, under the rather thin cover of being a "lecturer on Latin American affairs." In a speech he gave in 1956, he warned Americans "against our unfortunate assumption that maintenance of the status quo abroad is an effective barrier against the spread of Communism. Secure and comfortable among our supermarkets and Cinemascope screens, we fail to realize that for most people of the world, *anything* [emphasis in original] seems better than what they now know." In a passage that disturbed some at CIA headquarters, he said Batista's rule seemed "well-intentioned" but amounted to dictatorship. He returned to the island in 1958, under the slightly more robust cover of running a public relations firm called David Phillips Associates, which had an office on Humboldt Street, near the University of Havana. Among the CIA operatives working on the operation, he was the only one who had any firsthand contact with the Cuban leadership, and it was not extensive. Phillips happened to meet Che Guevara in a Havana coffee shop late one night in 1959 and introduced himself as an American businessman. He asked Guevara about his plans for governing Cuba. Guevara, he recalled, "launched into a ten-minute lecture on the plight of the underprivileged of the world and on the inevitable triumph of Marxism which would unshackle them from their misery. He said nothing memorable or even new. His speech was a litany of clichés which I had heard from many Latins before." Somewhat incongruously, Phillips claimed to have concluded on the spot that Guevara would become "the most successful revolutionary of our time."

By comparison, his colleagues knew little of Cuba. Win and Ray Leddy had been stationed on the island in the early 1940s but had not lived in the country since. Howard Hunt had never lived in Cuba. He had visited for a conference of station chiefs in 1956 and returned briefly in early 1960 to familiarize himself with its realities. Upon departure for his second visit to Cuba, he promised Phillips that he would think of him "when I have a few mulatas," meaning black prostitutes. In the eyes of Operation Zapata's chief political officer, Cuba beckoned as a white man's sexual playground.

Operation Zapata embodied the dangerous folly identified by Robert Lovett and David K. Bruce in their secret report on CIA covert operations: a band of men let loose in the world to wreak havoc against "anti-Western" political forces who had no experience of paying a price for failure. The CIA men actually held their own Cuban allies in disdain. Hunt called the AMCIGARs "shallow thinkers and opportunists." Dulles told Eisenhower there was "no real leader" among them, that they were "prima donnas." The Cuban communists, by contrast, were battle-trained. Guevara, who had lived in Guatemala in 1954, had seen firsthand the psychological warfare campaign behind Operation Success and he had learned. He and Castro knew what to expect from the CIA, and they set out systematically to deny the North Americans the ability to repeat it. Washington constantly underestimated the ability of Cubans to see through the CIA's machinations. In the summer of 1959, Carlos Todd, the pro-American editor of the English-language *Times of Havana*, figured out that Phillips was a CIA man and told him so to his face. Phillips had to leave the island by plane. But Phillips's confidence in his ability to trick Cuban communists remained unshaken.

Win carelessly assumed that his budding friendships with Lopez Mateos and Díaz Ordaz guaranteed that the agency's favorite Cuban counter-revolutionaries could come and go through Mexican territory as they pleased. The experiment did not start promisingly, according to the cable traffic of the day. The AMCIGARs complained about having to go to Mexico City to Howard Hunt, known by the alias "Eduardo." As was often the case, Hunt's sympathies lay more with his Cuban friends than with the suits in Washington. But orders were orders, and the Cubans started to trickle into Mexico. Dave Phillips was determined to make the best of things. He informed headquarters that the Cuban exile leadership group "would need the assistance of Station Mexico in improving the public and political climate in which anti-Castro people can work effectively." He said, "A tremendous publicity drive should be made."

Phillips was full of plans. One agency asset would produce *El Mundo in Exile,* an "ostensibly independent" newspaper that would also generate "satirical, humorous radio tapes for broadcasting over Radio Swan," a broadcast entity that the CIA had set up on an island in the Gulf of Mexico. The Cuban visitors had their own plans. They set up a shortwave radio communication link to their allies on the island. This was not only a breach of CIA security but also a violation of Mexican law. Of course, the Defensa Federal de Seguridad picked up on the transmitter's signal and took action to keep the Cubans off the air. The Cubans complained to Hunt about Mexican interference. The Mexicans stepped up the pressure, sending a succession of tax examiners, bank detectives, and immigration officers to inspect the AMCIGAR's Mexico City headquarters with ostentatious care. Hunt cabled Washington to say he had a rebellion on his hands.

"HQ should understand that AMCIGAR members are seizing upon any and all factors to substantiate their conviction that AMCIGAR location in MEXI is untenable," Hunt wrote.

Win and the Cubans alike had assumed the AMCIGARs would be able to travel to Miami and back as they saw fit, completely ignoring that the Cuban Revolution had substantial support in Mexico, even in the ruling PRI party. The Cubans soon discovered all requests to enter the country were being referred to the highest offices in Díaz Ordaz's ministry of government. This had the effect, Win informed Washington, "of prohibiting the legal entry of Cubans into Mexico except after long delays and / or extra-legal payments to secure preferred attention." Overnight, the agency's Cuban allies found themselves barred from boarding commercial airline flights to Mexico. One of the most promising exile leaders, a twenty-seven-year-old psychiatrist from Havana named Manuel Artime, wound up stuck in the Detroit airport for three days. He bombarded Hunt with telephonic complaints.

Hunt asked Win to take up the issue with Lopez Mateos. The president assured Win he wanted to be helpful. He said that Díaz Ordaz's people at Gobernacion would approve the Cubans "provided [there is] no evidence of

Cuban-[CIA] connection and Cubans lived within Mexican laws." But, of course, the Cubans' U.S. connections were obvious, as was their inability to operate within Mexican law or CIA security practices. In his next cable to Washington, Win enumerated a half dozen security violations by the AMCIGARs. Perhaps the most outrageous faux pas occurred when Cuban leader Tony De Varona visited Ray Leddy at the embassy and openly talked about his CIA connections. Leddy was appalled. Then voluble Varona paid a visit to the ambassador—and did the same thing. Within weeks of their arrival the Cubans were proving a daily disaster. Win wanted the AMCIGARs gone, and soon they were. Hunt and the Cubans bought one-way tickets back to Miami. "As we flew east across the Gulf," Hunt later wrote, "it seemed as though we could hear a sigh of relief from Los Pinos," the Mexican presidential residence where Lopez Mateos lived.

Win managed to patch up the situation within a few months. Lopez Mateos and Díaz Ordaz were practical men. They did not care to suffer accusations of cozying up to the yanquis, and Win had no intention of creating problems for them. They agreed that if he, Win, had a specific request that a certain Cuban friend be granted an entry permit, Gobernación would honor it, according to an elaborate five-step procedure. Subsecretary Luis Echeverria would handle the details. Win thought it was a reasonable suggestion. His concession to Mexican courtliness yielded the first real intelligence accomplishment of the LITEMPO program. "A special channel was set up in November 1960 through LITEMPO-1 and LITEMPO-2 which enabled us to secure entry permits," he told Washington.

Dealt a bad hand, Win played it well. He recognized early that a visible anti-Castro Cuban presence in Mexico City was not viable. He let the Mexicans solve their political problems and get rid of the Cuban interlopers without having to refuse a direct U.S. request. The agency had lost a base for the AMCIGARs, but the station had obtained Mexican cooperation on travelers to and from Cuba, a not unimportant intelligence collection priority. The Mexicans had protected their pride and sovereignty. Win had mastered a nuance of their politics. LITEMPO was working.

One sign was a private meeting on January 14, 1961, between President Lopez Mateos and Allen Dulles. The graying spymaster came to sound out Win about possibly replacing J. C. King as the chief of the Western Hemisphere division. With the election of Massachusetts senator John F. Kennedy, Dulles knew the White House would want new blood in senior positions. Dulles knew King had little enthusiasm for covert operations and that Operation Zapata was going to be launched within months. Win, with his wealth of experience in Mexico, might be just the man to take over the division. Together they paid a call on Los Pinos, where Dulles gave the Mexican leader a model pistol for his gun collection. The men talked for two hours with Win serving as interpreter. "Cuba," Dulles opined, "is now definitely communist and it is a problem for all of Latin America as well as for the U.S.A." In other words, the United States was expecting Mexico to help topple Castro. Lopez Mateos replied that Mexico had a tradition of noninterference in the affairs of other nations. "I hope the Cubans can get rid of Castro and communism and settle their problems for themselves," he said, adding that he did not feel the Cuban people could endure hardships and be as disciplined as, say, the Chinese. He said Mexicans could live for ten years on herbs and still fight for their revolution. "The Cubans lack fiber of this kind."

Lopez Mateos told Dulles that it was easy for the United States to look at the Cuba problem as one of international character because there was no chance of Castroism having any real internal effect. "Mexico, on the other hand, has to consider the possibility of internal security problems," he said. "There is a lot of sympathy for Castro and his revolution in Mexico. This factor has to be weighed by me in all actions concerning Cuba. For this reason Mexico cannot take any overt action."

Covert action was a different story, said the president. He offered to consider any action Dulles wanted. He said he would analyze any proposals with Win to determine if he could take action. "There are many things we should be able to do under the table," he allowed.

Dulles was not appeased. "Private enterprise in the United States has become frightened, or least concerned by the loss of nearly one billion dollars in Cuba, which they will probably never recover," he said. "Speaking frankly, some U.S. businessmen have become wary over certain statements and actions even in Mexico."

There was no mistaking Dulles's dig. Amid the adulation of Castro in Mexico, Lopez Mateos had sought to position his administration as a kindred, though not communist, government. The Mexican government, he had famously said, is "of the extreme left within the constitution."

His comment, Lopez Mateos countered, "has been misrepresented by the press. They usually leave out 'within the constitution,' making it look like I meant merely a government of the extreme left and hence communistic." He said his domestic political problems were real, including a communist-sponsored Latin American Peace Congress, upcoming negotiations with the railway workers, and so forth.

This just irritated Dulles more. The American spy chief cut off the Mexican president. "Why couldn't you prevent this peace conference from being held here?" he demanded. Lopez Mateos cited the Mexican constitution, hastening to add that he would do whatever he could to help the CIA disrupt and hamper the conference.

Dulles was not mollified. "Our new government in Washington and American businessmen find it hard to understand why Mexico would allow these communists to assemble in Mexico and attack the United States," he said. "I want you to know I am with the United States," Lopez Mateos reassured him. "There is a Mexican saying, 'Each person has his own method of killing fleas.' Sometime my methods of killing fleas will be different from yours."

"Just so long as we both kill them," Dulles barked, and the meeting was over.

Such was the state of U.S.-Mexican relations at the time President Kennedy took office. The CIA, not the State Department, spoke for the U.S. government.

The idea of promoting Win to division chief went aglimmering. Win had little desire to return to a desk job at headquarters. He could be more helpful in the field. J. C. King stayed on in Washington. As Lopez Mateos had promised Dulles, the Mexicans did provide "under the table" help to the CIA's campaign to overthrow Castro. Win's lieutenant George Munro boasted that he and Emilio Bolaños, LITEMPO-1, had delivered 50,000 gallons of Mexican oil to fuel the exile armada.

But Operation Zapata proved to be a perfect failure. The finest minds and roughest hands of the agency followed the model of Operation Success to the letter. The campaign to overthrow Castro began to buckle in early 1961 as reality weighed on its brittle assumptions that the Guatemalan formula could be transplanted to Cuba. A band of CIA men operating in the remote Central American countryside could keep their operations secret and dictate sympathetic news coverage from inexperienced reporters. Mounting an operation across the open seas against a popular government headed by a battled-hardened military leadership and an accomplished populist orator was a proposition of a different magnitude. And there was the much-noted inability of the Cubans to keep a secret.

President-elect Kennedy, who had been filled in on the broad outlines of Operation Zapata before he took office, had no objections. Within weeks of his moving into the White House, reporters and editors in Washington got word in Miami that an invasion of Cuba was coming. Castro's security forces already knew it. On April 15, 1961, Operation Zapata was launched, not quite seven years after Operation Success. The exiles' small air force bombed Castro's planes on the runways. In Washington, Dave Phillips wrote the invaders' communiqués, and his clients dutifully broadcast them. As in Guatemala, his scripts emphasized the size of the invading force and the weakness of the government. The Cuban leadership, well versed in how the Guatemalan operation succeeded, expected that this psychological warfare campaign would be followed by a pseudo-invasion with the goal of splintering the Cuban leadership and bringing pro-American forces to power. Castro's security forces started arresting everybody known or suspected of involvement in antigovernment groups. When the exile invasion force landed at the Playa Girón (Bay of Pigs) on the night of April 17, 1961, Phillips's propaganda claims vastly exceeded the actions of the U.S. allies on the ground. The anti-Castro student leadership that Phillips had cultivated in Havana was either in jail or hiding in European embassies. The University of Havana campus, the political heart of the capital, was dominated by defiant Castro supporters, pledging their lives to defense of the homeland. On the battlefield, Castro and his military commanders deployed their forces to the Bay of Pigs area on the island's south coast, where the exile invasion force was landing. The incoming rebels, arriving under heavy fire, called for more air support. The planes that had made the initial bombing run returned to Florida. Agency officials simply assumed Kennedy would authorize more flights to support the rebels, as had President Eisenhower during Operation Success. The president had assumed the operation would succeed without U.S. intervention. Both were wrong. Taking Kennedy aside at an elegant diplomatic party at the White House, top CIA officials asked if he would authorize air support. He said no.

The exile brigade was routed on the Playa Girón. Scores were killed. A few escaped into the surrounding swamps, but most were captured. Within a couple of days, the U.S.-backed invasion was defeated. Castro looked like a Caribbean David who had bested the American Goliath. He flaunted his triumph with a propaganda barrage of his own. The captured exile leaders were brought out for the cameras. Howard Hunt's friend Manuel Artime admitted publicly that the CIA planned and directed the invasion. He even spoke of Hunt, saying that an American named "Eduardo" had recommended him to be the overall political and military leader of the brigade and that he had worked closely with him. The agency had been stripped naked in public, its secret operations obscenely on view.

The agency's humiliation was complete. Win kept his mouth shut. He was not one to talk about politics and certainly not one to criticize his superiors, much less a president. His political views were conventional and conservative. He venerated great men like Hoover, Churchill, and Dulles and sought to follow their example. His colleagues were not as restrained. Dulles blamed a failure of nerve in the White House. Richard Bissell, chief of covert operations, blamed "political compromises" imposed by President Kennedy and his advisers. Win's successor as inspector general, Lyman Kirkpatrick, stirred anger by blaming the agency, not the White House. Win's old friend Dick Helms quietly cited the limitations of the plan jointly developed by the agency and the White House.

In the middle ranks of the CIA, the reaction was even more visceral. Back in Washington, David Phillips was drinking heavily.

"I went home," he later recalled in his memoir. "I peeled off my socks like dirty layers of skin—I realized I hadn't changed them for a week. . . . I bathed, then fell into bed to sleep for several hours. On wakening, I tried to eat again, but couldn't. Outside the day was sheer spring beauty. I carried the portable radio to the yard at the rear of the house and listened to the gloomy newscasts about Cuba as I sat on the ground, my back against a tree."

"Helen [his wife] came out of the house and handed me a martini, a large one. I was half drunk when I finished. . . . Suddenly my stomach churned. I was sick. My body heaved."

"Then I began to cry . . ."

"I wept for two hours. I was sick again, then drunk again."

"Oh shit. Oh shit."

When he sobered up, Phillips came away with a simple conclusion. "Secret shenanigans couldn't do what armies are supposed to do," he wrote in his memoir.

In the Mexico City station, George Munro, principal agent on the LITEMPO program and a personal friend of Win's, was seized with a loathing for Jack Kennedy that would never leave him. "From the Bay of Pigs until the end of his life, he hated Kennedy with a passion," said one person who knew Munro well.

Win loathed Castro almost as much as the rest of the disgruntled CIA men, but Cuba was not his obsession. He had other things on his mind. He had fallen in love.

9

Spy as Poet

A slender volume that sat unread for years on the shelf above Michael Scott's desk in his Los Angeles home yielded the story. The book, called *My Love,* told in a coded poetic way the story of Win's most covert operation, falling in love with a woman not his wife. The book's author, "Ian Maxwell," was actually Win himself. His poetic muse, last active fifteen years earlier in war-torn London, had returned. Win was not a brilliant versifier by any means. In fact, some would say he was a terrible poet. His meters sometimes stumbled, and his syntax often clanked. But the depth of his emotions was unmistakable.

Win's life as a spy was often lonely and alienating. Not many spies were capable of admitting that, even privately. But he could say poetically that he had found a woman who eased his inner plight. In love, he escaped darkness. In love, he could express all that emotion generated and suppressed by the formal deceit of the spying life. It was during this season that he began to write to her, for her, of her:

> The luscious toll
> of all you say and do repays
> For weary waiting, pining years
> For heartbreaks, doubts and fears.

In this woman he found a way to live in truth. She did not just remind him of that. She embodied that other way to live. He could be a spy and live in truth.

You are the mirror and reflection too,
The picture and the reality
All things lovely are centered in you;
Beauty, love and spirituality.

He had to have her. He delighted in her presence. Of course, he hurt too because of the damage he was doing.

a dream
Of wine, laughter and faith; a young girl
With dark eyes; and with sweet music
Bearing the couch away!
That night, so filled with thrills;
The weather warm, turned me from
My quiet life; and, now,
I await, My Love, other moments
When pleasure and pain coincide!

Win was writing about Janet Leddy, wife of his longtime friend Ray Leddy.

At work, Win's burden was not small. The embassy had moved into a modern building on Reforma that announced the American government's presence much more openly than it ever had before. Each day, he went to his neat modern desk and tended to the complex task of covertly collecting intelligence. It was a tough time back at headquarters. It was not just that his friend Allen Dulles's job was in jeopardy. The CIA itself faced scrutiny and criticism like never before. In the wake of the Bay of Pigs, JFK had sworn to aides that he wanted to splinter the agency into a thousand pieces and scatter it to the winds. He was just venting. If the United States truly wanted to get rid of Cuban communism and Fidel Castro—and JFK's hawkish younger brother Bobby certainly did—then the job required an intelligence agency. Kennedy furiously signed three national security memoranda, restricting agency involvement in paramilitary operations, but rejected a State Department proposal to strip the CIA of its covert operations function. At headquarters, Dick Helms recalled "a busy interregnum marked with flashes of abrupt change, dampened by the anxiety most of us shared about the shape and the future of the Agency."

In Mexico City, Win attended to Adolfo Lopez Mateos, who was becoming a friend. Every Sunday, Win's chauffeur delivered him to Los Pinos, the Mexican presidential house nestled in Chapultepec Park, to have breakfast.

An American who knew about those meetings was Brian Bell, who served as the press attaché at the United States Information Agency office. He worked closely with Tom Mann, the new ambassador who succeeded Robert Hill. Bell recalled Mann saying, "I tell Win to let me know about the things I should know and don't tell me anything more. As far as I know, he has always done that."

The qualifier said it all: *As far as I know*. In fact, there was a lot Tom Mann did not know about what Win was doing, and Mann knew that he did not know.

Dulles wanted to exploit Win's access to Lopez Mateos. The CIA director, now into his seventh year on the job, was struggling to hang on to it in the wake of the Bay of Pigs fiasco. He was anxious to ingratiate himself with President Kennedy, who could forgive but not forget the Bay of Pigs debacle that, at least so far, defined his presidency. Dulles wanted to show the president that the agency could be useful to him. In a White House meeting with JFK in August 1961 he sought to impress him with the opportunity that Win's friendship afforded. Dulles shared a cable from Win with JFK and explained that while contact with Lopez Mateos was "fully coordinated" with Ambassador Mann, diplomatic protocol did not always have to be observed. Dulles said the Mexican president "desired covert routes for certain types of planning and action." This seemed to echo Lopez Mateos's offer to Dulles in their meeting eight months earlier for "under the table" action against Castro. If this was a hint that JFK might ask the Mexican president to help in renewed secret operations against Castro's Cuba, JFK did not pick up on it. He asked whether Lopez Mateos would support the U.S. bid to block China's admission to the United Nations.

Win's long-standing friendship with Jim Angleton was not so productive. Angleton had built the Counterintelligence Staff into an extraordinarily secretive power center within the already secretive CIA. Demanding absolute security, he ran operations and compiled files that could not be reviewed by anyone, even Dulles. With the imperative of preventing communist penetration, he repelled all efforts to share information with colleagues. By sheer force of brilliance and reputation, he usually got his way. Angleton assumed that Win, like most everybody else at the agency, would do his bidding. But Win had the clout and the personal history with Angleton to say no, and when Angleton attempted to venture onto his turf, Win responded forcefully.

For Angleton, Mexico City was a war front, rife with threats of communist penetration but also loaded with opportunities for creative espionage. His counterintelligence mission was considerably complicated by Castro's embassy in Mexico City. The Cubans established a presence and opened up fraternal relationships with the embassies of the communist bloc. The Cubans, in short, had broadened and deepened the KGB's beachhead in the Western Hemisphere. Angleton wanted to respond. He wanted Win to create an "outside" unit that could mount counterintelligence operations against the KGB under so-called deep cover, with no visible connection to the U.S. government. Anne Goodpasture, a protégé of Angleton's, liked the plan. The idea was to establish a model project that would, as Goodpasture put it, "benefit C.E. [counterespionage] work and standards throughout the region."

Win hated the idea. He flew to Washington to lay down his demands to Jim. He said he wanted only career officers for the new counterintelligence unit, not contract employees. He asked that all the officers be fluent in Spanish, and specified that they would concentrate on the Soviet Union and its allies. When two officers from the Western Hemisphere desk came to Mexico City to work out the details, Win escalated his demands and downplayed Angleton's scheme. He wanted a unit staffed mostly by junior officers who would do both covert action and counterintelligence. The headquarters men returned to Washington without attempting to resolve the differences. They conferred with Angleton and sent a dispatch to Win explaining how the project would proceed. Win replied curtly. Angleton's proposed CI unit would have "too much independence from the station," he wrote. He insisted counterintelligence operations had to be run from official cover positions, meaning out of the embassy and under his personal control, not Angleton's. The incident crystallized a change in Win's friendship with Angleton, said one man who knew them both. Once a friend to Win, Angleton was now a rival.

"They were like two boxers in the ring, eyeing each other, who's going to strike," this man said. "They were two tigers who are looking at each other, who was going to pounce first. Win didn't say much about Angleton. He wasn't someone to make statements about other people that were derogatory. He was a very fair guy, but I don't think he trusted Angleton."

Angleton was retreating into his own mind. The counterintelligence chief lived within a proverbial "wilderness of mirrors" in which he tried to figure out how the Soviets were trying to penetrate CIA operations. Haunted by memories of affable Kim Philby, Angleton spared no effort and respected few laws in his effort to make sure that the Soviet Union did not have a "mole" in the ranks of the CIA. Because of the secrecy of his position and its perceived importance, he could circumvent the legality without much difficulty. In 1956, he had established a program called HTLINGUAL to intercept the mail of U.S. citizens. An office in New York opened, read, and copied a thousand letters a month. His staff informed other U.S. intelligence and law enforcement agencies that they would have to "vigorously deny" any such activity because there was no possible legal justification for the program. Angleton also had special files of intercepted communications involving "elected officials." By some reports he had files on thirty to forty congressmen, and perhaps on President Kennedy himself. The commander in chief habitually indulged his taste for women not his wife but returned again and again to his favorite mistress, Mary Meyer. She was a beautiful artist and free spirit who had formerly been married to a CIA man named Cord Meyer, a good friend of Angleton's. Meyer had theories about the beneficial uses of recreational drugs, and JFK, the leader of the free world, was dallying with her. Angleton would later say that JFK and Meyer had once taken LSD together. Meyers's biographer concluded that "no evidence exists that he [Angleton] taped Kennedy or Mary Meyer but Angleton boasted of it."

For Win, the spy in love in Mexico, each day offered new wonders that could only be captured in poetry. Michael wondered when his father did his writing. Did he close the door to the insistent business of the station and snatch a moment at his desk to write out his equally insistent emotions? Or did he retreat to the study of their home on Avenida Avila Comacho? Wherever Win composed his verse, the subject was the same. "How to measure this love," he wrote, almost mystified. "How to weight it and figure it out?"

> How to balance the sound of a song
> Frame the scent of a flower?
> These impossible solutions
> Are the measure of my love.

Love opened the heavens and the abyss of nonexistence, too.

> My Love! Cure my desire;
> Cut apart the pain
> Rend to bits the ache
> I feel for you!
> I cannot stop the
> Thoughts I have of you
> The thoughts which press my brain
> Void entry of all else.

His passion, his moods, his words echoed the epistolary record of his love for Paula Murray fifteen years earlier. But now Paula, his wife, was forgotten, left to the comforts of the country club, her girlfriends, and gin. The spy-poet felt his own pain but not hers.

Paula took out her anger on little Michael. At least that is the way it would seem in retrospect. Michael sensed something was wrong with his mother. "I have one very vivid memory of Paula," he says. "I don't know how old I was, but I had homework in penmanship. To improve your handwriting, you had to trace over the script, and then mimic what you had traced. The tracing of the letter was [supposed to be] thin and thick."

Paula was not satisfied with the way he wrote.

"I was not doing the thin and thick aspect of it. I was just doing the script, and she got angry at me because I wasn't doing it the way it was supposed to be done. We had a big tangle about it. I just thought it was so odd. I remember thinking, 'This doesn't make sense.' She was not fully rational. It was not worth getting upset about. I think back and I think she was having issues."

No wonder Michael shied away from the self-published volume on the shelf above his desk. Not just because the prose sometimes read like doggerel but because, even if he did not care to think about it, the words evoked a love affair between his father and his stepmother, an affair that had wounded his mother. It was all too personal. At the same time, Michael had always found it easy (sometimes too easy, his wife, Barbara, allowed) to transcend family trauma with objectivity. His profession was filmmaking. He was practiced in looking at the drama of life through different lenses, in thinking about how stories come into view. It was not that he avoided emotion. In his professional life Michael was skilled at making the kind of fraught family or crime dramas featured on cable television networks aimed at women. He knew how to explore and evoke feelings. So when he found Paula's friends later in life, he gingerly asked them what had happened, and they told him the story.

In the fall of 1961 Paula had yet another problematic pregnancy, and it reverberated in her Irish Catholic soul. Just because she had miscarriages and those miscarriages made her sad and sadder did not mean she would not keep trying to get pregnant with Win's child. As ever, she could not stay pregnant. At the suggestion of Win's brother Morgan, she flew to Atlanta and checked into Emory University Hospital, where, according to a medical record that Michael stumbled across decades later, the Emory surgeons "removed a mass on her uterus relating to 10–12 week pregnancy."

"When they went in to operate on her to find out what was wrong," Uncle Morgan told Michael, "they found that she had tuberculosis masses in her abdomen." Michael could only imagine the vast sorrow for his mother in those antiseptic terms. She was forty years old. She would never have a child.

"She went downhill from that time," Morgan said.

All the while, Win presented an image of comfortable authority. "He always wore a dark suit and a white shirt every day," recalled Anne Goodpasture. "He had white hair. He looked like a grandpa. His voice was very soft, barely above a whisper. He had a stocky build. He claimed that he had been a baseball player but he didn't look like that." He basked in the approbation of headquarters. A team of four inspectors came from Washington, and they had the run of the station, the right to flip through files and ask about sensitive operations. They spent a few weeks pulling out file drawers and squinting at explanations they found dubious. They came away impressed. The Mexico City station was clearly the best in the Western Hemisphere, they reported, and probably one of the best in the world. The station was "aggressive and well-managed," they wrote. The technical facilities and capabilities were extraordinary and impressive. The results could be quantified. Win's staff had produced no fewer than 722 intelligence reports in the past year, 45 percent of which came from telephone tap operations.

Win's access to President Lopez Mateos remained invaluable. When Ambassador Mann wanted to know about Lopez Mateos's position on agrarian reform, Win just asked. The issue concerned U.S. officials because Fidel Castro had just expropriated 70,000 acres of property owned by U.S. sugar companies, including 35,000 acres of pasture and forests owned by United Fruit Company in Oriente province. Various left-wing political movements were pressuring the Mexican government to take the same sort of action. Via Win, Ambassador Mann sent Lopez Mateos the message that the U.S. government was keen to extend covert U.S. assistance to the Frente Civico Mexicano, a businessman's group that sought to combat the leftist tide. Lopez Mateos replied he did not want the United States to give money to the Frente or any other anticommunist group in Mexico. "He thought internal politics was the business of Mexicans and that Americans should not get themselves involved," Win reported.

Lopez Mateos preferred to talk of President Kennedy's upcoming visit. He recommended Monterrey as the easiest place to avoid embarrassing demonstrations. He said Mexico was likely to face trouble in the months ahead, particularly in March. He asked Win for help, to "keep communists covered." When the meeting was over, Win asked Mann not to mention in his cable to the State Department that the CIA station chief was present at the meeting. Mann agreed. It was a deft move. Diplomatic protocol required that all meetings with the Mexican chief of state be coordinated by the ambassador. By deferring to Win's request, Mann ceded control of contacts with Lopez Mateos to the CIA. The CIA station chief, not the new ambassador, was in charge of the U.S. relationship with the Mexican chief of state, an unusual arrangement that would endure for years.

Then came word that Win was losing his patron in Washington. Allen Dulles had been fired as CIA director, another casualty of the Bay of Pigs. In November 1961 Kennedy named John McCone, a successful businessman and conservative Republican, as his replacement. For the first time in ten years, Win was not working for his great good friend. His consolation was that the deputy director job, the chief of the Directorate of Plans, would be filled by Dick Helms, his old pal from OSS days. Helms took over the job with a mandate from JFK: get something done about Cuba. His first move was to call in the agency's most effective covert operator, Win's old friend Bill Harvey, to serve as the chief of the Cuba Operations.

In Clearwater, Florida, Janet Leddy paced in a rented house while talking on the phone to her lawyer. In 1961 she and Ray had moved to the Army War College in Carlisle, Pennsylvania, where Ray took a job as a senior adviser. Her marriage already failing, Janet hated the rural military town and its conservative and conformist values. One day, she left her husband with her five children in tow to attend a wedding in Washington, D.C. Instead of returning, she moved to Florida. The kids, mercifully liberated from dreary Carlisle, were confused nonetheless. Her oldest son, Gregory, recalls making a dollar a week helping set up beach chairs. John, the sensitive second son, recalls being angry, missing his dad. Ray Leddy came to visit once. Ever the gentleman, he said nothing bad about their mother.

"He faced all of his challenges in life, stoically, without complaint, and in the case of protecting his children from the unseemly side of adult foibles and transgressions, discreetly," said John Leddy. "My dad thought it was a sign of weakness to become angry, to become inebriated, and to betray a friend. He treasured his friends, his mentors, his colleagues, unless they broke one of the other rules."

John Leddy once asked his father directly to talk about some of the details of his divorce.

"He simply held up his hand and said: 'No, John, I will not do that,'" the son recalled in an e-mail. "To do so (to contest a years-old portrayal of him by my mother favorable to herself and Win Scott but very unfavorable to my father) would require me to go into details and to say things about others that I will not do (i.e., he would not go down a path of discussion or argument that might require him to criticize his former wife to their children). And then he just smiled, and lowered his hand down to the arm rest of his favorite leather wing back chair."

He took Win's betrayal like a gentleman.

In Mexico City, Win was moping, composing interior landscapes of a lover in waiting.

> . . . this far-off love
> Makes an impossibility of our present lives.
> Like a magic storm which stirs the skies,
> When all else is fair

At night his situation seemed even starker.

> Night has lost its charm
> And now is nothing
> Since we're apart.
> Night is obscure while now you're away;
> Unknown and cloudy skies hold sway
> Night confuses, no longer intrigues;
> Dark follows endless dark.
> Stars dim and do not light
> The lonely path on which I walk
> With only shadows of remembrance.

His advancing age—Win was now fifty-three years old—made him impatient.

> Love will conquer, they say,
> But my youth is in flight.
> What is a half-year
> Out of a whole life-time?
> It is a hundred lovings,
> One thousand dreams;
> Which could have become realities.

In the summer of 1962, after school let out, Janet and the kids returned to Mexico City. Win greeted them at the airport. He helped them move into a small apartment off Reforma. Janet's oldest son, Gregory Leddy, recalled the truth as seen through his thirteen-year-old eyes: "Scottie was a friend of the family who was helping us out." Gregory remembered the apartment because that is where he was when he heard that Marilyn Monroe had died.

Win was still married to Paula but bringing Janet and her kids into his life. As covert operations went, this was a delicate one.

At the office, the central irritant of Cuba remained. With the Mexicans, it had to be handled carefully. Win knew what he could and could not expect from Lopez Mateos, whose priority was balancing the leftist and rightist forces in the ruling party. When the White House persuaded fourteen of the twenty-one ministers in the Organization of American States to expel Cuba from the organization in January 1962, Mexico abstained.

In Washington, the Kennedy brothers wanted to overthrow Castro's government, but they did not want to rely on the CIA. On the advice of his favorite military adviser, General Maxwell Taylor of the U.S. Army, Kennedy brought in another general, Edwin Lansdale, to run what amounted to a secret war against the Cuban communists. Lansdale had made his reputation in the Philippines in the early 1950s where he rallied a popular national force in a counterinsurgency campaign that put down a communist rebellion. The Kennedys liked the idea because Lansdale's campaign, in contrast to Operation Success in Guatemala, had bolstered, not destroyed, local nationalists and enhanced the U.S. reputation. Lansdale drew up a fanciful timetable that had the U.S. prevailing in Cuba within the year.

Dick Helms was skeptical. He had ascended to the deputy director's chair on the strength of his quiet but visible refusal to join in the illusions that doomed the Bay of Pigs operation. He believed Cuba policy planning lacked realism. Lansdale was a military man, with little experience in secret operations and running agents. He had never worked in Latin America, knew nothing of the mercurial character of Cubans nor the workings of Soviet-trained security forces that U.S. policy makers confronted on the island. As McCone's man for everything Cuban, Helms had to serve the White House, meaning Bobby Kennedy, the attorney general whom the president whimsically assigned to oversee his Cuba policy. In CIA communications, RFK was dubbed GPFOCUS. He focused what Helms described as "relentless pressure" on the agency to build an underground movement in Cuba that could mount effective and widespread sabotage operations. In Helms's private view, the Kennedy brothers seemed to be avoiding the facts and acting rather amateurishly.

"The steady flow of intelligence data and National Intelligence estimates showing that Castro's military and the internal security and foreign intelligence services were continuing to gain strength did not lessen the Kennedys' determination to even the score with Castro," Helms would later write. "However ambitious, our sabotage efforts never amounted to more than pinpricks. The notion that an underground resistance organization might be created on the island remained a remote romantic myth."

In Mexico City, Win did his part. He had the Cuban diplomatic compound at the corner of Calle Francisco Marquez and Calle Zamora in Tacabuya covered with a photographic surveillance program known as LIERODE. From the Mexico City airport, Anne Goodpasture regularly retrieved the product of a joint program with the Mexican security forces known as LIFIRE: passenger manifests and photographs of the passports of Castro sympathizers traveling to the island. A network of agents dubbed LIMOTOR generated a steady stream of reports on pro-Cuban groups and personalities on the campus of the Universidad Nacional Autonoma de Mexico. LIEVICT supported a national Catholic student group that was anticommunist; the group's president met biweekly with a station officer.

Some of Win's operations assumed the blessing of heaven. LILISP paid 95 percent of the costs of a Catholic Church periodical whose articles included features on "Christianity vs. Communism, the true face of communism, dialogues between a campesino and a more politically sophisticated friend on land reform and education, the menace of Castroism as it affects the Mexican countryside, [and] what the Sino-Soviet conflict means to the average Mexican." Others took place in the gutter. The men behind LITAINT planted stink bombs ("stench devices") in the Cuban consulate.

Best of all, from Win's point of view, was the arrival of David Phillips, the veteran of the Guatemala and Bay of Pigs operations whom Helms had sent to oversee all the covert operations run out of the Mexico City station. Within six months of his arrival, Phillips was guiding thirteen propaganda projects and had seven more in development. He assisted Win in all station matters concerning propaganda and political action and served as liaison to the State Department and U.S. Information Agency. Win thoroughly enjoyed Phillips's presence. "He is intelligent, imaginative; is interested in his work and is a leader," Win cabled Washington. "He originates ideas and vigorously works toward attainment." And Phillips, after eleven years as a deep-cover operative outside of CIA offices, appreciated Win's relaxed and pleasant tutorials on "inside" work—how a station really functioned. Win, in turn, could not help but be impressed by this astute, energetic man.

"I think he trusted me, trusted my judgment," Phillips said later. "It was a relatively close professional relationship. Mr. Scott is a man who if he likes someone, it is obvious that he likes them and I felt that he liked me." Phillips wrote how impressed he was by Win's photographic memory and his unique filing system, even if it was "the despair of management experts in Washington," those paper pushers "who winced at the mountains of paper Scott accumulated in defiance of Agency practices." Win's system worked very well, Phillips noted slyly, "as long as you had a photographic memory."

Most of Phillips's work in his first year in Mexico involved support to CIA projects in third countries and was relatively routine, allowing him some leisure to observe other CIA officers working against the station's "hard targets"—the Soviets, Cubans, Czechs, and other communist countries—and also its "soft targets," the Mexican and Latin American communist parties. "It was new to me," said Phillips, "and a valuable learning period."

While Phillips absorbed new dimensions of espionage, Win had bigger things to worry about. The White House had at long last accepted the invitation from Lopez Mateos. President Kennedy and First Lady Jacqueline Kennedy were coming to Mexico City.

10

Knight

And so the ideological struggle between the United States and Cuba was joined in the heart of Mexico City. After the embarrassment of the Bay of Pigs, John Kennedy wanted to present his Alliance for Progress as the benign face of American power willing to help the people of Latin America. Win Scott was determined to make his visit a success.

The Mexican Left responded without delay. Disorders broke out in rural areas in early June 1962, "believed provoked by the Communists in connection with President Kennedy's forthcoming visit," according to the *New York Times*. Police clashed with campesinos near Cuernavaca in a dispute over lands occupied by squatters. In Sonora, farmworkers carried out a hunger march. Win thought the LITEMPOs were prepared to maintain order during Kennedy's visit. So did headquarters. The agency sent the White House a Special National Intelligence Estimate titled "Security Conditions in Mexico" describing the political situation as "remarkably stable."

"In the name of the continuing Mexican Revolution, the Institutional Revolutionary Party (PRI) maintains absolute control over the political life of the country," said the estimate. "Mexican security forces are experienced and effective. The Mexican government expects to derive great benefits from President Kennedy's visit and is determined to ensure its success."

The estimate did not shy away from the realities of Mexican society. Although the economy was growing at the rate of 6 percent, industry was reaping investment profits of 15 to 20 percent, and the middle class was growing, the benefits to campesinos were minimal—and the ruling party knew it. "Most of the PRI's leaders are seriously worried over the government's failure to make more rapid progress with social and economic reform in the countryside, where about half the population still lives under substandard conditions."

The communists sought "to agitate the general public, to obtain national and international publicity, and to provoke brutal repression on such a scale as to embarrass both the Mexican government and its guest," said the estimate. But Win insisted Kennedy would not be embarrassed in Mexico City. Díaz Ordaz and Gutiérrez Barrios knew what to do. "Federal District police agencies have a good capacity to detect subversives and extremists," the estimate said. "These agencies have a pickup list of 2,000–3,000 potential troublemakers who will be arrested and jailed three days prior to President Kennedy's arrival and held until completion of the visit. The various civil police and organizations in the Federal District number about 10,000 men and have in the past proved effective in controlling disturbances. . . . Local US capabilities for providing warning of planned hostile actions against the Presidential party are excellent." As the *New York Times* reported, "Diverse forces in Mexican official, economic and religious life have united to insure the success" of JFK's visit.

Kennedy's arrival on the morning of June 29 was triumphant. Lopez Mateos greeted Kennedy and wife at the airport. Sitting side by side in an open-air car, the two presidents drove along a nine-mile motorcade route thronged by an estimated 1 million people. It took more than an hour to reach Los Pinos, and not a single anti-Kennedy or anti-American sign appeared along the way. The two men attended a luncheon and then spoke privately for about two hours.

The visit proved to be a huge success for both presidents. At a state banquet the next day Lopez Mateos touted Mexico's revolutionary heritage and successful development. He endorsed the Alianza Para el Progreso "as a movement in which all the Republics of this hemisphere that desire to participate in it have responsibility." He emphasized that it was "not just a unilateral program of aid from the United States of America." JFK replied that the United States sought to reinforce the principle of "sovereignty and independence of every nation" and to reject "subversion," a jab at Cuba. He likened the American and Mexican revolutions as movements for individual freedom that were a model for the hemisphere. He recognized criticism of the United States with the assurance that "we are devoted to increasing social justice." Jackie offered up a bouquet of roses at the Shrine of Guadalupe, the patron saint of Mexico, and charmed a luncheon audience with a speech in passable Spanish. Everywhere the Kennedys went, they were greeted effusively. "This seems more like a giant United States–Mexican fiesta than a state visit by President Kennedy," said the *New York Times* in a front-page story.

Michael Scott remembered Kennedy's visit. He and his father were standing in a reception line in the courtyard of the embassy in the evening. His mother was not there. "When our turn came up, he held me up in his arms and we stepped forward. I shook JFK's hand. I remember us being apart from the crowd for quite a few minutes," he said. "I don't recall the conversation, but I do remember getting a warm and embracing feeling from JFK. He was very friendly to me and I remember his smile. I asked Win later how it was that he was able to speak to the president. He said that he was in charge of the president's security while in Mexico City."

David Phillips, too, would recall JFK's visit, albeit not so fondly. By his own account, he had been devastated by the defeat of the exile brigade at the Bay of Pigs. He felt personally responsible. Phillips was a liberal-minded man, but he did not like how Kennedy had abandoned his allies as they came under communist fire on Playa Giron. He brooded about the Bay of Pigs. David Groves, a public relations man who knew Phillips both in Havana and in Mexico City, had the same impression. "I never heard him complain about his job," he said, "except about Kennedy and the Bay of Pigs."

"It took him a long time to get over that," Phillips's ex-wife, Helen, said in an interview decades later. "I think he was very . . . " She paused, looking for the right word. "He thought a lot about what had gone on. He didn't say a lot to me. I think he was bothered a lot by it."

Phillips had an exalted conception of his profession. In his essay collection, *Secret Wars Diary*, Phillips approvingly quoted Plato's definition of the ideal guardian spy: "swift, strong, spirited and philosophic." He regarded himself as one of the men who stood sentry against America's enemies in the darkest hours. "The Night Watch," as he dubbed his job, was not a post for the faint of heart. He had seen revolutionary street fighting in Havana. In his own fictions, which he claimed were based on personal experience, he spoke of firing guns in anger, of stuffing a urine-soaked rag into the mouth of a man who wanted to kill him, of blackmailing a Soviet counterpart. Maybe it was all imaginary. Helen Phillips never knew him to carry a gun. But he was not averse to projecting the image of ruthlessness. He once turned to a woman at a dinner party in Mexico City and said, with trembling contempt, "Madam, you have no *idea* what I do in my job." One young officer in the station at the time described him as "more of a smooth talker and operator" than Win, "a guy with a good imagination, an understanding of the business and how it should be done, a man who would listen and take his own counsel."

In such a dangerous line of work, Phillips expected support from the leadership for whom he was risking his neck. He viewed his job as "peculiar service" with noble overtones. In CIA communications Dick Helms was known as "Fletcher Knight." In what Phillips proudly regarded as "the ultimate accolade," the deputy director bestowed this moniker on his friend and protégé. Phillips could also call himself "Knight." When Phillips finally met President Kennedy in person during his Mexico City visit, this "Knight" concealed his feelings of disdain for his king. As Phillips recounted somewhat peevishly in his memoir, his standing as the number three officer in the station did not merit an invitation to most exclusive functions for JFK. He had to settle for joining 2,000 other guests at a reception in the Foreign Ministry. In his book, Phillips sketched the scene with clever venom.

"Jackie was queen-like, lovely in a turquoise evening gown," he wrote. "Jack Kennedy was a king that night and acted like one. To the regal he added a touch of the politician, striding about the great hall to meet and shake hands with the guests. As Kennedy made his triumphant round of the ballroom he was chased by a pack of reporters and photographers. Some forty members of the international and Mexican press stayed as close as they could to the handsome young visitor as he stopped to introduce himself and chat, with a pretty woman here, a portly diplomat there, another pretty woman elsewhere." The imputation of a man in search of sexual conquest may have had a personal animus. One of those pretty women whom JFK sought out was Helen Phillips, standing by David's side.

"Suddenly the President headed straight for me," Phillips wrote. "He put out his hand."

" 'Hi,' said the President of the United States, 'I'm Jack Kennedy.' I was surprised that, at close range, he was a much larger man than I had imagined from photographs and that his face was not only ruddy, but downright red." (The implication was that Kennedy's natural color was enhanced, whether by embarrassment, exertion, or drink he did not say.)

" 'Sir.' I shook hands. 'My name is David Phillips.' "

" 'What do you do here, Mr. Phillips, in Mexico?' "

"The forty newspaper reporters behind the President were jostling for a place near him, those winning out jotting down notes on their pads."

" 'I work for you, Mr. President. In the embassy.' "

" 'I see.' Obviously Kennedy preferred more definitive answers to his straightforward questions."

"'What do you do in the embassy, Mr. Phillips?'"

"'I work in the Political Section, sir.' Flashbulbs popped, reporters' pencils scribbled. Mr. President, I thought to myself, please stop asking questions. Would I be the first intelligence officer in history to have his cover blown by his own President?"

"Kennedy was persistent," Phillips wrote. "He wanted a straight answer. 'Mr. Phillips,' he said, a tinge of the imperial in his voice, 'What do you do? Precisely.'"

"Precisely? God! Would I be forced to lie to my commander-in-chief?"

"'I write reports, Mr. President.' Kennedy's face hardened, reddened even more. I continued, lamely, 'Reports which I hope will be useful.'"

"'Mr. Phillips, I—' the President stopped abruptly. His jaw dropped. He finally realized my dilemma. He touched his lips momentarily with the tips of his fingers, as a little girl might do when caught out. Then, in clear tones, 'I see, good luck to you, Mr. Phillips.'"

"Then the President looked at me, his eyes softening in apology. Soundlessly, he mouthed an 'I'm sorry.' Then Jack Kennedy continued his royal rounds. The reporters swept after him."

In Phillips's account the president comes off as a flushed, skirt-chasing aristocrat revealing himself to be immature, even effeminate ("like a little girl caught out"), although the slavish press pack is too busy to notice.

Helen Phillips remembered meeting President Kennedy that night. She recalled that when he entered the room, he immediately spotted her elegant, full-length dress of white silk crepe with one shoulder bared and came over at once. "Of course, he saw it," she said. "He made a dash right for it," she said with a touch of pride. She endorsed her ex-husband's suggestion that Kennedy pursued female companionship with compulsive attentiveness. But she thought David's account was perhaps embellished. "I don't remember David having a conversation that long with Kennedy and him going on and on about it. I don't remember Kennedy ever saying, 'Where do you work' and all that. I think David added that for a little intrigue."

Helen had no way of knowing what such intrigue might entail because David did not tell her about his work. But agency records, declassified decades after Phillips wrote his memoir, suggest his portrait of a clueless president and a canny CIA man was founded in fact. JFK really was in the dark about what Dave Phillips did, especially when it came to Cubans with guns.

In his visible actions, David Phillips certainly served President Kennedy. After JFK and Jackie had returned to Washington, the White House sent a message to Ambassador Mann, asking him to thank his staff for making Kennedy's visit such a success. Mann relayed the compliment to Phillips, adding his own praise. "I understand you handled a particularly useful assignment adroitly and efficiently," he said, without citing any details.

Phillips's secret propaganda operations in the summer and fall of 1962 were a different story. His paid assets mounted a series of actions less friendly to Kennedy. They publicly challenged his Cuba policy by engaging in unauthorized armed action and generated misleading newspaper and TV stories to create pressure for a more aggressive Cuba policy—all without disclosing Phillips's own hand.

Win played no role in these operations. He probably did not know much about them because they did not take place in Mexico. The requirement that covert actions be "compartmentalized" meant that he had no need to know. Yet Phillips's covert action agenda would, within little more than a year, shape the Mexico City station's response to an American traveler to Cuba named Lee Harvey Oswald and to the assassination of President Kennedy. Sometimes what Win did *not* know about David Phillips was as important as what he did.

The stick that Phillips used to poke the White House was a CIA-funded group called the Directorio Revolucionario Estudiantil or DRE. North American newspaper editors called it the Cuban Student Directorate. The group was one of Phillips's favorites. Its leaders had first come to his attention in February 1960 when he was still running his phony public relations business out of an office in downtown Havana. Soviet vice minister Anastas Mikoyan paid a visit to the Cuban capital, an early sign of Castro's intention to align his government with Moscow. A group of University of Havana students took the occasion to lay a wreath at the statue of Jose Marti in the Old City, expressing concern about the future of Cuban independence. Their leader was Alberto Muller, an eloquent young student from a good family who had supported Castro but feared the revolution's direction. Castro supporters appeared and started swinging pipes and sticks at Muller and his friends. The police did not intervene.

Phillips liked the courage of these anti-Castro Cuban students. He made contact with some of them, invited them into his office, and offered money and advice. When Castro's campus enforcers expelled Muller and his friends from the university, Phillips helped them make their way to Miami. He also arranged for agency funding to sustain their activities. By calling themselves the Directorio, they self-consciously linked themselves to the freedom-fighting student directorates at the University of Havana that had taken up arms against Batista in the 1950s and the dictatorship of the 1930s. In CIA communications, the DRE was known as AMSPELL.

Working out of Miami, the DRE leaders impressed Phillips and Hunt as energetic, independent, and mercifully immune to the political intrigues that consumed many exiles. Alberto Muller, who had first gone to the countryside in a literacy campaign, returned to the island and traveled to the Sierra Maestra, where he organized campesinos opposed to the collectivization of life in the countryside. Another wing of the DRE returned covertly to Havana to organize young people unhappy with the revolution and also to mount sabotage operations. They planted bombs that disrupted a campus speech by Castro. They used napalm to burn down El Encanto, Havana's largest department store. Phillips liked their freewheeling style. He gave the DRE boys a show on Radio Swan, the rebel station that he ran from an island off of Honduras.

But the Bay of Pigs fiasco devastated the DRE's network in Cuba. In the run-up to the exile invasion, Muller had waited in vain for promised airdrops of weapons to be used in the planned uprising. He was picked up in a massive security sweep right before the invasion. By the summer of 1962, he was languishing in jail, facing a possible trip to *el paredon,* the firing squad. Phillips took care to respect the freedom of his young Cuban friends. It was not true, as one agency memo later asserted, that the CIA "conceived, funded and controlled" the DRE. The Cuban students had come together on their own and attracted a sizable following with their message of student unity against Castro's communist orthodoxy.

Passionate and headstrong, the young leaders of the DRE often defied the CIA's wishes. More than one officer in Miami wanted the agency to cut off their subsidy. Over time, though, the DRE learned to accommodate the wishes of their CIA allies enough to stay in the anti-Castro fight. Perhaps the fairest description of the group came from Paul Bethel, a retired State Department hand who had served in Havana and was a friend of Phillips's. He praised the DRE as "an instrument of U.S. policy."

Phillips used that instrument to maximum effect in 1962 and 1963, directing the group's propaganda activities first through a Miami-based case officer named Bill Kent. Phillips visited Miami "quite often," Kent later said, and communicated by cables and telephone as well. Kent also conferred daily with Ross Crozier, a hard-drinking contract officer who had responsibility for personal contacts with the DRE leaders. Crozier also reported to Phillips. "There was a mutuality of interest," Kent said of his AMSPELL allies. They had "good respect for the U.S. and realized that we were their only hope for the future." Crozier regarded the DRE as one of the few

Cuban groups that could keep a secret. Their standing was equally high at headquarters. "This [was] the new generation," Nestor Sanchez, then a deputy to Helms, said in an interview. "If anything happened down there, these [guys] are the young generation that are going to go back there to be the new leaders of Cuba." Sanchez said the deputy CIA director took a personal interest in Phillips's passionate protégés. "Absolutely Helms was interested. These aren't the old worn out politicians. This was the new group coming in there."

In the summer of 1962, Bill Harvey, the agency's chief of Cuban operations, was doing his best to help build a resistance movement inside Cuba—though it was not as easy as Bobby Kennedy believed. Harvey loathed the president's younger brother for his increasingly active role in Cuba operations. According to one of Harvey's biographers, he "began suggesting that some of the Attorney General's actions bordered on the traitorous." Miami station chief Ted Shackley recalled Harvey complaining, " 'I need authority. I need guidance but I can't get it by myself from the political level.' " With Manuel Artime, Alberto Muller, and the most capable Cubans sitting in Castro's jails, Harvey and Helms's people had to rely on younger recruits willing to act on their own. With foolhardy courage, the DRE's new leader, Luis Fernandez Rocha, stepped into the breach. He ventured into Cuba to reassure the DRE's increasingly isolated supporters and rebuild the group's capabilities for action. As the plans for a joint uprising at the end of August 1962 fell apart, the DRE leaders began contemplating taking action on their own. From Ross Crozier on up through the ranks of the agency's clandestine service, few cared to discourage Cuban patriots who wanted to take action to stop the consolidation of Cuban communism.

On the night of August 24, 1962, the DRE struck. A pudgy former law student named Manuel Salvat led two boats carrying twenty-three DRE militants across the Straits of Florida to the Cuban shoreline. When they saw Morro Castle overlooking Havana harbor, they veered west toward their target, the ten-story Icar Hotel in the suburb of Miramar. Once a tourist redoubt, the Icar was now home to the engineers and doctors arriving from Eastern European countries to build Cuban socialism. The boats pulled up to within 200 yards of the shoreline. At 11:20 P.M., they opened fire with a twenty-millimeter cannon, aiming for the hotel and the Chaplin Theater across the street, where they thought Castro might be meeting with Russian and Czech comrades. The assault went on for seven minutes. Frightened guests scrambled from their beds as windows shattered and concrete fragments sprayed. No one suffered injuries, only a bout of fright. The Cuban coast guard gave chase, but the DRE boats escaped into the night. In

New York, a DRE spokesman, Tony Lanuza, announced the attack while talking live on the air with popular WABC talk radio host Barry Gray. His appearance had been arranged by the Lem Jones public relations agency, on whose services Phillips often relied.

The attack made headlines around the world. "Havana Suburb Is Shelled in Sea Raid by Exile Group," proclaimed the front-page headline in the *New York Times* the next morning.

"Havana Area Is Shelled; Castro's Charge of U.S. Aid in Sortie Rejected," declared the banner headline in the *Washington Post*. The accompanying story described the attack as "the most dramatic anti-Castro move since the ill-starred Bay of Pig invasion 16 months ago." A DRE spokesman in Miami said, "The Russians are on our soil. We cannot stand by and do nothing."

President Kennedy, vacationing in Hyannis Port, Massachusetts, "consulted by telephone with members of his staff in Washington," according to the *Post,* while Castro denounced the attack as the work of "mercenary agents . . . who operate with impunity from the coast of Florida." The State Department described it, inaccurately, as a "spur of the moment" attack in which the U.S. government had no involvement or prior knowledge.

Dave Phillips had made the whole incident possible. The records of the AMSPELL program, declassified thirty-five years later, show that the CIA was giving the DRE $51,000 a month to fund its intelligence and military operations (worth more than $300,000 a month in 2008 dollars). The DRE students would later say in interviews that the idea for striking the hotel was theirs alone, and that might be true. But they did not deny that they could not mount such operations without the confidence of their closest allies in the agency. The agency, after all, had made it possible for them to announce their coup on national radio.

Phillips was no rogue operator, at least not in the context of CIA operations. AMSPELL was fully funded and authorized. Win probably knew about the DRE program, at least in its broad outlines. There was a DRE delegation in Mexico City, which occasionally made headlines with its reports on Cuban prisons and sabotage operations. AMSPELL might have been one of the thirteen propaganda and paramilitary operations Phillips ran from his desk across the hall from Win's office. If Win did not concern himself with all the details, it was because he trusted Phillips and shared his outlook on the Cuba problem.

Phillips's agents in the DRE had called attention to the soft core of JFK's policy toward Castro. Publicly, Kennedy denounced Castro and described his communist experiment as unacceptable. But when the DRE raiders acted on the president's language by attacking Castro himself, the White

House disowned them and ordered the FBI to curb its activities. The DRE boys and their agency allies thought they were more faithful to the goal of bringing down Castro than the Kennedys themselves.

Dick Helms said as much to Attorney General Robert Kennedy a few weeks later. When Bobby voiced dissatisfaction to Helms with the lack of progress in overthrowing Castro in mid-October 1962, the deputy CIA director responded with a lecture. He said Kennedy should explain exactly what the administration's goals were, "since the Cubans with whom we have to work were seeking a reason for risking their lives." He told the attorney general that the DRE was "willing to commit their people only on operations which they regarded as sensible." By "sensible," Helms continued, the DRE meant actions that "would contribute to the liberation of their country, another way of saying that the United States, perhaps in conjunction with other Latin countries, would bail them out militarily." Helms was voicing in the bureaucratic language of Washington what Dave Phillips said more colloquially: "Secret shenanigans can't do what armies are supposed to do." If the Kennedys wanted to get rid of Castro, they should prepare for the eventuality of U.S. military action. Anything else was self-deception.

With the attack on the Icar Hotel, Dave Phillips and his Cuban assets had sent their message to the president: that freedom-loving Cubans wanted him to act against Cuban communism. JFK did not know that the headlines of the day had been orchestrated by that theatrically handsome man with the pretty blond wife whom he had met at the reception in Mexico City two months earlier. For David Phillips, knight of the Cold War, Cuba was not a theoretical exercise. It was about letting Fidel Castro know he might die in a hail of bullets and prodding the commander in chief to take decisive action.

II

Darkness

Michael was not surprised by the deadly realities of his father's work. Win lived at the front lines of the Cold War. But Michael could also tell that Win differed from some of his colleagues. He was not a theoretician of intelligence like Jim Angleton, who sought to discern fiendishly hidden threats in labyrinths of raw data. He was not an adventurer like Dave Phillips, who relished operating under deep cover on the far side of the law. He was not a mandarin like Dick Helms, whose clean desk and impeccable cocktail party manners signaled the presence of a power broker. Win was no less anticommunist or pro-American than Angleton, Helms, and Phillips. If anything, he was more conservative in his politics. Anne Goodpasture has said that Win's political views were "to the right of George Wallace," the segregationist governor of Alabama. "He was extremely conservative," she said. "He didn't leave any doubt about this." But precisely because he was a southern populist, Win lacked the ideological fire and finesse of his East Coast contemporaries. Although it might not have been obvious from the outside, he was also more emotional. At that time in his life, he was trying to find a new equilibrium. He was less concerned with Cuba than with mundane matters like Janet Leddy and her children in the apartment off Reforma and his son's upcoming seventh birthday. Most of all, he was coming to terms with the fact that he had fallen out of love with his wife.

Paula knew her marriage to Win was dead, and she too was coming to terms. She went away to Acapulco with her sister Deirdre, who was visiting from London. She told her sister she was unhappy; Win was distant and uncommunicative, she said. She suspected that he was having an affair. Deirdre could see that her sister's health was not good. Others saw nothing amiss. When Paula returned to the city, she played golf with Anne Goodpasture and shot a seventy-five. Goodpasture thought she looked fine.

On September 1, 1962, Michael turned seven, an event he remembered well, if only because the birthday was captured on the family Kodak 16 millimeter movie camera wielded by Win. Michael came home, the big black iron gates around the Italianate house at Paseo de la Reforma 2035 swung open, and there was Win's friend George Munro outside on horseback with a pony in tow. The pony, named Mechero, was for Michael. He was surprised and amazed. For a boy living south of the border, having his own pony was better than a dream.

Anne Goodpasture recalled hearing the news. "I had just come to the office in the morning, and I think one of the officers told me that Paula had died of a heart attack, the night before. I was shocked. I knew that she had been ill. But I didn't think it was serious." It had happened just before eleven o'clock the previous night. Win and Paula were at home. Michael was asleep in his bedroom at the end of the long hallway on the first floor. Win called the embassy with the news that Paula had died, and soon people were on their way.

The death certificate, which Michael obtained from the Mexican Archivo General de Nacion forty-five years later, stated that she had died at 11:00 P.M. on September 12, 1962 and gave the cause of death as "infarto de miscardio tuberculosis intestinal" (heart attack intestinal tuberculosis). That contradictory diagnosis was not what a physician would have written. Paula did have intestinal tuberculosis, but such a condition could not have caused sudden death.

One embassy official who was at the Scotts' house that night recalled having received a phone call from Win speaking in a voice of shock. Paula had died. Could he come over? The official came right away.

"Win was not himself. He was pacing around and saying things, but he wasn't coherent in the sense that he wasn't speaking in coherent paragraphs. What he said made sense, but his thoughts were disjointed. He was distraught," this man recalled in an interview.

"There were one or two other people there, I don't recall who. The house was dark. Win was moving about, saying a lot of disjointed things. I was very uneasy about the whole situation."

The visitor, who did not see Paula's body or have any indication where it was, left after twenty minutes.

Michael has no memory of that night. He does recall spending the next day at the home of a playmate, Tommy Haslet, whose father worked for Win in the station. "I spent the day at their house but had to stop at home to pick something up, and when I walked in the house there were a dozen men standing around in dark suits. They were conferring in the living room and none spoke to me. It seemed very odd, but I got what I needed and went back out with the Haslets. I had a hunch something was up."

For Michael, memories of his mother were few. He wanted to believe that she loved him. Her friends praised her as a mother. But he wondered how many of the memories he had emanated from photographs or what other people had told him.

The nature of Win's work forced Michael to take seriously all the stories he heard about Paula's death. Clare Petty, a friend of Jim Angleton's, claimed to know what happened that night, albeit indirectly. Years later Petty had the opportunity to read one of Win's fictions, a short story called "A Time to Kill." The thirty-one-page story languished in a CIA vault for several decades before being destroyed.

Petty said the story concerned a U.S. intelligence official in Washington who is approached by a Soviet diplomat whom he knew casually years before when stationed in London. When the Soviet tries to recruit his friend, the American obtains the permission of a top-level group within the CIA, involving the likes of Dulles, Helms, and Angleton (though Petty said the real names were not used), to act as though he was accepting Soviet recruitment. The Russian and the American develop a close friendship, so close that the Russian falls in love with the American spy's wife. At that point, Petty said, the story got "kinda weird."

"Scott comes home one night and discovered his wife murdered in the bathtub, all cut apart—he knows he did it. Then Scott ostensibly murdered the Soviet, took him down highway ninety five, someplace south out of DC, and dumped him over a culvert."

Petty said the facts of Scott's life and service matched the story so closely that he did not have the slightest doubt that Win's story narrated real events from his life. "It was autobiography," he declared.

Not quite. The short story as Petty described it did include some events resembling events in Win's life. Win had played a role in a double agent recruitment plan in London in the late 1940s, said his former colleague Cleveland Cram. In Cram's account, a Soviet agent approached Win with a recruitment pitch. Win got approval from his superiors to respond in a certain way that Cram said he could not reveal but which was intended to advance U.S. intelligence goals. The operation never amounted to much, Cram added, nor did it have any deadly repercussions as far as he knew.

In most respects, the facts of Win's life did not match events in "A Time to Kill." Win had fallen in love with a friend's wife, but the friend was an American foreign service officer, not a Russian spy. Win and Paula did not live in Washington at the time of her death. There is no evidence Win killed a Soviet intelligence officer. (The local KGB chief, Nikolai Leonov, no fan of the CIA, never mentions the violent death of a Soviet intelligence officer in Mexico City in his memoir of the period.) Paula Murray did not die in a bloody bathtub. Win's story was, in all probability, just that: a work of fiction based on his experience, his imagination, and his desire to be a published author. For Michael the subject was not exactly inviting. He had little reason and less desire to investigate his father for foul play. His father was a warm and loving man. There was something obscene and awful about contemplating one's father as the murderer of one's mother, especially when the evidence did not warrant it. In the end, he rejected the idea. "Everything I ever heard about Paula's death or Win's supposed involvement has been supposition or hearsay," he said.

How credible was Clare Petty? Like a lot of people who made a living in counterintelligence operations, Petty had a paranoid streak that ran deep and wide. He succeeded by seeing the worst scenarios woven into incomplete fact patterns. Later in life, he would come to believe that Jim Angleton was an agent of international communism. Michael thought his Uncle Morgan a more reliable source, though he knew that Morgan could spin a yarn, especially in defense of southern family honor. Morgan said that Win told him Paula had committed suicide. "This was covered up," Morgan told Michael years later. "In the Catholic Church, you lose your chance to go to heaven if you commit suicide. So it was never admitted."

Morgan was in a position to know. When Win called him and told him Paula had died, he had flown to Mexico City immediately. Did she leave a note? Michael asked, boyish hope rising involuntarily in his throat.

"I think so," Morgan said, "but I think that was destroyed. I don't think it does any good to bring up those things."

Why not? Michael wondered. It only occurred to him years later, listening to a tape recording of the conversation, long after Uncle Morgan had passed on. And again, intellectual curiosity led to emotional disorientation. Maybe he was just attaching too much importance to Morgan's choice of words, "covered up."

Sure, the phrase had connotations of wrongdoing, but just as surely it might refer to a shameful or embarrassing event as well. Michael felt that pondering the imponderables was a dead end. Whatever happened to Paula, Win had the power to publicly present it as he wanted. It was unlikely that Michael would be able to pierce the veil decades later.

He felt more certain that his father's commanding self had faltered on that shocking day. Win could not bring himself to tell their son that Paula was gone forever, Uncle Morgan said.

"It was so covered up to you that when I got down there, they hadn't even told you that your mother was dead," he recalled. Morgan said he got mad at his big brother. "You better tell him," he warned. "I said, 'this boy has to know.' This was one of Win's big things, he just didn't . . ."

Morgan could not finish the thought any more than Win could confront unpleasant emotions. He just did not want to tell his seven-year-old son that he would never see his mother again. Over the years, Michael picked up other bits and pieces from friends of Paula's. One person heard that she had been addicted to painkillers. Others said she had a heart attack. "There was a cloud there," said another.

"You've got to understand that the president of Mexico was his good friend. Lopez Mateos hated most Americans. He was one of the nastiest guys I ever saw," this friend said. "But he had Win over to his residence every Sunday morning for breakfast when they were both in town. Talk about being close. So Win could shush anything up."

As the idea echoed—*It was so covered up to you*—Michael returned to it. In his tape-recorded talk with Uncle Morgan, Michael pressed his line of inquiry.

"So Dad told you then that it was a suicide?"

"Yeah."

"In the house?" Michael asked.

"She had been very depressed for a long time," Morgan said.

"You know when a person drinks a certain amount and then takes some pills," he went on, "you never know if they're actually intending to commit suicide, or if it's just unintentional. She had overdosed before. Plus, the fact that when she took alcohol and left off her antituberculosis drug, that made things worse."

A good friend of Paula's heard the same story. This woman's daughter, then a teenager, recalls that Paula's sister, Deirdre, came to Mexico City for the funeral. Deirdre "took my mother aside in the kitchen, and said, 'My feeling is that Paula committed suicide.' I don't think it was beyond belief given what my mother knew [about Win's affair with Janet Leddy]. If you couple her female problems with the reality of 'My replacement is on green seven' or having a drink at the bar, that would be very hard. Women know these things."

Three thousand miles away, in a small town outside of Dublin, a young mother named Terry Murray Duffy remembered the day she received a phone call from the U.S. Embassy in Mexico City. She was Paula's younger sister.

"Am I talking to a Mrs. Terry Duffy? You are a sister of Paula, Mrs. Winston Scott? Is there anybody there with you?"

There wasn't.

"I am sorry to tell you that Paula died a few hours ago."

"I was terribly shocked and incapable of questioning her at that time," Terry recalled in a letter to Michael decades later. At this time, she was living in Ireland. Her son, Gary, was a producer for the BBC. When she received a letter from Michael, Gary prodded her to answer it with as much detail as she could. Terry Duffy supplied the details and the pain too.

"I was certain that there would be an explanatory note from Win, but nothing came," she wrote. "We had no personal message or details of her death which the family found extremely hurtful and insensitive."

Terry contacted another sister who was living in Africa, and she was devastated, as were all the family.

"We were convinced, a conviction which has never left us, that the circumstances of her death were extremely suspicious."

Months later a trunk containing Paula's evening dresses was delivered to Terry's home in Dublin. There was no note from Win.

Forty years later, Terry was offended by the notion that Paula might have committed suicide. Such an action would have been "out of character with her personality and totally contrary to all the tenets of her Catholic upbringing," Terry said.

"Paula was an exceptional human being. She was extraordinarily beautiful, warm and affectionate. She nurtured her siblings with great love and was forever faithful to her siblings and friends. She was very perceptive to the feelings and needs of others. She had the happy knack of springing affectionate communications on those she loved, telegrams being the favorite medium. She laughed a lot and was adored by many. She was taken from us too young and her death has left a permanent void in our family. That her passing merited neither a post mortem (as far as we know) nor a brief note from Win strengthened our feelings of suspicion which time has not removed."

Terry was not a paranoid. She knew nothing of Win's work or Jim Angleton or the ways of the CIA. She said what any loving sister would have said under the circumstances. No, she was not as close to Paula as her other sister Deirdre, but no matter. She said, belatedly, what no one else cared or dared to say. No one took a second look at the circumstances of Paula's death because Win was a powerful American spy.

Michael absorbed the uncomfortable facts. His mother's sudden death was suspicious, and so were his father's actions. All Michael could conclude was that whatever happened on the night of September 12, 1962, in the big house on Reforma, it started with the fact that Win no longer loved Paula, and she knew it.

What is more, Win had helped Janet Leddy, Paula's friend who had the good fortune to have lots of children, to return to Mexico City. And now Janet was divorcing her husband. If, hypothetically speaking, Win had told Paula on that night that he wanted a divorce so that he might marry Janet, she might have believed that the life she knew and wanted to live was over. Under the influence of gin and the seductive buzz of barbiturates, she might have concluded that killing herself would both end her pain and punish Win for his betrayal.

Michael was sure of only one thing, his one clear memory of the events around his mother's death. His father came to him late one night, at least a day after Paula actually died. He hugged Michael, told him that his mother had died, and wept in the darkness.

12

Wedding in Las Lomas

After Paula's death, Win took refuge in work and numbers. Anne Goodpasture said she saw a man "in deep distress." In his memoirs, Dave Phillips later wrote that he sometimes saw his boss leaving the office "carrying a bulging satchel of books and abstruse mathematical journals which had arrived in the day's mail." Win suffered insomnia and confided to Phillips that he endured it with intellectual stoicism. "At night he would play bridge with himself but without cards—mentally dealing and playing until sleep came," Phillips said.

His workload was unrelenting. In October, the Cuban problem culminated again in crisis. U.S. surveillance photos confirmed that missile bases under construction in the Cuban countryside were designed for Soviet long-range nuclear missiles. As President Kennedy and his advisers considered a preemptive attack on Cuba, the State Department sent a message to U.S. embassies all over the world instructing them to brief their personnel on the latest developments. Tom Mann called a meeting of his top staff. Win did not show up, one senior State Department hand told Mel Proctor, a colleague who had served in the embassy in the 1950s. The perception, said Proctor, was that "he was arrogant, a power unto himself and played by his own rules."

But he delivered. As the crisis went on, his friendship with the LITEMPOs proved valuable. Mann wanted to know what position Mexico was going to take. President Lopez Mateos had gone to Hawaii, so Mann called on Díaz Ordaz. What was Mexico going to say publicly? he wanted to know. Díaz Ordaz replied that Mexico always supported Cuba's right to have defensive weapons, but these missiles were clearly Russian-controlled offensive weapons, which could threaten the United States, or Mexico, for that matter. Díaz Ordaz called Lopez Mateos, who stated the same position publicly. Win's friendship with both men helped ensure statements favorable to Washington's position.

In Washington, President Kennedy presided over a team of deeply divided advisers. Kennedy chose not to take the advice of Secretary of State Dean Rusk and chairman of the Joint Chiefs of Staff General Lyman Lemnitzer, who wanted to invade Cuba immediately and remove the nuisance once and for all. He need not fear nuclear war, they said. The Soviets were not going to risk Moscow for a bearded adventurist. Rather, Kennedy took the counsel of his brother Bobby and others who proposed to buy time by establishing a naval blockade, diplomatically dubbed a "quarantine," on the high seas around Cuba. Kennedy demanded that Soviet premier Nikita Khrushchev withdraw the missiles. Khrushchev balked. The Americans could not threaten war over the missiles in Cuba, any more than the Soviet Union could threaten war over U.S. missiles in Turkey, he said. Kennedy dispatched his brother Bobby to tell the Soviet ambassador privately that he could not hold out much longer against the generals demanding an invasion of Cuba. To avert war, Khrushchev relented. On October 28, he announced the withdrawal of the missiles.

Khrushchev's concession letter to Kennedy, written that day, was a backhanded compliment to the effectiveness of David Phillips's operations, testifying to the strategic impact of the CIA man's audacious work and confirming his unseen influence on the Kennedy administration's Cuba policy. In the letter, the Soviet leader attempted to justify the introduction of the missiles to Cuba with a reference to the DRE's attack on the Icar Hotel back in August. He told Kennedy that the Soviet Union had only aided Cuba because

> the Cuban people were constantly under the threat of an invasion. A piratic vessel had shelled Havana. They say that this shelling was done by irresponsible Cuban émigrés. Perhaps so, however, the question is from where did they shoot. It is a fact that these Cubans have no territory, they are fugitives from their country and they have no means to conduct military operations.
>
> This means that someone put into their hands these weapons for shelling Havana.

Khrushchev's rationale was not entirely convincing. After all, he had persuaded Castro to accept the missiles in May 1962, three months *before* the DRE's headline-grabbing attack. But Khrushchev was right that the hotel attack disclosed the reality of U.S. policy toward Cuba. David Phillips did not literally put the weapons used in the shelling of the hotel into the hands of the DRE. (A young militant, Jose Basulto, bought the cannon for $300 at a Miami pawnshop.) But Phillips had recruited, funded, managed, and sustained the DRE as an instrument for the purposes of advancing the U.S. policy of getting rid of Castro. The hotel attack signaled the existence of a faction in Kennedy's administration that was serious about taking violent and subversive action against the communist regime above and beyond what the White House wanted. These were the men whom Khrushchev and Castro sought to deter with the most powerful weapons at their disposal.

Phillips was not done with his covert efforts to forge a tougher line on Cuba. A week later, the DRE got Kennedy's attention again, not with a cannon but with a sensational headline on the front page of the *Washington Star*, the capital city's largest-circulation newspaper: "Exiles Tell of Missiles Hidden in Cuba Caves / Refugees Give Location of 7 Camouflaged Sites for Rockets." Staff writer Jerry O'Leary Jr. quoted DRE sources as saying that some of the Soviet missiles in Cuba had not been returned to the Soviet Union but had been stashed in underground installations. Luis Fernandez Rocha, the DRE's secretary general, had seen two of the sites and had received firsthand intelligence on others, according to the *Star* story. "The free world is on the verge of being victim of a new swindle by the Soviet Union," the DRE declared. "We have in our hands sufficient information that there exist on Cuban territory bases of missiles like the ones that have caused the present crisis and some of even greater range in the subterranean installations that cannot be photographed by reconnaissance aircraft." O'Leary's scoop suggested that Kennedy had been duped again, that the missile crisis was not really over.

O'Leary was close to David Phillips. He was a hard-drinking, straight-up former U.S. Marine colonel who had turned to journalism as an outlet for his conservative political convictions. They had first met in Chile a decade earlier when Phillips was running the *South Pacific Mail* and O'Leary was a roaming foreign correspondent. They had renewed their acquaintance in the run-up to the Bay of Pigs when they talked about Cuban politics and what JFK was going to do about Cuba. "We liked each other and we had dinner together and we were friends," Phillips later said in a sworn deposition.

"They were good friends," said Maria O'Leary, Jerry's widow, in an interview. She rejected published accusations from the 1970s that her late husband had accepted money from the CIA. "He never was a paid informant," she said. "He had information that he passed along to CIA people and they in turn gave him information."

O'Leary's story, based on information from Phillips's favorite young Cubans, angered President Kennedy. At a meeting of his National Security Council, Kennedy interrupted a discussion of a draft reply to Khrushchev's latest letter on the Cuba situation to demand an explanation from John McCone. The CIA director said the source of the *Star's* story had been interviewed, but he did not know anything more. (In fact, the DRE leaders quoted in the story had not been interviewed and would not be for another week.) Kennedy coolly suggested that McCone talk to the editors of the *Star* and other papers and tell them to check such stories with the government before printing them.

The pressure on the White House from the DRE program continued. A few days later, Luis Fernandez Rocha appeared on the nationally televised *Today Show* and repeated the allegation that the Cubans had stashed nuclear missiles in caves. In the White House, Kennedy blew up. He ordered the CIA to interrogate every Cuban refugee who was making statements about arms in Cuba. "The refugees are naturally trying to build up their story in an effort to get us to invade," he complained. "We must get to the people the fact that the refugees have no evidence which we do not have. Such refugee statements, if they continue, could make the problem almost unmanageable."

As usual, Dick Helms did the president's bidding as consistent with the CIA's agenda. He moved to bolster agency control over the Cuban Student Directorate. He summoned leaders Luis Fernandez Rocha and Jose Lasa from Miami for what one aide described as a "Dutch uncle" lecture. The deputy director grilled the two young Cubans about the sources of the "missiles in cave" story. He told them he wanted "to work out a slightly different way of doing business." He wanted a "reasonable collaboration," which would be handled by a new contact, he said.

"This new man will be able to come to me for any clarification needed regarding the relationship," he told the young Cubans. He said he understood their political concerns that Kennedy's policy was weak. The policy toward Cuba, he said, was under review. He said it would take a month to clarify the future course of U.S. policy.

The new man assigned to handle the DRE/AMSPELL program was an up-and-coming forty-year-old officer named George Joannides. A lawyer and journalist from New York City, he was a protégé of Helms's trusted deputy, Tom Karamessines. When Joannides replaced Ross Crozier as the case officer for the DRE in Miami in late November 1962, he was serving as the deputy chief of psychological warfare operations in Miami. He introduced himself to the Cuban students as "Howard." It was his job to keep the DRE boys under control, probably on behalf of David Phillips, the agency's psychological warfare specialist par excellence.

In Mexico City, Win let it be known that he and Janet Leddy were going to get married in December. The announcement, sent out to a select group of friends, said the ceremony would be held at the house of Paul Deutz, a tall, handsome scion of a Mexican American family that owned a steel mill. His wife, Dorothy, and Janet were best friends. Tom Mann heard the news only a few days before the event and blanched at this most public development in the station chief's private life. For many in and around the embassy, the shock of Paula's death had not worn off. The news that Win was remarrying so soon was another shock, and the fact that he was marrying Janet Leddy, whom most people still knew as the wife of Ray, Win's ostensible State Department colleague and supposed longtime friend, was even harder to comprehend. "It hurt Win's reputation," said Mann's former assistant Bill Pryce. "It was so gross."

Brian Bell, the press attaché at the Information Service, was stunned. He did not know that Janet Leddy had left her husband, only that Ray Leddy had left Mexico before the end of his tour. "It was too bad because he was one of the most competent political officers I ever met in the Foreign Service," Bell said. When Bell heard Win and Janet were getting married, he assumed Win's job was in jeopardy. "Everybody thought they would transfer Win because it was real embarrassing," he said.

The women of Chapultepec Golf Club were more offended. How could he? they gasped to each other. How could she? Every day they missed Paula, and that keen loss made some loathe the sight of Janet Leddy with Paula's husband. She was a scavenger of men, said one to her daughter. She had been after Win for years. "It's like Hamlet," she cried. "Couldn't they have waited?" Another woman recoiled at Win's choice, believing that Paula had committed suicide. "It was like he married the motive."

Back in Carlisle, Pennsylvania, Ray Leddy was fighting back. In response to Janet's unilateral divorce filing from Florida, he hired Eddie Hidalgo, a prominent attorney in Mexico City who had been a classmate of his at Xavier High School in New York City in the 1930s. He filed suit against Janet in a Mexican court for "abandonment." He demanded custody of their five children. He also appealed, via friends in the State Department, to have Win transferred back to the United States. Mel Proctor, then serving in the Inter-American Affairs division of the State Department in Washington, was sent to see Tom Mann in Mexico City. "I made the pitch that Ray Leddy wanted access to the kids and we were wondering if Win hadn't been in Mexico long enough. This is a legitimate concern by the State Department." Mann told Proctor, "You can get me out of Mexico easier than you can get Win Scott out of Mexico." Win stayed put. Mann told another State Department friend he feared the conflict between Win and Ray might end with an "explosion."

Win, by all accounts unperturbed, ignored his former friend and tended to his future wife. He had never been one to dally on the way to the altar. Thirty years earlier, when he was a college student and brought Besse Tate home to meet his parents, he had demanded his father find the justice of the peace in the middle of the night. He would not and could not wait. Twelve years later, when he was climbing fast in the new U.S. intelligence service, he insisted Paula marry him, less than a month after he hastily signed the divorce papers in the office of Besse's lawyer. In those times that Win found himself without a mate to woo and win, life lost meaning, and the sheer passage of empty time afflicted his soul.

Now that Paula was gone, Win would not delay in making Janet his wife. His bride, for her part, did not care about a big or elaborate ceremony. She wanted what Win wanted. Yes, she wanted to get married right away, for the sake of the children. For more than a year, they had been moving from rented house to apartment, from school to school. She wanted them to have a stable home again, and she knew Win would be a good stepfather. As for the wedding arrangements, she turned to her good friend Dorothy Deutz. Dorothy and Paul had a beautiful home in the swank Las Lomas Chapultepec section of Mexico City. Dorothy knew how to play hostess, to arrange for parking, to find the caterers, to stock the bar. Win would do the guest list.

Win had a vision of a ceremony, both grand and practical. He wanted an event that would fuse his personal and political power, impress the world, and gratify his new wife. His first move probably came at one of his breakfast meetings at Los Pinos when he invited Lopez Mateos to serve as *padrino* (chief witness) at his wedding, a gesture that said the president was the closest of friends. Lopez Mateos agreed. Díaz Ordaz said he would attend, as would the rest of the cabinet.

When Tom Mann heard about Win's wedding plans, he balked. The ambassador was a correct and conservative man, and he did not care to bless Win's brazen ways by attending the ceremony. He relied on the sensibilities of his wife, Nancy, in all aspects of his life. She was as offended as the other women around the embassy by the news of Win's impending nuptials. But when Mann heard that Lopez Mateos was going to attend, he had to reconsider. If El Presidente was there, the American ambassador could not very well stay away. Mann decided he had to go.

Win had a knack for getting his way, which is to say Win had a knack for power and its preservation. And nothing preserved his moment of power like the 16 millimeter home movie of his wedding that Michael retrieved from a Mexico City storage locker decades later. The civil ceremony was an orchestrated display of power that Win wanted to capture in images and memorialize.

When the wedding day came, December 20, 1962, Win arranged for an unknown cameraman to mingle among the guests. On ten minutes of celluloid, alternately grainy, gloomy, and garish, the Kodak camera captured the ease and style of Win's heyday. For Michael the home movie was family memorabilia. When he showed it to Mexican friends, he realized it was also a political document of the highest order, a revelatory glimpse of secretive gringo power in mid-twentieth-century Mexico.

Mann was the first to arrive, at least in the cinematic version. A score of guests, many of them Janet's female friends, had arrived earlier, but the cameraman, perhaps on Win's instructions, had not filmed their entry. Mann came in, a trim man in a suit and bow tie, accompanied by Nancy, wearing a handsome black and emerald faille dress. They shook hands with Paul and Dorothy Deutz, who did the greeting by the door. Win and Janet, also hovering at the entrance, then escorted them down the receiving line. Win and Janet made a dignified couple. Win came dressed in his usual dark suit and white shirt; Janet wore a white sequined dress and sparkling earrings. If she looked serious, he looked almost grim, as if he was at work, which of course he was. The house was modern and elegant, with the furnishings both old and new that reflected the fact that the Deutzes had both money and style. But for anyone who knew the nature of Win's work—and more than a few in the room did—the event had a brazen quality.

No one could have appreciated or worried more about Win's audacity than Dave Phillips. In the film, he can be seen standing with Helen, in front of a massive wooden armoire displaying an array of delicate white china figurines. They, too, made a handsome couple. His dark suit, white shirt, and skinny silver tie, with a white handkerchief peeking out of his breast pocket, set off her more decorative black and white patterned dress, with a single strand of small pearls around her neck. But he hardly looked relaxed, and he eyed the camera warily. He was, after all, a spy, a specialist in propaganda, a man skilled in invisibly perpetrating images and information to maximum advantage, and here he was, out of loyalty to his boss, exposed to a camera. The composed look in his eyes glinted with awareness of vulnerability. No wonder that Helen looked more comfortable. Her identity was not being betrayed by the whirring camera of Win's reckless love.

A squat photographer circulated, taking snapshots of the guests. Here was Benito Coquet, the minister of social security, in charge of distributing pensions to tens of millions, standing shyly to one side. He would be touted as a possible future president of Mexico. There was a sleek functionary with Indian features nodding knowledgeably to Ambassador Mann. Here was Carlos Trouyet, owner of a telephone company and one of the richest men in Mexico, pudgy and shrewd, smiling by the stairs. He built the Las Brisas luxury hotel in Acapulco that helped turn that modest seaside resort town into a synonym for global glamour. He wore a diamond-studded lapel pin. Nancy Mann perched on the arm of a couch, looking older, plainer, and wiser than the elegant women with plucked eyebrows who listened to her.

"We had secret service personnel galore as every minister brought his own entourage," recalled Paul Deutz in an interview. "When the whole cabinet was present and it was time for the president to arrive, he did so without any escort and in his personal Porsche. He was a car nut. He drove himself."

Lopez Mateos swept in, and the glare of the popping flashbulbs tinted the film green for a moment. Win walked right beside him, hands in pockets, his casual gait ceding attention to El Presidente but also announcing himself as the discreet compadre of his honored guest. Lopez Mateos's face, creased with the pressures of power, broke into an easy smile at the sight of familiar faces. When Win introduced him to those he did not know, he nodded hard and mouthed words that elicited smiles.

Right behind them came Díaz Ordaz and Janet, walking side by side but not looking at each other, each accustomed to playing a secondary role to these leading men. Janet ushered him to guests who had just met the president. Díaz Ordaz extended a tentative paw, and his shy smile revealed an unfortunate row of buckteeth.

And so the essence of LITEMPO, a top secret CIA operation, was captured on film. As Dave Phillips surely knew, Win was violating every rule of espionage tradecraft. From their first day of service, these men had been taught that to reveal real names and the true nature of relationships would threaten nothing less than the national security of the United States. Every day he and Win and the many officers who reported to them took elaborate precautions to avoid being observed with their agents. Station protocol forbade any meetings in public. Even forty years later, when many of the people who had been in Paul Deutz's living room that day were dead, the identity of Lopez Mateos as LITENSOR and Díaz Ordaz as LITEMPO-2 was still censored from publicly released documents. At Win's whim, all professionalism was abandoned at Paul Deutz's door. Tradecraft, it seemed, mattered less than love and power.

The ceremony itself was solemn. Win and Janet, flanked on the right by Lopez Mateos and Díaz Ordaz and on the left by Paul Deutz and George Munro, stood before the justice of the peace. Win's carriage was erect and immobile, his eyes looking steely. Janet sneaked a peak at the camera with the flicker of a smile, as if thinking this is funny, if not fun, and I'll enjoy it however I can. Vows were exchanged. If there was a kiss, the camera did not record it. Win signed the marriage certificate, then Janet took the pen, then Lopez Mateos scrawled his name with a flourish, and looked up with a grin of satisfaction. Two marriages, one of man and woman, the other of Mexican and American power, had been consecrated. The party began.

A stunning blond woman, an artist friend of Janet's who also ran an exercise class for the women of Las Lomas, came up to kiss her and Win. Janet turned around to introduce her to the president.

"This is my friend Gudrun Edwards," she said. "She is from Sweden and she is a sculptress."

Lopez Mateos took one look at Gudrun's low-cut dress, her bare alabaster shoulders, and lithe neck graced with a diamond necklace, and objected warmly.

"No," he said to Janet. "She is not a sculptress. She is a sculpture."

Win had a word with Carlos Trouyet, then with Mann. Dave Phillips tried to step out of the camera's view when it approached again. On the couch, Lopez Mateos was chatting up Gudrun, holding up his hand, fingers entwined as if holding up a precious thing for inspection, and she laughed in demure delight.

"The gathering was relatively small, but I thought it went well, and the president certainly had a good time," said Paul Deutz. "Humberto Romero, his personal secretary, kept telling him that it was time to go to a cabinet meeting. He finally told Humberto for them to go ahead and he would catch up to them later. That cleared just about all of the security, and the president stayed for another couple of hours and enjoyed his champagne and Delicado cigarettes."

When Lopez Mateos made his exit on the film, all eyes were on him. Framed by the doorway, he gave an *abrazo* to Ambassador Mann and spoke of something serious. Mann laughed, perhaps too readily. Win, standing in the vestibule, pulled the president to his chest for a manlier hug and then escorted him out the door. When he returned a few moments later, the room began to relax. The buffet dinner was served. As the guests held out their plates for mounds of mashed potatoes, the movie ended.

Decades later, Michael could watch the footage of the wedding with pleasure, just to solidify the sometimes tenuous memories of his father or to soak up the details of sixties style: the bouffant hairstyles and the carefree smokers, the plucked eyebrows and skinny ties. He could parse its implications for Mexican politics, or, as a filmmaker, he could appreciate that the unknown cameraman had a steady hand and probably some experience behind the viewfinder. But like so many things in his father's life, there was something about the film that did not quite cohere.

Why would Win stage such a flamboyant scene? he wondered. Why parade his friendships with Lopez Mateos and Díaz Ordaz in front of the world? Everything Michael had learned about Win suggested that he served the CIA without question, that he craved the approval of Allen Dulles and worked late into the night for Dick Helms. He might have had his private insecurities, but he would not flout the agency's rules and practices carelessly or out of vanity. The home movie, in and of itself, did not blow his cover with Mexican authorities, but the article that appeared four days later, on Christmas Eve, in the *secion sociales* of *Excelsior,* the broadsheet of the Mexican political establishment, certainly invited attention to their friendship.

"Enlace de Janet Graham y Winston MacKinley Scott" (The Joining of Janet Graham and Winston MacKinley Scott), declared the top-of-the page headline, over a photo of the bride and groom clinking glasses with Lopez Mateos. The caption announced that the president of the country had been the witness to the gringo wedding.

Michael could understand why Lopez Mateos would want to do a favor for his American friend. What he could not understand was why Win would jeopardize his secret relationship to the president by publicizing their friendship in the society pages. There did not seem to be any intelligence or political advantage in that.

Win's wedding show never made sense to him until he heard the explanation given by Bill Pryce, Tom Mann's assistant at the time. Pryce may have been a peach-faced aide in 1962 but in the fullness of time would become an ambassador himself. He did not lack insight into the motives of men of power. Pryce said in an interview that Win staged the wedding show to fortify Janet in her custody battle with Ray Leddy.

"Remember, the law was on Ray's side," he explained. "This was Mexico. The father was presumed to have rights to the kids. Win knew this, which is why he arranged to have Lopez Mateos as the witness. So that if Ray's case ever was heard in a Mexican courtroom, Win could show the marriage certificate to the judge. The judge would see the president's signature, and he wouldn't dare to question Win's rights as a father and husband. The wedding was set up to show how powerful Win was." Lopez Mateos and Díaz Ordaz might have been flattered to be asked to participate, Pryce said, but they did not really have the choice of turning him down. "Win could tell them about the Soviets and the Cubans. He had the money and the information."

In other words, Win had deployed his political power in service of Janet's desire to keep her children.

"I thought it was unprofessional, using his position for a personal matter like that," Pryce said. "He was a real swashbuckler. He was playing fast and loose."

Michael could not be so judgmental. His father's brashness had forged the family he would have for the rest of his life. His marriage to Janet gave him a stepmother to replace Paula, as well as the companionship of four brothers and a sister. Michael recalled staying at a rented house in Cuerna-vaca over the Christmas holiday that year and his new siblings inviting him to their room late one night to welcome him as their new brother.

Gregory Leddy, the oldest of Janet's children, had an even more specific memory. After all the changes of the past year, he wanted to make the new family work. He recalled going to the house in Cuernavaca while his mother remained in the city. One day before Christmas, she called him.

"'Gregory, I want you to know that I have to marry Mr. Scott,' she said."

"I was like, 'What?'" Gregory remembered. "I think I said, 'You have to marry him?' She said, 'No, I want to.'"

"I think I said, 'Why?' She said, 'Because I love him very much.'"

Unlike his brother John, who was hurt and baffled by the loss of his father, Gregory remembers being eager to please his mother. On Christmas Eve, the day the wedding story appeared in *Excelsior*, Win and Janet drove down to Cuernavaca in his big black Mercury. When they arrived Janet told the children to go outside and help their stepfather. Gregory ran outside. Up until then, he had always called his mother's friend "Mr. Scott."

Win opened the trunk of the car. It was full of Christmas presents.

"I said, 'Hi, Scottie,'" Gregory recalls with a smile. "It was the first time I called him that. He loved it. It absolutely melted him."

13

"You Might Have Had a Seven Days in May"

One day around the time of the wedding, Win walked into Dave Phillips's office and closed the door behind him. "I'm going to tell you something which you must never tell anyone," whispered the silver-haired station chief.

Phillips gamely agreed.

"If you do tell anyone, I'll kill you," Win said.

Phillips, suddenly alert and curious, agreed again.

"I read a while back about a poetry competition in the States," Win stammered. "There's a national prize for the best new volume of . . ."

Phillips watched as his boss blushed.

" . . . love poems."

Win, said Phillips, threw a manuscript onto his desk. He wanted Phillips's opinion. Phillips read the poems and recommended he enter the contest. A few weeks later Win dropped by Phillips's office and gave him a thin volume. "I won that competition," he grunted. "Thanks." The book's dust jacket, Phillips later wrote, "revealed that the poet, an unknown, had won one of America's most prestigious literary competitions. I kept my word to Win and did not reveal that the Laureate was a CIA station chief."

It was a nice story. It may have actually happened. But Win had not won a literary competition, prestigious or otherwise. Either Win fibbed or Dave was embellishing or maybe both. Win's suite of his love poems, *My Love,* was published by Dorrance, a Philadelphia company that catered to determined authors who lacked other outlets. The "competition" to which Win referred was probably the bait for aspiring authors who wanted to see their name in print.

Typically, the authors received a hundred or a thousand copies and had to sell the books themselves. How many Win bought is unknown, but it is certain that *My Love* was registered at the Library of Congress the week after Win and Janet's wedding. Win gave the first and most important copy to his new wife as a wedding gift while they and their six children spent a satisfying, if chaotic, first Christmas together in Cuernavaca.

Michael could forgive Win for fibbing about his literary accomplishments. Win's volume, after all, had won the prize he cared about most: Janet's love and affection. The book's audience was not much wider than the family, which did not bother Michael at all, given its sometimes embarrassing contents. In all the years the book had been on his shelf, he had only skimmed it. And he was not alone in his reluctance. Anne Goodpasture allowed as she had never even opened her copy.

Phillips's anecdote about Win's private passion indicated he had gained Win's personal confidence. That was no small accomplishment for a man looking to get ahead. Phillips had sported a sterling reputation as a clever "deep cover" operator in Guatemala, Havana, and Miami. He impressed all who met him on Operation Zapata. He was energetic and astute, an aspiring writer, an amateur actor playing the real-life role of spy. Win was less dazzling but had time on his side. He had dodged Hitler's rockets in the streets of wartime London, helped unmask Philby, run the Western Europe division, served as inspector general in Washington, and run the Mexico City station long past the usual four-year limit on a station chief's tenure. Phillips envisioned himself as a station chief one day, and maybe more. From Dick Helms's point of view in the deputy director's chair, Win and Dave made a natural pair, an experienced veteran bringing along a rising star. Phillips had free rein within the limits of Win's vigilant control of every aspect of the station's operations.

No one could have known at the time that the partnership of Win Scott and Dave Phillips would come to play a central role in the massive intelligence failure, still obfuscated by CIA secrecy four decades later, that would culminate in the murder of President Kennedy in Dallas on November 22, 1963.

For Michael, understanding his father's role in a national catastrophe was part of his mission. For him personally, 1963 held mostly the amusing memories of a whole new family dynamic. After Win married Janet in December 1962, the trauma of Paula's passing was succeeded by the sudden appearance of four brothers, a sister, and a strong-minded stepmother. Dave and Helen Phillips and their children inhabited Michael's happy childhood memories. Like Win and Janet, the Phillipses enrolled their children at the Greengates, a private school in Las Lomas favored by English-speaking expatriates. Maria Phillips, at age thirteen, was the oldest and like her mother she was strikingly pretty. She was a classmate of Michael's new sibling, Gregory Leddy, who had just turned fourteen. David Phillips Jr., nicknamed Buzzy, was ten. Another Phillips girl, Atlee, was friendly with the only Leddy girl, Suzanne. Michael was in second grade, as was his new stepbrother George Leddy. His life as the only child of a reclusive mother and hardworking father gave way to the daily scramble of six kids looking for food, attention, and adventure.

As for David Phillips, Michael recalled him as the father of his playmates and a family friend. He did not have a strong interest in pursuing the theories of JFK conspiracy writers who thought Phillips had some role in the assassination. His interest was more personal. From the very start, no small part of his quest to learn more about his father's professional life had been propelled by that singular fact: *Win's unpublished memoir had a chapter on Oswald, and the agency had seized it.* As a filmmaker he could appreciate a plot twist, and this was a doozy. Michael had no desire to implicate (or exculpate) his father (or David Phillips or anyone else) in grand and dirty deeds. He just wanted to locate Win in the Kennedy assassination story: what did he see, hear, talk about, and do as the tragedy approached?

What Win did *not* know in late 1963 were details of David Phillips's anti-Castro operations outside of Mexico. Win did not figure in that story, but those operations were essential to understanding Win's role in the events that led to Kennedy's murder.

Win admired Phillips almost without qualification. "He is the most outstanding Covert Action officer that this rating officer has ever worked with," Win wrote in his April 1963 evaluation of Phillips's work. His performance was "superior in every respect." From his earliest days under the tutelage of Kim Philby and Norman Holmes Pearson, Win understood that the key to running agents was psychological sensitivity—and Dave Phillips had it. "His comprehensive understanding of human beings combined with a thorough knowledge of covert action techniques and his fluent Spanish make him unusually valuable." Anne Goodpasture saw "a close friendship" developing between the spy-poet and the former public relations man. She said Win tried to promote Phillips to the job of deputy station chief in early 1963. But Helms, who had other plans for Phillips, vetoed the idea.

In the wake of the missile crisis, Cuba policy was in flux again. Kennedy may have forced Khrushchev to back down on the missiles, but Castro, despite his fears and fulminations, had emerged ever stronger. The fact that the United States had not attacked Cuba, despite the provocation of the missiles, suggested to many that the Kennedy administration had a de facto policy of coexistence with Havana. Some at the State Department and White House rationalized the possible benefits of learning to live with Castro, but the vast majority of men and women in the upper ranks of the CIA and Pentagon balked at the notion of accommodating communism in the Western Hemisphere.

The Kennedys moved to reorganize the CIA's Cuba operations yet again. Helms agreed to bring in Desmond FitzGerald, director of the agency's Far East division and a friend of the Kennedy family, to oversee a new component within the CIA with the bland name of Special Affairs Staff (SAS), dedicated solely to Castro's overthrow. The Cuba Coordinating Committee was established at the State Department to orchestrate a diplomatic offensive. The Joint Chiefs were tasked with developing contingency planning for military intervention in Cuba. Inspired by their successful handling of the missile crisis, the Kennedy brothers set up an executive committee of top officials from all the national security agencies to handle Cuba. The Ex-Comm, as it was dubbed, would be strictly hush-hush. No assistants or deputies would attend the meetings. "Unleashing" the exiles was not a solution, said JFK publicly. Privately, his brother aimed to bring down Fidel Castro himself. In his more hubristic moments, Bobby thought of himself as "second commander in chief," the man forging a new Cuba policy and perhaps his own future presidency.

Helms sent the new chief of SAS, Desmond FitzGerald, to give the new order of battle to the men and women in the field. He traveled to Mexico City, where he drank brandy with David Phillips and informed him he had been promoted to the new chief of Cuba operations, with writ to roam the entire Western Hemisphere mounting secret operations to get rid of Castro. The ever-gracious Win ordered up an engraved silver platter as a gift for FitzGerald; Anne Goodpasture took care of the shipping.

In his memoir, Phillips would credit his new assignment mainly to CIA director John McCone and, with characteristic misdirection, leave his patron Dick Helms out of his narrative. After the October crisis was over, McCone had "another canny premonition," Phillips wrote. "He was concerned that the agreement with Khrushchev—a pledge by Kennedy that the United States would stay out of Cuba—would leave Fidel Castro in a strengthened position to pursue subversion in the other countries of Latin America." In Phillips's view, Kennedy's resolution of the crisis, while politically pleasing, had actually fortified and emboldened Castro. McCone could only prepare the CIA "for the period when it must fight Castro's surge to export the Cuban revolution."

The truth was that McCone did not make Cuba personnel decisions. From the start he had designated Dick Helms as his point man on Cuba policy. It was Helms, not McCone, who sent Phillips to his new post in the summer of 1963.

Phillips loved a stage, and now he had one. From the Bay of Pigs humiliation, he had returned to a central role in the operational execution of Kennedy's waning war on Castro. "He thought he was a real James Bond," said Phillips's first wife, Helen. "He wanted to live that life." His new job assignment, he later explained, "was to gather intelligence about Cuba and about Cuban activities abroad." He had a large staff and received reports from all over the Western Hemisphere and elsewhere. His office, he said, served as "a point of reference . . . a place where guidance could be obtained for Cuban activities anywhere in the world." He also took over responsibility for monitoring the Cuban embassy in Mexico City, especially "any nexus it might have with pro-Castro groups in the hemisphere." Each day Phillips received the transcripts from all the conversations picked up by LIENVOY audio operations that concerned Cuba. He also oversaw the observation post, which photographed visitors to the Cuban embassy. There were few spaces that Phillips knew better than the much-photographed entrances to the embassy and the neighboring consulate.

Dave wanted Anne Goodpasture on his team. Because of Anne's reputation for reliability, Phillips hoped she could handle the photographic take on the Cuban embassy, just as she handled the photo take from photo surveillance programs of the Soviet embassy. Goodpasture begged off.

"When Scott came and said, 'Dave wants you'—I believe it was Dave . . . 'to do the same thing for him that you're doing for the Russians' [to identify people coming and going], and I said, ' . . . I just can't do it because I don't know anything about what else is going on. And so many little things were—pieces would fit together easier—so it has to be someone who's working with it,'" she recalled. "And he said, 'Well, I think you're right.'" Phillips had to hire another woman to handle that chore.

There was one aspect of his new Cuba responsibilities that Phillips never spoke about: impersonation operations aimed at visitors to the Cuban embassy. On July 19, 1963, for example, a man named Eldon Hensen called the Cuban embassy for the second time in a week, saying he wanted to make contact with the embassy but did not want to come in person because "an American spy might see him." Hensen left a phone number. LIENVOY picked up the conversation, which was forwarded to the Cuba desk at the station. Phillips read it and authorized one of his agents, an exiled Cuban journalist, to return Hensen's call. Phillips's man told Hensen that he was a Cuban embassy officer and wanted to meet at a hotel restaurant where they might talk more privately. Hensen came to the meeting, happy to have evaded U.S. intelligence. He explained to Phillips's friend that he was willing to help the Castro government in the United States. He said he had "good contacts" and could help move "things from one place to another." The CIA man listened attentively. So did deputy station chief Alan White, who was sitting nearby listening. Someone would get back to him, Hensen was told. He should never call the Cuban embassy again. Win relayed the story to Washington. When Hensen returned to Texas, the FBI prosecuted the man. The Eldon Hensen story, not revealed until 1996, shows how David Phillips used an impersonation operation in a counterintelligence maneuver against the Cuba embassy. JFK conspiracy theorists would later speculate that someone had impersonated Lee Harvey Oswald in Mexico City, a claim that many journalists and historians scoffed at. But the Hensen story confirmed that the CIA station in Mexico City did mount impersonation operations on visitors to the Cuban embassy.

As always, Phillips's portfolio also included anti-Castro propaganda operations. He had made his professional reputation in the psychological warfare campaign that drove Operation Success in Guatemala. He was widely regarded within the agency as a master of media operations. He ran anti-Castro propaganda operations in 1963. "I had some degree of responsibility for them," he said in a sworn deposition, "in the sense that such a thing would have always been—" He stopped at the word *always,* perhaps not wanting to boast that *every* secret anti-Castro propaganda operation was brought to his attention in late 1963.

"I was a consultant," he explained modestly.

David Phillips took over responsibility for Cuba operations outside of the United States at a time of profound discontent in the ranks of the agency, especially in Miami. From the point of view of Win and his colleagues, Kennedy's handling of the missile crisis had postponed the Cuba problem, not solved it. Whether the commander in chief might have used the opportunity to eliminate the dangerous Castro without excessive loss of life was a hypothetical question left for historians to debate. Four out of five Americans approved of Kennedy's statesmanship, but JFK's right-wing critics and Castro's exiled foes saw another failure of nerve. Once again, the liberal president had squandered the opportunity to eliminate Castro. In Washington,

Kennedy's handling of the crisis would be mythologized in tomes with appropriately portentous titles: *The Missiles of October* and *Thirteen Days* and *Eyeball to Eyeball*. In Cuban Miami, they called the showdown over missiles on the island *La Segunda Derrota*, the second defeat.

Kennedy's rhetorical commitment to the exiles' cause had not wavered. When he welcomed home the Bay of Pigs prisoners at Miami's Orange Bowl stadium at Christmas 1962, he declared the brigade's flag would someday fly over a free Havana. But he refused to commit himself to the ideological and strategic proposition that Castro had to go. To the contrary, his political advisers wanted less "noise" around U.S. support for the exiles. A number of State Department officials privately thought the United States should accommodate itself to the reality of the Castro government. A policy of "coexistence" was anathema to many in the State Department, and to most in the Pentagon and the CIA. Much to JFK's annoyance, the Joint Chiefs of Staff continued to make clear their conviction that only a U.S. invasion would solve the Cuba problem once and for all.

The question for the Cuba hawks was how to bring about the political conditions to justify a U.S. attack. In early 1962, the Joint Chiefs had begun developing the idea of creating a pretext for an invasion of Cuba in a set of proposals dubbed Operation Northwoods. The generals stated that there was no possibility of internal revolt in the next nine to ten months, meaning that the overthrow of Castro "will require a decision by the United States to develop a Cuban 'provocation' as justification for positive U.S. military action."

Preliminary proposals were drawn up with the recommendation that the Joint Chiefs of Staff pick the ones they thought had the best chance of succeeding and ordering their implementation. A host of proposals were offered. One planner suggested bribing one of Castro's commanders to launch an attack on the U.S. naval base at Guantánamo, a proposal that historian James Bamford described as tantamount to treason. Another proposal called for staging a contrived "Cuban" attack on one of Cuba's neighbors. The attacked country could then "be urged to take measures of self-defense and request assistance from the U.S. and OAS." Another idea was to "develop a Communist Cuban terror campaign in the Miami area, in other Florida cities, and even in Washington."

When these plans surfaced thirty years later, some news reporters and intelligence analysts characterized them as "Keystone Cops" scenarios, with the implication of bureaucratic silliness. Nothing could be farther from the truth. As James Bamford notes, these were not idle schemes but plans approved by the country's military leaders. They were close to official policy.

They were described as preliminary in the full expectation that more fully developed schemes would follow.

President Kennedy had no appetite for such "pretext operations," as they were known. Nor did defense secretary Robert McNamara, who vetoed the Northwoods proposals. When Lyman Lemnitzer, the reactionary chairman of the Joint Chiefs of Staff, pressed for reconsideration of "plans for creating plausible pretext to use force" at a meeting in March 1962, the president interrupted him. "We were not discussing the use of U.S. military force," he snapped. Lemnitzer's rage against Kennedy's policy made him useless to McNamara, and he was relieved of his chairmanship of the Joint Chiefs later in 1962. Yet, according to Bamford, planning for pretext operations continued well into 1963. The authors of the Northwoods proposals understood both their sinister nature and what it would take to execute them. One planner noted in early 1963 that contriving a pretext for war was "inherently extremely risky in our democratic system. . . . If the decision should be made to set up a contrived situation, it should be one in which participation by U.S. personnel is limited only to the most highly trusted covert personnel."

Jack and Bobby Kennedy wanted to get rid of Castro, but they did not want an invasion or a public campaign against the Cuban leader. While the president privately sent out feelers to Castro, the CIA was supposed to assist Bobby. The Kennedys' new Cuba policy took shape in May and June in a series of meetings of the president's national security advisers. On June 19 they approved a National Security Council directive ordering a campaign of sabotage and harassment by armed Cuban organizations operating outside of the U.S. territory and thus beyond the reach of the Neutrality Act. The idea was that these "autonomous groups," under guidance of the CIA, could and would disrupt the Cuban government's ability to rule. Handpicked political figures would present a progressive political message that would inspire the people to rise up. To deputy director Dick Helms and other CIA men, Kennedy's new Cuba policy resembled nothing so much as his old policy, in both its premises and its particulars. The difference, it seemed, was that this time the Kennedy brothers said they were serious— really serious—about fomenting an internal rebellion, and that determination would make the difference. The Kennedys had two strikes against them—the Bay of Pigs and the missile crisis. Were they serious? Or were they just using the agency and its personnel for cover as they edged toward coexistence with Castro?

Helms was close to being appalled. The whole concept depended on repudiation of the CIA's own 1963 National Intelligence Estimate on Cuba, which said that Castro was secure in power, popular enough to repel all challenges with an increasingly sophisticated Soviet-trained security apparatus. Worse yet, Bobby Kennedy was taking the lead in this new old policy by playing case officer with his favorite Cubans. He thought he could organize a more progressive political cadre than the CIA without the grandiose schemes of Lansdale. The notion that a senior government official could moonlight as a case officer struck Helms as absurd. The president's younger brother, he wrote, had only "a slight idea of what was involved in organizing a secret intelligence operation. He appeared to equate the director of Central Intelligence position with that of the chief of the General Staff." Two years after the Bay of Pigs, the president and his brother still had not absorbed the central lesson of that defeat as voiced by David Phillips: *secret shenanigans couldn't do what armies are supposed to do.*

Helms also had to indulge Bobby's demands for a plan to assassinate Castro. There is no written proof of this, say Kennedy admirers. But there is good reason to believe Bobby Kennedy was comfortable with the idea of using the CIA to kill Castro. When RFK learned in May 1962 that Bill Harvey was relying on his sleek Mafioso pal Johnny Rosselli to kill Castro, he objected to the choice of assassins, not the idea itself. Helms later told Henry Kissinger that RFK had been deeply involved in Castro assassination plots. Helms, of course, was a self-interested witness, but the claim is plausible because of the CIA's choice of assassins. He was Rolando Cubela, a hero of the Cuban Revolution, known in the CIA by the code name AMLASH. Cubela was the sort of romantic figure that Bobby Kennedy admired. He had won repute as a leader of the Revolutionary Directorate, a nationalist and Catholic group that had fought alongside Castro's July 26 movement. After the triumph of the revolution, Castro named him to oversee the University of Havana, where his armed exploits made him a legend. A revolutionary but not a communist, he had no problem expelling young critics of the Castro government. But he did not thrive in his post. He came from a middle-class family and did not feel comfortable with the class rhetoric and strong socialistic policies of the new government. He thought he was due more power. The CIA picked up on his discontent early. In the summer of 1961, when Cubela visited Mexico with a university delegation, one of Win's men had pitched him on the idea of cooperating with the agency. Cubela had rejected the pitch. He disliked Fidel's communistic ways, but he disliked the Americans even more.

When Helms called for the AMLASH file again in the summer of 1963, he knew the odds of success were only middling. Cubela had one successful assassination to his credit. In 1956, he gunned down Batista's chief of military intelligence in the Montmartre nightclub and eluded capture. He had battlefield nerve. In the decisive battle of Santa Clara, he fought shoulder to shoulder with Che Guevara in routing Batista's forces and guaranteeing Castro's triumph. But Cubela drank and was prone to bouts of moodiness. In addition, as the counterintelligence officer in the anti-Castro operation frequently pointed out, he still had some kind of personal relationship with Fidel. Helms sent a couple of emissaries to meet secretly with Cubela and gauge his interest in a plan to overthrow Castro. Cubela, despondent over Castro's socialist orientation, forbade the use of the word *assassination* but said he wanted to meet again.

Bobby's larger plan was dubbed AMWORLD. The attorney general, with the reluctant assistance of Helms, was putting together yet another Cuban leadership group, the best of the Cuban exiles, who were nominally more attractive to the Cuban people than the Batistano-dominated cliques previously favored by the agency. Bobby's chosen allies were Cuban politicians of the usual varying quality. The most attractive was Enrique Ruiz Williams, a former Havana bus driver and union leader who had been taken prisoner at the Bay of Pigs and recently released. Known as Harry, Williams had become a personal friend of Bobby's. Manolo Ray was a moderate leftist who had served briefly in Castro's government. The resilient Manuel Artime, friend of Howard Hunt, had not let the AMCIGAR follies disrupt his relations with the CIA. He gained Bobby's confidence with his substantial following among the armed exile groups. Bobby's idea was that Ray and Williams would take the political lead in Miami and Washington, and Artime would organize the exile military force in Nicaragua. The military planning for a U.S. invasion of Cuba would be stepped up. The idea came from the Operation Success formula: that the United States would intervene militarily if Castro faced an internal challenge from dissident officers like Cubela or a popular uprising. Desmond FitzGerald, one of the CIA officers most sympathetic to the Kennedys, thought Bobby was serious. He wagered with a friend that Castro would be gone by August 1964.

Helms bit his tongue and followed his orders. Always a master of distancing himself from policies he did not like, Helms asked division chief J. C. King to deliver the details of the AMWORLD operation to CIA hands in the field. They were the ones who were going to have to tolerate the White House freelancing in their domains. Win received the cable on June 30, 1963.

King made clear that CIA support should have definite limits. The agency would support Artime with money, logistics, and advice only, he said. "Any manifestations of KUBARK [CIA] participation in the planning and execution of the program will be kept to a minimum." King acknowledged operational security would probably not meet CIA standards. The White

House, he wrote, "is willing to accept the risks involved in utilizing autono- mous [Cuban] exile groups and individuals who are not necessarily respon- sive to [CIA] and to face up to the consequences which an unavoidable lowering in professional standards adhered to by autonomous groups (as compared with fully controlled and disciplined agent assets) is bound to entail." King made clear the White House wanted political cover. "This is the price [the U.S. government] is willing to pay to enable it to deny publicly any participation in the activities of autonomous groups no matter how loud or even accurate reports of [U.S.] complicity may be." Win was in- structed to keep "aloof from involvement in operational activities which you have reason to believe are somehow related to AMWORLD." Since Artime might occasionally meet his CIA contacts in Mexico and other coun- tries, "we cannot rule out that the local service will learn of his presence and activities." In that event, King said, "nothing should be said or hinted at which could in any manner be construed as implying [U.S. government] of- ficial condonment [sic] let alone sponsorship of his activities."

Win delegated AMWORLD to Dave Phillips. When Artime passed through Mexico City on his way to the exiles' military bases in Nicaragua, Phillips arranged a safe house and kept his profile low. When Artime started getting bad press as an American agent, headquarters called on Phillips to plant stories in the Mexican press casting his offshore crusade against Castro in a more positive light. Win wanted no repeat of the AMCIGAR fiasco.

At the same time, Win was stepping up his anti-Cuban operations. He hired four more secretaries to transcribe the mass of information generated by LIENVOY and other surveillance programs. In May 1963 he reported to headquarters that the station had tapped six phone lines in the Cuban em- bassy, compared with five in the Soviet embassy and two in the Czech em- bassy. He passed along eighty-seven pages of transcripts of conversations of people in the Cuban embassy.

While Phillips focused on the Cuban embassy, Win kept a close watch on all Americans traveling to Cuba, an increasingly important task as Castro sought to persuade American public opinion that his revolution was benign. In January, for example, the LIFIRE operation at the Mexico City airport provided proof that Vincent Lee, the head of the pro-Castro Fair Play for Cuba Committee (FPCC), based in New York, had traveled through Mexico to Cuba and spent three weeks there. To Washington, Win boasted accu- rately that his surveillance operations had obtained "the usual great amount" of "personality and operational material."

His pride spoke to a subtle technical difference in the kind of secret in- formation that the Mexico City station gathered. As Anne Goodpasture later explained, the station's intelligence collection efforts yielded two very different kinds of product. "Positive intelligence," she explained, concerned the plans, policies, and course of action of other governments, in this case, the Soviets, Cubans, Mexicans, and Czechs. This information was sent to Washington, where the agency distributed it to "customer agencies," meaning other U.S. government offices that could judge the usefulness of the information when they compared it with their other sources.

"Security information," by contrast, interested the CIA, Goodpasture said. This kind of intelligence, generated "in response to Agency internal requirements or in pursuit of obvious, but not necessarily formalized, security objectives," was closely held by the agency. It "received limited distribution to a few other agencies with security responsibilities, if it was disseminated at all." Its importance might not become known for months or even years. In her secret history of the Mexico City station, Goodpasture defined "security intelligence" with her usual precision. It concerned "the identities, activities, contacts and movements of U.S. and foreign subversive personalities, foreign intelligence personnel, and other persons known or suspected of engaging in activities inimical to the United States." She cited three specific examples: "U.S. citizens initiating or maintaining contact with the Cuban and Soviet diplomatic installations; travel to Cuba by U.S. citizens or residents; [and] activities of Cuban and Soviet intelligence personnel." In short, the Mexico City station was intensely interested in American visitors to the Cuban and Soviet embassies who wished to travel to Cuba and who had contact with Soviet or Cuban intelligence officials.

As the Kennedys' efforts to chart a new Cuba policy foundered in the spring and summer of 1963, disenchantment among senior CIA officers and their allies in Cuban Miami was evolving into disobedience. Win was not one to articulate political arguments, but his politics were deeply conservative and not out of tune with those of his fellow cold warriors. Happily remarried and immersed in the vast complexities of running the Mexico City station, he stood slightly apart from the struggle over Cuba policy in Washington. But his new friend David Phillips and his old friend Jim Angleton were immersed in it.

This mood of rebellion was strongest on the streets of Cuban Miami. In the spring of 1963, Phillips's young friends in the Cuban Student Directorate came to believe that the administration's low-profile policy since the missile crisis amounted to slow-motion abandonment by the Kennedy administration. In an open letter that received wide distribution in south Florida, the DRE leaders declared their intention to keep striking Cuban government targets. They sent word to Helms via their new case officer, George Joannides, that they planned a new attack on Cuba along the lines of the raid on the Icar Hotel. As they schemed, another exile group, Alpha 66, seeking to attack a Soviet freighter, struck a Spanish ship by accident. The Cubans and the Soviet Union accused the United States of condoning piracy on the high seas, exactly the kind of noise that the White House did not want. Bobby Kennedy, while intent on getting rid of Castro, was not going to tolerate freelancing. He ordered the Immigration and Naturalization Service to confine the most militant exiles to metropolitan Miami. Eighteen leading militants, including the top leaders in the AMSPELL program, could not leave the area without written permission.

The sense of betrayal deepened. Kennedy's Cuba policies have "always culminated in abandonment, treachery and broken promises," DRE leader Luis Fernandez Rocha, one of the blacklisted militants, told the *New York Times*. He accused JFK of abetting Castro's tyranny. "The United States has effected a blockade to stop the attacks against the Communist regime in Cuba and are, thus, strengthening the Communist position," he declared. Ted Shackley, the ambitious Miami station chief who never liked the DRE, had heard enough. He moved to cut off agency funding for the AMSPELL program. Helms overruled him. As Helms's trusted aide Nestor Sanchez explained later in an interview, Helms admired the DRE's style. Yes, the headstrong young Cubans were freewheeling in their unauthorized attacks on Castro and indiscreet denunciations of JFK, Sanchez said. "But sometimes you want freewheeling." The Cuban students most vocally opposed to JFK's policy remained on the agency payroll.

It was not just hotheaded youth who defied JFK. Howard Hunt, back in Washington as the chief of the Domestic Contacts Division, minced no words about Kennedy's dishonorable policy. "Instead of standing firm, our government pyramided crucially wrong decisions and allowed Brigade 2506 to be destroyed," he later wrote. By the summer of 1963, Hunt said Kennedy had "moved shamefacedly into the shadows and hoped the Cuban issue would simply melt away."

And it wasn't just mediocre midlevel operatives like Hunt. Win's old friend Bill Harvey, the former chief of the anti-Castro effort, was flouting Kennedy's Cuba policy—and with Jim Angleton's blessing. Harvey had been fired by Bobby Kennedy during the missile crisis for preparing to insert CIA action teams into Cuba in advance of the expected U.S. invasion. RFK rescinded Harvey's order, which he regarded as dangerous insubordination. Helms transferred Harvey to Italy, where he drank heavily. According to Ted Shackley, he began traveling to Miami to meet with his friend Johnny

Rosselli, the dapper mobster whom he had enlisted to kill Castro, every four to six weeks. Other times, Rosselli visited Harvey in Washington.

In June 1963, FBI agents tailing Rosselli watched in surprise as he disembarked from a flight at Washington's National Airport and got into a car with Harvey. The agents called Sam Papich, the bureau's liaison to the CIA, who happened to be visiting Angleton at his house in Arlington. Angleton called Harvey's wife and found out her husband and Rosselli were dining at Duke Ziebert's restaurant in downtown Washington. Angleton called the restaurant, and Harvey took the call. When the conversation was over, Angleton put down the phone and turned to Papich, saying, "I said, look, let's go very easy on this." Angleton claimed he did not know about Harvey's friendship with Rosselli. "But I did know him well enough to know that he was not a frivolous man," he said. In the eyes of Angleton, Harvey could not be blamed for using all his contacts to try to solve the Castro problem.

Angleton had reached the peak of his power and influence. He had recovered from an unidentified illness that forced him to take a six-month leave of absence in 1960. Besides his interest in Castro's intelligence services, he had a larger concern. The story told by Anatoly Golitsyn, a Soviet intelligence official who defected in December 1961, justified his worst fears about the Soviet Union, germinating ever since Philby's betrayal a decade earlier. Golitsyn said that the Soviets had insinuated a spy into the upper ranks of the CIA, just as they had managed to insert Philby into a leadership position in the British secret service. If so, Moscow might actually gain the ability to influence, if not control, the CIA's actions. Angleton called it the "Monster Plot." If true, its implications were indeed monstrous: the Soviets might be in a position to control the agency's operations. Angleton was trying to figure out who the mole was. He was looking for another Philby in the Soviet Russia division. As for Cuba, he felt the United States had a debt of honor over the Bay of Pigs debacle that had to be repaid. "We owed a deep obligation to the men in Miami," he said. He also felt no obligation to respect all of Kennedy's policy directives. "It is inconceivable," Angleton told a congressional committee years later, "that a secret intelligence arm of the government has to comply with all the overt orders of the government."

The disenchantment with JFK's Cuba policy penetrated right into Dick Helms's corner suite on the second floor of CIA headquarters in Langley, Virginia. Ever correct and attentive to the White House, Helms knew how to voice his objections to Kennedy's Cuba policy in tart asides and then get on with the business at hand. His aides could afford to be more candid. One of them was Nestor Sanchez, a fluent Spanish speaker from a prominent family in New Mexico, who handled a wide variety of tasks for Helms in the summer of 1963 and would eventually become chief of the Western Hemisphere division of the clandestine service in the 1970s. "You don't get involved in covert-type operations unless you are willing to go the distance," Sanchez said in an interview. That kind of commitment "was lacking in the Kennedy administration and it happened twice: the Bay of Pigs and the second one [referring to Operation Mongoose, the secret plan to overthrow Castro that died during the missile crisis]. They backed out of both."

Sanchez grew more emphatic. "The buck stops with the president on operations like that. There's no one else. He says yes or no. All the other conspiracies of the agency was running amok, that's baloney. . . . God damnit you do it or you don't, and if you don't feel you can do it you either get yourself out, take 'em out, or get someone else."

By the summer of 1963, he felt Kennedy's Cuba policy was not serious. Said Sanchez, "The waffle was already in there."

Helms's top aide, Sam Halpern, spoke even more candidly. Halpern served as Helms's executive assistant for many years and in retirement came to serve as a spokesman for his former boss. While Helms saved his historical observations for selected journalists and historians, he often sent working reporters to talk to Halpern. A quick-witted man, credited by many with having a photographic memory, Halpern reliably presented a perspective on the agency that reflected Helms's own views.

Thirty-five years after the fact, Halpern was openly contemptuous of the Kennedys' competence. "You're dealing with two guys in the White House who made a botch of things at the Bay of Pigs and haven't a clue what it means to run clandestine operations or covert operations or whatever you want to call them," he said in an interview about the events of 1963. "They've got their fingers all over the place trying to make amends, and the more they try to make amends, the worse it gets. Kennedy wouldn't listen. They believe in keeping on doing all this, busy-ness, busy-ness, busy-ness."

Halpern was referring by memory to the minutes of a meeting of Kennedy's National Security Council in May 1963. NSC adviser McGeorge Bundy had opened the meeting by forcing discussion of the failure of the U.S. policy of overthrowing Castro. He said he was coming to believe that the U.S. government could not be certain it was ever going to get rid of the bearded revolutionary. "We should face this prospect," he said. Defense secretary McNamara said one option was to "buy off Castro," that is, end the U.S. embargo of the Cuban economy in exchange for Castro breaking his ties to the Soviet Union. Desmond FitzGerald tried to rally with a list of all the covert operations that might still be launched. As he spoke, Bobby Kennedy walked in and said, "The U.S. must do something even though we do not believe our actions would bring him down." Bundy said, "We can give an impression of busy-ness in Cuba and we can make life difficult for Castro." For Halpern, that prissy word, *busy-ness,* encapsulated the defeatism, if not treachery, lurking beneath the surface of Kennedy's low-key Cuba policy. Men were risking their lives every day so that the White House could hide its unwillingness to "pay any price, bear any burden" to get rid of Cuban communism. Halpern argued that the deceptiveness of Kennedy's policy virtually justified extraconstitutional correction. "I'll tell you one thing," he said, sitting forward in his seat, finger jabbing the air. "I didn't know that word 'busy-ness.' It was never mentioned by Des [FitzGerald] when he came back from that meeting, and it was a good thing he didn't, because you might have had a *Seven Days in May* at that point."

Halpern was talking about one of the best-selling books of 1962, a popular thriller written by two journalists who had picked up on the rage against Kennedy's foreign policy among military men in Washington. Their book featured a handsome, young, liberal president trying to fend off a military coup by a clique of generals opposed to his pursuit of peaceful coexistence with the Russians. It struck a chord with the reading public and went through many printings. JFK himself thought the threat of a coup was real and privately urged John Frankenheimer, a Hollywood producer and friend, to make the book into a movie. Halpern's allusion was neither facetious nor metaphorical. He described a point of honor.

"If that word 'busy-ness' had gotten out to the military forces as well as to all of our troops and everybody else in the U.S. government that was knocking their balls off trying to do this nonsense [the pinprick raids of the autonomous groups], there might have been a revolt of some kind," he said. "I might have led it."

Dick Helms himself did not engage in such bluster. He sought to thwart the Kennedys' amateurish Cuba policy with that favorite weapon of the Washington bureaucrat warrior: the newspaper leak. When Bobby traveled to south Florida in July 1963 to hold what he thought would be a secret meeting with Manuel Artime and other Cuban allies who wanted to take military action against Castro, Hal Hendrix, a Pulitzer Prize–winning reporter for the Knight-Ridder newspaper chain in Miami, blew his cover in a story called "Backstage with Bobby."

"There is growing speculation here and in Washington that Attorney General Bobby Kennedy has once again donned an invisible warrior's helmet and is embarking quietly on a new anti-Castro operation with hand-picked Cuban exiles," Hendrix wrote. He highlighted the fact that the Kennedy administration was backing away from the once-prevalent notion that the United States should simply invade Cuba. "No large invasion force is envisioned. . . . Instead, in line with the Kennedy Administration's enforcement of the Neutrality Act, hit and run attacks from a base outside the U.S. would be the role of 'Bobbie's Boys.'"

If the attorney general thought he could keep his private Cuba policy secret, he thought wrong. Hendrix, not coincidentally, was friends with Dave Phillips. They had first met when Phillips was stationed in Cuba in 1958. Hendrix was willing to work with the agency. Nine months earlier, at the height of the Cuban missile crisis, he told Miami station chief Ted Shackley over lunch that he was researching a story about inconsistencies in Kennedy's Cuba policy, to wit, how Bobby Kennedy promised one Cuban exile ally that the United States was committed to liberating Cuba while simultaneously making guarantees to the Soviets about not invading the island. After that meeting, Shackley cabled headquarters promising to "continue development of Hendrix as source."

Bobby Kennedy was undeterred. He continued pushing his AMWORLD allies on the CIA and the Pentagon, determined that Castro would yet be ousted. His older brother was less interested. As 1963 wore on, the president preferred to talk about the nuclear test ban treaty and Berlin and Martin Luther King's March on Washington, almost anything but the Cuba issue. Helms went along stoically with the administration's ambiguous, uncertain policy. Many, many people in the upper ranks of the CIA and Pentagon felt the resentments that rankled the likes of Halpern, Sanchez, and Angleton: *Kennedy wouldn't listen. . . . Busy-ness was not a policy. . . . Goddamnit, you do it or you don't. . . . A secret agency does not have to comply with all of the government's overt orders. . . . There might be a revolt of some kind.*

As the mood of patriotic rebellion simmered in the ranks of the anti-Castro cause late in the summer of 1963, a mysterious stranger named Oswald came to Win's attention.

14

A Blip Named Oswald

Like many Americans, Michael Scott had often wondered about the assassination of President Kennedy. He had debated conspiracy theories in dorm rooms and at the dining room table, wondering all the while what his father knew. He thought about his visit to CIA headquarters and the CIA's admission that it had censored what his father wrote about Lee Harvey Oswald. But it was almost a decade after he first asked the CIA to return the memoir before Michael began to learn more. In 1994 Michael heard of a new kind of JFK investigation, overseen by an entity known as the Assassination Records Review Board. The board was established by Congress in the wake of the furor over Oliver Stone's film *JFK*. While Washington journalists savaged Stone for taking liberties with the historical record, the combative director scored with a telling reply: if the government had nothing to hide, why were most of the government's records on the subject still classified? The Congress responded by unanimously approving the JFK Assassination Records Act, which mandated the declassification of virtually all the government's assassination-related records. A civilian review board was charged with enforcement. The five-member board, chaired by federal judge John Tunheim, got to work in 1994 and soon heard the story of Win Scott's manuscript. In 1995, the board ordered the public release of an eight-page Oswald chapter. For Michael, it was the first additional revelation from his father's memoir since his visit to CIA headquarters almost a decade before. It proved somewhat anticlimactic. In those pages Win recounted his actions in 1963 and argued there had been some kind of Soviet conspiracy behind

Oswald. Michael found the chapter fascinating but defensive and hardly definitive.

As the board pushed hundreds of thousands of other long-suppressed CIA files into the public record, the context of the story that Win told about his own role in the events leading up to the Kennedy assassination began to emerge. Only when Michael understood how the Mexico City station worked, and the nature of Win's relationships with Jim Angleton and David Phillips at the time, did the story begin to become clearer. It was not a tale of conspiracy or of a "lone nut" but a saga that eluded all five official investigations of JFK's assassination and all the hundreds of writers who had explored the subject. In the last hundred days of his life, Lee Harvey Oswald came to the attention of four different CIA collection operations. Their code names were AMSPELL, LIERODE, LIENVOY, and LIEMPTY. Win ran two of them (LIENVOY and LIEMPTY), Phillips oversaw the other two (AMSPELL and LIERODE). At the time, Oswald's file in Washington was held by the Special Investigations Group in the Counterintelligence Staff. Any questions about Oswald were answered by men and women who reported to Jim Angleton. In other words, Win and two friends were at the heart of the epic intelligence failure that culminated tragically on November 22, 1963.

If that sounded damning to his father, Michael did not feel disloyal. He could not imagine his father talking about such things, but he felt certain Win would not have discouraged his search for the truth.

In the summer of 1963, Lee Harvey Oswald was twenty-three years old, living in New Orleans with his wife, Marina, and their baby daughter, June. He had led an unusually interesting life. Raised by a single mother in Fort Worth and New Orleans, Oswald moved along with his family to New York City and back to New Orleans in his adolescence. He had enlisted in the marines out of high school, served two years, wrangled a discharge in 1959, and traveled to Moscow, where he proclaimed his sympathy for communism and tried to renounce his U.S. citizenship. This highly unusual move made news in his hometown of Fort Worth and attracted the attention of Angleton's Counterintelligence Staff. Officially, it took the CI staff more than a year to open a file on Oswald, a procedural lapse that some say reflected the agency's lack of interest. Dick Helms said under oath that the delay "amazed" him and he could not explain it. A former marine who defected to the Soviet Union was not someone whom Angleton would likely overlook.

The Soviets sent Oswald to Minsk. Headstrong but resourceful, he managed to learn Russian and fit in among a group of young people there, dating local girls and going on at least one hunting trip. Oswald asked a Russian girl named Marina Prusakova to marry him. She agreed. Oswald soon tired of the regimentation of Soviet life. In May 1962 he returned to the United States with his new wife, saying he was disillusioned with Soviet-style communism though still supportive of Marxism. The CI staff followed that move, too, just as they kept up with the dozen or so other Americans, including some military personnel, who had defected to the Soviet Union and returned. Unlike those defectors, however, Oswald was never interviewed, or so the CIA claims. Upon his return, the FBI would keep track of him.

Lee and Marina settled in Fort Worth, Texas. Oswald impressed those who met him there as intelligent, if difficult. He spoke good Russian and read a lot of books but had trouble holding a job. In April 1963, seven months before the assassination of President Kennedy, he and Marina moved back to his hometown of New Orleans, where he became active on the issue of Cuba. While the local Cuban exile community seethed at Kennedy's passive post–missile crisis posture, Oswald set out to publicly defend Castro, a rare stance in a conservative southern city. He stayed aloof from local Castro supporters but had many contacts with anti-Castro exiles. He drank at a bar run by a Cuban exile named Oreste Pena, who saw him in the company of government employees from Customs and the Immigration and Naturalization Service. Other credible eyewitnesses saw him visiting the offices of Guy Banister, a former FBI agent turned anticommunist crusader, at an office building located at 544 Camp Street in downtown New Orleans. Although there is no proof that Oswald was a government informant, the details of his interest in Cuba—his activities, contacts, and travels—would soon be noted by the FBI and delivered to top CIA officials—while President Kennedy was still alive.

Win was one of these officials, although he certainly did not know the full scope of CIA intelligence on Oswald at the time.

The first CIA operation to pick up on Oswald in late 1963 was the DRE, aka the Cuban Student Directorate, aka AMSPELL, Dave Phillips's favorite young Cubans, who had jarred Kennedy with their attack on the Havana hotel in August 1962 and irked him with the "missiles in caves" story in November of that year. By the summer of 1963, these militants had come under greater CIA control, according to officials in Miami. They were still subsidized by the agency. DRE/AMSPELL was receiving $51,000 a month, according to an agency memo sent to the State Department in April 1963. George Joannides, the case officer whom Dick Helms had sent to Miami to rein in the group, had done "an excellent job in the handling of a significant student exile group which hitherto had successfully resisted any important degree of control," one CIA supervisor noted. On July 31, 1963, Joannides was promoted to be chief of psychological warfare operations at the agency's Miami station.

Perhaps coincidentally, the next day Oswald acted on a plan to ingratiate himself with the Fair Play for Cuba Committee. The FPCC was then the best-known *pro*-Castro group in the country, and the object of intense interest from the CIA and FBI because it received funding from Castro's operatives at the United Nations. On August 1, 1963, Oswald wrote a letter to Vincent Lee, the executive director of the FPCC in New York, boasting that he had taken on the local anti-Castro forces, fought them on the street, and won favorable publicity for the pro-Castro cause. None of this was true—yet. A few days later, Oswald took action to make good on the scenario. On August 5, he walked into Casa Roca, a store in downtown New Orleans run by Carlos Bringuier, a twenty-seven-year-old lawyer who served as the DRE's spokesman in the city. Like most of the DRE's leaders, Bringuier came from an upper-middle-class family and had attended Belen, the most prestigious secondary school in Havana. Oswald chatted up Bringuier, saying he had served in the marines and could train anti-Castro commandos to fight in Cuba. Bringuier was noncommittal about this offer.

Bringuier's public declarations of support for the DRE's Havana raid had won him a visit from the FBI the previous summer. Warren DeBrueys, a senior FBI agent responsible for keeping track of pro- and anti-Castro activists, warned Bringuier he was being watched. Ever since then, the voluble Cuban had been wary of government informants. Oswald returned the next day to repeat the offer. He produced his Marine Corps manual as proof of his expertise and gave it to Bringuier as a demonstration of his good intentions. Bringuier rebuffed him again. He later said he suspected that the FBI or the CIA might have sent Oswald.

Oswald then reverted to his pro-Castro ways and carried out the actions he had already described to Vincent Lee of the FPCC. On August 9, he spent the afternoon handing out FPCC pamphlets on Canal Street, not far from Bringuier's store. This appearance provoked an altercation much like the one he described in his letter to Lee. Bringuier and the three other members of the DRE delegation spotted Oswald. Bringuier called him on his double-dealing. Loud words were exchanged. One of the DRE boys grabbed Oswald's FPCC pamphlets and tossed them to the wind. A crowd gathered.

Oswald dared Bringuier to punch him. A passing policeman broke up the shadowboxing by issuing summonses to all the participants. Francis Martello, a New Orleans police lieutenant who followed up on the incident, thought the fight was contrived. Oswald, he wrote in his report, "seemed to have set them up, so to speak, to create an incident, but when the incident occurred he remained absolutely peaceful and gentle."

There was nothing contrived about Carlos Bringuier's reaction. He acted as a good delegate of the DRE would. He sought to combat this duplicitous Castro supporter. He wrote to Tony Lanuza, the Miami-based coordinator of the DRE's chapters in North America, telling him of his plans to expose and denounce Oswald. Lanuza says he shared the news with DRE secretary general Luis Fernandez Rocha, who was meeting regularly with CIA handler George Joannides at the time. Fernandez Rocha, who would go on to a distinguished career as an obstetrician in Miami, said in an interview he may have told Joannides about Oswald but has no specific recollection of doing so. Bringuier also notified his friend Isidro "Chilo" Borja, an engineer who led the DRE's clandestine military section. Borja and Bringuier, who had grown up in the same section of Havana, had been friends since childhood. Bringuier passed Borja a report on one of the DRE members who had helped confront Oswald. In the margin, Bringuier wrote, "This is one of the Cubans who collaborated with me against the Fair Play for Cuba Committee here in New Orleans." Borja filed the report in the DRE's confidential "military-intelligence" archive.

In New Orleans, Bringuier deployed his friends to collect intelligence on Oswald. He sent another DRE member, a young man named Carlos Quiroga, to visit Oswald's house posing as a Castro supporter. According to Oswald's landlady, Quiroga delivered a stack of FPCC pamphlets, apparently to enhance his credibility as a Castro supporter. Quiroga, who was also an informant for Warren DeBrueys, reported back to Bringuier that he had heard Oswald speaking a foreign language to his wife. Bringuier made inquiries with a local ally, Ed Butler, who ran an organization called Information Center for the Americas (INCA), dedicated to combating communist influence in the Americas. The CIA had relied on INCA publications in the propaganda blitz that preceded the invasion at the Bay of Pigs. The agency, explained one officer, "did not fund this organization though we had contacts with some of its members." Butler, in turn, called the House Un-American Activities Committee (HUAC) in Washington to see if it had a file on Oswald, which it did. A HUAC staff member reported Oswald's defection to the Soviet Union and his return in 1962. Oswald had certainly succeeded in attracting attention to himself—all the way to Washington.

When Oswald and the DRE Cubans appeared in court, a local TV news camera crew was there. While the charges against the Cubans were dismissed, Oswald received a ten-dollar fine. Local radio talk show host Bill Stuckey, another friend of Butler and Bringuier's, jumped on the Oswald story. He had been trying to find FPCC supporters in New Orleans for the past year. He interviewed Oswald for a brief news report. When the FPCC man said he had lived in the Soviet Union, Stuckey thought he deserved a bigger story. Oswald's past seemed to confirmed what congressmen and senators had been saying for months: the FPCC was not an independent group interested in "fair play" but a communist front. Stuckey invited Oswald to appear on his show. On August 21, Stuckey hosted Oswald, Butler, and Bringuier in a debate about the Cuba issue on his new weekly program, *Latin Listening Post.*

"Tonight we have with us a representative of probably the most controversial organization connected with Cuba in this country," Stuckey intoned. "This organization has long been on the Justice Department's blacklist and is a group generally considered to be the leading pro-Castro body in the nation. As a reporter of Latin American affairs in this city for several years now, your columnist has kept a lookout for local representatives of this pro-Castro group. None appeared in public view until this week when young Lee Oswald was arrested and convicted for disturbing the peace."

When Stuckey turned to his guests for comments, Bringuier attacked Oswald. "I'd like to know exactly the name of the organization that you represent here in the city because I have some confusion, is [it] Fair Play for Cuba Committee or Fair Play for Russia Committee?"

"Well, that is a very provocative request and I don't think [it] requires an answer," Oswald said.

Bringuier launched into an explanation of how the Cuban economy had declined under Castro's rule. "I think that Cuba right now is a colony of Russia and the people of Cuba who is living in Cuba every day who is escaping from Cuba every day they disagree with you that you are representing the people of Cuba."

Stuckey asked Oswald about his nonexistent FPCC chapter. Oswald lied and said he could not reveal its membership. "Is it a secret society?" asked Ed Butler. Oswald defended the principles of the FPCC, even though he had no formal relationship with the organization. "We are striving to get the United States to adopt measures which would be more friendly toward the Cuban people and the new Cuban regime in that country," he said. "We are not all communist controlled regardless of the fact that I had the experience of living in Russia."

Stuckey felt sorry for Oswald, who had not expected to be required to talk about his Soviet past. He gave Bringuier a tape of the show, and the energetic DRE delegate proceeded to write a declamatory press release in florid Cuban revolutionary style, delivering it to the newspapers and wire services. "We Cubans who want to regain our freedom in Cuba, and at the same time protect your freedom, ask you Americans for four things," Bringuier declared. One of them was, "Write to your Congressman asking for a full investigation on Mr. Lee H. Oswald, a confessed 'Marxist.'" For some reason, this prescient call for an investigation of the thoroughly obscure Oswald, made by a representative of a group secretly funded by the CIA, did not make it into the agency's normal reporting channels.

Bringuier also distributed an "Open Letter to the People of New Orleans" to local civic groups, stressing "the danger that the FPCC represents to you and your family." He salted the missive with details of Oswald's life in the Soviet Union and the communist loyalties of the FPCC. He added references to newspaper articles to illustrate Cuban government support of the FPCC. He urged the people of the city to write to their congressmen "expressing your concern over the activities of the FPCC pressure group." He issued the open letter in the name of six other anti-Castro organizations, including the Cuban Revolutionary Council, Alpha 66, and Cuban Revolutionary Rescue, all groups subsidized by the CIA. The notion that Oswald posed a "danger" also failed to reach the AMSPELL files. What, if anything, George Joannides, the DRE's handler, reported about the DRE's encounters with Oswald is unknown. But a wide variety of circumstantial evidence indicates that Dave Phillips knew or should have known of the DRE's contacts with the oddball ex-marine.

AMSPELL was Dave Phillips's baby. In his memoir he praised the DRE's leaders. In congressional testimony he described the DRE as "a very important group both in Havana and Miami." He had helped the group's top leaders—Alberto Muller, Manuel Salvat, and Chilo Borja—to resist Castro's orthodoxy while they attended the University of Havana. He had helped them escape to Miami and arranged for funding of their sabotage raids and propaganda operations during the run-up to the Baby of Pigs. In 1961 and 1962, he had received regular reports on the group from case officers Ross Crozier and Bill Kent. When JFK investigators asked Howard Hunt about the DRE in 1978, he blurted out, "Dave Phillips ran that for us . . . but I think that's classified."

Phillips also kept up with the anti-Castro cause in New Orleans in 1963. He had spent a lot of time at a military training camp in the suburb of Belle Chase during the run-up to the Bay of Pigs. He knew Warren DeBrueys, the senior agent in the New Orleans FBI office, who was monitoring both the DRE and Oswald's one-man FPCC chapter, and whose informant, Carlos Quiroga, had paid a visit to Oswald's house. When he was asked about De-Brueys, Phillips said, "Yes. I remember having been in touch with him."

The former leaders of the DRE say Oswald's approach to the group seemed relatively unimportant at the time, but they also say that the CIA paid close attention to their network of delegations in North and South America. "That was what the CIA wanted," said Tony Lanuza of the DRE. "Castro was organizing students all over Latin America. We were the only ones who could counter that with a network of our own." The records of the DRE, now in the University of Miami's Richter Library, support Lanuza's and Borja's story that Phillips's colleague George Joannides paid close attention to the DRE's far-flung delegations.

In early August 1963, the same week that Bringuier mobilized DRE supporters in New Orleans to confront Oswald, Joannides visited the group's headquarters to adjudicate a dispute among members of the group's chapter in San José, Costa Rica. Borja, an engineer who ran the DRE's clandestine military section in 1963, says he is certain that Joannides learned about Oswald's FPCC antics at the time they happened. "That's what the money was for," said Borja, referring to the CIA's funding of the group. "Because we gave them that kind of information." Yet no reference to the Oswald-DRE episode appears in publicly available CIA records.

Most significantly, the DRE's efforts to combat the FPCC in New Orleans fulfilled the CIA's mission for the group. The AMSPELL project, said one agency document from July 1963, involved "political action, propaganda, intelligence collection and a hemisphere-wide apparatus." When Carlos Bringuier and his friends confronted Oswald, the AMSPELL apparatus delivered, engaging in intelligence collection, the generation of propaganda, and the mounting of political action. When it came to the DRE and Oswald, the CIA got what it paid for

None of this necessarily implied that Dave Phillips had ordered the DRE to do any particular thing when it came to Lee Harvey Oswald. All the former DRE leaders emphasized that they did not take orders from the CIA, and there is good reason to take them at their word. In 1963, they were passionate young anticommunists who feared their homeland was in danger of slipping under one-party control forever. They did not need a CIA man from Washington to tell them to take action against a public supporter of Castro like Oswald.

David Phillips did not need to issue orders to get the results he wanted. The whole point of the CIA sponsorship of the DRE via the covert

AMSPELL channel was to wield the hidden hand in the realm of psychological warfare. The point was to confuse and confound the Castro regime with actions that the U.S. government could plausibly deny.

In two interviews, Sam Halpern claimed he could not recall the name of the case officer who ran the DRE for Helms in 1963. Few senior CIA men cared to remember Joannides, at least not on the record. Halpern, who died in 2006, scoffed at the notion that anybody in the clandestine service would have been interested in Oswald's antics in New Orleans. Asked why no information about the DRE's efforts to combat the FPCC in New Orleans ever reached the AMSPELL file at CIA headquarters in Washington, Halpern said, "There's no reason why it should. Lee Harvey Oswald was a totally unknown name. It was like Joe Schlipmagilda. You know, it's a name. Doesn't a mean a damn thing to anybody. . . . We wouldn't play games with that kind of stuff. Wouldn't even be interested in it."

For anyone with a passing familiarity with CIA operations in 1963, Halpern's claims were more smoke than substance. David Phillips was *always* interested in the FPCC, according to CIA records declassified in the 1990s. Phillips had read the transcripts of wiretapping operations against the group since its inception in 1960. In 1961, he had persuaded a colleague to join an FPCC chapter in northern Virginia and report back on its activities. Phillips was fully aware that such informal spying might fall on the wrong side of the law forbidding CIA operations on U.S. soil. He asked his colleague James McCord of the CIA Security Office, later notorious as one of the Watergate burglars, if he needed to inform the FBI of what he had done. McCord said no.

Halpern's dissembling ignored the fact that one of Phillips's most valuable agents in Mexico City in 1963 was a fetching and informative woman named June Cobb, who specialized in penetrating FPCC operations by romancing its leaders. By the summer of 1962, her friend, FPCC executive director Richard Gibson, was a CIA informant himself with a file in Langley running to 400 pages. Halpern's claim that David Phillips would not have been interested in Oswald's FPCC activism lacks credibility, to put it politely. All the evidence shows that Phillips was deeply interested in the Fair Play for Cuba Committee.

The official story that it was sheer coincidence that Oswald, a sociopathic loner, chose the CIA's favorite young Cubans as the target for his attempted infiltration finds no support in the agency's records of the AMSPELL program. The DRE's case officer George Joannides never made any such claim. Fifteen years later, Joannides would be called out of retirement to serve as the CIA's liaison to congressional investigators. At that time Joannides did *not* take the opportunity to say that the accused assassin had been in contact with his assets. Rather, he concealed his working relationship with the DRE in 1963. He provided only a handful of miscellaneous AMSPELL documents to investigators looking into Oswald's contacts with anti-Castro Cubans, and he said nothing of his own knowledge of the group. In fact, four decades after the fact, the most important AMSPELL records are missing from CIA archives—perhaps intentionally.

In the early 1960s, the agency's internal procedures required the case officer handling Cuban exile groups to file monthly reports. These reports, filed by case officers Ross Crozier and Bill Kent from September 1960 to November 1962, detailed AMSPELL's generous budget, their extensive propaganda operations, their continuing military activities, their responsiveness to agency direction (or lack thereof), and their general effectiveness in furthering U.S. policy goals. Such reports were also submitted by DRE case officers in May 1964 and later. In the 1990s, the Assassination Records Review Board declassified these documents. But the board was unable to locate any monthly AMSPELL reports from December 1962 to April 1964. There was a seventeen-month gap in the AMSPELL records, which coincided exactly with the period in which George Joannides handled the group on behalf of Phillips and Helms. As a result, it is hard to draw any firm conclusions about the contacts between the DRE and Oswald, other than that the CIA has never explained them. Deep-sixing the AMSPELL file was the kind of work for which Joannides won a Career Intelligence Medal. Joannides was never questioned by investigators about his knowledge of Oswald. When he died in 1990, he took what he knew about Oswald and the DRE to a grave in suburban Washington. His obituary in the *Washington Post* described him as a "Defense Department lawyer." A good spy, he stuck to his cover story as he passed into the next world.

Five weeks after his encounters with the DRE, Oswald came into contact with a second CIA collection program run by David Phillips, this one codenamed LIERODE. Oswald had ceased all pro-Castro activities in New Orleans after the August 21 radio debate. He spoke to his wife about hijacking a plane to Cuba. He toyed with a rifle all the while planning a more conventional means of reaching the island. On September 17, he went to the Mexican consulate in New Orleans to apply for a visa. A week later he apparently caught a Trailways bus to Mexico City. "The last I heard was that he had left the city," said Carlos Bringuier.

Oswald arrived in the Mexican capital on Friday morning, September 27. He checked into a room in a cheap hotel, then headed for the Cuban diplomatic compound on Calle Francisco Marquez, where he paid a visit on the consulate. Oswald's arrival brought him into view of Win Scott's hidden cameras. The combination of the Oswald chapter of Win's manuscript, declassified CIA records, and the testimony of two former colleagues strongly suggests a conclusion that the agency still denies: that the CIA took a photograph of Oswald as he contacted the Cubans.

Win insisted this was so. One of the central points of his long-suppressed Oswald chapter was that the Warren Commission report on the assassination of President Kennedy had misstated the facts. Win was especially irked at a passage in the Warren Report that stated: "In October 1963, the Passport Office of the State Department received a report from the Central Intelligence Agency that Oswald had visited the Soviet Embassy in Mexico City. The report said nothing about Oswald having visited the Cuban Embassy in Mexico City, a fact which was not known until after the assassination."

Win knew this was evasive. He did not report Oswald's visit to the Passport Office. He reported it to Dick Helms, the CIA's deputy director of operations, and it was he who passed it along to the State Department. More important, Win disputed the claim that his people had missed Oswald's contacts with the Cubans. The Mexico City station had a hard-won reputation for knowing everything about the Cuban embassy. His operations were designed to ensure that every phone line was tapped, every visitor photographed. The Warren Commission's statement implied the station had failed in one of its strongest areas. Win rejected the notion.

Oswald, he wrote in his memoir, "was a person of great interest to us during this 27 September to 2 October 1963 period." He was specific about the station's response to his visit in Mexico City:

Every piece of information concerning Lee Harvey Oswald was reported immediately after it was received to: US Ambassador Thomas C. Mann, by memorandum; the FBI Chief in Mexico, by memorandum; and to my headquarters by cable; and included in each and every one of these reports was the entire conversation Oswald had, so far as it was known. These reports were made on all his contacts with both the Cuban Consulate and with the Soviets.

Because we thought at first that Lee Harvey Oswald might be a dangerous potential defector from the USA to the Soviet Union, he was of great interest to us, so we kept a special watch on him and his activities. He was observed on all his visits to each of the two communist embassies; and his conversations with personnel of these embassies were studied in detail, so far as we knew them.

Win's account is far from infallible. He wrote from memory, not from the documents, and it showed. He sometimes scrambled the sequence of events in Oswald's trip. He got some details wrong. He wrote "November 23" when referring to the events of November 22. Anne Goodpasture noted that his reporting to headquarters sometimes exaggerated his accomplishments. But on the question of whether Oswald was photographed during his visits to the Cuban embassy in September 1963, a wide variety of evidence supports Win's version of events.

The station's program of photographic surveillance of the Cuban diplomatic compound in Mexico City, called LIERODE, was housed in an apartment across the street. David Phillips, as the chief of Cuba operations, had responsibility for reviewing the photographs of all visitors and deciding if their contacts with the Cubans warranted further action. In a September 1963 report to the photographic branch at headquarters, Win noted that photographic surveillance of the Cubans had been *expanded* on September 27, the very day of Oswald's visit. Up until then, the observation post had only one employee, who took pictures of visitors coming and going through the embassy's main gate. But then the Cubans reopened the public entrance to the consulate, halfway down the block. A lone photographer could not take pictures of visitors to both the embassy's main gate and the consulate door, so a second camera, with a shutter device called a VLS-2 that automatically snapped a picture whenever someone came into the viewfinder, was installed.

"On the morning of 27 September, PARMUTH [code name for the photo technician] installed VLS-2 Trigger Device at the LIERODE base house and used the 500mm lens issued with this system," Win wrote. He reported that the VLS-2 device had been examined the day before and needed new batteries, "but otherwise the system tested well." There was a slight mechanical problem that required the remachining of a screw on the trigger device. The station requested that the new system be tested for four days. In his next report on LIERODE in November, Win wrote that "the VLS-2 broke down after 4 days of photographing." That suggests that the camera was working on September 27 and broke down on October 1. "The VLS-2 Trigger Device, installed at the LIERODE base house to cover the Consulate entrance," he wrote, "is performing well with little false triggering." If anything, the camera was overly sensitive, according to Win. "During the first two weeks of operation, the VLS-2 would trigger traffic entering and leaving the target entrance."

No photo of Oswald's comings and going has ever surfaced, but two of Win's colleagues later told congressional investigators they had seen such photos of Oswald. Stanley Watson, who served as Win's deputy chief of station from 1965 to 1969, said he reviewed the station's Oswald file at one point and found a photo of Oswald, which he described as a "three quarters from behind photo—basically an ear and back shot." Watson was not alone in such memories. Joseph Piccolo, a counterintelligence officer who did two tours in Mexico City in the 1960s, told investigators he saw two surveillance photos of Oswald in the station's files. Piccolo was quoted as saying "that these two pictures had been taken of Lee Harvey Oswald either entering or leaving the Cuban Embassy/Consulate in Mexico City. The first picture was a three-quarters full shot of Oswald exposing his left profile as [he] looked downward. The second photograph which Mr. Piccolo recollected seeing was a back of the head view of Oswald."

Dave Phillips denied knowing of any such photo or anything about Oswald's actions in the Cuban consulate. In his entertaining if unreliable 1975 memoir, *The Night Watch,* he contended that Oswald's appearance had aroused little interest when it occurred. No one in the station, Phillips wrote, "knew anything about Lee Harvey Oswald: that he had previously lived in the Soviet Union and married a Russian wife. He was just another blip." He insisted that the station's cameras had not captured Oswald's comings and goings. "Yes, there was a photographic coverage of the Cuban embassy," he told the House Select Committee on Assassinations in 1976. But the surveillance "did not work on the weekend and sometimes the camera had to be pulled out. The camera was pulled out either because of malfunction or something. It was not there on the day that the intercept indicated Oswald was in the Cuban Embassy, and consequently there was no picture of Lee Harvey Oswald that we ever saw in Mexico."

Phillips's comments were evasive. Oswald first visited the consulate on Friday, not the weekend. The LIERODE camera was not "malfunctioning or something" on September 27, at least not according to Win's contemporaneous report. Phillips was correct that the camera was "pulled out," but that did not happen until October 1, according to Win.

For CIA insiders attentive to fine factual points, Win's memoir had long been disturbing, especially the statement that Oswald "was observed on all his visits to each of the two communist embassies." The agency's top lawyer worried about its implications.

"The underlying problem," noted CIA general counsel Scott Breckinridge in 1978, was that Win's first-person account refuted the agency's preferred narrative of Oswald's visit to Mexico City. The CIA's story, as Breckinridge faithfully detailed it to Congress, was that "other than a telephone call on 1 October 1963" that led to a "routine report to Headquarters," the agency and its personnel had "no real knowledge of [Oswald's] presence there until after the assassination of President Kennedy." Breckinridge had no choice but to share the Oswald chapter with congressional investigators who had learned about it from other sources. But he made a point of impugning Win's credibility by quoting John Horton's view that Win had "gone to seed" and drank too much. The CIA did not much care for Win's account because it called into question the agency's position that Oswald was but a blip in their eyes.

No CIA surveillance photographs of Oswald have ever surfaced.

Oswald arrived at the Cuban consulate around 11:00 A.M. on Friday, September 27; he expressed his desire to travel to the Soviet Union via Cuba. Informed that he needed passport-style pictures to apply for a visa, he left, giving the new LIERODE camera a second chance to take his photo. He returned about an hour later with the passport photos, again passing through the door surveilled by the CIA's cameras. Inside, he said he wanted to travel to Cuba the following Monday, September 30. To persuade the Cubans to grant him a transit visa, he produced evidence of his clash with the DRE in New Orleans, a newspaper clipping about his encounters with the exiles, and a Fair Play for Cuba Committee membership card. Sylvia Duran, a Mexican employee in the consulate, explained that Oswald would first have to contact the Russian embassy about his planned travel to the Soviet Union before she could issue an "in-transit" visa. Oswald departed again and walked to the Russian embassy a few blocks away. There he was admitted to speak with Vice Consul Oleg Nechiperenko, who told him that his request for a visa would have to be sent to the Soviet embassy in Washington and could not be processed for four months. Oswald returned to the Cuban consulate around four o'clock that afternoon, passing for a fifth time through the viewfinder of the newly installed LIERODE camera. Inside, he spoke to Duran again and lied, telling her that the Soviets had no problem with his visa application. Duran called the Soviet embassy to check his story.

Duran's call triggered another CIA surveillance program, this one known as LIENVOY. This was Win's massive audio intercept operation that listened in on thirteen telephone line into various communist embassies.

"There is an American here who has requested an in-transit visa because he is going to Russia," Duran said. "I would like to know to whom he spoke at the Russian Embassy because I sent him to you thinking if he got a Russian visa then I could issue him a Cuban visa without any more processing. Who did he speak to? He claims he was told there were no more problems."

The man on the line in the Russian embassy said someone would call her back. Twenty minutes later, a Soviet official called and explained, "We cannot give a visa here without asking Washington. He says he belongs to a pro-Cuban organization and the Cubans cannot give him a visa without his first getting a Russian visa. I do not know what to do with him. I have to wait for an answer from Washington."

Oswald exchanged sharp words with Duran and another Cuban consulate employee and left.

It did not take long for the news of this American visitor to the Soviet and Cuban offices to reach Win's desk. At the end of each day the tapes at LIENVOY monitoring center were transcribed and, if necessary, translated into English by a station employee named Boris Tarasoff and his wife. On Monday, September 30, they passed their work on to Anne Goodpasture as was their routine. After scanning and sorting the fifty pages of material, Goodpasture delivered the transcripts to the appropriate desks in the station. Duran's conversations with the Soviets went to Bob Shaw, an officer who monitored the Cuban audio and photographic surveillance programs for Dave Phillips. When he read that Duran had contacted the Soviets about an unnamed American visitor who wanted to travel to the Soviet Union via Cuba, he recognized these conversations for their counterintelligence interest right away. As Goodpasture noted, the two types of "security" information that most interested the station concerned "U.S. citizens initiating or maintaining contact with the Cuban and Soviet diplomatic installations" and "travel to Cuba by U.S. citizens or residents." Shaw routed the transcript of Duran's conversations back to Goodpasture, and to the Soviet desk and to Win. Tarasoff and the typist who had produced the transcript later told a *Washington Post* reporter that the station's top officials were "hot" for the conversation about the unnamed American. When Win read the transcript of Duran's September 27, 4:25 P.M. call to the Soviet embassy about the American traveler, he wrote in the margin, "Is it possible to identify?"

It was possible. That next day, Tuesday, October 1, Win learned that an American named Lee Oswald had just paid a visit to the Soviet embassy. He had called the Soviet military attaché at the Soviet embassy at 10:30 in the morning and said, in Russian, "Hello. I was at your place last Saturday and I talked to your consul. They said that they'd send a telegram to Washington, and I wanted to ask you if there is anything new?" The Russian voice answering the phone in the Soviet attaché's office asked Oswald to call back on another line and gave him the number. At 10:45 A.M., in another call to the Soviet embassy, the same voice was heard saying, "This is Lee Oswald speaking. I was at your place last Saturday and spoke to a consul, and they said that they'd send a telegram to Washington, so I wanted to find out if you have anything new. But I don't remember the name of that consul."

The man answering the phone was a guard named Obyedkov whom the station believed to be a KGB man.

"Kostikov," the guard guessed. "He is dark?" Valeriy Kostikov was a consul at the embassy, and he was unusually dark-skinned for a Russian.

"Yes," came the reply. "My name is Oswald."

There was a pause, and Obyedkov came back on the line. "They say that they haven't received anything yet."

"Have they done anything?" Oswald asked.

"Yes," came the reply. "They say that a request has been sent out but nothing has been received as yet."

Oswald started to ask, "And what . . . " Obyedkov hung up on him.

The caller had mentioned his name. That was key, said Goodpasture. The monitors of the LIENVOY lines had standing orders from Win to report at once any conversation in which a visitor to the Soviet embassy was identified by name. What made the call doubly interesting was that the man who identified himself as Oswald indicated he had visited with the Soviets on Saturday and talked to Kostikov. Goodpasture and others suspected Valeriy Vladimirovich Kostikov was a KGB officer. The station's files indicated he had first come to Mexico in late 1959, traveled to Cuba in January 1960, and arrived at the Soviet embassy as vice consul in September 1961.

The CIA tape of the Oswald call was marked "urgent" and delivered to the station within fifteen minutes. "I am certain that the Oswald call came to our attention from the Soviet line," Goodpasture told colleagues later. "[The tape] was picked up and taken to Boris [Tarasoff] for translation because the caller was trying to speak Russian." Per usual practice, Goodpasture arranged for the Oswald exchange on the tape to be duplicated onto another tape. In an interview in 2005, Goodpasture explained that the most interesting conversations were copied for future reference. The duplicate tape, or "dupe," as she called it, went into the files while the original tape would be reused within a couple of weeks. Goodpasture then delivered the transcript to the Soviet desk officer. The desk officer in the station who handled day-to-day issues related to the Soviet embassy testified the transcript of Oswald's call "was brought to my attention by the chief, the head of the Soviet section and by Anne Goodpasture who was discussing this and who was going to notify headquarters and whose responsibility it was."

It was the translator Boris Tarasoff who ultimately connected Oswald's call to the Soviets on Tuesday with a phone call picked up over the weekend by LIENVOY. In the margin of the transcript of Oswald's Tuesday October 1 call, Tarasoff wrote, "The same person who phoned a day or so ago and spoke in broken Russian." That was a reference to an intercepted call made from the Cuban consulate to the Soviet embassy at 11:51 on Saturday morning, September 28. In that phone call, a woman, later identified as Sylvia Duran, put a man on the line who spoke "terrible, hardly recognizable Russian," according to Tarasoff. The man said he had just visited the embassy and wanted to give them his address. The Russians hung up on him.

Win pushed Tarasoff to come up with the answer. Who was the American who visited the Cuban consulate? Win wanted to know. It took Tarasoff two weeks to come up with the answer.

Far in the future, Dave Phillips would have trouble fashioning a coherent account about what he knew of Oswald. In the late 1970s, he offered four not entirely consistent versions of the story of Oswald's visit to Mexico City. First, in his memoir, written in 1976 and published in 1977, he said Oswald was "a blip" of no interest. Second, in November 1976, he added remarkable details not found in the book. He told Ron Kessler of the Washington Post that Oswald had offered his services to the Cubans during his visit to the consulate. The next day, Phillips was grilled, under oath, by Richard Sprague, the general counsel of the House Select Committee on Assassinations (HSCA), and supplied a third version. When Sprague challenged him to back up the story of Oswald's offer, Phillips recanted the story he had told Kessler the day before, a move that Sprague described as slithery. Confronted with the paper trail while under oath, Phillips admitted the Warren Commission's claim that the station missed Oswald's Cuban contacts was wrong. He acknowledged he was informed right away about Oswald's presence in Mexico City because he was an American who wanted to travel to Cuba. He said he drafted a cable for Win about Oswald. Two years later, confronted with still more documents, Phillips changed his story again and said he had "exaggerated" his involvement in the response to Oswald's visit and was not involved in the drafting of the cable. This shifting testimony leaves the strong impression Phillips tried to obscure what he knew about Lee Harvey Oswald's travel and intentions before President Kennedy was killed.

In his first HSCA appearance, Phillips initially offered a mea culpa. "After this whole thing [JFK's murder] was over," he said, "I noted certain weaknesses in my performance, one of them being, damn, why didn't I know more about this before the assassination? So I think what may have happened is, I indeed did see the [October 1] transcript and didn't recognize that it pertained to the other [September 27] transcript."

"So I went back into the file," he said. "Let's look at everything." Only then, he claimed, did the conversation of the unidentified American make sense. "By goodness, that's talking about Lee Harvey Oswald." Was there a measure of nervousness in his mixed-up language? He might have wanted to say "My goodness," or "By God," but it came out "By goodness."

"So it is quite possible that I saw it and didn't recognize the value or the connection with Oswald because it was just a case—" Phillips stopped, apparently deciding that he did not want to commit himself to any particular story. "Well that is possible," he finished lamely.

In fact, it was not possible. If he indeed knew "that Oswald wanted to go to the Soviet Union via Cuba," as he testified, then he knew of Oswald's Cuban contacts at the time they happened. If true, that assertion was doubly damning to the Warren Commission's passage to which Win objected. Phillips knew not only that Oswald had contacted the Cubans but also that he intended to travel to Cuba.

Phillips might have conceivably learned about Oswald's plans to travel to Cuba not from the surveillance recordings but from Oswald himself. Antonio Veciana, the leader of the exile group Alpha 66, which opposed the Kennedy White House's Cuba policy, told congressional investigators that he saw his case officer, a man who called himself "Maurice Bishop," with Oswald in Dallas in early September 1963. The investigators interviewed CIA officer Ross Crozier, who had handled DRE matters for Phillips from 1960 to 1962. He said that Phillips sometimes used the alias "Maurice Bishop," a statement he later recanted. Veciana described "Bishop" in some detail to an artist who produced a sketch of a man whom Phillips acknowledged bore some resemblance to him. Veciana, now in his late seventies, still lives in Miami, where he helps his son run a boating supply store. In an interview, he retold the story of the CIA man who used the name "Maurice Bishop" exactly as he told it thirty years ago. But he said, as he has always said, that he did not know if "Bishop" and Phillips were the same man.

Phillips did eventually concede under oath that the Mexico City station learned of Oswald's visit to the Cuban consulate at the time it happened. And once he conceded the point, his story changed. Oswald, "the blip" who attracted only "normal" attention became a man who raised questions. The fact that an American was attempting to travel to Russia via Cuba, Phillips told the HSCA, "escalated the importance" of Oswald's visit in the eyes of the station. "As far as the Cuban Embassy was concerned, as I recall it, we then tasked our agents, 'What do you know about a man named so and so with this and that and the other,' and asked them if they knew about his visit or something like that."

What matters less than Phillips's inconsistent accounts and factual mistakes (which, given the passage of time, might have involved some honest failure of memory) was the convergence of his account and Win's on the question of Oswald's visits to the Cuban consulate and Oswald's plans to travel to Cuba. The Warren Commission's assertion notwithstanding, they agreed that the CIA station knew about Oswald's contacts with the Cubans at the time they happened. They differed over whether those contacts had been reported to CIA headquarters—Win said yes, Phillips said no—but they both admitted that they knew of the contacts.

The tapes of Oswald's calls might have clarified what they knew, especially the duplicate tape of Oswald's October 1 call to the Soviet embassy that Anne Goodpasture made. This was the tape to which translator Tarasoff listened. After Kennedy was killed, Goodpasture said she gave a duplicate of the original Oswald tape to Win and suggested that he might have "squirreled it way" in his safe. John Whitten of the CIA and J. Edgar Hoover and Gordon Shanklin of the FBI later reported independently that U.S. officials had listened to a tape containing the voice of a man who said he was Oswald. But these tapes were never made public. In 1964, Goodpasture herself wrote a note for the files saying that a "voice" comparison of the Oswald tapes had been made. In an interview, Goodpasture said she had no memory of the notation about Oswald's voice on the tape and could not explain it.

Michael would later learn the CIA had probably destroyed the Oswald tapes in 1986, just a few months after he launched his search for his father's stolen memoir.

Oswald's calls and visits to the Soviet embassy in pursuit of a visa brought him into view of a fourth CIA collection program, a photo surveillance operation code-named LIEMPTY. Supervised by Win's good friend George Munro, this operation was housed in an apartment across from the embassy's massive gated entrance on Avenida de la Revolucion. The LIEMPTY technicians had instructions to photograph all persons who approached the guardhouse. Oswald had approached at least twice, once on Friday, September 27, and once the next day. According to Anne Goodpasture, Win was reluctant to send a cable to Washington about the would-be traveler to the Soviet Union and Cuba unless he could include a photo. Combing through the LIEMPTY contact sheets, Goodpasture could find no pictures of an American on Friday, September 27, and there was no photo coverage on Saturday, September 28, but she did find an image of a man, possibly American, taken as he came out of the Soviet embassy gate on October 2. He appeared to be about thirty-five years old. He was heavyset and slightly balding. She gave the photo to Win, saying she could not vouch that the man was Oswald, only that he was the only American visitor in recent days.

In his published memoir, Phillips wrote that a station officer (whom he called "Craig") took his time drafting a query to Washington about the visitor. "The circumstances were such—Oswald wished to return to the Soviet Union *via Cuba* [emphasis added]—that a cable to headquarters was required asking for a Washington file check on Oswald," Phillips wrote. "Craig procrastinated as he was busy with other things. . . . Finally, Craig's wife typed out a cable herself, dropping it on her husband's desk for his review before it went to Win Scott for release." In his testimony before the HSCA in 1978, Phillips let slip a detail he had omitted from his previous accounts. He said that he had personally approved "Craig's" draft cable to headquarters on Oswald. "During that process, it did come to me, also to sign off on," he said. "Because it spoke about Cuban matters."

It took a week, but on October 8 Win was ready to report to headquarters about Oswald. He had a transcript from LIENVOY, a photograph from LIEMPTY, and a draft cable approved by "Knight," aka David Phillips. Late on the afternoon of October 8, Win sent the following cable to CIA headquarters:

> According to LIENVOY 1 Oct 1963 American male who spoke broken Russian said his name was Lee OSWALD at the SOVEMB 28 Sept when he spoke with Consul who he believed be Valeriy Vladimorovich KOSTIKOV. Subj[ect] asked Sov guard Ivan OBYEDKOV upon checking said nothing received yet but request had been sent. Have photos male appear be American entering Sovemb 1216 hours leaving 1222 on 1 Oct. Apparent age 35, athletic build circa 6 feet, receding hairline, balding top. Wore Khakis and sports shirt Source: LIEMPTY.

Win was prudent not to claim that the man in the photo was Oswald. The LIEMPTY images depicted a man emerging from the Soviet embassy who was ten years older and forty pounds heavier than Oswald. It is certain that Oswald visited the Soviet embassy on September 27 and 28 because Oleg Nechiperenko, the vice consul with whom he met, wrote a book about it. The man in the photo was never identified. No LIEMPTY photograph of the real Oswald coming or going through the Soviet embassy gate on Avenida de la Revolucion has ever surfaced.

In terms of CIA competence, an even bigger problem with the reporting on Oswald was what Win's cable did *not* say. Why didn't Dave Phillips tell Win Scott to mention Oswald's contacts with the Cuban consulate? After all, the American visitor was a subject of obvious interest. In Phillips's own description of his duties as chief of Cuban operations, he said he was interested in "any nexus" between the Cuban embassy and "pro-Castro groups in the hemisphere." Oswald had told both the Cubans and the Russians that he belonged to a pro-Cuban organization. Oswald's public support for the FPCC attracted the interest of Phillips's friend Warren DeBrueys in the FBI's New Orleans office. Oswald had also attracted the attention and indignation of his AMSPELL allies in Miami and New Orleans. And Phillips, by his own admission, knew Oswald wanted to travel to Russia via Cuba.

So why did Win's October 8, 1963, cable fail to mention Oswald's Cuban contacts? That was something Dave Phillips had trouble explaining.

"Do you have any explanation as to why that would be omitted?" HSCA general counsel Richard Sprague asked as he questioned Phillips in 1976. Phillips said he did not know why. The information "should have been there," he acknowledged. "It was a grievous omission."

Sprague, an experienced federal prosecutor, had worked his way around many a white-collar conspiracy. He sensed Phillips was being evasive. "Would that just be an omission or would that be more likely a decision by someone . . . ?"

Phillips tried to dodge the question. He did not want to admit the possibility he knew about Oswald's Cuban contacts and chose not to tell Win. "It certainly could be somebody decided not to do it for one reason or another, but of course, that is an assumption," he said. Phillips was in a legal box. His CIA oath required him to conceal all information about secret operations. But if he had omitted mention of Oswald's appearance at the Cuban consulate because he wanted to conceal an authorized operation about which Win had no need to know, then he could neither confirm nor deny his actions.

Phillips wouldn't say who made the decision not to mention Oswald's Cuban contacts in the cable. But he insisted Win Scott had approved. "No one else would dare make that decision without Win Scott's knowing about it and approving it," he said. Phillips's account could not be verified because by the time he offered it Win was dead. But even at its most evasive, Phillips's account dealt yet another blow to the CIA's cover story that Oswald's visit to Mexico City drew only "routine" interest at the time and that the station had failed to detect his Cuban contacts. To the contrary, Phillips knew of those contacts and did not share them with his own friend and boss.

For Michael, the totality of Win's Oswald chapter and the new records declassified in the 1990s by the JFK review board posed a very basic question about his father. Although Lee Harvey Oswald had passed through various CIA surveillance programs in the weeks before he allegedly murdered JFK, much of the evidence had never seen the light of day. Four decades on, the 1963 AMSPELL reports on DRE at the time of its encounters with Oswald are still missing. The surveillance photos of Oswald outside the Cuban consulate that Joe Piccolo and Stanley Watson say they saw are missing. Transcripts of the LIENVOY tapes are available, but the tapes themselves were never aired publicly and were most likely destroyed by the CIA. The surveillance photos of the visitor to the Soviet embassy were erroneously identified as depicting Oswald. And Win Scott had failed to report Oswald's contacts with the Cubans.

Michael could overlook the CIA's lavish praise of his father and indict him for sloppiness, incompetence, and possible dereliction of duty about the man who was arrested for killing the president of the United States. But while his father might have been prone to exaggeration (as Anne Goodpasture said) and had betrayed wives and friends, he had no history of carelessness in intelligence collection or counterintelligence operations. To the contrary, CIA inspectors said he set the standard for the Western Hemisphere, if not the world. Win, like Dave Phillips, was a vigilant and accomplished anticommunist who was unlikely to conceal intelligence, deliberately or accidentally, about a pro-communist, pro-Castro troublemaker who sought to violate U.S. law by visiting Cuba.

There is another, simpler possibility: that Win blurred the story of Oswald and the Cubans consciously and deliberately at the behest of his superiors. This was not necessarily sinister. Espionage professionals constantly share—or do not share—information on a need-to-know basis. They would not—legally could not—share the product of their intelligence collection efforts if the information would reveal the sources or methods of an authorized covert operation. That would violate their CIA oaths. Most likely, they were discreet about what they knew of Oswald in October 1963 because that was their duty.

This conclusion does not imply that Win or anybody else acquiesced or participated in a plot to kill Kennedy. In fact, the opposite seemed more likely to Michael, who had a hard time believing his father would have ever countenanced such treachery. He had no trouble believing, though, that his father would have covered up an authorized intelligence operation—even one that involved Oswald—that had a legitimate purpose in the eyes of the CIA.

A careful reading of the CIA headquarters response to Win Scott's cable about Oswald bolsters the notion. The record shows that top officials digested the information on Oswald with care and deliberation. In their reply to their own station chief, Jim Angleton's Counterintelligence Staff and

Dick Helms's top deputies opted not to share everything they knew with their own man in the field. When it came to the details of Oswald's recent activities they decided Win did not have a "need to know."

As one of Angleton's aides was to admit decades later, this was no accident.

15

Out of the Loop

When Michael thought back to what he was doing in the fall of 1963 as his father wrote cables about Lee Harvey Oswald, the first thing that came to mind were the family dogs.

"We lived in a large home at Paseo de la Reforma 2035 in Mexico City which had expansive gardens and a roof top patio," he recalled. "Arete, the German shepherd that had come to join the family when Janet married Win, had the privilege to roam the yard for the morning and early afternoon, while Chato, Win's bulldog, remained on the roof top patio. At around 2 P.M. there would be a shift: Chato would be allowed to have yard privileges while Arete would be confined to the patio. It worked most of the time, but every now and then there would be a mishap and the two dogs would tangle in a fight to the death."

It was September 1963. Michael had just turned eight years old.

"It was a horrifying scene—to be present while these two creatures went at it. The bulldog would instinctively try to latch himself to attack the throat of Arete, as he in turn would bite at any part of Chato that he could get a hold of. The sound of their terrifying struggle is something I will never forget. The end would come when some brave adult, usually my father or Antonio, his driver, would step in and open up Chato's jaws with their hands and pull him away while someone else restrained Arete. I recall seeing Chato unable to walk for days after being pulled out of the fight by his hind legs."

For the boy, what stuck in his mind was the rage of canines and the courage of his father. For Win, what endured about that time September 1963 was the more subtle and lethal business of Lee

Oswald and the deceptions that enshrouded it. In the difference, Michael glimpsed how his father's secret profession and deliberate character had shaped his boyhood. Amid deadly struggle, his father exhibited a reassuring calmness.

Win received the answer to his query about Oswald via cable on October 10, 1963, a week after Oswald returned to the United States and settled in Dallas. Defenders of the CIA and those who exclude the possibility of conspiracy in Kennedy's assassination contend that this communication document is "routine." Read in the context of Win Scott's and David Phillips's operations, however, the cable shows that as the diverse streams of intelligence about Oswald were absorbed at headquarters, Win Scott was cut out of the loop.

The response came from Dick Helms's trusted assistant, Tom Karamessines. A former OSS man like Win, Karamessines had distinguished himself as a frontline operator supporting the anticommunist forces in the vicious Greek civil war of 1946–1948. He went on to become the chief of the CIA station in Athens and patron for a generation of Greek American spies, including George Joannides, the handler of the DRE/AMSPELL account in Miami. In the cable, Karamessines passed on what headquarters purported to know about Oswald.

The three-page message stated that Oswald had defected to the Soviet Union and attempted to renounce U.S. citizenship in Moscow on October 31, 1959. He married a Russian woman, Marina Prusakova, in April 1961 and had second thoughts about becoming a Soviet citizen. His U.S. passport was returned to him in 1962, and he left the Soviet Union in May 1962 to return to the States. The cable passed along the view of the U.S. embassy in Moscow that "twenty months of realities of life in Soviet Union had clear maturing effect on Oswald." According to the cable, the last thing the agency had heard about Oswald was that the chastened young man was trying to come home. Then came this line: "Latest HDQS info[rmation] was [State Department] report dated May 1962 stating [it] had determined Oswald is still U.S. citizen and both he and his Soviet wife have exit permits and Dept. of State had given approval for their travel with infant child to USA."

Latest headquarters information. This seemingly authoritative and innocuous phrase was, in fact, intended to mislead, as one of its authors would later concede. Concocted by Angleton's Counterintelligence Staff and sanctioned by anti-Castro operations officers, this morsel of misinformation kept Win in the dark about Oswald's recent past. It was deceptive and it was intentional. The reconstruction of the paper trail shows that top CIA officials were deliberately concealing from Win all they knew about Lee Harvey Oswald.

When Win's name trace request first arrived at headquarters on October 9, Charlotte Bustos, the majordomo of WH/3, the Mexico and Central America desk of the CIA's Western Hemisphere division, located the agency's basic personality file, known as a 201 file, on Oswald, which had been on loan to the Counterintelligence Staff. As a former Soviet defector, Oswald was a natural subject of interest. Had he been "turned" by Soviet intelligence operatives during his time in Minsk? Was he sent back as a "sleeper" agent? Such questions were the province of the specific office within Angleton's staff, the Special Investigations Group (SIG), that possessed Oswald's file. The SIG had a broad mandate from Angleton to conduct research "into the long-range validity of CIA operations in terms of known or potential hostile capabilities, including penetrations, and of Agency Security." The chief of CI/SIG was one of Angleton's top aides, Birch D. O'Neal, who had served as station chief in Guatemala City during Operation Success.

Bustos sent a draft reply to Win's query about Oswald to Counterintelligence Staff because CI had the longest-standing interest in his activities and travels. Three different CI offices reviewed the draft. O'Neal's assistant in the SIG, a woman named Ann Egerer, looked it over. So did Jane Roman, head of CI Staff's liaison office, which handled the communications with other federal agencies. Given this level of staff review, it seems likely that Angleton himself was familiar with Oswald's name, if not biography, in October 1963.

The draft reply was also shown to the Counterintelligence office in the Special Affairs Staff, known as SAS/CI, which was run by former FBI agent Harold Swenson. "As Chief of Counter Intelligence for the Special Affairs Staff," Swenson later told investigators, "I was responsible for protecting the CIA's Special Affairs Staff against penetration by foreign intelligence services, particularly the CUIS [Cuban intelligence service] and for mounting SAS Counter Intelligence operations intended to penetrate the Cuban Intelligence Service." Their input was consistent with a David Phillips operation. Phillips served in SAS, had responsibility for counterintelligence operations against the Cubans outside the United States, and had visited CIA headquarters in the days before the cable was drafted.

The involvement of Swenson's office in the preparation of the Oswald cable indicated that Oswald was either regarded as a threat to anti-Castro operations—perhaps because of his contacts with the DRE/AMSPELL delegation in New Orleans—or because he was somehow part of a counterintelligence operation in Mexico City intended to penetrate the Cubans.

Otherwise, there was no reason for SAS/CI to review Win's name trace request. In any case, the seemingly obscure Oswald was getting a thorough look-over in Langley.

The final draft of the cable went to John Whitten, chief of the desk responsible for overseeing all covert operations in Mexico and Central America. Then it went to an even higher level. Standard agency procedure at the time required that every cable sent from headquarters have an "authenticating officer," who vouched for its accuracy. In the case of Win's name trace request, the responsibility would normally have fallen to J. C. King, the veteran chief of the Western Hemisphere division. As often occurred in covert action matters, however, King chose not to get involved. One of Helms's deputies, William J. Hood, the chief of covert operations for the Western Hemisphere, signed instead. The "releasing officer," tasked with ensuring that the communication followed agency policy, was Karamessines.

This level of scrutiny was hardly routine. Questioned about the October 10 cable years later, Karamessines said he had signed off because Win's inquiry involved the CIA in disseminating information about an American citizen. Not true, said John Whitten. In secret sworn testimony not declassified until 1997, Whitten said headquarters had often done name traces on Americans in contact with communist embassies and released the information without bothering a senior official such as Karamessines. Whitten said he could not explain why the release of information about Oswald request had to be approved at such a high level.

The truth only came out thirty-two years later, when one of the drafters of the October 10, 1963, cable talked about how it was prepared. That happened in 1995, after the JFK Assassination Records Review Board started declassifying large batches of long-secret, preassassination records on Oswald. Among them was a copy of the October 10, 1963, cable that revealed for the first time that Jane Roman had helped prepare the cable. Roman, a retired CIA officer who had worked for Angleton since the late 1940s, was well connected and well regarded. Her husband, Howard, also a CIA officer, had helped Allen Dulles write his book *The Craft of Intelligence*. In 1995, the author tracked her down at her home in the Cleveland Park neighborhood in Washington, where he arranged to interview her on tape with historian John Newman, who, in his first career, spent twenty years as a U.S. Army intelligence analyst, specializing in examining cable traffic. Roman was shown the new records and asked for her assessment.

Newman started with the routing slips attached to three FBI reports on Oswald that had circulated in the agency in September 1962 and September 1963. They were covered with signatures of people from the various offices who had signed for the document. "Is this," Newman asked, "the mark of a person's file who's dull and uninteresting? Or would you say that we're looking at somebody who . . ."

"No, we're really trying to zero in on somebody here," Roman acknowledged. "Our interest would stem mainly from the Cuba angle."

Newman then reviewed the routing slips on two documents about Oswald that Roman had signed for in September 1963. They had come to her because they pertained to Oswald's interest in Cuba. The first was an FBI report from agent James Hosty in Dallas, who had responsibility for monitoring Oswald's activities there. Hosty reported that Oswald had left Dallas in April 1963 and moved to New Orleans, noting his recent leftist political activities, including his subscription to the *Socialist Worker*. FBI director J. Edgar Hoover sent Hosty's report to the agency on September 24, 1963—just two months before Kennedy was killed—and it had gone immediately to the Counterintelligence Staff. The routing slip attached to the document displayed the initials "JR"—for Jane Roman.

The second FBI report concerned Oswald's clashes with the DRE in New Orleans. The routing slip showed that Roman had signed on October 4. In other words, Roman had seen the latest FBI report on Oswald less than a week before she participated in the drafting of the October 10 cable to Mexico City about Oswald. Roman, if she was doing her job and reading the material she signed for, knew a lot about Oswald's personal and political life that week, including:

- that he and his wife had returned from the Soviet Union to live in Fort Worth, Texas, where he was questioned by FBI agents and refused to take a lie detector test.
- that he had then moved to New Orleans and that he had agitated on behalf of the Fair Play for Cuba Committee as recently as August 1963.
- that he had attempted to infiltrate and then gotten into a fight with members of the New Orleans delegation of the DRE, a leading anti-Castro group that was funded by the agency under the AMSPELL program.

In other words, the "latest HDQS info" on the visitor to the Cuban and Soviet embassies was not seventeen months old, as the cable to Win had said. It was less than a month old.

Shown these documents, Roman explained that she did not have ultimate responsibility for the cable about Oswald. The CI liaison office would not have dictated the final contents of the cable, she said. Given Oswald's background and his recent activism for the FPCC, the Special Affairs Staff, which oversaw all anti-Castro operations, had the most interest in Oswald. "The only interpretation I could put on this [the language of the cable and the identities of the drafters] would be that this SAS group would have held all the information on Oswald under their tight control," she said.

Roman stressed, no doubt accurately, that she was not privy to such operational matters, that running a name check was routine. "All these things that you have shown me so far before the assassination would have been very dull and very routine," she said. But then she qualified her remarks. "It's interesting that this guy tries to defect in Russia, then he comes back to the United States, [inaudible] turn him over to the FBI," she said. "Then he gets in touch with the Fair Play for Cuba Committee and all the—the [CIA] Cuba task force, they got word how to handle this. . . . Well, I mean they hold it within themselves."

Roman was describing how the anti-Castro operatives inside the agency did not share information about Oswald. *They hold it within themselves.* Newman pressed the point that Roman herself had to have known that information about Oswald was being handled selectively. She had read the FBI reports on Oswald in September and October 1963, he noted. Less than a week later, she reviewed a draft of the cable to Mexico City. She must have known the "latest HDQS info" message—the line sent to Win in Mexico City—was not accurate.

"Well, I had thousands of these things," Roman protested.

"I'm willing to accept whatever your explanation is," Newman allowed, "but I have to ask you this—"

Roman was getting testy.

"And I wasn't in on any particular goings-on or hanky-panky as far as the Cuban situation," she added.

"Right, so you wouldn't have"—Newman groped for the right words—". . . tried to examine it that closely?"

"Yeah, I mean, this is all routine as far as I was concerned," she answered.

That was the word the agency preferred to rely on when it came to talking about Oswald. Nothing unusual was noticed; CIA interest was *routine*.

"Problem though, here," Newman noted. He pointed to the words "latest HDQS info." Roman finally conceded the point. "Yeah, I mean I'm signing off on something that I know isn't true," she said.

I'm signing off on something that I know isn't true. Roman was acknowledging that somebody high up in anti-Castro operations was interested in Oswald six weeks before the assassination of President Kennedy. She accepted too that somebody in Cuba operations had made a decision to withhold information about Oswald from other CIA personnel—including Win Scott—before November 22, 1963. Newman put it to Roman that she had participated in drafting a cable in which officers higher up in the clandestine operations division had chosen not to tell the whole truth.

"I may have not noticed it or anything," she said. "And normally I wouldn't be moving the cable . . . I mean, higher-ups than me. I'm a desk [officer], not a division chief." That was certainly true. It was Tom Karamessines's cable.

Newman asked, "What does this tell you about this file, that somebody would write something they knew wasn't true? . . . I guess what I'm trying to push you to address square on here is, is this indicative of some sort of operational interest in Oswald's file?"

"Yes," Roman replied. "To me it's indicative of a keen interest in Oswald held very closely on the need-to-know basis."

A keen interest in Oswald. Held very closely. Need-to-know basis. This trifecta of intelligence jargon suggested the sort of activity usually associated with a covert operation. It certainly begged a few more questions.

In intelligence jargon "a keen interest" in Oswald meant that one or more persons involved in anti-Castro operations were focused on the man who would be accused of killing Kennedy. A likely candidate was Dave Phillips, who said under oath that he was interested in Oswald in the first week of October 1963. If the chain of command in anti-Castro operations was functioning, his man in Miami, George Joannides, had reported back in August on AMSPELL's efforts to discredit Oswald's one-man chapter of the Fair Play for Cuba Committee in New Orleans. Phillips certainly knew that Oswald had been in contact with the Cubans in Mexico City on September 27. And he had visited Washington after Oswald's presence was detected and before the misleading October 10, 1963, cable was drafted. But if, as Phillips would claim, Oswald was a mere "blip," why would senior officers at headquarters handle information about him on a "need-to-know" basis?

Jane Roman took on the difficult question.

"There has to be a point," she said, "for withholding information from Mexico City."

Newman offered his belief that "somebody made a decision about Oswald's file here," meaning one or more of Roman's colleagues in Washington. Roman mulled the possibilities.

"Well, the obvious position, which I really can't contemplate, would be that they [meaning the people with final authority over the cable] thought that somehow . . . they could make some use of Oswald," she said. "I would think that there was definitely some operational reason to withhold it [the information at headquarters on Oswald], if it was not sheer administrative error, when you see all the people who signed off on it."

Roman's candor illuminates the enduring problem posed by the October 10 cable. The most plausible explanation for the deception of Win Scott perpetrated by the Counterintelligence Staff and the Special Affairs Staff was "operational." CIA officers with a "keen interest" in Oswald did not want to share what they knew with Win because they did not want to commit details of a deniable operation to the record. If there was such an operation, it would explain the otherwise inexplicable failure of Win to mention Oswald's contacts with the Cubans in his October 8 name trace query. In any case, Jane Roman's candor and the declassified paper trail show that when it came to the CIA's latest reports on Lee Harvey Oswald, Win was deliberately cut out of the loop.

The only other signatory to the October 10 cable who ever spoke about it was William J. Hood, the retired CIA hand who coauthored Dick Helms's memoir. Still sharp in his eighties, Hood did not hesitate to comment on a fully declassified copy of the October 10 cable in a recorded interview. He scanned its identifying markers and vouched for his signature.

"It comes to me and I sign for King, and it goes to Karamessines, which is unusual, but the reason for that is obviously that . . . " Hood paused in his reading. "It's unusual that that would go to Karamessines," he acknowledged. Thus he confirmed John Whitten's testimony that it was not routine for such a request to go to a senior official such as Karamessines. Then he ticked off the names of Jane Roman and the other officials who had contributed to the cable about the utterly obscure Lee Harvey Oswald. "Jesus Christ," he whistled, "it goes all over the place. That's a lot of coordination." Thus he confirmed what CIA spokesmen and more than a few historians have long denied: that information about Oswald's visit to Mexico City circulated widely at the top of the agency while Kennedy was still alive.

Hood could not explain why Oswald received such high-level attention. He told me he was puzzled that "latest headquarters information" on Oswald had been omitted after such extensive consultation. Was it possible that Karamessines had omitted the latest information on Oswald because somebody at headquarters was running an operation involving him?

"Absolutely not," Hood said. "There's no reason to. If it was something at Helms's level there would be a reason not to tell somebody in the field. But not at this level."

But the October 10 cable had reached the level of Tom Karamessines, who was Helms's most trusted deputy. Hood conceded that "the information that is left out is pretty significant." The omission of Oswald's encounter with the DRE, he said, was "an anomaly. . . . It really should have been sent in the cable."

Thus significant information about a man who would go on to kill the president of the United States six weeks later was deliberately denied to the CIA's top man in Mexico. Hood could not explain why, save to say, "I would like to think that 80 percent [of CIA cables] would be more competent."

But he insisted, "I don't find anything smelly in it."

Thanks to the selective reporting in the October 10, 1963, cable, Win did not learn about Oswald's FPCC activism or his encounters with the DRE when President Kennedy was alive. David Phillips had not shared his knowledge that Oswald had visited the Cubans. But Win did learn—from his diligent translator Tarasoff—that Oswald had contacted the Cuban consulate on his way to the Soviet embassy. As Anne Goodpasture explained, "The caller from the Cub[an] Emb[assy] was unidentified until HQs sent traces on Oswald and voices [were] compared" by the translator.

Win wrote in his memoir that all of Oswald's contacts with the Cubans were observed immediately, and in this he was probably right. His assertion that these contacts were immediately reported to Washington is less certain. There is no cable from late September or early October 1963 about Oswald's visit to the Cuban consulates, only about his visit to the Soviets. Ray Rocca, Angleton's longtime deputy, later told JFK investigators that he recalled a cable about Oswald's travel plans—"there was someone down there who wanted to go to Cuba," he said—but no such document has ever surfaced.

The first solid evidence that Win knew Oswald had contact with the Cubans came a week after headquarters sent the traces on Oswald. On October 16, 1963, Win passed a memo to Ambassador Mann reporting that an American named Oswald had visited the Soviet embassy on both September 28 and October 1, concerning his request to travel to Cuba. Why didn't Win then report to Washington that Oswald had visited the Cubans as well as the Soviets? Goodpasture said headquarters had "no need to know" about the visit. Once again, information that probably should have been reported about Oswald was withheld.

To be sure, there was no reason for the Mexico City station to suspect a lone FPCC activist trying to travel to Cuba and Russia was a threat to the president. But Oswald certainly fit the definition of a threat to U.S. national security as defined in the Mexico City station's mission statement. He fit the top three priorities for "security intelligence" as defined by Goodpasture: First, he had initiated contacts with the Cubans and the Soviets. Second, he had attempted to travel to Cuba, a violation of U.S. law. And third, he was in contact with Cubans and Soviets believed to be intelligence officers. If Win had also known in October 1963 that Oswald had also recently proselytized for the FPCC and attempted to infiltrate the DRE, he would have been even more suspicious. He certainly would have been more aggressive in seeking to figure out what Oswald was up to.

Instead, Win could only act on the outdated information he was given. On October 16, the same day that he notified Mann about Oswald, Win asked headquarters to send him a photo of Oswald to compare with the man in the surveillance photo. Win explained he wanted to know more about "attempts of Lee Oswald and wife to reenter U.S." In other words, upon learning that Oswald had contacted the Cubans, Win immediately tried to find out what Oswald had been up to since his return from the Soviet Union in May 1962—the very information that headquarters had denied him. His photo request was routed to Jane Roman at the Counterintelligence Staff, which was handling all inquiries about Oswald. Roman replied that she had asked the Department of the Navy for two photos of Oswald. "We will forward them to our representative in Mexico who will attempt to determine if the Lee Oswald in Mexico City and subject are the same individual," Roman told the Navy on October 23. Goodpasture never received a picture of Oswald, and she felt headquarters' lack of action was deliberate. "They refused to send us a photograph," she said. "It may have been some reason that they didn't have one or couldn't get one. And we couldn't understand that."

Win continued to think about Oswald in the weeks before Kennedy's assassination. On November 7, in his monthly report on the LIENVOY program, he noted "a contact by an English-speaking man with the Soviet Embassy in Mexico City," a clear reference to the man identified as Oswald.

It was hardly surprising—and not necessarily sinister—that the anti-Castro operatives and Angleton's minions on the Counterintelligence Staff took an interest in Oswald. His clumsy efforts to infiltrate the DRE (as reported by the FBI), his desire to travel to Cuba (as noted by David Phillips), and his contact with Kostikov (as noted by Goodpasture) all identified him as a continuing potential penetration threat. What was more surprising were the revelations in a critical CIA study of Angleton's Counterintelligence Staff that was declassified in the late 1990s. It showed that the files maintained by the Special Investigations Group were not part of the agency's regular record-keeping system but were maintained in an archive controlled by Angleton. The program, said another internal report, sought to generate leads for new covert operations to be mounted by Angleton himself.

"CI operations were frequently conducted without the knowledge of the respective . . . Division Chiefs or Station Chiefs," notes one agency historian. Angleton had made his reputation as a theoretician and practitioner of counterintelligence. But his successor, George Kalaris, reviewed his files and concluded that "Angleton viewed himself more as chief of an operational entity than a staff. Few gave him high marks as an effective staff, as opposed to operations, officer." Angleton had preferred to conduct operations "in which the local station would be effectively cut out" of the picture, Kalaris wrote. He liked to establish "command channel and communications" that bypassed CIA stations and flowed directly to his office in Washington. Whatever Angleton's interest in Oswald, no trace of it remains. After Angleton was forced out of his job in late 1974, the CIA destroyed all of his files on Kennedy's assassination.

At times, questions about the Kennedy assassination became the focus of Michael's journey into his father's life. The totality of the historical record decisively refuted the CIA's long-standing claim that Oswald was an obscure figure of little interest before Kennedy was killed. But what was the alternative suggestion? Had top CIA officials deceived his father about Oswald's most recent political activities on a mere whim? Or had they used Oswald in some authorized but innocuous operation against the Cuban Embassy in Mexico City or the FPCC in New Orleans, only to realize too late that they had underestimated a madman? Or had some of the many U.S. national security operatives disenchanted with Kennedy's Cuba policy orchestrated a scenario along the lines of Operation Northwoods, the top-secret Pentagon program that proposed deploying the most trusted covert action operatives to create a pretext for a U.S. invasion of Cuba by staging a violent attack on a U.S. target and blaming it on Castro?

Win and Dave Phillips came to differing conclusions about Kennedy's assassination. In his unpublished memoir, Win claimed his people had watched Oswald everywhere he went in Mexico City and reported everything to Washington. He wrote that he suspected Oswald was part of a conspiracy organized by the Russians. Phillips sounded a less confident note. When asked by a congressional investigator to summarize the story of the Mexico City station's handling of Oswald's visit, he said, "At the very best, it [was] not professional. At the very best." In his published memoir, Phillips wrote that he felt "confident that Oswald was not recruited in

Mexico City by the Soviets or the Cubans to assassinate President Kennedy." He added, though, "I certainly can't be sure Oswald was not involved in some sort of conspiracy back in Dallas." Phillips expanded on that observation in 1985, when he told researcher Kevin Walsh that "my final take on the [JFK] assassination is there was a conspiracy, likely including American intelligence officers."

Though Michael did not rule out the possibility of a conspiracy involving CIA people, he doubted his father was party to it. He figured that Dave Phillips was right that the CIA's handling of intelligence about Lee Harvey Oswald in late 1963 was unprofessional—and it was far from certain that the failure was unintentional. The barely concealed hostility to JFK among other officers and assets in the anti-Castro operations in 1963 made the enigmatic circumstances of the Dallas ambush seem ominous.

It all felt a little personal to Michael. As a boy, he had shaken JFK's hand, and his father had been responsible for the president's security during his June 1962 visit to Mexico City. Whatever had happened on Win's watch in late 1963, it culminated in a spectacular crime.

16

"The Effect Was Electric"

On the morning of November 22, 1963, Win's chauffeur took all the boys—Michael, George, John, Gregory, and Paul—to the Greengates school. He then returned to the house at Reforma 2035 and took his boss to the embassy. At his desk, Win read a report on foreign businesses in Cuba. He arranged for a military identification card swiped from a soldier in Cuba's Revolutionary Armed Forces to be sent via pouch to Langley. Headquarters could use it to make fake identification cards for anti-Castro guerrillas. In the next office, David Phillips was waiting to hear from a man named Tony Sforza, who was scheduled to arrive that day on a Pan Am flight from Miami. Sforza, who traveled with a fake passport in the name of "Henry Sloman," was a legendary deep cover agent who had spent twenty years operating throughout Latin America, Europe, and Asia pretending to be a Mafia-connected smuggler. For his work, Sforza reportedly received several CIA commendations.

A thousand miles to the north, in Dallas, Texas, Lee Harvey Oswald arrived at the Texas School Book Depository, a redbrick building on Elm Street, with a package under his arm that he said contained curtain rods. President Kennedy was in town. Texas was not altogether hospitable territory for the liberal leader. Just a few weeks before, UN ambassador Adlai Stevenson had been roughed up and spat on by conservative Texans angered by what they said was Kennedy's pro-communist foreign policy. But besides a hostile full-page advertisement in the *Dallas Morning News,* the reception in the city could not have been friendlier.

As Kennedy's motorcade rolled through the streets of Dallas, the president and the First Lady, seated in the back of the open limousine, chatted with Texas governor John Connally and his wife, Nellie, who were seated on the jump seats in front of them. A Secret Service agent drove, and another rode in the front seat. The crowds thinned out as they approached a green open space named Dealey Plaza. Then, as the motorcade passed the Book Depository, coasting down Elm Street toward a railroad underpass, gunfire erupted.

John and Nellie Connally, both hunters and familiar with the sound of gunfire, agreed that the first shot came from behind. "My God, I am hit," cried Kennedy, raising his arms up to his throat. As Connally turned to see, he was blasted in the right shoulder. "My God," he shouted. "They're going to kill us all!" A bullet struck a granite sidewalk curb down the street, sending a fragment of concrete into the face of a bystander. The forty-six-year-old president was now slumped forward, eyes agape in surprise. As Jackie turned to look at her husband, another bullet smashed into the right side of his head, shattering his skull, slamming him backward into his wife's arms. A ghastly pink cloud of bone, blood, and brains spattered the surrounding Secret Service men and policemen who were supposedly protecting the president. For all intents and purposes, John Kennedy was dead.

The bystanders on either side of Elm Street roiled in panic. Many pointed up to the high floors of the Book Depository. Others ran up a grass embankment along the motorcade route toward a wooden stockade fence that rimmed a parking lot. A policeman ran inside the Book Depository and asked a supervisor for help searching the premises. They came upon Oswald standing by a soda machine in the second-floor lunchroom. The supervisor vouched for Oswald, and they ran up the stairs. Oswald ducked out of the building amid the confusion and caught a bus. When the bus got stuck in traffic he disembarked and hailed a taxi. He went to his room in a boardinghouse a mile away, picked up a jacket and a pistol, and then left on foot.

The news reached the CIA station in Mexico City within thirty minutes.

"I believe it was around lunchtime when there weren't too many people there and as they all filtered back in, there was office gossip," Anne Goodpasture recalled. "I have tried to remember. I've heard so many people say 'I can remember, I was standing at the telephone' or 'I was in the drugstore,' or 'I was in church.' I really don't remember who all were there at the time. David Phillips said that someone from the military attaché's office came up and told him about it, and I don't remember that." Phillips and Goodpasture gathered with others in Win's office to listen to the radio and watch television.

At CIA headquarters in Langley, transistor radios were turned on everywhere to follow the tragedy. Around four o'clock came word that the Dallas police had arrested a suspect named Lee Harvey Oswald. "The effect," said John Whitten, "was electric."

For some at the CIA, Oswald's name induced a jolt of awareness because he had long been a person of interest. Jane Roman had been reading reports about him since he defected to the Soviet Union in October 1959. Now we know, thanks to the declassification of records on the AMSPELL, LIERODE, LIENVOY, and LIEMPTY surveillance programs, that there was no shortage of people in the clandestine service who recognized the suspect's name. When Jim Angleton got a phone message from the FBI saying Oswald was the possible assassin, he ordered his staff to run a trace. Paul Hartman, a senior official in the Counterintelligence Staff, knew which CIA office had been most interested in Oswald. "You know, there's a 201 file on this [expletive]," Hartman told his boss, "and SIG has it."

Ann "Betty" Egerter, Birch O'Neal's assistant in the Special Investigations Group, went running down the hallway for Oswald's 201 file. So did Charlotte Bustos, from the Mexico desk in the Western Hemisphere division, who also recognized the name. Egerter won the foot race to retrieve the file. When it came to Lee Oswald, Jim Angleton's staff was a step ahead of everybody else.

Oswald's name also rang a bell in the Mexico City station.

"My first reaction was somebody by that—[a] guy by that name went to the Soviet embassy," said Anne Goodpasture. "When we heard that, the first thing that happened was we . . . checked the cards and then someone told Win."

Win was seated at his very neat, modern desk.

"That's the man we sent the cable about," he said quietly. From memory he gave his secretary several file numbers, and she went off to fetch them. Goodpasture knew to go to look for the photographic and audio coverage of the embassies.

In Miami, the Cuban exiles leaders of the DRE also recognized the name of the obnoxious Castro sympathizer who had tried to infiltrate their New Orleans delegation. They called their CIA contact, George Joannides, saying they knew all about the suspected assassin. They had exposed his support for the Fair Play for Cuba Committee in New Orleans. They even had a tape of him defending Castro on the air. They wanted to go public, they told their CIA handler.

"He said he had to consult with Washington and that we should not do anything," recalls Tony Lanuza. "We went ahead anyway." The DRE leaders began telling people that Kennedy's killer was a Castro supporter who had lived in "the home of the Soviet foreign minister for two months."

In Washington, word of Oswald's Cuban connections jolted Bobby Kennedy. When he learned about Oswald's pro-Castro history that afternoon, he felt certain it was a façade. He called his best Cuban friend, Harry Williams, who was in Washington to attend a meeting about Cuba at the Pentagon. "One of your guys did it," Bobby said flatly, meaning CIA-supported anti-Castro exiles.

Even unflappable Dick Helms felt a surge of concern. He was lunching with CIA director John McCone when he heard the news that the president had been shot. At that moment, he admitted many years later, he had wondered fleetingly if CIA operatives might be involved. As the deputy director and his colleagues headed to their battle stations, he took an aide aside. "Make sure we had no one in Dallas," he said.

Anne Goodpasture returned to Win's office with the surveillance photos of the only American-looking man who had visited the Soviet embassy in early October. She also had the duplicate tape of one of the Oswald phone calls. "I think I brought a tape in and gave it to the [name deleted]," she said in sworn testimony to the Assassination Records Review Board in 1997. "I'm sure that they would have sent it to Washington. What happened from there, I don't know."

Win called Western Hemisphere division chief J. C. King in Washington and asked for permission to give the FBI the photographs of the man thought to be Oswald. King balked. So did Goodpasture. She told Win the photograph might actually be of someone else. "I felt that it should not be sent out, that he should ask Washington to send us a photograph of Oswald," she said. Win did not take her suggestion. He cabled Washington with word that he had photos of a man believed identical to the suspect in Dallas. He took Goodpasture's suggestions in that he also asked headquarters for a photo of Oswald—the one he had been requesting since October 16.

By six o'clock that night, ambassador Tom Mann decided the photographs were important enough that someone from the legal attaché's office should take them to Dallas right away. A flight was arranged, but by then photographs of the suspected assassin had appeared on television and it was clear that Oswald was not the man in the photograph. Nonetheless, FBI agent Eldon Rudd departed on a special 10:00 P.M. flight to Dallas with two copies of the unidentified man emerging from the Soviet embassy and of the tape of the October 1 call. One set went to the FBI in Dallas. The second set went to CIA headquarters in Washington. "Enclosed are photos of a person known to you," Win wrote in his cover letter to King.

A person known to you. When Win's memo was finally declassified in the late 1990s, that line drew attention. King was a longtime friend of Win's, though not a close one. Both had started their careers as FBI men in Latin America. Win had arranged a meeting for King with Government Minister Gustavo Díaz Ordaz just two months earlier. Díaz Ordaz asked King for information about terrorists traveling through Mexico and promised the same kind of information about American subversives in Mexico. Did Win mean that the man in the photo was known to J. C. King? Or was he saying that Oswald was known to King?

Win's cryptic notation may not be significant. Or it may constitute more evidence that Oswald was known to top CIA officials before Kennedy was killed.

The flight from Mexico landed at Dallas's Love Field at 3:46 in the morning of November 23, then proceeded on to Washington. Win's package of tapes and photos made a splash that rippled all the way to the White House. By then the capital city was a city in a daze. A light rain fell, and people wandered about seemingly lost, unable to comprehend the impossible news that the president had been shot to death in broad daylight, apparently by a communist. The morning edition of the *Washington Post* had a front-page story, "Pro-Castro Fort Worth Marxist Charged in Kennedy's Assassination." It quoted Carlos Bringuier of the DRE as saying that Oswald had been in New Orleans for two months as the chairman of the pro-Castro Fair Play for Cuba Committee when he was arrested "for allegedly distributing pro-Communist propaganda." Another *Post* story told of Oswald's appearance on the New Orleans radio program in which he denied being a communist. Yet a third dispatch, headlined "Castro Foe Details Infiltration Effort," quoted Bringuier describing Oswald's approach to the group. "I was suspicious of him from the start. But frankly I thought he might be an agent from the FBI or the CIA trying to find out what we might be up to," he said, adding, "He was a very, very cold blooded one." In this way, the DRE, funded under the covert CIA program called AMSPELL, shaped the first day's coverage of the assassination.

In the White House, Kennedy's successor, Lyndon Johnson, was meeting with John McCone. Johnson wanted to know one thing: what exactly the CIA knew about reports that Oswald had visited the Soviet embassy in Mexico City a few weeks before. Twenty-four hours earlier, Johnson had been widely regarded as a political has-been. He was dodging scandalous reports about a former aide and facing the prospect that Kennedy might dump him from the 1964 ticket. Kennedy's assassination had delivered him into the office he had always dreamed of holding. But it also raised the specter of war with Cuba and the Soviet Union.

After McCone departed, FBI director J. Edgar Hoover called Johnson. The new president's first question was, "Have you established any more about the visit to the Soviet embassy in Mexico in September?"

"No, that's the one angle that's very confusing for this reason," Hoover replied. "We have up here the tape and the photograph. That picture and tape do not correspond to this man's voice, nor to his appearance. In other words, it appears that there is a second person who was at the Soviet embassy down there."

Hoover was not the only one who spoke about the voice on the CIA surveillance tape. Later that morning, Hoover's aide Clyde Belmont spoke to Gordon Shanklin, special agent in charge in Dallas, who said the same thing: "Inasmuch as the Dallas agents who listened to the tape of the conversation allegedly of Oswald from the [deletion] and examined the photographs of the visitor and were of the opinion that neither the tape nor the photograph pertained to Oswald," Belmont reported.

Who in the FBI or the CIA actually listened to the tape that Win sent up from Mexico City has never been determined. But the apparent discrepancy between the voice on the tape and the voice of the real Oswald raised the disconcerting possibility that "a second person"—as Hoover put it—had used Oswald's name in Mexico City, that Oswald had been impersonated. At CIA headquarters, one prescient bureaucrat noted in a memo that if there had been a conspiracy to kill Kennedy, Oswald's life was in danger.

In Mexico City, Win was back at his desk early on Saturday morning, reading a cable from Dick Helms. The deputy director wanted answers about the accused assassin's contacts with Soviet officials. Overnight, the CIA's Soviet Russia division had checked its records on Valeriy Kostikov, the consul and KGB agent with whom Oswald had met. Kostikov had been tentatively identified as the case officer in an operation sponsored by the KGB's Thirteenth Department, the section of Soviet intelligence responsible for sabotage and assassination operations. Helms wanted everything the station knew about Kostikov's travels inside and outside Mexico, all the details of his activities during November, names and backgrounds of his contacts. He wanted an hour-by-hour account of Kostikov's whereabouts on November 22 and surveillance of all his future contacts and activities.

Win already knew Kostikov was a KGB man. The revelation that he had assassination experience was ominous. Win put Anne Goodpasture on the case, and she reported back promptly. All of Kostikov's travel had been previously reported. He was at the Soviet embassy every day between November 6 and 19 and showed no recent unusual activities. Win ordered surveillance on Kostikov and other suspected Soviet intelligence officers, as well as on the switchboard of the apartment building where several of them lived. Win cabled Helms with the latest information, and Goodpasture continued to check unerased tapes for more Oswald calls.

Birch O'Neal, head of Angleton's Special Investigations Group, weighed in, via cable, with a suggestion. He told Win that it was "important you review all LIENVOY tapes and transcripts since Sept 27 to locate all materials possibly pertinent." O'Neal thought correctly that such material would date to September 27, the day Oswald first contacted the Cuban consulate in Mexico City. But how did he know that? It was either a lucky guess or, more likely, SIG knew of Oswald's Cuban contacts in advance of Kennedy's assassination.

Another key question: Where were the surveillance tapes of Oswald, aside from those of his October 1 call to the Soviet embassy? Headquarters demanded an answer from Win, and David Phillips came up with one. They had been erased. More than a decade later, Phillips told the Church Committee exactly when it happened. "It was not until after 5 pm on November 23, 1963 that Agency headquarters cabled its station in México City as to whether the original tapes were available," the committee stated in its final report. "David Phillips recalls that this inquiry precipitated CIA station's search for the tapes which confirmed that they had been erased."

Phillips's recollection was technically accurate. It was true that the originals had been erased. Phillips did not know or did not say that Anne Goodpasture had a duplicate of at least one of the Oswald conversations. Win said the same thing. He relayed three of the transcripts of Oswald's phone calls to Helms in Washington. He did not send the transcript of the call about Oswald's travel plans made by Cuban consulate employee Sylvia Duran on September 27. About the Saturday, September 28, conversation, he wrote, "Subj[ect] is probably OSWALD. Station unable compare voice as first tape erased prior to receipt of 2nd call." With that dubious claim, the CIA's false story that there were no LIENVOY tapes of Oswald's conversations came into being.

The issue of Oswald's visit to the Cuban consulate was, as always, handled with the utmost discretion. One pressing question for Win was, what did Sylvia Duran know about Oswald? The station already had a "substantial interest" in her before the assassination, Phillips later admitted, not the least because surveillance had revealed that she had had an affair with Carlos Lechuga, the former Cuban ambassador in Mexico City, who was now serving as Castro's ambassador to the United Nations. At least one Mexican source on the CIA payroll had told his case officer that "all that would have to be done to recruit Ms. Duran was to get a blonde, blue-eyed American in bed with her."

Win called Luis Echeverria, the trim, self-effacing subsecretary to Díaz Ordaz, the minister of government, whom Win had recruited into the LITEMPO network. Echeverria, as LITEMPO-8, had shown the ability to get things done. Win asked him to have his men arrest Sylvia Duran. Then he called Díaz Ordaz, expecting full cooperation from the Gobernacion minister. He asked that Duran be held incommunicado until she gave all details of her contacts with Oswald. Díaz Ordaz agreed. Within an hour, President Lopez Mateos himself called. Win was expecting condolences for Kennedy's death, but his friend wanted to share some intelligence. His people working in the LIENVOY joint operations center had located the transcript of Oswald's September 28 call.

But when Win reported his aggressive police work to CIA headquarters, he was rebuked. Mexico desk chief John Whitten called on a nonsecure phone line with urgent orders from Helms's top deputy, Tom Karamessines: call off the Mexicans. *Don't arrest Sylvia Duran.* Win told him it was too late, but not to worry. The Mexican government would keep the arrest secret and make sure no information leaked.

Not reassured, Karamessines followed up with a cable to make sure Win understood his instructions.

ARREST OF SYLVIA DURAN IS EXTREMELY SERIOUS MATTER WHICH COULD PREJUDICE [U.S.] FREEDOM OF ACTION ON ENTIRE QUESTION OF [CUBAN] RESPONSIBILITY. WITH FULL REGARD FOR MEXICAN IN-TEREST, REQUEST YOU ENSURE THAT HER ARREST IS KEPT ABSO-LUTELY SECRET, THAT NO INFORMATION FROM HER IS PUBLISHED OR LEAKED, THAT ALL SUCH INFO IS CABLED TO US, AND THAT FACT OF HER ARREST AND HER STATEMENTS ARE NOT SPREAD TO LEFT-IST OR DISLOYAL CIRCLES IN THE MEXICAN GOVERNMENT.

A decade later, when investigators discovered this cable and asked for an explanation, Karamessines said he had no recollection of it. When pressed on why he might have issued such an order, he said that the CIA might have "feared that the Cubans were responsible [for the assassination] and that Duran might reveal this during an interrogation." He further ventured that "if Duran did possess such information, the CIA and the U.S. government would need time to react before it came to public attention." But Karamessines could not explain why he sought to prevent Win from using his Mexican contacts to learn what Duran knew.

John Whitten, chief of the Mexico desk, wrote a rare memorandum for the record stating that he opposed Karamessines's order. When Senate investigators asked him about his objections in 1976, he too said he had no recollection of the memo he had initialed. But he did attempt an explanation. "We were concerned about blowing the—revealing our telephone taps, prematurely revealing our knowledge that Oswald had been in the Cuban consulate at all," he told investigators. "Of course, that all came out later in the papers and so on but at this juncture, . . . the 23rd, the next day. We were keeping a lid on everything because we didn't know which way the thing was going to go." Might the United States attack Cuba in retaliation for the murder of the president? That question did not need to be asked at CIA headquarters, Whitten said. "It was just in the air."

Two years later, Whitten came up with a more incisive explanation. "At the time we were not sure that Oswald might not have been a Cuban agent, and the arrest of a foreign consular person was quite a serious matter under international law. Although Sylvia Duran was a Mexican, . . . Karamessines may not have known at the time and simply felt that this breach of international law, violation of her immunity, might have made it awkward for the United States, if we wanted to let out a roar of outrage if we discovered that Castro had been behind the assassination. In other words, Karamessines feared that this whole thing [the arrest of Duran] might be laid at the United States doorstep."

But why wouldn't American officials want to question a communist who had contact with the man who had apparently killed the president?

Jim Angleton did not want to answer that question. He told congressional investigators he had a "vague recollection" of Karamessines's order. "All I would say is that usually if Tom intervened it was for good reason . . . because he had superior information."

Karamessines's order to Win showed that within twenty-four hours of Kennedy's assassination, top CIA officials were maneuvering to preserve their "freedom of action" to blame the crime on Castro—an option that would have generated the U.S. invasion of the island that Cuba hawks had long favored. The command evoked the mind-set that generated Operation Northwoods, the Pentagon pretext operations conceived and rejected by JFK in 1962 and 1963: if Castro could be blamed for a horrible crime against American interests, then the U.S. government might be able to justify an invasion to overthrow him. The Karamessines order also illuminated the difference between Win and his superiors in Washington. By having Sylvia

Duran arrested, Win sought to investigate the crime. His bosses in Washington sought to control the investigation.

In Miami, David Phillips's young allies in the DRE wanted to pin the responsibility for Kennedy's death on Cuba. A *New York Times* story on November 24, reporting on Oswald, quoted Bringuier extensively. The *Miami News* reported, "Suspect Oswald Is Known Here," quoting DRE leaders about Oswald's pro-Castro ways. The group also rushed to distribute a special issue of its monthly newspaper, *Trinchera* (Trenches), which featured photographs of Oswald and Castro under the headline "The Presumed Assassins." The accompanying text recounted Oswald's encounters with Bringuier and the DRE in New Orleans. The front page highlighted a telegram that the group sent to President Johnson. "We express our deepest sorrow at the death of the President of the United States of America, John F. Kennedy," it said. "May God enlighten the government of this country at such difficult moments."

The DRE's scenario was the first JFK assassination conspiracy to reach public print, and it was paid for with CIA funds from the AMSPELL budget administered by George Joannides, chief of psychological warfare operations in Miami. The AMSPELL assets focused on what interested Karamessines: "the entire question of Cuban responsibility." They generated what seemed to be evidence of Cuban involvement without disclosing the hidden hand of the CIA.

In Havana, Fidel Castro was alarmed by the news reports out of Dallas and Miami about Oswald's pro-Castro connections. On the afternoon of November 23, the Cuban leader delivered a long discourse on Cuban television about Kennedy's death. "Malas noticias" (bad news), he called it, sounding shaken. As a revolutionary, he said, he hated systems, not men. Yes, Kennedy had sought to destroy his revolution, but he had also shown moderation and statesmanship in the face of fierce criticism.

"What is behind the assassination of Kennedy?" Castro asked. "What were the real motives . . . ? What forces, factors, circumstances were at work behind this sudden and unexpected event that occurred yesterday? . . . Even up to this moment, the events that led to the murder of the President of the United States continue to be confused, obscure and unclear."

Castro felt he was being set up to take the blame for the crime and spoke specifically of the early reports from the DRE about its clashes with Oswald, the Castro supporter. "We foresaw that from these incidents there could be a new trap, an ambush, a Machiavellian plot against our country; that on the very blood of their assassinated president there might be unscrupulous people who would begin to work out immediately an aggressive policy against Cuba, if the aggressive policy had not been linked beforehand to the assassination . . . because it might or might not have been. But there is no doubt that this policy is being built on the still warm blood and unburied body of their tragically assassinated President."

Castro indignantly read a series of wire service reports, generated by the DRE's claims: that Oswald had been the chairman of the Fair Play for Cuba Committee, that he was a "Marxist supporter of Cuban Prime Minister Fidel Castro," and that was he was a "Castro-communist." He scorned Carlos Bringuier's statement, published in the *New York Times,* that the DRE had spurned Oswald's advance because it thought he "might have been an FBI or CIA agent."

"How curious! . . . " Castro scoffed. "They say he is a Castroite, a communist, an admirer of Fidel Castro. And now it appears . . . he tried to enter the organization [the DRE] and was not admitted because they thought he belonged to the FBI or CIA. They must know pretty well the kind of agent the FBI and the CIA have, since they deal with them a lot."

Castro did not know that CIA man George Joannides had been in contact with the DRE leaders just hours before but he intuited as much. He stopped short of charging that Kennedy's assassination was the work of anticommunist conspirators. "For the time being, without affirming anything because we cannot affirm anything, since Oswald could be guilty or innocent, we can't tell. He could be a CIA or FBI agent, as those people [the DRE] suspected, or an instrument of the most reactionary sectors that have been planning a sinister plot, who may have planned the assassination of Kennedy because of disagreement with his international policy. Or [Oswald] could be a sick man now being used by U.S. reactionary sectors."

In Mexico City, Win's priority was to find out what Sylvia Duran knew. At six o'clock on Saturday, November 23, Luis Echeverria reported back to Win. Duran, her husband, and five other people had just been arrested at her brother-in-law's house. Echeverria had just come from seeing Lopez Mateos, whose instructions about the prisoner had been as simple as they were brutal: "Proceed and interrogate forcefully."

At 7:15 that night, Win told Clark Anderson, the FBI legal attaché, about the arrest and passed along the CIA's desire for secrecy. He also informed Ambassador Mann, who was "very pleased." The ambassador thought the Soviets were too sophisticated to have been involved but deemed the Cubans "stupid enough" to have hired Oswald.

Later that night, Echeverria paid a personal visit to report the results of the interrogation of Duran. She had been "completely cooperative," he said. She had given a written statement attesting to two visits by Oswald on Friday, September 27. She said Oswald had shown her a U.S. passport indicating a long stay in the Soviet Union. He had said he was a communist and an admirer of Castro, and he wanted a transit visa to go to Cuba and then the Soviet Union. She had told him she could issue the visa only after the Soviets issued one for his final destination. When Oswald returned, he told her the Soviets had approved his request, which turned out to be a lie. She had called the Soviet embassy and been told approval would take several months. Oswald had become angry and left. "He never called back," she told her interrogators. This account matched the story in the surveillance transcripts, with one exception. The tapes indicated that a woman from the Cuban consulate had called the Soviet Embassy on Saturday, September 28, and put an American on the line who spoke almost incomprehensible Russian. The female voice was later identified as Duran, the male voice as Oswald. *But if Oswald had never come back after Friday, who made the Saturday phone call from the Cuban consulate to the Soviet embassy?* Four decades later, that question remains unanswered.

Late that night, Win's driver took him home. Janet and the kids were watching the continuing coverage of the tragedy on the big black-and-white TV in the downstairs family room. Win kissed his wife, hugged the kids, poured himself a Jack Daniels mixed with ginger ale, and sat down in his big red leather lounge chair. When bedtime came, the kids filed by to say good night. Michael Scott has no specific memory of what his father said, but he is sure that he did not disclose that he had first learned of the world-famous Lee Harvey Oswald some six weeks before.

17

"A Transparent Operation"

As the jaws of the big black steel gates on the driveway at Reforma 2035 opened up late on Sunday morning, November 24, and Win's big black car emerged, the Mexico City station chief was heading toward a watershed in twentieth-century history. This was a time in which men of power in the United States of America would choose between war and peace. As the Mercury cruised down the Mexican capital's main boulevard in the light Sunday traffic, the man in the backseat did the calculus of counter-intelligence.

Who was Lee Harvey Oswald? Had Win's station failed to pick up some sign that the man who called on the Soviet and Cuban diplomatic offices six weeks ago was a communist agent? A threat to the president? Was he a disturbed individual? Someone's agent? Or a double agent? And why would someone kill him? That was the new stunning fact that Win had to deal with: the leftist interloper whom he had written a cable about six weeks earlier, the man whose presence at the Cuban consulate he had chosen not to report, the man who had apparently gone on to kill Kennedy, was now as dead as the president.

Win and Janet and the kids had spent all morning watching television in the bedroom, talking and staring at the bleak, majestic images on the screen. World leaders were converging on Washington. The president's coffin was going to lie in state in the U.S. Capitol. Solemn crowds were gathering. Men and women were weeping openly. Gravelly voiced announcers supplied a steady stream of repetitious details. Back in Dallas, Oswald was going to be transferred to another prison. The cameras cut away from Washington to a parking garage as Oswald, in handcuffs, was brought out by a phalanx of stocky detectives. A man in a suit darted out of the crowd, jabbed a pistol in Oswald's stomach, and shot him. Baffled at the sight, Michael and his siblings watched the chaos, the shouts, the men writhing on the floor of the parking garage. They looked at each other and talked about their disbelief. He shot him. They heard the name Jack Ruby. The guy who shot the president was dead. It was so unbelievable. Win left immediately for the embassy. Upon his arrival, Tom Mann told Win he thought that Kennedy's assassination would lead the United States to invade Cuba.

In Washington, President Johnson feared the assassination would lead to war. Thirteen months earlier, Johnson had watched as all the generals and a majority of Kennedy's national security advisers had advised an invasion during the missile crisis. Only Kennedy's resolute statesmanship had diverted the consensus of the brass into a peaceful resolution. He did not want to find himself in a similar situation. He had talked with Hoover the previous morning about the possibility of an imposter in Mexico City. He might be facing a communist dirty trick or a right-wing provocation from those who hated Kennedy for the Bay of Pigs fiasco. More than anything, LBJ needed some answers about Oswald's contacts with the communists in Mexico City. He needed the agency to get him the story. He needed Win to deliver.

Johnson spent an hour that morning with John McCone, who presented Win's preliminary findings as written up by John Whitten, Mexico desk chief. Oswald had not only visited the Soviet embassy, McCone told the president. He had also gone to the Cuban consulate. The station now believed the voice on the tape was Oswald. "The search for Oswald data on November 22 found technical operations material the subject matter of which showed the speaker to be Oswald," Whitten wrote. "Our expert monitor says the voice is identical with the voice of 1 October known to be Oswald's." In other words, the CIA had listened to the October 1 tape of Oswald, and "an expert monitor" had compared them. The identity of this expert has never been revealed. It is also possible that the expert did not exist, that Whitten was simply reporting what he had been told by Win or someone else. Whitten's comment was the third reference by a senior CIA or FBI official in less than 48 hours to the existence of Oswald tapes. Win and Dave Phillips were insisting no such recordings existed, but John Whitten, J. Edgar Hoover, and Gordon Shanklin thought they did. Anne Goodpasture would later say the same thing—under oath.

Win went down to the ambassador's office, where Mann and Mexican foreign minister Manuel Tello were meeting. Legal attaché Clark Anderson was there, along with deputy station chief Alan White. Win shared the latest from Luis Echeverria on Sylvia Duran. She had been "completely cooperative" with the Mexican authorities, he said, not mentioning that she had been beaten. Duran had bruises on both her arms from being shaken by her interrogators, she told a colleague at the embassy a few days later. The Mexican authorities had pounded her again and again on one question. Had she slept with Oswald? Didn't she have sexual relations with him? She denied it. That line of questioning was significant for two reasons. First, CIA officers in the Mexico City station had discussed the possibility of obtaining information from Duran by getting her into bed with an American, and because four years later, Duran would admit to a close friend that she had dated Oswald while he was in Mexico City, but that she had no inkling of his plans to shoot Kennedy—a story that Win Scott believed was true. According to Echeverria, Duran denied sleeping with Oswald.

The bland but efficient FBI legal attaché Clark Anderson reported what the FBI had learned about the accused assassin. Oswald had ordered a rifle of the same type used to kill the president from the Klein mail-order company in Chicago. He had used the name "Alek Hidell" to order the weapon, a name that also appeared on Fair Play for Cuba Committee propaganda found in his room. The FBI did not yet know if Hidell existed or was just an alias. Win ordered a name trace on "Alek Hidell." Nothing.

Win cabled headquarters with a summary of the meeting he had just come from. He reassured headquarters that it did not have to worry about Duran's arrest being attributed to the U.S. government. Echeverria said that Duran had spoken freely about Oswald's visits. She did not know where Oswald stayed in Mexico. She had the impression that Oswald had or believed he had some arrangements in Washington where he could get the Soviet entry visa without actually visiting the Soviet embassy. She said he was simply "a comrade who could not live comfortably under rigors of capitalism and wanted to return to spiritual home in the USSR." Echeverria said that Duran and her husband would be released but kept under surveillance.

Win advised headquarters that he would ask for Duran to be questioned again, if headquarters so desired. He also said he had transcripts of all calls believed connected to Oswald, but no recordings. "Regret tapes for this period already erased," he repeated.

Win viewed the situation through the lens of counterintelligence, which was very different from a law enforcement perspective. For the FBI, the following questions were significant: Had Oswald, an average marksman in the marines, managed to unleash a volley of accurate rifle shots from a sixth-floor window, pegging President Kennedy square in the neck at 160 feet, Governor Connally in the shoulder, and—ready, aim, breathe, squeeze the trigger—blasting the side of the president's skull, killing him almost instantly? And, if Oswald had pulled off that not inconsiderable feat of shooting skill, why had he done it? Or did Oswald and his own killer, Jack Ruby, just pull the trigger for the sheer psychotic hell of it?

As an officer trained in counterintelligence, Win would have focused on a narrower question: Was Oswald a communist agent? Win felt certain Oswald's political sympathies had played a role. Oswald had lived in the Soviet Union. He leafleted for the Fair Play for Cuba Committee. Win would come to reject the notion that Oswald acted alone, concluding that Oswald was a person of more than average intelligence and not a proverbial "lone nut." From his point of view in the days after JFK was killed, the question of communist control turned on the substance of Oswald's contacts with Duran and Kostikov at the Cuban and Soviet embassies. Duran portrayed his communications with the Cuban consulate as routine and minimal. Oswald had also made contact with Kostikov, but Win's men had no way to talk to him. The possibility that Oswald was a communist agent could not be ruled out on such evidence.

Or was Oswald what he said he was? "I'm a patsy," the accused assassin had shouted to reporters in the Dallas police headquarters the night before he was killed. Castro suggested Oswald might be "a cat's paw" in a counter-revolutionary provocation. Win rejected the idea, not the least because the Cuban communists immediately embraced it, according to a surveillance transcript delivered to Win.

"It is all a plot," an unidentified caller to the Cuban embassy said. "Those guys wanted to make it appear" that Oswald was "a Communist sympathizing with Cuba, etc etc. Sure he was once in the Soviet Union. He subjected himself to a dirty game [there]. . . . It is obvious they had to liquidate him so he wouldn't talk." The Cuban official on the line agreed. Oswald had been killed "precisely so that he wouldn't talk. The job [of finding out who killed Kennedy] has become more difficult." The Cuban diplomat said he was "very worried" about the international situation.

So was Lyndon Johnson. The new president knew that only one answer would soothe a grieving nation, stunned and baffled by the two homicides in Dallas, and forestall pressures for him to go to war: that Oswald had no accomplices of any sort. J. Edgar Hoover had reached the same conclusion. Around four o'clock on the afternoon of November 24, Hoover spoke with Walter Jenkins, one of Johnson's aides, who wrote a memo about the conversation. He quoted Hoover as saying, "The thing I am most concerned about, and Mr. Katzenbach, is having something issued so that they can convince the public that Oswald is the real assassin."

Katzenbach, the deputy attorney general who also had Johnson's confidence, explained Johnson and Hoover's goal in a memo to press secretary Bill Moyers the next day. "It is important that all of the facts surrounding President Kennedy's assassination be made public in a way which will satisfy people in the United States and abroad that all the facts have been told and that a statement to this effect be made now," he wrote. "The public must be satisfied that Oswald was the assassin; that he did not have confederates who are still at large; and that the evidence was such that he would have been convicted at trial. Speculation about Oswald's motivation ought to be cut off, and we should have some basis for rebutting thought that this was a Communist conspiracy or (as the Iron Curtain press is saying) a right-wing conspiracy to blame it on the Communists. Unfortunately," Katzenbach added, "the facts on Oswald seem too pat—too obvious (Marxist, Cuba, Russian wife, etc.)."

But as the imperative to cut off inquiry into Oswald's motivation flowed down from the top of the government, the Mexico City station came up with a sensational story about Oswald's Cuban connections that demanded looking into. The next day, November 25, a young Nicaraguan man named Gilberto Alvarado came forward to say he had seen Oswald taking money in the Cuban embassy in September. When Dave Phillips vouched for Alvarado's story, Win relayed the story to headquarters, which passed it to the White House. President Johnson, fearing the United States was being pushed toward war, redoubled his efforts to control the JFK assassination investigation.

Phillips's central, if invisible, role in promoting Alvarado's story continued his uncanny record of covertly promoting a more aggressive U.S. Cuba policy in 1962–1963. Like the DRE's raid on the Havana hotel and the "missiles in caves" story, Alvarado's story was promoted by Phillips's hidden hand. It resulted in public pressure on the man in the White House to take more forceful action against Castro. The Alvarado story failed when Johnson adroitly used the fear of war to forge the creation of the Warren Commission. Win navigated the crisis by going along with Washington's disinterest in Oswald's associates. He relied on his Mexican friends to coerce Alvarado into recanting. Win emerged unscathed. His partnership with Phillips would not.

Of the many untruths that David Phillips told about his own role in the Kennedy assassination story, few were more curious or revealing than his version of the Gilberto Alvarado story. In his memoir, *The Night Watch*, Phillips said he wanted to refute "the swarm of skeptics who have found a lucrative profession in conning lecture audiences and writing ludicrous books with bizarre explanations" of the president's murder. He said the critics of the Warren Commission "combined the true with the false in coming up with conspiracy theories on the 'Mexico City connection' of Oswald."

One story that had been misunderstood, he said, was that of Gilberto Alvarado. Phillips said he wanted to set the record straight.

"After President Kennedy was assassinated there was a walk-in to the American embassy in Mexico City," Phillips wrote. "He was a young Nicaraguan, who said that he had been inside the Cuban embassy when Oswald visited there, and that he saw a red-haired black pay Oswald $6500 in American money, an advance payment presumably for his role as the hired gun in killing Kennedy." Phillips said he was surprised to learn, via a cable from the CIA station in Nicaragua, that the Nicaraguan intelligence service had identified Alvarado as a prominent communist. Phillips and a colleague were assigned to interrogate him, he recalled. "It soon was apparent that he was lying, and not very well," Phillips wrote.

CIA records declassified in recent years show that Phillips's version of the Alvarado story was misleading at best. To be sure, Alvarado had told the story of a red-haired Negro who supposedly gave Oswald $6,500, and, yes, Alvarado was eventually discredited. But Phillips had distorted the rest of the story, including his own role in it. In a less ethically flexible world than the one Phillips inhabited, one would say that the CIA man told a series of bald-faced lies.

The story began on the afternoon of Monday, November 25, when Alvarado, a twenty-three-year-old Nicaraguan man, called the U.S. embassy and said he had some important information about Oswald. The next morning, deputy station chief Alan White and another CIA officer picked up Alvarado, drove him to a random spot on the southern edge of Mexico City, and listened to his story. Alvarado explained that he belonged to a group of leftists sent to Mexico by the Frente de Liberacion Nacional (FLN), a Castro-style guerrilla group in Nicaragua. The FLN wanted him to obtain Mexican citizenship and go on to Cuba, where he would be trained in sabotage. During a visit to the Cuban embassy, he said he had overheard a North American—a man he now recognized as Oswald—talking with a red-haired Negro man. Oswald said something about being man enough to kill someone. He said he saw money change hands. Alvarado said he had phoned the embassy a few times to report his belief that someone important in the United States was going to be killed. He was finally told, "Quit wasting our time. We are working here, not playing." Now Kennedy had been killed, apparently by the man he saw. Alvarado said he was outraged by Kennedy's assassination and that he was 80 percent sure it was a communist plot. The CIA men listened but did not question him in detail. They told him if they needed to speak with him again, he would get a phone call from "Rodolfo Gabaldon."

The question of whether the pro-Castro Oswald had Cuban confederates was obviously of interest to Win. At the very same time that Alvarado was telling his story, Win was reading the transcript of a conversation picked up that morning on one of the Cuban embassy lines covered by LIENVOY. The Cuban ambassador to Mexico, Joaquin Hernandez Armas, had called Osvaldo Dorticos, the figurehead president of Castro's government at 9:40 A.M. They talked about Duran's interrogation. Dorticos wanted to know if Duran had been asked anything about "money" by the Mexican authorities. Hernandez Armas said the Mexicans wanted to know if she "knew" Oswald in the sense that she had "intimate relations" with him. She denied it. The story that Duran had been questioned about sleeping with Oswald was getting around.

By early afternoon, deputy station chief Alan White had returned to the embassy. He met with Win and Tom Mann in the ambassador's office. He recounted Alvarado's story about Oswald and the red-haired Negro. Mann recalled the tape of the Cuban president. Dorticos's preoccupation with the money angle tended to corroborate the authenticity of Alvarado's story. The three men talked about how they might investigate further. Mann thought Sylvia Duran should be arrested and confronted with Alvarado's story. He asked Win to forward his recommendation to CIA director John McCone, FBI director J. Edgar Hoover, and Secretary of State Dean Rusk. This was telling in two ways. In a crisis, the CIA station chief, not the ambassador, was the main channel to the leaders of the American government; and the "question of Cuban responsibility," raised by Karamessines on Saturday, was kept alive by Alvarado's story on Monday.

"Duran should be told that as the only living non-Cuban who knew the full story, she was in exactly the same position as Oswald prior to his assassination," Mann wrote in his message. "Her only chance for survival is to come clean with the whole story and cooperate fully. I think she'll crack when confronted with the details. . . . The Mexicans should be asked to go all out" to break her, he said. Mann also told Win that he wanted another FBI officer to be detailed to his office to help in the investigation.

Win hesitated. He intuited Washington did not want to know too much about Oswald. He felt Mann was pushing too hard. And he certainly did not want an FBI officer running around the embassy with the job of investigating the station's handling of Oswald. But Mann was technically his boss, so he could not openly object. Instead, he went back to his office to let Dick Helms know of Mann's desire for help. He said he was passing along "this info only because it indicates Amb[assador]'s feeling he is not being fully enough informed of aspects of these cases in USA." Helms replied that he did not like the idea either.

As for Alvarado, Win wanted to check out the story himself. He cabled Langley asking for a name trace on Alvarado. Headquarters responded that Alvarado "is a known informant [for] Nic[araguan] Intel[ligence] Service." In fact, Alvarado was quite friendly with the man who served as Nicaragua's liaison to the CIA's Managua station.

In the early evening, the LIENVOY monitors picked up another call from President Dorticos in Cuba to the embassy. Again, the transcript went to Win. Again, Dorticos wanted to know if Duran had talked about money. Was it possible that Alvarado's story was true? Had Oswald gotten paid in the Cuban embassy? Win wanted Alvarado to be questioned in more detail, and he wanted Dave Phillips to do it. Phillips immediately called Alvarado and arranged to meet him in a safe house, where they talked until two in the morning.

Phillips, according to his own contemporaneous account of the interrogation on the night of November 26, 1963, listened carefully to Alvarado's story. The Nicaraguan reenacted the conversation and the money-passing scene in the Cuban embassy. He said the black man had broken the paper band on a quarter-inch-thick pack of U.S. bank notes and counted out $1,500 for extra expenses and $5,000 as an "advance." As best he could recall, the meeting had taken place around noon on September 18. In his cable on the meeting, Phillips wrote that he had asked Alvarado to look at surveillance photos of no fewer than seventeen different Cuban embassy employees and questioned him about each one. Alvarado did not know any of their names, Phillips reported, but he did give "partial descriptions such as duties, height, skin coloring, condition of teeth, disposition, accent, etc. not discernible from photos." Far from questioning Alvarado's veracity, Phillips implied in his report that he had verifiable knowledge of Cuban embassy personnel. Phillips described Alvarado as "completely cooperative, showing some signs of fearing for safety." At the end of the interview, he gave Alvarado 600 pesos so that he could relocate to another hotel, indicating that he thought he deserved protection and that his story merited further attention.

Ambassador Mann continued to press Washington. He wanted to arrest Duran again and confront her with Alvarado's story. Win remained noncommittal. Dick Helms said he thought that Alvarado's story needed more investigation. The deputy director said that the Nicaraguan intelligence agency was insisting they had dropped Alvarado as an informant back in August. And the FBI had interviewed Oswald's landlady, who said Oswald was in New Orleans on September 18, casting doubt on Alvarado's claim that he had seen Oswald in Mexico City on that day.

Then came a surprise. Luis Echeverria called Win with the news that his people had rearrested Sylvia Duran because she was trying to leave Mexico for Cuba. Win furnished some questions he wanted asked during the interrogation but, sensitive to Mexican feelings, said the decision whether to hold or release her was theirs alone. When Win reported Duran's detention to Mann, the ambassador demanded action yet again. Possessed of considerable self-confidence, Mann pushed back against the go-slow stance of his colleagues. He wrote another memo, for Win to send to McCone, Hoover, and Rusk, emphasizing the developments of the last twenty-four hours. He did not mention Phillips by name, but he noted the CIA had been "impressed by Alvarado who has offered [to] make himself available as a witness. . . . It will not have escaped your attention that the wealth of detail Alvarado gives about events and personalities involved is striking."

"Washington should urgently consider feasibility of requesting Mexi[can] authorities to arrest for interrogation: Eusebio Azcue, Luisa Calderon and Alfredo Mirabal," he said. The first two names were consular officers while Calderon was a secretary in the consulate. According to Mann's reading of U.S.-Mexican diplomatic agreements, "they would all seem to be subject to arrest, provided Mexican law defines their apparent conspiracy with Oswald as a crime, not a misdemeanor. They may all quickly be returned to Havana in order to eliminate any possibility that Mexi[can] government could use them as witnesses. . . . While I realize enormous difficulty in giving us instructions, I nevertheless feel obliged to point out again that time is of the essence here."

Win was less impressed with Alvarado's story than was Phillips. He cabled headquarters to say the young Nicaraguan's account proved only "that he has been in the Cuban embassy and knows some of the employees by sight, name or both. Nothing more." Win suggested the "outside possibility" that Alvarado's story might be a gambit by the right-wing Somoza regime in Nicaragua to build support for an invasion of Cuba.

The unstated message emanating from the White House was by now clear to Win—though not to Mann. Speculation about Oswald's motives was to be cut off, not pursued. The usually astute ambassador failed to take the hint when the CIA, the State Department, and the FBI deflected his proposal that Duran be confronted with Alvarado's story. Instead, he continued to press for more aggressive action. Shortly after noon the next day, November 28, he sent another telegram to Rusk and his top aide, Alexis Johnson, again asking for instructions. He said the Mexicans had to be told immediately if Washington wanted them to continue the investigation into Oswald's contacts with the Cuban consulate. What should he say if Mexicans wanted to turn Duran loose but watch her closely? And what about Alvarado? Should they turn him over to the Mexicans? Ship him to the States? Or polygraph him in Mexico?

Helms replied that he would pass along the suggestions but warned Mann not to expect an immediate response. FBI had the lead on the assassination investigation in Washington, he said. J. Edgar Hoover did not have the slightest interest in Mann's ideas. In fact, Hoover derided Mann for trying "to play Sherlock Holmes." Helms told Win that Mann "is pushing this case too hard and that we could well create [a] flap with Cubans which could have serious repercussions." Helms said he had enlisted the State Department to send Mann a message "attempting to give him better perspective on this whole problem. We hope this will be of some assistance in reducing his pressures on you."

Win was navigating in complex political currents. Oswald's activism on behalf of the Fair Play for Cuba Committee, officially identified as a "subversive" organization, raised the possibility he might have had pro-Castro coconspirators. Yet, from Hoover at the FBI, to Helms at the CIA, to Katzenbach at the Justice Department, senior U.S. officials sought to deflect Mann's effort to investigate the possibility of Cuban involvement and made no effort to question Duran themselves.

The reluctance to pursue an obvious lead that might connect Oswald to the hated Castro bordered on the bizarre. Helms felt the need to defer to Angleton's staff about the handling of the Oswald investigation. He consulted with Birch O'Neal, chief of the SIG. They decided the decision about who would question Alvarado should be made by the FBI. Sam Papich, the FBI's liaison to the agency, did not want to handle this hot potato. He replied that the decision should be made by the CIA, since Alvarado was an agent "under the control" of the agency. That was another blow to Phillips's claims later that Alvarado was a lying communist. In fact, the FBI identified Alvarado as a CIA agent.

Finally, Hoover ended this odd dance by deciding Win should hand over Alvarado to the Mexicans. At the same time, he sent a highly regarded agent named Larry Keenan down to Mexico City to kill Mann's efforts to investigate. Keenan, just returned from a tour of duty in Paris, spoke good Spanish. He was told he was going to assist the ambassador, but Hoover's aides prepared him to deliver the message that the FBI had already concluded Oswald acted alone.

At 2:30 in the afternoon of November 28, Win delivered Washington's decision. He called Echeverria and explained that the U.S. government wanted the Mexicans to interrogate Alvarado. Echeverria expressed his gratitude. He said Fernando Gutiérrez Barrios, deputy director of the Defensa Federal de Seguridad, Mexico's equivalent of the FBI, would handle the questioning. Gutiérrez Barrios was a paid agent of Win's in the LITEMPO program. Win asked him to keep his sidekick George Munro, who handled LITEMPO matters, informed about what they learned. Washington awaited word from Win's intelligence gathering with barely concealed impatience. When Win arrived at the office early on the morning of November 29, there was a cable from the tireless John Whitten saying, "Please continue to keep us filled in on status of interrogations of Sylvia Duran, Alvarado and others implicated as fast as you can get info." The vigilant Birch O'Neal asked the FBI to keep him posted.

In the White House, President Johnson met with his top national security advisers to discuss the latest reports from Mexico City. With Secretary of State Rusk at his side, he called Senate Majority Leader Mike Mansfield, a key congressional ally, at eleven that morning to talk about "several investigations" that he said "could have some very dangerous implications." He said he and Rusk agreed there should be a "high-level commission" to investigate Kennedy's murder.

Johnson and Hoover's decision that it would be best for all concerned if Oswald was found to be the lone gunman was taking effect. In Mexico City, Win went to a meeting in Tom Mann's office with David Phillips and Larry Keenan, Hoover's messenger from Washington. The FBI's legal attaché, Clark Anderson, introduced the visitor to the ambassador but not to the CIA men. "I sensed I was not receiving the Legat's full cooperation," Keenan wryly recalled.

Ambassador Mann opened the meeting by predicting war. "The missiles are going to fly," he declared. He expressed his belief that members of Castro's Direccion General de Inteligencia (DGI) were involved in Kennedy's murder, possibly with Soviet connivance. The U.S. government was on a countdown to invading Cuba, he said. His colleagues were not so excited. Anderson expressed doubt that the Soviet leaders and the KGB, known for their professional expertise and rigid chain of command, would have had any involvement. Win said he concurred with Anderson.

When it was Keenan's turn, he dropped the bomb from Washington. He told Mann that Hoover had already concluded the accused assassin was "a dedicated communist" who had acted alone, adding Hoover's claim that Lyndon Johnson and Bobby Kennedy shared his view. Seeking to sugarcoat the bitter pill, Keenan added that he was otherwise available to help Mann's investigation. At the time, Keenan said he did not fully appreciate how he had been used. "Clark Anderson worked for Mann. He couldn't tell him that Hoover didn't want to investigate. Mann wanted FBI assistance with the CIA investigation. It was my job to get him to back out of the request, [to tell him] that we were not going to investigate any possible Cuban involvement. I think Mann felt quite chastised."

He was certainly taken aback. He responded that he had known Lyndon Johnson for a long time and was prepared to accept Hoover's finding. But he never believed it. Years later, Mann would express bafflement at the order to cease investigating Oswald's Cuban connections even before Alvarado's veracity had been determined. "I hadn't reached any conclusion" about Oswald's contacts and motivation, Mann told author Dick Russell, "and that's why it surprised me so much. That was the only time it ever happened to me—'We don't want to hear any more about that case—and tell the Mexican government not to do any more about it, [not to do more] investigating, we just want to hush it up.'"

"I don't think the U.S. was very forthcoming about Oswald," the retired ambassador said. Washington's termination of his efforts to investigate Oswald's Cuban connections, Mann said, was "the strangest experience of my life."

Strange indeed. Why would senior U.S. government officials, every one of whom professed to loathe Fidel Castro and more than a few of whom had countenanced conspiracies to murder him, refuse to investigate contacts between his government and the man who just killed the president with a gunshot to the head? Why would they want to prevent examination of the seemingly pregnant possibility that the pro-Castro Oswald was part of a communist plot, especially at a time when Gilberto Alvarado, vouched for by David Phillips, the chief of Cuba operations in Mexico, was still being questioned?

Clearly, part of the reason was that Lyndon Johnson thought the Alvarado story, on top of Oswald's stint in the Soviet Union and his public support for Castro, might force him to wage war on Cuba or the Soviet Union. Johnson's fears rose when Win delivered an update from Mexico City later that day. Gutiérrez Barrios had emerged from the interrogation room around 11:30 that morning to report that Gilberto Alvarado was sticking to his story about the red-haired Negro delivering money to Oswald.

Confronted with the fact that Oswald was in New Orleans on September 18, Alvarado said the date might have been September 28. Gutiérrez Barrios told Win that he thought Alvarado might be confused on the dates but telling the truth and promised to get tougher. Win relayed the ambiguous news to Washington and the FBI. Hoover had killed Mann's investigative efforts, but he still could not explain away Alvarado's story, not with Phillips vouching for it.

When President Johnson called the FBI director at 1:40 that afternoon, Hoover said his report on Oswald's guilt would be delayed.

"This angle in Mexico is giving us a great deal of trouble," Hoover told the president. "Now the Mexican police have again arrested this woman, Duran, who's a member of the Cuban embassy and will hold her for two, three more days. And we're going to confront her with the original informant [Alvarado]—who saw the money pass, so he says—and we're also going to put the lie detector test on him. Meantime, of course, Castro's hollering his head off."

The Cuban leader had given another speech asserting that the assassination was most likely the work of "ultra rightist and ultra reactionary sectors" of American society.

That, very likely, was the other reason that U.S. officials flinched from investigating Oswald's Cuban connections, especially his contacts with anti-Castro operatives. Men of power in Washington knew full well that a Castroite conspiracy was not the only plausible scenario for what had happened in Dallas. It was not just that Oswald had been killed while in police custody. It was not just that, as Nicholas Katzenbach had noted, the facts of Oswald's communist background seemed "too pat—too obvious." An investigation of a possible Castroite conspiracy would require examination of Oswald's contacts with anti-Castro forces in New Orleans and Miami—most of which had financial and personal ties to the CIA.

Bobby and Jackie Kennedy knew, if the American public did not, that Castro's charge that the assassination was a provocation by Kennedy's rightwing foes was all too plausible. In fact, the slain president's younger brother and widow suspected that JFK had been ambushed by domestic conspirators. That same day, November 29, an artist friend of Jackie's named William Walton left Washington for Moscow on a previously scheduled trip. He carried a message from Bobby and Jackie for a Russian diplomat, Georgi Bolshakov, who the year before had served as a back-channel link between the Kennedy White House and the Kremlin during the missile crisis. Walton met with Bolshakov not long after arriving in Moscow. According to

Bolshakov, who told the story to historians Aleksandr Fursenko and Tim Naftali, Walton said the president's brother and widow wanted the Soviet leadership to know that "despite Oswald's connections to the communist world, the Kennedys believed that the president was felled by domestic opponents."

Bobby Kennedy knew better than anyone that his brother's Cuba policy had bred a deep anger among the exiles, as well as the resentment of CIA officers like Sam Halpern, Bill Harvey, and Howard Hunt. He knew that provocation was regarded as a legitimate policy tool in the anti-Castro cause. In Operation Northwoods, the Joint Chiefs of Staff had contemplated staging violent deceptive operations on American soil to build public support for a U.S. invasion of Cuba. Even Dick Helms had instinctively feared agency operatives might have been in Dallas on that day.

Helms and Hoover did not share RFK's suspicions, but they knew CIA and FBI intelligence gathering on Oswald in the three months before the assassination had been far more extensive than the stunned and grieving American public could imagine. They could not investigate the possibility that Castro's agents had helped Oswald without investigating their own people in Mexico City, Miami, and New Orleans. The problem was not theoretical. If the CIA and FBI wanted to know about Oswald's visit to the Cuban consulate in Mexico City, they would have to examine Win Scott's and Dave Phillips's surveillance operations. They would have to examine the actions of the AMSPELL assets in New Orleans and what George Joannides knew about them. There was every reason for the barons of Washington to drag their feet. As for President Johnson, he did not know if Alvarado's story was true or a deliberate falsehood. It hardly mattered. Either possibility would only encourage those who wanted to use Kennedy's assassination as a rallying cry for an invasion of Cuba, a prospect he deeply feared.

Late that afternoon, Johnson welcomed Chief Justice Earl Warren into the Oval Office. Warren had just spent a couple of hours fending off Johnson's aides, who were asking him to serve as the head of a presidential committee that would preempt the various congressional investigations in the works. Warren insisted it would not be appropriate. Johnson wasted no time on formalities. He told Warren that he had to head the commission. He said competing congressional investigations would leave the public more emotional and confused than ever. Warren tried to object, saying a sitting Supreme Court justice should not engage in outside investigations. Johnson cut him off.

"Let me read you one report," he said. He pulled out a memo describing Alvarado's allegation that Oswald had been paid in the Cuban embassy in

Mexico City. This story, Johnson said, could lead to war, a war that could kill up to 40 million people. He conjured up the image of mushroom clouds over America. Only a presidential commission could head off the peril.

"You were a soldier in World War I, but that was nothing comparable to what you can do for your country in this hour of trouble," Johnson said, his voice now quavering. "When the president of the United States says that you are the only man who can handle the matter, you won't say 'no,' will you?"

Warren, by his own account, had tears in his eyes.

"Mr. President, if the situation is that serious, my personal views do not count. I will do it."

Johnson had prevailed with a masterful display of political jujitsu. He had used the Alvarado allegations, which he knew would increase pressure on him to take military action against Cuba, to force America's leading liberal statesman into heading an investigation whose purpose was as much to prevent a war as to find the truth.

In Mexico City, Win was disturbed to learn that Fernando Gutiérrez Barrios could not shake Alvarado's story. On the evening of November 29, the Mexican cop told Win he had spoken with the young Nicaraguan for an hour in the morning, and three more hours in the afternoon. After the first session, the Mexican said he thought Alvarado's story was "a fantastic lie," but he could not shake him in the second session. His preliminary conclusion was that "either Alvarado is telling the truth essentially or is the best liar I have ever talked to in my many years, and I have talked to some of the biggest." Gutiérrez Barrios said he was "inclined" to believe Alvarado was telling the truth generally but was mixed up on the specific date he saw Oswald.

Alvarado's handler from the Nicaraguan intelligence service arrived from Managua. He met Gutiérrez Barrios at the hotel where they were holding Alvarado. He described Alvarado as "seventy five percent accurate" in his reporting. He had provided good information on communists in the past but had a tendency to "go off on his own" at times and was impossible to control. The questioning continued and got rougher. At 10:30 the next morning, Gutiérrez Barrios called Win to say that Alvarado had recanted and signed a statement admitting that his story of seeing Oswald in the Cuban embassy was "completely false." He had not seen any money change hands. He had not called the U.S. embassy to warn someone might be killed. He said his motive was to try to get the United States to take action against Castro, whom he hated.

Win relayed the news to headquarters. Everyone was relieved. Helms asked Win to express his thanks to Gutiérrez Barrios. He also asked Win to "ascertain and cable details of how the confession was obtained. What threats, promises, inducements and tactics were used by the LITEMPO-4 [Gutiérrez Barrios]. Was Alvarado physically mistreated?"

A few days later Alvarado reverted to his original story. He told his Nicaraguan handler that he had confessed only because he was "mentally mistreated" by the Mexicans, who he said had threatened to hang him by his testicles. He expressed resentment that the U.S. embassy had turned him over to the Mexicans after he had volunteered to help. But when an agency polygraph specialist came to Mexico City a few days later, he found that Alvarado's statements about Oswald were deceptive. Alvarado recanted again.

Dave Phillips concluded his misleading account of Alvarado's story with a curious observation. "I have a theory, almost a conviction," Phillips wrote in his memoir, "that in fact this man [Alvarado] was dispatched to Mexico City by the Somoza brothers, the authoritarian but pro-American rulers of Nicaragua, in what they considered a covert action to influence the American government to move against Cuba. If so, it was a nice try, but a transparent operation."

In fact, Phillips knew all along about Alvarado's service as a CIA informant. Even the FBI said he was under CIA control. Phillips's dissembling in print suggested an alternative explanation: that he knew all along that Alvarado intended to provoke, to make claims that would create a political atmosphere more conducive to a U.S. attack on Castro. The results certainly served Phillips's agenda. Alvarado's bogus story served to develop and advance the story generated by Phillips's other assets in the previous three months. First came the AMSPELL publicity blitz against Oswald's antics in New Orleans. Then came the LIEMPTY/LIENVOY surveillance of his visits to the Cuban consulate. Then came Alvarado's story of Oswald receiving money. All three reports tended to corroborate the insinuation first made by the AMSPELL spokesmen in the wake of Kennedy's death: that Oswald and Castro were the "presumed assassins."

There is, to be sure, no proof that Phillips masterminded these developments, but the circumstantial evidence is suggestive. Three CIA reports demonstrate conclusively that Alvarado was a CIA informant in the spring of 1963. The Nicaraguan intelligence agency that employed him was the CIA's creation and client. Phillips specialized in devising psychological warfare operations that would confuse or confound the communist enemy. Just to force Castro to make headlines denying that Oswald had taken money in the Cuban embassy would isolate him in American and world opinion, and perhaps advance a U.S. policy of overthrowing his government, something that Phillips and most of his colleagues thought was overdue.

As the facts emerged over the years, Michael Scott turned them over in his mind but could reach no firm conclusions about what was actually going on. Rather than spin conspiracy theories, he wondered what his father would have said had he lived long enough to face interrogation about Gilberto Alvarado's "transparent operation."

18

"I Share That Guilt"

November 22 helped make Win Scott a legend in the annals of the CIA. The Mexico City station's handling of the assassination and its aftermath enhanced Win's already considerable reputation in the upper reaches of the U.S. government. Kennedy's murder had exposed the sorry state of the Secret Service, the Dallas police, and the FBI, all of which failed in their duties to protect the president. By contrast, the performance of the Mexico City station, while not perfect, was a matter of immediate pride inside the agency. Few knew that Win had helped perpetrate a wide-ranging cover-up of CIA operations around Oswald that, as it came to light in coming years, would enmesh the agency in conspiratorial suspicions.

On December 16 the chief of the Western Hemisphere division, J. C. King, thanked Win for the station's assistance in the assassination investigation, praising "the really outstanding performance of Mexico City's major assets and the speed, precision and perception with which the data was forwarded. Your LIENVOY data, the statements of Sylvia Duran, and your analyses were major factors in the clarification of the case, blanking out the really ominous specter of foreign backing." Win stashed a copy of King's commendation in his office safe, along with other tapes and documents that he valued highly.

King's choice of words reflected Washington's priorities in the weeks after the assassination. The "blanking out" of possible foreign involvement was at the very top of the priority list. For Jim Angleton, the priority was even more specific: ensuring that the Warren Commission learned the absolute minimum about the Cuban angle to the Oswald story and the way the CIA had handled it. Angleton's first step was to marginalize John Whitten, chief of the Mexico and Central America desk, whom Dick Helms had assigned to review all the agency's Oswald files. Brilliant if overbearing, Whitten had a track record of success in complex counterespionage investigations. With a staff of thirty people working up to eighteen hours a day, he read every report related to Oswald, no matter how ludicrous or trivial. As he drafted his findings, Angleton grew annoyed.

"In the early stage Mr. Angleton was not able to influence the course of the investigation, which was a source of great bitterness to him," Whitten said in secret sworn testimony in 1978. "He was extremely embittered that I was entrusted with the investigation and he wasn't. Angleton then sandbagged me as quickly as he could."

Whitten soon discovered that he, like Win, had been cut out of the Oswald loop by his superiors. In early December 1963, he attended a meeting at the Justice Department and came away stunned by what he had not been told. "For the first time I learned a myriad of vital facts about Oswald's background which apparently the FBI had known throughout the initial investigation and had not communicated to me," he said. "For the first time I learned that the FBI was in possession of diary-like material which Oswald had had in his possession and was found after the assassination. I learned for the first time that Oswald was the man who had taken a pot shot at General Edwin Walker, two key facts in the entire case."

"None of this had been passed to us," he said. Whitten was specific about the information denied him. "Oswald's involvement with the pro-Castro movement in the United States was not at all surfaced to us [meaning him and his staff] in the first weeks of the investigation." Whitten had never received the FBI reports on Oswald from Dallas and New Orleans, nothing from the AMSPELL files on the DRE. All Whitten knew about Oswald's encounters with the Cuban students in New Orleans came from the *Washington Post*. When Whitten complained to Helms at a meeting on Christmas Eve 1963, the deputy director relieved him of all JFK responsibilities on the spot. "Helms wanted someone to conduct the investigation who was in bed with the FBI," Whitten said bluntly. "I was not and Angleton was."

As Angleton took over as the agency's liaison to the Warren Commission, he made sure its investigators never saw a key piece of paper: John Whitten's November 23 memo on how Tom Karamessines had ordered Win not to seek the arrest of Sylvia Duran so as to preserve "U.S. freedom to maneuver." Whitten had noted his objections. When commission general counsel Lee Rankin asked the CIA in February 1964 for the cables summarizing the incident, Angleton stonewalled. His deputy Ray Rocca told Helms, "Unless you feel otherwise, Jim would prefer to wait the commission out on the matter." The commission never got the cables.

Win had no trouble reading the bureaucratic breezes. With more experience and closer friendships at the top than Whitten, he understood the Oswald investigation was going to be limited, not thorough. He knew Angleton would be interested in Oswald's Soviet past but would never share what he learned with anyone. He knew Dulles, called out of retirement to serve on the Warren Commission, would not allow outsiders to second-guess operations. He knew that Hoover and the FBI did not care to look into Oswald's Cuban connections, having joined them in blocking Ambassador Mann's investigation.

So when three lawyers from the Warren Commission came to the Mexican capital in April 1964, Win was prepared with a story that was both true and untrue. The most senior of the visitors introduced himself as Bill Coleman. He was a forty-two-year-old lawyer from a Main Line Philadelphia law firm, with a law degree from Harvard, a Supreme Court clerkship on his résumé, and the black skin of an African American. Win's personal politics, said Anne Goodpasture, were "to the right of George Wallace," the populist Alabama governor who championed racial segregation. But if Win was uncomfortable with Coleman, he showed no trace of it. Taking notes was W. David Slawson, another Harvard law graduate; Howard P. Willens, an assistant attorney general in the Justice Department, mostly listened.

Win knew how to handle the staff of fact-finding commissions from his days of holding hands with Generals Doolittle and Clark back in the fifties. "I understand you all have been cleared for Top Secret material," he began. "I trust you will not disclose to anyone outside of the commission and its immediate staff without first clearing it with my superiors in Washington." There were nods and agreement all around.

The story had begun last September, Win said, "when we first picked up information that Oswald had appeared at the Russian and Cuban Embassies." Two months earlier, Dick Helms had told the commission that the CIA in Mexico had learned of Oswald's contacts with the Cuban embassy only *after* Kennedy was killed. This was the cover story used to prevent public knowledge of the CIA's surveillance of foreign and diplomatic missions. It served to prevent review of David Phillips's operations in and around the Cuban consulate specifically. It also served to cover up the fact that Counterintelligence—Angleton's shop—maintained a more than routine interest in Oswald between 1959 and 1963. Win knew the position to be taken for public consumption. Now, though, behind closed doors with trustworthy interlocutors, he preferred to tell the truth: the station had known from the start that Oswald had been in contact with the Cubans when he was in Mexico City.

Win brought out the surveillance transcripts of the phone conversations involving Oswald and contact sheets of the photographic take from the observation posts outside the embassies. Win's remarks "disclosed immediately how incorrect our previous information had been on Oswald's contacts," Slawson wrote later. "The distortion and omissions to which our information had been subjected had entered some place in Washington because the CIA information we were shown by Scott was unambiguous on all the crucial points."

Unambiguous perhaps but not necessarily accurate. Were there photographs of Oswald coming or going from one or both of the embassies? Coleman wanted to know.

No, Win said. Photographic coverage had been limited by and large to the daylight weekday hours because of lack of funds and because no adequate technical means for taking photographs at night from a distance had been developed. This was evasive. Nighttime photography was not a real issue because Oswald had never visited the Soviet or Cuban offices in the evening. The lack of funds was nonsense. Win's own report showed that the LIERODE operation was expanded, not shortchanged, in September 1963. At least one camera, and perhaps two, had been functioning in the observation post on Calle Francisco Marquez in the days of Oswald's visits. And the CIA's own Stanley Watson and Joe Piccolo, as noted earlier, recalled having seen two photos of Oswald taken there.

Coleman asked Win the question that the whole world wanted answered: "Do you think there was a conspiracy behind Oswald?"

"In my professional opinion, there probably was not a foreign conspiracy connected with Mexico," Win said carefully.

What about the letter that Oswald wrote to the Soviet embassy in Washington ten days before Kennedy was killed? they asked Win. This was a letter, dated November 9, 1963, from Oswald to the Soviet embassy in Washington. In it Oswald had told the Soviets about his visit to Mexico City, requested a visa, and mentioned his contacts with "Comrade Kostin," probably a reference to Kostikov, the KGB man. It had been opened and read in Washington while Kennedy was still alive. Didn't the letter open the possibility that Oswald had Soviet help? Coleman asked.

"I've never seen that letter," Win said. Slawson found it curious and noteworthy that the agency in Washington had not even told Win about the letter that was information directly related to Oswald's visit to Mexico City.

Then there was the matter of Sylvia Duran, the Mexican consular aide whom Oswald had confronted at the Cuban mission. Win told his visitors a good deal about her. Duran had long been a target of opportunity, he said, because surveillance showed that she had been romantically involved with the ambassador. "A Mexican pepper pot," someone said appreciatively when Win produced a photo of the woman. Banter aside, the Warren attorneys insisted on authenticating Duran's story about Oswald's visits to the consulate. They wanted to be certain there was no substance to Alvarado's story. And they were especially interested in what Duran said about Oswald's physical appearance. Win said he thought Luis Echeverria, the ever-helpful subsecretary at the Ministry of Government might help arrange a meeting with Duran. He escorted the three visitors to Echeverria's office.

Echeverria suggested that the Americans interview Duran and any other Mexican witnesses over lunch or coffee. The Americans said they preferred a more formal setting for such a serious matter. After more small talk and courtesies that went nowhere Echeverria excused himself to lunch with Queen Juliana of Holland. The commission lawyers went back to the embassy, where they met in Win's office, sensing they had been—ever so politely—deflected. Echeverria's office did send over a copy of Sylvia Duran's signed statement, in Spanish, about Oswald's visit. The CIA provided an English-language translation. The lawyers went home. Duran, a critical witness, was never interviewed by the Warren Commission, and some basic questions went unanswered.

For example, how many times had Oswald spoken with Duran? Slawson had made a chronology of all of the recorded phone calls involving Oswald. There had been three calls, to the Cuban consulate, following his arrival on Friday, September 27. There were two calls on Saturday, September 28. In one of these, a woman identified as Duran called the Soviet embassy and put a man on the line who asked about his visa request. Duran had told the Mexicans that Oswald had visited the consulate twice on Friday and *had never returned*. The question was, did Duran assist Oswald in making a phone call to the Soviets on Saturday—as the CIA transcript indicated—or not, as Duran claimed. She noted that Saturday was her day off. If Duran denied having seen Oswald on Saturday, was she hiding a relationship between the accused assassin and the Cubans?

David Phillips preferred to obscure this question, not answer it. Phillips was responsible for the CIA's translation of Duran's statements, according to Anne Goodpasture. In that translation, Duran's unambiguous denial that she had seen Oswald after Friday, September 27—"He never called back"— was translated as "she does not recall whether or not Oswald later telephoned her at the Consulate number on Saturday." Did Phillips, whose actions and connections raise questions in so many areas of the JFK story, deliberately see to it that Duran's statement was mistranslated?

The change occurred on a crucial point and could hardly have been accidental. Phillips was fluent in Spanish. And even if someone else had done the translation, he was responsible for its contents. Would Phillips have abetted an attempt by Duran to minimize her relations with Oswald? That seems unlikely. She was a dedicated leftist and Castro supporter, not the kind of person the chief of anti-Castro operations for the CIA in the Western Hemisphere was inclined to coddle. If Duran was telling the truth when she said Oswald did not visit the Cuban consulate on Saturday, September 28, then the CIA—and Cuba surveillance chief Phillips—had a huge problem.

The problem was the voice on the surveillance tape. It wasn't Oswald. One of the CIA translators, Boris Tarasoff, had noted that the voice of the Saturday, September 28, caller was the same one heard in the Tuesday, October 1, conversation in which the caller said his name was "Oswald." Tarasoff also noted at the time that the Saturday caller spoke "terrible, barely recognizable" Russian. In fact, Oswald spoke Russian fairly well. If Tarasoff's observation that the Saturday caller barely spoke Russian was true and Duran's original testimony that Oswald never came back to the Cuban consulate after his Friday, September 27, visit was true, then Lee Harvey Oswald did not make *either* call on Saturday, September 28, or on Tuesday, October 1. Someone else made the Tuesday, October 1, call and said, "My name is Lee Oswald." That would be consistent with J. Edgar Hoover's initial report to President Johnson on the CIA intelligence about Oswald in Mexico City: that "the picture and tape do not correspond to this man's voice, nor to his appearance."

But the discrepancy begs the question of who—other than Oswald—had used his name. And why? As previously noted, Phillips and his men had orchestrated an impersonation operation around a visitor to the Cuban embassy in July 1963. If Phillips indeed changed a crucial point in Sylvia Duran's testimony, he was removing a contradiction from the record, one that the Warren attorneys might have otherwise insisted on pursuing. He was also, at a stroke, preventing any informed probe into the possibility that Oswald had been impersonated.

Such subterfuge cannot, however, be ascribed only to Phillips. Win himself had failed to report to headquarters the fact that Oswald had visited the Cuban consulate. Anne Goodpasture said headquarters had "no need to know" about it. One plausible explanation for the serial deceptions that Win and David Phillips practiced on the subject of Oswald's presence at the consulate is that they were showing discretion about an authorized, compartmentalized CIA operation whose source and methods they were obliged to protect—not the least after things went horribly awry on November 22.

The notion that David Phillips or Angleton and his Counterintelligence team ran a closely held operation involving Oswald in the weeks before Kennedy was killed has become less implausible as more records have come into public view. Phillips himself entertained such a scenario later in life. In addition to two nonfiction memoirs, Phillips also wrote novels of espionage. When he died in 1987, he left behind an outline for a novel about the Mexico City station in 1963, entitled "The AMLASH Legacy." The leading characters were explicitly based on Win Scott, James Angleton, and David Phillips himself. The role of the Phillips character in the events of 1963 was described as follows:

> I was one of the two case officers who handled Lee Harvey Oswald. After working to establish his Marxist bona fides, we gave him the mission of killing Fidel Castro in Cuba. I helped him when he came to Mexico City to obtain a visa, and when he returned to Dallas to wait for it I saw him twice there. We rehearsed the plan many times: In Havana Oswald was to assassinate Castro with a sniper's rifle from the upper floor window of a building on the route where Castro often drove in an open jeep. Whether Oswald was a double-agent or a psycho I'm not sure, and I don't know why he killed Kennedy. But I do know he used precisely the plan we had devised against Castro. Thus the CIA did not anticipate the President's assassination but it was responsible for it. I share that guilt.

The outline for a novel cannot be taken as proof of anything save the workings of Phillips's imagination, but it is tantalizing. *The CIA did not anticipate the President's assassination but it was responsible for it. I share that guilt.* Phillips was not one to impugn the agency just to make a buck. After his retirement he founded the Association of Foreign Intelligence Agents and served as its chief spokesman, ably defending the CIA from its critics without much compensation. He always insisted that his espionage fiction was realistic and denounced those who sought to cash in on JFK conspiracy scenarios. The outline for the novel suggests that the notion that a CIA officer like himself would recruit a schemer like Oswald in a conspiracy to kill Castro did not strike Phillips as too improbable to sell or too unfair to the agency to market under his own name.

The scenario offered in the outline, moreover, conformed to fact in at least one verifiable way. Phillips *had* helped "establish Oswald's Marxist bona fides" via his DRE exile protégés in the AMSPELL program. The DRE's publicity blitz against Oswald in New Orleans in August 1963 generated most of the evidence later used to identify the alleged assassin as "pro-Castro." Did Phillips, in real life, feel guilty about those contacts? If he did, he left no other trace of it. Phillips died before he could start writing "The AMLASH Legacy."

Win Scott never spoke ill of David Phillips. But their relationship changed after the assassination of President Kennedy. In his evaluation of Phillips's work in 1963, Win did not repeat his judgment of the year before that his colleague was "the finest covert action officer he had ever met." He damned Phillips with some routine praise but downgraded his performance in two out of three performance categories. Only in covert action did Win think Phillips had matched his performance of the previous year. Phillips's supervision of surveillance operations against Cuban targets, he thought, no longer merited the highest possible grade of "outstanding." Instead, Win gave him the next highest grade, "strong." The fact that an accused presidential assassin with Cuban contacts had passed through Phillips's collection operations unnoticed, at least in official reporting channels, was a job performance issue, no matter how benignly one viewed it. Phillips's recruitment and handling of "foreign intelligence and counterintelligence personnel" also received a lower mark, perhaps because he had initially vouched for the credibility of Gustavo Alvarado, whose story about Oswald getting money in the Cuban embassy turned out to be fictional. Win knew his colleague's actions in regard to the Oswald case were questionable, and he said so in the quietest possible way.

Despite this relatively unfavorable fitness evaluation, Phillips received a promotion. In 1965, Helms named him the new station chief in the Dominican Republic. But something, perhaps the Oswald business, had come between Win and David. After Phillips's departure in the spring of 1965, Win did not keep in touch with him. Win remained in Mexico City, his clout and reputation still growing. Nonetheless, his Oswald problem had not gone away. Far from it.

19

An Anonymous Warning

The Warren Commission Report on Kennedy's assassination, issued in late September 1964, found that Oswald alone and unaided had killed the president for reasons known only to himself. Privately, the commission members had been deeply divided on the interpretation of the bullet evidence. Commission counsel Arlen Specter posited that Oswald, from a window perch on the sixth floor of the Book Depository, had fired a first shot that passed through President Kennedy's neck and struck Governor Connally, causing seven nonfatal wounds, and a second shot that hit Kennedy in the head. If this was not true—if three or more bullets had caused the two men's wounds—then there had to have been a second gunman. Three commissioners—Georgia senator Richard Russell, Kentucky senator John Sherman Cooper, and Louisiana congressman Hale Boggs—had serious doubts about the bullet evidence. Russell wanted a dissent included in the published version of the report, but Warren struck it from the record. President Johnson himself told Russell privately that he did not believe the report's finding on the bullets.

In Mexico, Win Scott did not believe the case was closed. A couple of days after the Warren Report was released, he learned that a friend of his wife's, a woman named Elena Garro, claimed to have seen Oswald and two other Americans at a party thrown by people from the Cuban embassy in September 1963. Garro, married to the Nobel Prize–winning poet Octavio Paz, was an accomplished poet in her own right. She described Oswald and his companions as "beatnik boys" who mostly kept to themselves. A week later, Win heard much the same story from June Cobb, a CIA informant who was also friends with Garro. Then Garro told the story to a political officer in the embassy, adding more detail. When she saw Oswald's picture on November 22, she and her daughter remembered that he was the man they had seen at a party a few months earlier. Garro explained that Sylvia Duran, whose husband was her cousin, had invited her to the party. She said that she, too, had been told that Duran had slept with Oswald. After Kennedy was killed, she went to the Cuban embassy and shouted, "Assassins!" only to be picked up by a Mexican security official who told her not to talk about what she knew.

Win knew full well that when the Mexicans first questioned Duran after Kennedy was killed, they focused on the question of whether she had slept with Oswald. Now a credible witness, a woman who attended Win and Janet's dinner parties, was saying as much. Win sent the gist of the story to Washington. When he got no reply, he did the bureaucratically prudent thing: he wrote a memo for the file.

In Washington, Dick Helms and Jim Angleton suffered a shock in October 1964 when Mary Meyer, an artist and ex-wife of a senior CIA officer, was murdered on the C&O canal towpath in Georgetown. Angleton had been good friends with her. He admired her freethinking ways, even as she carried on an affair with President Kennedy. He knew that she kept a diary, and he knew of its potential for blackmail. Meyer trusted Angleton and told a friend that if anything happened to her, she wanted him to have the diary. Angleton was not taking any chances. The day after she died, *Washington Post* editor Ben Bradlee, who was married to Meyer's sister, went to Meyer's house looking for the diary. He said he bumped into Angleton, who was carrying a toolkit and looking very much like a man trying to burglarize the house. Angleton was red-faced but came away with the diary, which he read and did not destroy. Angleton, observed one journalist, was a collector of secrets who was "well placed to manipulate the flow of information from the CIA about Kennedy and the assassination."

The subject of Kennedy's death hovered in Win's world. Bobby Kennedy visited Mexico City in November 1964 to dedicate a housing project named after his slain brother and to meet with labor leaders. He did not meet with Win or ask any questions about Oswald's visit to Mexico. Security agents reporting to the Mexican DFS followed all his movements. Asked by a Mexican reporter if he agreed with the Warren Commission Report, RFK said he believed in its veracity, "as far as the investigation went," an unobtrusive qualification that spoke to his private doubts that the investigation had gotten very far.

When Elena Garro continued to tell her story about seeing Oswald at a party, Win reacted with skepticism. "What an imagination she has," he scrawled in the margin of a 1965 memo about her story. "Should we send to HQs?" Win's new deputy, Stanley Watson, said yes. Win made a point of clipping any article about Kennedy's assassination in the *Mexico News*, a local English-language newspaper. By the end of 1966, he had articles about three books criticizing the Warren Commission. Across the political spectrum, from leftist lawyer Mark Lane to right-wing columnist William F. Buckley, people were calling for the reopening of the investigation.

In the spring of 1967, the JFK story reached a new crescendo as New Orleans district attorney Jim Garrison announced he was investigating the possibility that Oswald had been part of a murder conspiracy emanating from New Orleans. Win was feeling stressed. On March 3, 1967, *Mexico News* reporters Robert S. Allen and Paul Scott reported on the existence of a "still secret CIA report on Oswald's September 1963 activities" that was dated October 11, 1963, and might shed some new light on the Mexico trip of the accused assassin. Win cabled Washington immediately to say the story probably referred to the October 10 headquarters cable about Oswald that arrived in the station on October 11. Win recommended that the cable not be declassified for newspaper reporters because it would "blow LIENVOY and give grounds for criticism" of the agency. Ten days after sending this cable, Win started having chest pains and checked himself into a hospital with high blood pressure. The life of a spy was not conducive to good health and longevity.

The droplets of fresh information on the Oswald case continued. A newspaper reporter in the coastal city of Tampico, Oscar Contreras, told a U.S. consular official that back in September 1963, he had had a chance encounter with Oswald. At the time, Contreras had attended Mexico's main university and belonged to a leftist student group. He said Oswald had approached him and a group of friends and told them that he was trying to go to Cuba and that the Cuban embassy had denied him a visa. Could they help? The Mexicans did not trust the American and did not help him, but they had spent the day with him. The station knew nothing of such contacts. Win asked his most trusted field man, George Munro, to look into the allegation, a sign of how seriously he took it.

Win received a new revelation about Sylvia Duran. A trusted Mexican source for the CIA—code-named LIRING-3—had become close to Sylvia and her husband over the years. Sylvia had admitted to LIRING-3 that she did date Oswald when he was in Mexico City. "She had first met Oswald when he applied for a visa and had gone out with him several times since she liked him from the start," the source reported. "She admitted that she had sexual relations with him but insisted she had no idea of his plans." After Kennedy was killed, Duran said she was "interrogated thoroughly [by Mexican authorities] and beaten until she admitted that she had had an affair with Oswald."

Win did not doubt the report. Duran's confession was consistent with what the station knew of her love life and the story that the sane, if excitable, Elena Garro had been telling for years. "That Sylvia Duran had sexual intercourse on several occasions with Oswald . . . is probably new but adds little to the Oswald case," Win wrote to headquarters. His complacent tone belied the fact that he had to worry that he and the station might have missed something important about Oswald. He knew better than to ask a lot of questions.

David Phillips also had a problem in the spring of 1967. Recently returned from the Dominican Republic, Phillips had been promoted to chief of the Cuban Operations Group, the last bureaucratic vestige of the CIA's secret war against Castro. "He told us at the first staff meeting, 'we are going to peel Castro like an onion, leaf by leaf, until there is nothing left,'" recalled one colleague. Phillips's problem was that one former officer in the Miami station had written a memo recalling that some of Phillips's favorite young Cubans in the DRE had an "animus" against President Kennedy and recommended they be checked out.

With JFK assassination questions now arising from the ranks of the CIA itself, Dick Helms was feeling defensive. Less than a year earlier, he had been promoted from deputy CIA director to the very top job, director of Central Intelligence. The navy lieutenant whom Win had first met twenty years earlier now sat in Allen Dulles's old chair, which was fine with Win. One Washington columnist described Helms as "the ultimate prudent professional of the intelligence game." In his rare appearances on Capitol Hill, Helms spoke in assuring generalities while puffing an ever-present cigarette. In private, he felt the critics of the Warren Commission were nothing less than a threat to the CIA itself.

On April 1, 1967, Helms launched a secret campaign to discredit critics of the Warren Commission. He approved a "book dispatch" to CIA stations all over the world written by Western Hemisphere division chief Bill Broe. Criticism of the Warren Report, the dispatch declared, "is a matter of concern to the U.S. government, including our organization. . . . The members of the Warren Commission were naturally chosen for their integrity, experience, and prominence . . . efforts to impugn their rectitude and wisdom tend to cast doubt on the whole leadership of American society." In addition,

"Conspiracy theories have frequently thrown suspicion on our organization, for example, by falsely alleging that Lee Harvey Oswald worked for us." The dispatch came with no less than nine different documents to help in "countering and discrediting the claims of the conspiracy theorists" with the public and with journalists.

Win absorbed headquarters' orders, but he did not abandon his own conspiratorial suspicions. One incident that stuck in Win's mind was the story of a Cuban airliner that waited on the runway of the Mexico City airport on the night of November 22. During LBJ's April 1966 visit to Mexico City, Win and advance man Marty Underwood had talked about Kennedy's assassination. Win told Underwood that he had asked Dallas authorities to check out the flight. "I've always wondered who the occupant was—was he armed and was he sent by Castro to be an observer. As you know, the assassination rumors were numerous that week in Texas." Nothing came of the report.

In June 1967, Win was warned by a top headquarters official to watch what he said about Oswald, even in private conversation. The message came from a colleague—a senior official—using the cover name "Thomas Lund." Judging by his tone, he knew Win personally. But he was not willing to use his real name.

"Dear Willard," this correspondent wrote, referring to the name Win used in CIA communications. "As you are aware, the Garrison investigation of the Kennedy assassination has prompted a rash of spectacular allegations and charges, some against the CIA."

"In this situation you understand, of course, that it is essential that all of us be particularly careful to avoid making any kind of statement or giving any indication of opinion or fact to unauthorized persons. In this regard, we have received from a very sensitive source two pages only of a letter (Attachment A) almost certainly by LIOSAGE to his home office reporting on comments he claims made by you."

The tone was collegial, but the substance was a loaded gun. LIOSAGE was the cryptonym for Win's longtime friend Ferguson Dempster, the chief of British intelligence in Mexico whom Win had known since his days in London. The agency's "sensitive source" was probably Angleton's HTLINGUAL program, which culled all international mail for sensitive information. Whoever he was, "Lund" was issuing an unsubtle reminder that the agency had eyes and ears everywhere and that Win should watch his mouth.

"We recognize that any such remarks by you could well have been misinterpreted, enlarged upon, or taken out of context no matter how carefully made," the author went on. "Possibly even a nod of your head to another person's comment might have been given undue weight. Nevertheless, you should be aware the letter was written and be guided accordingly. After reading the letter should be destroyed."

"Lund" wanted Win to keep investigating. Oscar Contreras's story about Oswald consorting with leftist students "might well represent the first solid investigative lead we have on Oswald's activities in Mexico. . . . the matter warrants your personal attention with the best resources at your command." That sounded like an order.

The "Lund" letter was a turning point for Win. It marked the moment when he realized the official story of Oswald in Mexico was no longer credible. It illuminated how little confidence senior CIA officials really had in the story that Oswald had passed through Mexico attracting only "routine" interest from the agency. Had that been the truth, "Lund" would have had nothing to worry about. It looked as though top CIA officials knew the Warren Report's account of Oswald's activities in Mexico was not true, and they were concerned that Win knew it was not true—and was privately saying so. Win took measures to protect himself. He stashed a copy of the "Lund" letter in his personal safe, along with the Oswald tapes and, probably, the Oswald surveillance photos.

The JFK assassination story had become a recurring nightmare, both for Win and for the agency. It posed a lurid, looming threat to his reputation and the agency's legitimacy that would not go away. Win ordered a review of the Oswald file. In the margin of "Lund's" letter he scrawled a note to Anne Goodpasture: "Suggest we may have to do a complete analysis of the Oswald file and point out to Hq. (and to Mexi Govt.) all the people who are now claiming to have been w/ Oswald that day beginning with much as we know."

Goodpasture went to work. Over the next few months, she read everything in the station's files on Oswald, compiling a chronological summary of all important information. Eventually, the document ran to 133 pages of legal paper, every sheet covered with single-spaced summaries of cables, dispatches, memos, reports, and newspaper stories about Oswald, complete with names of operation, like LIENVOY, and the identities of sensitive sources, like the LITEMPOs, Win's high-level government confidants. By February 1968, Goodpasture had looked at every significant piece of paper about Oswald or Kennedy's assassination that Win had filed in the past four and a half years. As she read and typed, her own doubts about the Warren Commission grew. She noted all the interesting leads that had never been followed up, all the obvious questions that had never been asked.

"The Warren commission did not do an adequate investigative job," she commented in the margin at one point. "It is hard to believe the Commission served the public well. Instead of ending all the rumors, they set the stage for a new and more serious era of speculation."

Goodpasture's chronology of the Oswald file confirmed the dimensions of the JFK problem that faced the clandestine service in the late 1960s, especially the anti-Castro warriors and Angleton's counterintelligence operatives. Dick Helms was trying to shore up the Warren Commission by mounting a propaganda offensive against its critics, but the doubts about the commission's lone gunman finding had infected even die-hard CIA loyalists like Anne Goodpasture. As for Win, he was tired of the whole business. If the story of the Oswald-Duran affair was true—and Win believed it was—the station had failed to pick up on the fact that Kennedy's accused killer had a lover in the Cuban embassy. Win found himself in a bureaucratic box he did not much like. His superiors were instructing him to say that the Warren Report was complete and authoritative, while he had to deal with a proliferation of tips indicating it was anything but.

For a long time Win suppressed his doubts. Keeping secrets was his job, and as station chief, he was regarded as one of the best in the world.

Spies on the rise: Win relaxes with James Jesus Angleton, future chief of Counterintelligence for the CIA, in Rome, probably in 1946 or 1947.

Win's friend: Raymond G. Leddy, seen here in Switzerland in 1941, served in the FBI, CIA, Defense Department and State Department. When his wife Janet left him and married Win, the friendship with his former colleague ended.

Cover: Win Scott's State Department identification card, issued in July 1956, when he became chief of the CIA station in Mexico City.

Dad: Win with fourteen-month-old son Michael in Mexico City in December 1956.

Colleagues: Win, back row on right, and Ray Leddy, front row on left, joined a group of U.S. embassy employees paying a visit to Mexican president Adolfo Lopez Mateos in January 1960.

Tragedy: Paula Murray Scott, Win's second wife, died under mysterious circumstances in Mexico City in September 1962.

Connections: Win introduces his third wife, the former Janet Leddy, to Mexican president Adolfo Lopez Mateos at their wedding reception on December 20, 1962.

Making friends: Win introduces President Lopez Mateos (center) to chief of Cuban operations David Phillips and his wife, Helen, at his wedding in December 1962. (Helen Phillips)

Workplace: Exterior of the U.S. embassy in Mexico City with inset photo of Win's office

Massacre: The Mexican security forces crushed a burgeoning democratic student movement in October 1968 by killing scores of people at a student demonstration in the Tlatelolco apartment complex in Mexico City. (AP Images)

Portrait: Win Scott at the height of his power in May 1966.

Mystery man: An unidentified man, photographed leaving the Soviet embassy on October 1, 1963, whom Win mistakenly identified as Lee Harvey Oswald in the hours after President John F. Kennedy was killed. The man was never identified. (JFK Lancer Archive)

Cold warrior: David Phillips, amateur actor and psychological warfare specialist, displays trophies from the Navy League, a club for American military officers and government officials in Mexico City. Phillips admitted under oath that the Mexico City station's handling of Oswald's visit was "not professional." (Helen Phillips)

Warning: Tom Karamessines, the senior CIA official who, in the panicky hours after Kennedy's assassination, ordered Win Scott not to take any actions that might "prejudice U.S. freedom of action on entire question of Cuban responsibility" for JFK's murder. (AP Images)

Oswald tape: In a 2005 interview in Dallas, Win's longtime assistant, Anne Goodpasture, said she gave him a surveillance tape recording of Oswald's voice. The tape was never shared with JFK investigators.

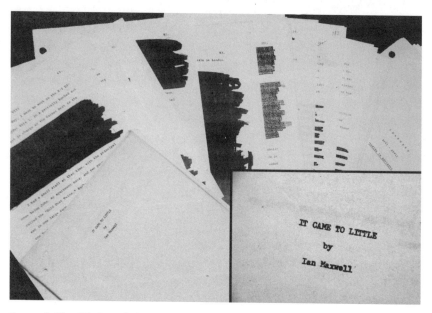

Censored: After Win Scott died, counterintelligence chief James Angleton flew to Mexico City and seized his unpublished memoir, which disputed a key finding of the Warren Commission about Lee Harvey Oswald. Decades later, much of the memoir remains top secret.

Future president: In January 1949, Win and his future wife Paula Murray met actor Ronald Reagan in London's Trafalgar Square, where Reagan was shooting a movie.

Spymaster: Allen Dulles, CIA director from 1953 to 1961, was Win's friend, mentor, and idol.

"Amigo": Adolfo Lopez Mateos, president of Mexico from 1958 to 1964, was known in Scott's cables as LITENSOR.

"Gran Amigo": Gustavo Díaz Ordaz, the hard-line president from 1964 to 1970, was known as LITEMPO-2.

President: JFK autographed this photo for seven-year-old
Michael Scott during the president's triumphant visit to
Mexico in June 1962.

Medal: In 1969, CIA director Dick Helms awarded Win Scott the Distinguished Intelligence Medal, one
of the agency's highest honors.

20

The Padrinos

Throughout the 1960s, Win's victories blazed without attribution in the headlines of *Excelsior*, the *New York Times*, and countless other newspapers. Inside the agency he was known as "Willard Curtis" and spoken of with admiration. His stewardship of the Mexico City station demonstrated almost daily how small developments could be turned into big victories for U.S. policy makers. His successes pleased presidents. His failures were undetectable.

Win delivered propaganda victories, along with espionage. In June 1964, the station got word that Fidel Castro's sister Juana wanted to leave Cuba. She was exfiltrated from Cuba and brought to Mexico, where she was spirited away to George Munro's ranch in Cuernavaca. According to one person who was there, she was handcuffed to a bed so she could be questioned at leisure about what she knew about the Cuban leader and what she would say about him if asked. When Win was convinced of Juana's reliability, she was turned loose. She made headlines by denouncing her brother's communistic ways.

He worked tirelessly. Anne Goodpasture, working at Win's side, saw how he maintained his grip on power by marginalizing each and every deputy chief of station who ever worked for him. "Win never trusted anyone," Goodpasture said in a rare criticism of her late boss. "The deputies were in a position that it was pretty much in name only because Win was there all the time." She said he knew what headquarters wanted to hear. "He was prone to exaggeration, and in retrospect, I felt that he probably didn't want to be away because they would find out that he was probably exaggerating things. There were numerous instances in which he changed figures. Somebody would describe a crowd of 500 in the newspaper; he would add another zero."

He was effectively untouchable. With the departure of Tom Mann to Washington in late 1963, Win faced a challenge from his replacement, a career diplomat named Fulton Freeman who wanted to take over all contacts with the Mexican president, as called for by diplomatic protocol. Win refused. One young CIA officer, Philip Agee, heard that the Scott-Freeman dispute went all the way to the White House. Freeman's "expectations of meaningful diplomatic relations with Díaz Ordaz collided with the President's preference for dealing with Scott," Agee wrote in his memoir. Freeman was relegated to protocol contacts with the president and had to expend his diplomatic talents on the foreign minister, who in the Mexican scheme of things was not that powerful.

Headquarters could not have been happier with Win. His old friend J. C. King had retired as Western Hemisphere division chief in 1964 and was replaced by Bill Broe, another old friend. Broe had first met Win twenty years before when they were both working in the FBI's Cleveland office during World War II. As Win's new boss, Broe was impressed. "He was one of our outstanding officers," he said in an interview. "It was a strong station. He ran a very good shop." And he had connections at the top. "He had a very good relationship with Dick Helms, there's no doubt about it," Broe said. "On the job and personally."

The station, which now had fifty employees and a reputed annual budget of $50 million, was described as "classic" by the agency's inspectors. Between April 1963 and June 1964, the station had provided no less than 615 reports to headquarters, they said. Win could order up mobile surveillance of any target in Mexico City, a venture appropriately named LIFEAT. Mexico City was, without question, the agency's best source of information on people traveling to Cuba. His agents had the Cuban embassy covered and penetrated, claiming even to have a microphone concealed in the love seat in the ambassador's office.

"He was a meticulous man, a taskmaster," said one young officer in the station. "He wanted to make sure things were done the right way. He didn't want surprises. But if you had some initiative and he thought it would go along with what he wanted to do, he was behind you 100 percent."

LITEMPO continued to function smoothly, ensuring almost complete harmony of interests between the U.S. and Mexican governments. President Lopez Mateos had anointed government minister Gustavo Díaz Ordaz as his successor. He was a friend of Win's and a paid agent too, known as LITEMPO-2. In July 1964, Díaz Ordaz received 88 percent of the vote and assumed the presidency. When it came to the wishes of the United States, Win assured his superiors that the new Mexican president "would act in most cases in the manner requested." Díaz Ordaz would certainly cooperate with CIA requests for action against foreigners such as "simple harassment, police interrogation, 'losing' the individual's papers and expelling them from the country for being without documents, possibly jailing an individual on trumped up charges for a short period before expelling him. There might be other refinements that could be worked out as we go along."

Win joked to his family about just how responsive Díaz Ordaz was. At the dinner table, he told of a discussion in the president's office on some point of business where Díaz Ordaz spoke so rapidly that Win could not quite understand. "Parase, parase," Win said, meaning, "Stop, stop." He wanted clarification. Díaz Ordaz, seated behind his desk, suddenly stood up. Win was puzzled. "What's wrong?" Win asked. "Why are you standing up?" "I thought you said 'Parase,'" said Díaz Ordaz. In Spanish, the injunction *parase* also means "stand up." So when the CIA man said, *"Parase,"* the Mexican president did not shut up. He stood up. Win found that hilarious.

Win's influence in the Mexican government extended far beyond the presidency. He had fourteen LITEMPO agents across the upper reaches of the Mexican government in his pay. As Díaz Ordaz moved up to the presidency, Luis Echeverria, LITEMPO-8, took over as minister of government. Another longtime friend, Fernando Gutiérrez Barrios, LITEMPO-4, had become the real power at the Defensa Federal de la Seguridad. He had revitalized the DFS by creating what Anne Goodpasture described as "the semblance of a genuine nonpartisan investigative agency." The Mexican leadership, said Ferguson Dempster, the British spy chief in Mexico City, especially appreciated the daily report on "enemies of the nation" that Win delivered to Díaz Ordaz. Agee said the "daily intelligence summary" included sections on activities of Mexican revolutionary organizations that helped the Mexican security forces "in planning for raids, arrests, and other repressive action."

Life for Win was also good at home. The conflict between Ray Leddy and Win and Janet was finally defused in 1965 by an agreement that the two oldest Leddy boys, Gregory and John, now fourteen and fifteen years old, would leave Mexico City and enroll at the Admiral Farragut Military Academy in St. Petersburg, Florida. John remained especially close to his father, and Gregory needed U.S. school credits for college. Ray Leddy, now serving as diplomatic adviser to the commandant of the Army War College in Carlisle, Pennsylvania, was pleased to have two of his children in the States where he could see them more often. Ever the gentleman, he refused to speak ill of his ex-wife or his former friend in front of his children.

Win encouraged Michael's budding interest in photography by giving him a Super 8 movie camera and asking Anne Goodpasture to show him around the station's darkroom. Goodpasture took a shine to the growing boy, now ten years old, and taught him how to develop photographs. For Michael, the process was imbued with the magic and mystery of his father's job at "the outfit." In the glow of the darkroom's red lights, he saw images materializing on white shiny paper, pictures of the world coming to light. Michael's lifelong fascination with film was born in a CIA film lab.

In 1967, Win and Janet moved the family to a new house. Located at Rio Escondido 16 in a gated suburban cul-de-sac on the west side of Mexico City, the new home was an American-style brick split-level ranch house with a front walk and ivy-covered walls. Janet decorated the rooms with European furniture and folk art. On the weekends Win took Michael to the Chapultepec Country Club and taught him to square his shoulders and swing through the ball. On holidays, the family drove down to George Munro's ranch in Cuernavaca or over to Las Brisas, the swank hotel in Acapulco owned by Win's friend Carlos Trouyet. There were only occasional glimpses into the nature of Win's work. One Christmas after the family had opened all the presents, someone spotted a last gift for Win from a senior Mexican government official. Win unwrapped the present and found himself holding a pistol in the presence of his children.

By the mid-1960s, Win was effectively the second most powerful man in Mexico, outranked only by Díaz Ordaz. He thought Mexico was in fine shape. Construction cranes loomed on the increasingly smoggy skyline. One hundred thirty-eight miles of boulevards and expressways had been built since his arrival in the city a decade earlier. President Lopez Mateos had boasted of having dedicated twenty-eight schools and fifteen municipal markets between 1958 and 1964. Díaz Ordaz sought to do even more in the way of public works because Mexico was going to host the Olympic Games in 1968. And the beneficiaries were ordinary Mexicans. The massive Tlatelolco housing project in the heart of the city was nearing completion. It featured fourteen apartment buildings, from four to twenty stories tall, that housed nearly 70,000 people. This city within a city included shopping centers, churches, schools, playgrounds, and the grand Plaza de las Tres Culturas, which celebrated Mexico's mixed heritage of indigenous, Spanish, and European cultures.

In the spring of 1966, President Johnson thought the conditions were ripe for a reprise of Kennedy's successful visit to Mexico in June 1962. He decided to join his wife and Secretary of State Dean Rusk on an already scheduled trip to visit Mexico City. An advance man, Marty Underwood, was sent to Mexico City to drum up a huge welcome. When Ambassador Freeman proved unhelpful, Underwood met with Win, who delivered what the White House wanted. The station chief arranged for the advance man to meet with no less than the minister of government Luis Echeverria.

"For the next thirty or forty minutes we discussed the importance of the 'trip' not only to my President but to his," Underwood wrote in a memo. "I impressed on him that the 'world would be watching'—that the future of our countries could be at stake. . . . He turned to his interpretator [*sic*] and said 'Ask him what he wants.' I told him two million people and all the glitter and glamour of a fiesta. He turned around and pulled open a door with six phones on it. He started punching buttons and after about ten minutes— he told the interpreter to tell me 'not to worry.' I told him we would supply balloons, confetti, flags etc."

Johnson and his party arrived a few days later and received a rousing welcome. Díaz Ordaz's Party of Institutional Revolution (PRI) had told government workers to turn out. The government unions bused in workers from local factories, and trains brought in campesinos from the countryside. The throng was plenty large and friendly. The motorcade was mobbed, the confetti flew, and Johnson's aides assured reporters that LBJ's reception matched JFK's. But it was largely a sham. Out of Johnson's sight protests had erupted across the city. Some 200 students from the National University gathered in front of the capital's popular monument to Benito Juarez, shouting, "Johnson out of Mexico, Johnson—Murderer, and Yankees out of Vietnam." Another group burned American flags in public without reproach from the often brutal police. The CIA had nothing but praise for Win's security arrangements during LBJ's visit. But Mexico's facade of benign power was beginning to show signs of stress. Opposition to President Díaz Ordaz was mounting.

Win had known the man for eight years now. Díaz Ordaz had been a witness at his wedding, which meant they were *padrinos,* the Mexican term for friends as close as family. Win understood how he saw the world. The president especially feared Victor Rico Galan, a well-known Mexican journalist of Spanish origins. In a widely read article in 1965, Galan called an abortive peasant uprising in the city of Madera "an act of suicidal desperation" that was justified by years of abuse. Peaceful change was impossible in Mexico,

Galan wrote. Win regarded Galan as a "prolific and ardent" apologist for Castro and put his mobile surveillance team on his trail. The DFS provided Miguel Nazar, a rising officer whom Win had known for years, to build a dossier. It proved easy for the Mexican and American spies to capture the voluble journalist's conversations. He was intensely and personally critical of Díaz Ordaz, but he was not trying to foment violent revolution. In the words of Anne Goodpasture, he was "trying to form a new leftist political party in opposition to the PRI." Win helped build the case against Galan. In September 1966 he and twenty-eight associates were arrested. After a show trial, Galan was convicted and spent the next seven years in the notorious Lecumberri prison.

Win's power was very real, yet it had isolated him from the realities of Mexico. He knew the country's men of power—Luis Echeverria, the new minister of government, was an occasional dinner guest—but he did not necessarily know that much about the land they ruled. The agency's Directorate of Intelligence (DOI), restricted to research and analysis, not secret operations, had a clearer understanding of Mexican reality. In 1967, DOI analysts warned that Mexico was failing in some basic ways that might not be visible to the power elite in the capital. Of the country's 45 million people, 40 percent were landless peasants. Thirty-five percent lived on what were known as *ejido* lands, communally held properties that were inefficient at best. Hunger, malnutrition, and misery were all getting worse, especially in the countryside. Desperation was breeding violent rebellion. Besides the suicidal attack at Madero, there had been clashes between campesinos and security forces in the states of Yucatán and Guerrero.

"The political establishment places a high premium on 'keeping the lid on' this explosive situation," the DOI analysis noted. The "brutally effective and politically astute" Mexican army dealt with peasant uprisings in its own way. They dispatched military units to scenes of unrest. After publicizing an imminent "training maneuver," they would "blast all standing objects to rubble."

To Win, in his office in the U.S. embassy, the fight was the same war he had been waging since the end of World War II, the struggle against international communism as directed by the Soviet Union. When a box containing rifles fell off the back of a truck in the heart of Mexico City, the station traced the manifest to a Guatemalan who had served as the chief of the Guatemalan armed forces in Jacobo Arbenz's government back in the early 1950s. With the help of a Cuban diplomat, the man was now shipping the weapons to a Guatemalan guerrilla group seeking to overthrow the CIA-installed military regime. Their Cuban patron was arrested, thanks to Win's work, and thrown out of the country.

Individual successes notwithstanding, Win's performance was slipping. He felt aggravated by matters large and small. The agency's inspection teams, once laudatory, now hassled him, pushing him to find more high-level agents among the various communist groups. Another survey team questioned the very foundation of his operation, the station's voluminous file room. What would happen if the embassy had to be abandoned? How would he get rid of secret records to keep them from falling into the wrong hands? The team estimated it would take approximately six days and nights of steady burning to destroy all the records that Win had collected over the years.

And, still nagging Win, year after year, were all the questions arising from Oswald's visit to Mexico shortly before Kennedy's assassination. Duty and conscience—what had guided him ever since he signed up for the OSS twenty-four years earlier—had begun to diverge as he reviewed the Oswald story. Anne Goodpasture completed her chronology of the Oswald file in February 1968. As Win flipped through it, he began planning to leave the agency. He made his first move a few weeks later when Allen and Clover Dulles came to Mexico for a personal visit. Win booked his old friends into one of the city's best hotels and arranged a visit to the impressive new Anthropology Museum. He and Janet threw a dinner party for the aging spymaster. Win took him to a natural salt bath to ease the pain of his worsening arthritis. Win was deferential as ever to his older friend. Gregory Leddy recalled his stepfather always addressed Dulles as "Mr. Director." "Certainly it was never 'Allen' or 'Mr. Dulles.' It was 'Mr. Director, yes sir, no sir, Mr. Director.'"

In private, Win told Dulles that he wanted to leave the CIA and take a job in the private sector. Could he use Dulles as a reference? Of course, said Dulles. On his return to the States, he sent Win a letter of recommendation.

"To whom it may concern," it began. "I consider Mr. Winston Scott a man of unique ability and outstanding accomplishment," Dulles wrote. "I have had an opportunity to be closely acquainted with his work over the last decade, and I can vouch for the fact that he has performed his work with diligence and success far above the ordinary call."

In his cover letter, Dulles added a postscript: "Jim A. came for dinner and I had a chance to tell him of the help you had been to us on our trip."

Win and Jim Angleton, it seemed, were no longer in touch. The young stars of the OSS had gone their separate ways over the years. Win had become a baron on his home turf, the spymaster of Mexico City. Angleton had achieved greater power, though it was now waning. His search for a Soviet mole paralyzed the Soviet Division for years until colleagues said his paranoid style was harming the agency. Increasingly isolated, Angleton fumed and stewed and—as ever—drank. About all Win and Angleton shared were memories of a friendship that had withered.

21

Night of Tlatelolco

One evening in the summer of 1968, Gregory Leddy went out to dinner in downtown Mexico City with his mother and stepfather. "After we finished, we were walking back to the car when Scottie said, 'Look they have music down there,'" Gregory remembered years later. "We were passing by what they call a *peña*, a coffee shop type of place. He said, 'Let's go listen.' I remember because I had just turned eighteen and it was the first time I'd been out to drink with them."

"So we're sitting there drinking our beers, and someone was singing a song about Castro that was popular at that time. The chorus went, *'Fidel, Fidel, ¿Que tiene Fidel / Que los americanos no pueden con él?'* (Fidel, Fidel, what does he have / That the Americans can't deal with him?). And Scottie's feeling good, so he starts singing along. He's holding his beer up and going, *'Fidel, Fidel, ¿Que tiene Fidel / Que los americanos no pueden con él?'*"

"My mother said 'Scottie do you know what they're saying?'"

"Oh, something about Fidel."

"She says, 'Yeah, they're saying, you can't handle him.'"

"Scottie said something like, it's only a song, and she said, 'You know, if somebody didn't know any better and saw you singing here, they'd think you were some kind of communist.' Scottie just laughed," Gregory recalled.

Janet, though, was not done. She wanted her husband to understand something.

"She said something to the effect that you guys at the CIA go around tagging people as commies and doing awful things to them, and you're singing the same song they do. She wanted him to see how innocent it can all be."

Win was at the zenith of his power, as Gregory Leddy found out late one night in the summer of 1968. Speeding on Reforma late one night, he wrecked his car and wound up in a police station. He called his stepfather for help.

"Next thing you know, Scottie pulls up in his big black Mercury," he recalled in an interview. "It had these red diplomatic license plates for the Olympics, which meant it was the car of someone important, and this big American gets out with a teenage girl. Scottie had brought my sister, Suzanne, along for some reason. The Mexican cops look at this man, and they start rethinking their position. *¿Ah chihuahua, quien es eso?* And Scottie hands the first cop he sees a hundred-peso bill. He hands the second cop he sees a hundred-peso bill. He asks me if I was OK. Was the car OK? I said I was fine and that he only had to pay the *jefe*. But he didn't care. He went around the room, shook everybody's hand and gave everybody a hundred-peso bill. He gave the *jefe* about 400. Then he looks around and says, '*¿Todos contentos?*' Is everybody happy? That was Scottie in his prime, this American who could do anything."

What Win could not do was understand the student demonstrations then spreading across Mexico. As he fitfully looked for work, Win had to keep up with the unprecedented displays of popular opposition to the government. In mid-June 1968 Ambassador Tony Freeman called a meeting with Win and other embassy staff. France had just been convulsed by student demonstrations so massive that the government fell. Win and the others concluded that would not happen in Mexico. "The government has diverse means of gauging and influencing student opinion," Freeman wrote in a cable about the meeting, "and it has shown itself able and willing, when unrest exceeds what it considers acceptable limits, to crack down decisively." But the demonstrations continued. In his meetings with Díaz Ordaz, minister of government Luis Echeverria, and DFS chief Fernando Gutiérrez Barrios, Win sensed their confidence and passed it on to Freeman, who cabled back to Washington to say there was "very little possibility that [the student protest] will take on critical proportions, at least in the coming years."

Just how wrong he was became evident a few days later, when tens of thousands of students gathered in the Zocalo, the central square of Mexico City. The police routed them with night sticks. Win saw the hand of international communism. In a secret report entitled *Students Stage Major Disorders in Mexico*, he said the violence represented "a classic example of the Communists' ability to divert a peaceful demonstration into a major riot."

In fact, the Cold War lens through which Win and his Mexican allies viewed the student movement distorted reality. To be sure there were communists, Trotskyites, and Maoists among the student leaders, but they hardly dominated. In fact, the movement was almost the antithesis of a disciplined Marxist-Leninist party with endless public deliberations, constant debates, and diverse publications. Win read an embassy study of forty separate incidents of student unrest since 1963. Twenty-three of the incidents—more than half—had been motivated by school grievances. Eight protests had concerned local problems. Six had been inspired by Cuba and Vietnam, and four of the demonstrations had denounced the authoritarianism of the Mexican system of political control. And the more violently the government cracked down on the demonstrators, the more rapidly the movement grew.

In Mexico City, a strike committee, representing all higher education students in the capital, was soon joined by a committee of professors who supported them. In July 1968, they jointly called for dissolution of the repressive security forces, respect for the university, compensation for those injured by the police, and release of political prisoners. For all the communist influence in the movement, its chief demand was nothing more radical than dialogue with the government.

Win went to see Díaz Ordaz and found him offended. "The Office of the Presidency is in a state of considerable agitation because of anticipated further disturbances," Win wrote in early August. "The pressure on Díaz Ordaz to restore calm, is particularly intense because of Mexico's desire to project a good image internationally" as host of the upcoming Olympic Games. Tourist and commercial interests were calling for "early action."

But it was far from clear what action Díaz Ordaz could take against an amorphous movement that had no headquarters, no single leader, no party affiliation—and growing public support. As the demonstrations grew in frequency and size in August, the government refused to concede anything. "The present impasse is due to the government's belief that a) giving in to students would invite further demands and b) ignoring situation most likely will lead to further disruption," Win wrote in a cable to CIA headquarters.

After Díaz Ordaz announced in his annual address to the nation on September 1 that "continued agitation would be suppressed," Ambassador Freeman told Washington to expect violence. He repeated his view that government "implicitly accepts consequence that this will produce casualties. Leaders of student agitation have been and are being taken into custody. . . . In other words, the [government] offensive against student disorder has opened on physical and psychological fronts."

In response to the government's tough talk, the student leaders held what they dubbed the Silent Demonstration. In mid-September, some 200,000 people marched through the city with white handkerchiefs over their mouths. The only sound was the shuffling of feet. "It seemed as though we were trampling all the politicians' torrent of words underfoot, all their speeches that are always the same, all their demagoguery, their empty rhetoric, the flood of words that the facts belie, the heaps of lies, we were sweeping them away beneath our feet," one strike leader told journalist Elena Poniatowska. "It was," said historian Enrique Krauze, "a time of infinite hope and delusion."

The army responded by moving 10,000 soldiers to occupy the university campus. At another university in the Tlatelolco housing complex, more radical students fired back with Molotov cocktails and rocks. After talking to Echeverria and Gutiérrez Barrios, Win reported that the government was "not seeking compromise solution with students but rather seeking to put [an] end to all organized student actions before Olympics. . . . Aim of Gov[ernment] believed to be to round up extremist elements and detain them until after Olympics."

On October 2, Win warned Washington the situation was volatile. "Any estimate, such as this one, of the likelihood of intentional acts designed to disrupt the normal course of events must take into account the presence of radicals and extremists whose behavior is impossible to predict," he wrote. "Such persons and groups do exist in Mexico." That might have been the voice of Win's intuition and considerable experience. More likely it was a tip passed along to him by friendly LITEMPOs who had reason to believe the normal course of events was about to be disrupted with a devastating display of violence.

At 5:00 P.M. that day the student protestors gathered at the Plaza de Las Tres Culturas in the Tlatelolco housing complex. Depleted by arrests, confronted by a hard-line government, and facing the opening of the Olympic Games in less than two weeks, the movement was struggling to keep up pressure on the government. Tanks surrounded the plaza, but that was normal for demonstrations, and the atmosphere was not tense. Soldiers sat on their tanks, cleaning their bayonets and watching people gathered around the loudspeakers, mounted on the third floor of the Edificio Chihuahua, a high-rise apartment building overlooking the plaza. By late afternoon, between 5,000 and 10,000 people had gathered in the plaza.

The military commanders on the scene received orders to prevent the rally from taking place. They were ordered to isolate the leaders of the meeting, detain them, and turn them over to DFS. A select group of officers in civilian clothes, known as the Olympic Battalion, had their own instructions. They were to wear civilian clothes with a white glove on the left hand and post themselves in the doorways of the Chihuahua building. When they got the signal, in the form of a flare, they were to prevent the entrance or exit of anyone to the plaza while the student leaders were being detained. Finally, a group of police officers got orders to arrest the leaders of the national strike council.

What virtually no one knew until more than thirty years later was that Luis Gutiérrez Oropeza, the chief of staff of the Mexican military, had posted ten men with guns on the upper floor of the Chihuahua building and given them orders to shoot into the crowd. He was acting on orders of Díaz Ordaz, according to a revelatory account published in 1999 in the newsweekly *Proceso*, by Julio Scherer and Carlos Mosivais, two of the country's best-known journalists. Oropeza was the link between Díaz Ordaz and Echeverria, according to Mario Moya Palencia, a Mexican political insider at the time. Oropeza was also a friend and occasional dinner guest of Win Scott's. He might have been a LITEMPO agent. There is no evidence that he acted on the CIA's behest in October 1968.

"No one could say precisely where the first shots came from, but the great majority of the demonstrators agreed that the Army troops suddenly began shooting without warning," wrote Elena Poniatowska in her classic account, *Noche de Tlatelolco*. "There were shots from all directions, from the top of a building in the housing unit and from the street, where the military forces fired round after round from the machine guns mounted on their light tanks and armored transports."

A wave of people ran to the far end of the plaza, only to meet a line of oncoming soldiers. They ran the other way—into the free-fire zone. It was a "closed circle of hell," said historian Krauze: a "terror operation." The shooting went on for an hour and then began to diminish. It started to rain. The tanks opened fire. "The hail of bullets fired at the Chihuahua building became so intense that around seven P.M. a large section of the building caught on fire," wrote reporter Jorge Aviles of *El Universal*. "All the floors from the tenth to the thirteenth floors were enveloped in flames and many families were forced to leave the unit, amid the heavy gunfire, carrying the children in their arms and risking their lives." Inside the floors of the hallways were sticky with blood. The shooting continued until eleven o'clock that night. Five thousand soldiers fired a total of 15,000 rounds. Two thousand people were arrested, many of them stripped, beaten, and abused. Lights were extinguished, telephone service was cut off, photographers were forbidden from taking pictures, and even ambulances were turned away.

"The dead bodies were lying on the pavement, waiting to be taken away," recalled one bystander. "I counted lots and lots of them from the window, about seventy-eight in all. They were piling them up there in the rain."

"Perhaps the most tragic sight of all," wrote Jose Luis Mejias in *El Diario de la Tarde* the next day, "was the blood-stained shoes scattered all over the Plaza, like mute witnesses to the sudden flight of their owners." Between 80 and 100 people had been killed in the course of the evening.

Win filed his first report around midnight. It was massaged at headquarters and passed to the White House, where it was read the next morning. Something big had happened at Tlatelolco, but Win could not say exactly what.

"A senior [classified source] counted 8 dead students, six dead soldiers but a nearby Red Cross installation had 127 wounded students and 30 wounded soldiers."

"A classified source said the first shots were fired by the students from the Chihuahua apartments."

An American classified source "expressed the opinion this was a premeditated encounter provoked by the students."

Another classified source said that "most of the students present on the speaker's platform were armed, one with a sub-machine gun . . . troops were only answering the fire from the students."

Virtually none of these reports turned out to be true. The morning newspapers in Mexico City gave a more accurate sense of the death toll, if not the perpetrators. *Excelsior* reported 20 dead and 75 wounded. *El Universal* had 29 dead and 80 wounded. *El Dia*, a leftist daily, declared, "Criminal Provocation at Tlatelolco Meeting Causes Terrible Bloodshed." The pro-government *El Nacional* said, "Army Forced to Rout Sharpshooters." The tabloid *El Sol* declared, "Foreign Interlopers Attempt to Damage Mexico's National Image."

Win stuck to the story of a left-wing provocation. His next situation report cited "trained observers" who believed the students instigated the incident. Díaz Ordaz told an American visitor—probably Win—that he believed the disturbance had been "carefully planned." "A good many people came into the country," he reportedly said. "The guns used were new and had their numbers filed off. The Castro and Chinese communist groups were at the center of the effort. The Soviet communists had to come along to avoid the charge of being chicken."

When President Johnson's national security adviser Walt Rostow demanded confirmation, Win's replies were less than convincing. Were

Mexican students using new rifles with numbers filed off from Chinese sources? Win said he had no verification of that claim.

Did individuals from outside Mexico participate in the student movement? While the Mexican press continually played on the theme of foreign involvement, Win noted, "no conclusive evidence to this effect has been presented."

What organizations outside the academic field participated in the student movement? There was "no conclusive evidence" of foreign support of arms to the students, Win replied.

Wallace Stuart, a counselor at the U.S. embassy in Mexico City, later said the CIA station had reported fifteen differing and sometimes flatly contradictory versions of what happened at Tlatelolco, "all from either 'generally reliable sources' or 'trained observers' on the spot!" Win had become so dependent on his well-placed sources that he had no independent means of getting accurate information about a hugely important political event.

Jorge Casteneda, the historian who later became Mexican foreign minister, interviewed many of the Mexican participants in the events of October 1968 and concluded that Díaz Ordaz and Echeverria had tacitly worked together to strike a decisive blow without leaving a paper trail of who gave the order. The massacre at Tlatelolco, wrote historian Sergio Aguayo, parted "the waters of Mexican history. It accented the turbulence of those years, served to concentrate power in the intelligence services dominated by a small group of men, hard and uncontrolled." A handful of Mexican men had entrenched themselves in power, acting with impunity against "an opposition that was weak but each time more bellicose and desperate to rebel against the apathy of an indifferent, if not complicitous, international community"—and Win had helped them every step of the way.

A week after the massacre, Win wrote a thank-you note to Echeverria for a gift the minister of government had just given him: a large, framed electronic map that displayed the correct time in every time zone in the world. "The marvelous clock you sent to me recently is a wonder to all who see it," Win wrote.

In the aftermath of the Tlatelolco massacre, Win's most trusted agents atop the Mexican government had delivered fictional accounts of a left-wing provocation and then a bauble. The puppet master had become a puppet.

22

"The Sludge of Spies and Knaves"

Michael's search for the story of his father's life led him to discover new dimensions of his own. After obtaining the documents about his adoption, he decided to seek out his biological mother, Martha Scruggs. A homemaker living in a small town in Georgia, she was now Martha Caldwell, married to the warden of a local prison. Michael could see the circumstances he would have grown up in had she not given him up for adoption. He marveled yet again at the accident of his life. Martha, a warm and effusive woman, was overjoyed to meet her son and especially delighted to introduce him to her other son. His name, she said, beaming, was Michael Scott Caldwell. Michael shook hands with his half brother, pleased somehow that they looked alike. Martha had married and given birth to him in 1960, five years after Michael was given up for adoption. She named him Michael, having no idea that that is what Win and Paula had named her first son. She gave him the middle name of Scott in honor of Win's brother, Morgan Scott, whose kindliness had helped her through the ordeal of an unwanted pregnancy and giving up a baby for adoption. Thus Michael had the singular experience of getting to know a brother of the same name. It was like meeting himself as a stranger.

And the odd sensation of self-discovery generated by meeting this other Michael Scott somehow echoed the story of his father's life: Win met his other self. He discovered, late in life, the difference between his identity as a spy and the person he called "his true self." It was a long time coming.

In June 1969, Win traveled to Washington to receive one of the highest honors that could be accorded to a CIA man: the Distinguished Intelligence Medal. He had been eased out of the station chief job. There was no specific reason. Headquarters, in the person of division chief Bill Broe, was adamant. The usual rotation for a station chief was four years. Win had been there for almost thirteen. Only one other station chief in the history of the agency had stayed in one place for so long. Win declined the offer of a job back at headquarters. No way was he moving back to Washington. Mexico was his milieu. He chose retirement. "Win's retirement didn't have anything to do with the events of October 1968," Broe said in an interview years later. "It was the long tenure. That was what we decided to do, to start changing and moving people. It wasn't because he had done something wrong. We just felt that we shouldn't have individuals there as long as that. Thirteen years is a long time."

Although Win harbored some bitter feelings when he arrived at headquarters, he stuck to his genial style. If he did not have something good to say, he would not say anything at all. The turnout was large. He had worked with lots of people over the years, and people liked what they remembered of him. The secretaries, the up-and-coming young men, the senior hands—they all had a story about the man with a file cabinet mind, his day-in-and-day-out approach, the scope of his operations, his capacious ability to digest information. There were few tales of derring-do but many of hard work and loyalty. Few knew how far he had come from rural Alabama. Everyone knew how much he had accomplished. Win shook hands, smiled, basked in the admiration of his fellows, felt satisfied. The Distinguished Intelligence Medal was reserved for those supergrade officers who had made a difference in the history of the agency. Everyone agreed Win deserved it.

Dick Helms presided in a dark suit with his usual aplomb. Jim Angleton, stooped and gaunt, was there to wish his old friend well. So was Anne Goodpasture, now living a less hectic life in northern Virginia and working on historical matters at the office. Allen Dulles, sadly, was not there, having passed away six months earlier. Jack Whitten, who never did make division chief, was there too. He would soon retire, move to Europe, and take up a new life singing in the Vienna Men's Chorus. Dave Phillips attended, now one of the leading men in the Western Hemisphere division. Win saw scores of other familiar faces, evoking memories of the K and L Buildings down by the Reflecting Pool, the lunches at the Army-Navy Club, the cocktail parties in Georgetown, and dinners at the Seaport in Alexandria. Win felt blessed but detached, too.

He went to Dick Helms's office, where a photographer snapped a picture of them shaking hands. At the ceremony, Helms read the citation: "In the formative years of our Agency, Scott developed and supervised intelligence relationships with nations allied with the United States in the cause of freedom—relationships which remain as enduring legacies to his vision and to his sincerity of purpose."

This nod to the "special relationship" with Great Britain warmed Win's Anglophilia. He knew he never could have made his way in the intelligence game without the irreplaceable support of his British friends—the bluff Tommy Robertson, who took him to see Churchill; the impressive Kenneth Strong, who built the War Room that served Eisenhower so well in the final push to victory; the brilliant Dick White, whom he introduced to American football. Memories of Kim Philby's deceit could not tarnish such men. Win's accomplishments in Mexico were comparable, said Helms. "In later years," the citation continued, "he initiated and brought to fruition an international alliance on this hemisphere which constitutes a foundation stone for achievements of great significance. During a career spanning more than a quarter of a century, Mr. Scott's performance has been marked by exceptional competence, integrity, and the stimulating leadership which has inspired his associates to their highest capabilities."

When the applause faded out and the ceremony ended, Win felt like a man returning to the human race. "I came away from that, my last official visit to headquarters happy and with a feeling of freedom," he later wrote. "I definitely decided to relax, talk about any work I engaged in the future, and try to get back my respect for and trust of people."

Back at his desk in his home office in Mexico City, he had no use for espionage. "I was happy to get out of the sludge of spies and knaves," he wrote, "pleased to believe that in the future, contacts could be made for friendship, or openly for business reasons; and I was very happy to get rid of the necessity to keep secret the work I did and the contacts I made."

Among other things, Win wanted to make money. He had always acted as if he had money even when he did not. Now he saw tuition bills coming due for the children and likely to grow. He wanted Michael and George to go to boarding school. He joked of sending Michael to Eton. So he would use his contacts to do business. He recruited Fergie Dempster, who had just retired from the British intelligence service and could not bear to leave sunny Mexico for dreary London. He brought in another agency man named Al Ulmer, who first met Win back in his Havana days and more recently had served as London station chief. Win's personal attorney, Bink Goodrich, put up the money to get started. He called their company

Diversified Corporate Services, DiCoSe for short, and opened an office a couple of blocks from the U.S. embassy on Reforma. "We established ourselves as consultants for people who wanted to do business in Mexico," Dempster later told Michael. "Win was loved and admired." Tom Mann said he thought Win was running "his own personal intelligence organization. . . . [The Mexicans] wanted to use his expertise and knowledge of Mexico, especially the intelligence side of it."

Win's contacts in the Mexican government generated business from the start. Díaz Ordaz and Echeverria, fearing more student and campesino uprisings, remained obsessed with the government's rapid reaction capabilities. They especially coveted a vertical takeoff aircraft, built by the British, that could take off and land like a helicopter. The Mexicans had no luck getting the U.S. military to approve a plane deal, so they turned to DiCoSe. Dempster used his London contacts to broker the sale. In a second deal, Dempster arranged the purchase of a private airplane for Díaz Ordaz. DiCoSe took in $60,000 in commissions on those two deals alone.

Win stayed in touch with old friends. He and Janet threw a dinner party for DFS chief Fernando Gutiérrez Barrios and his wife. Some people thought Díaz Ordaz might tap Gutiérrez Barrios to be the next president, but Win already knew that Díaz Ordaz had decided on Luis Echeverria, the man who chose not to compromise with the student movement. Of his friends in the Mexican government, Win personally liked Gutiérrez Barrios the most and invited him often to his home. Win's children noticed his mood brightening. "You could tell he was excited about the business," said Greg Leddy, his oldest stepson. Win hired Michael, then thirteen years old, to work as the office boy, making coffee and running errands. "It was my first job, and I got paid fifty pesos a week, which Janet thought was outrageously high," Michael recalls. He was beginning to see firsthand who his father's friends were.

The electronic wall map and clock that Luis Echeverria, long in charge of the Ministry of Government, had given Win in October 1968 hung on the wall. The gift from the future president no longer worked, but no one minded. It looked impressive. One of the secretaries was a young Mexican woman named Marta. She was the daughter of Miguel Nazar, now a senior official at DFS. Win complained mildly that she could not type, but he needed to do a favor for Nazar, so she stayed. It was an exciting time for Michael, getting to know his way around Mexico City on his own. He rode to the office every day with his father and often had lunch with him. One day when Win and associates took him to lunch, they ordered gin and tonics while Michael ordered a lemonade. When the drinks came, Michael received a gin and tonic. "I went along with the routine and said nothing,"

Michael recalled. "Then they brought me another and another. After lunch I had to run an errand and got thoroughly lost on various bus lines. I strolled back to the office around 6:00 P.M. after keeping everyone worried. By then the buzz had worn off. Win never knew I was drinking gin tonics. He thought it was lemonade."

Perhaps it was the literary success of former friend Kim Philby that inspired Win to think he could write a spy memoir that would sell. The British spy, still living in Moscow since his escape in 1963, had published a best-selling memoir, *My Silent War*, in 1967 in which he recounted how he betrayed the British and American services and why. Win read the book, no doubt relieved that it did not mention him. He might not have minded Philby's condescending portrait of the Americans in London, but he definitely disliked Philby's unkind portrait of Bill Harvey (whom Kim called "Bill Howard"). Most of all, he loathed Philby's silky defense of communism and his own treachery at a time when gullible young Americans seemed regrettably receptive to communist propaganda.

Win had always aspired to be a published author but never quite made it. His submissions, under the name "Ian Maxwell," for detective magazines had never seen print. *My Love*, his volume of poems for Janet, was virtually self-published. So was his fable of southern boyhood, *MacGee, MacGill and Me*. He believed he could write a memoir of his CIA career that would help the agency and the country. He brooded about his final years on the job, convinced that accountants had taken over the CIA, stifling effective secret operations with unreal budget formulas and intrusive demands. He wanted people to know how the CIA fought the good fight against a vicious and amoral foe and why America was losing.

He got some encouragement from a new friend, John Barron, an editor for *Reader's Digest* who had long been friendly with the agency. He visited Mexico City occasionally because he was writing a book about the KGB with the unofficial assistance from headquarters. As Win shared some of his spy stories with Barron, the editor expressed an interest in seeing anything he wrote of his own career.

Win had time on his hands, and the house was quieter than it had been in years. He and Janet sent Michael and George to the Taft School in Connecticut to prepare them for college. Win retreated to his home office and started tapping away on his Smith Corona typewriter. In November 1970, Win wrote to Barron, saying he was making progress. "I have taken a time of illness to try to put together items from my career which I am allowed to write about," he said.

Win touted some of the revelations he would provide. He mentioned his service in Havana, his work during the war and after with the British, including "my good friend Sir Kenneth Strong" and my "strong relations" with the General Communications Headquarters, the British cryptographic organization. He said he could write "plenty" about Kim Philby, whom he described as "the worst traitor in British history." He could relate "a great deal" about Lee Oswald's activities "from the moment he arrived in Mexico." He told Barron he wanted to call the book "It Came to Little." "If we are honest," he wrote, "communism is growing ever stronger and the U.S. government is more and more timid about confronting communism particularly in our own country."

He wrote to relive his life, the struggles with his father, and his improbable arrival in the OSS. As he looked back on his life, he focused more on personalities and events than politics. He recalled his encounters with great men, like Hoover, Churchill, and Dulles. He recalled the good times and hard times of London during the war with a lack of discretion that might have been lubricated by alcohol. Unlike Philby, he was neither a sophisticated polemicist nor an accomplished stylist. He did not much analyze the communist threat save to say that it was everywhere and it was bad. He wrote mostly to defend the agency and himself, to stake out his position on Oswald, to reconcile duty and conscience, and to improve the clandestine service.

He bared his soul selectively. He wrote more about "Anna," the beautiful Jewish mathematician who captured his heart in old Edinburgh in the summer of 1940, than he did about his first wife, Besse, to whom he was married for almost twenty years. He never mentioned Beau, the son he had loved and lost touch with. He did not write about his passion for Paula and made only brief mention of her death. He did not mention Janet or their blended family. He wrote about Kim Philby, Guy Burgess, and Donald Mclean because he wanted to deglamorize their treachery. He sketched the sterling qualities of Bill Harvey, whom Philby had traduced in his book precisely because he was the most able American intelligence officer, the first to see through his treason.

When it came to Kennedy's assassination, he wrote in self-defense. He read the theories and claims of people who knew a lot less about the subject than he did, and he wanted to establish some facts. He ignored Dick Helms's directive to pledge allegiance to the Warren Commission. Instead, he pointed out that irksome and untrue claim on page 777 of the commission's report, that Oswald's visit to the Cuban consulate "was not known until after the assassination."

That one line had come to rankle Win over the years. He thought Jim Garrison was appalling, but Win understood better than anyone that the agency's investigation of Oswald in Mexico City had been superficial. The Oswald file review proved that. He knew the investigation of Oswald had missed his fling with Sylvia Duran and perhaps his association with other leftists. He knew that people in Washington wanted to reopen the investigation. To accept the Warren Commission's "fact" implied his station had missed something basic and important: an American visiting the Cuban consulate. Win would be discreet about operations, but he did not want to let such criticism circulate without response.

"Every piece of information concerning Lee Harvey Oswald," he wrote, "was reported immediately after it was received to: U.S. Ambassador Thomas C. Mann, by memorandum; the FBI Chief in Mexico, by memorandum; and to my headquarters by cable; and included in each and every one of these reports was the entire conversation Oswald had, from Cuban Consulate, with the Soviet [Embassy]." Win was not going to mention tapes or photographs because that would blow the LIERODE and LIENVOY operations, but he had Oswald tapes and photographs in his home office to prove his point. When Oswald was unknown, Win had gone along with the headquarters' need to not report on his visit to the Cuban consulate. After Kennedy was killed, he had also gone along. But now that people were calling for a reopening of the JFK investigation, he was not going to feign ignorance or get stuck defending a story he knew was not true. Others might have had something to hide about Oswald's visit to the Cuban consulate. He did not.

Which is not to say that Win suspected his colleagues of conniving in Kennedy's death. He had spent the last twenty-five years in the clandestine service. He wanted readers to have the benefit of his experience, which told him Kennedy was killed by a conspiracy and Oswald was probably a communist agent. The suspected assassin's support for the Fair Play for Cuba Committee, his on-the-air defense of Castro in the New Orleans radio debate, and his contacts in Mexico City were "quite enough to cause a suspicion of Soviet involvement in the murder of President Kennedy," he wrote. Win was bothered that the possibility was not taken more seriously. "If a conservative or a member of a conservative group had shot President Kennedy and had been found to have had associations and conversations pertaining to escape a few weeks prior to the shooting, with members of that conservative group what would have been the reactions of communists, leftists and liberals in the USA? I believe that there would have been a great outcry advocating the abolition of the conservative group involved and declarations of guilt of all members of that organization."

Oswald's conspiratorial connections, he argued, had gone unexamined because of liberal bias. The fact that communist embassies dealt with and counseled this "assassin a few weeks prior to the time he murdered President Kennedy is treated as an irrelevant bit of news, not worthy of considering," he wrote. "This could be due to the fact that a serious investigation into the matter would offend the Soviets, with whom our foreign policy pundits, leftists and liberals are trying to be friendly while the Soviets stab us in the back and insult us to our faces."

Win's conclusion that there had been no "serious investigation" of Oswald's communist connections was well informed. His effort to blame "foreign policy pundits, leftists and liberals" was less persuasive. There were, after all, few such heretics at the top of the CIA. His friend Allen Dulles did not care to push the Warren Commission to look at Oswald's Cuban connections. His friend Jim Angleton could have mounted a serious investigation of possible counterintelligence failures around Oswald any time he wanted. Instead, he stalled the Warren Commission and indulged the suggestion of Anatoly Golitsyn, his favorite defector, that the Soviets were trying to hide a connection to Oswald. Likewise, his esteemed colleague Dick Helms could have ordered a closer review of the proliferating reports of Oswald's activities in Mexico. Instead, he ordered Win and other station chiefs to cut off and discredit all discussion of the alleged assassin's motives and contacts.

The peculiar truth that Win's conservative political faith could not absorb was that it was the impeccably patriotic Dulles, Helms, and Angleton, not deluded liberals, who blocked investigation of Oswald's communist connections, and his friend David Phillips who fudged the record. They stalled, avoided, and dissembled in the course of the Oswald investigation not because they were soft on communism, not to avoid offending liberal public opinion, but out of self-preservation. To investigate Oswald's connections required review of agency operations around the accused assassin, and that was something Helms and Angleton could not afford. The preassassination paper trail on Oswald was just too thick. The story of Oswald's encounters with Phillips's AMSPELL network; the missing LIERODE photos of his visit to the Cuban consulate; the misleading October 10 cable from headquarters; the illegal HTLINGUAL monitoring of Oswald's correspondence, not to mention Karamessines's panicky efforts the day after Kennedy was killed to "preserve U.S. freedom of action on the whole question of Cuban responsibility" and Phillips's promotion of Alvarado's provocative story, all tended to confirm what Fidel Castro alleged, what Win knew, and what supporters of the Warren Commission would heatedly deny: that "a person of great interest" to the CIA had killed the commander in chief.

The truth was, Win wrote his memoir to defend himself, not please his bosses. As he neared the end of his manuscript, he devoted a whole chapter to something that had proved unexpectedly difficult for him: getting back to normal. If he could not be candid about secret operations, he would be honest about the toll they took. He wanted future CIA officers to have the benefit of his experience. The profession had hidden perils that should not be ignored.

"The good clandestine intelligence officer should live two lives, all through his work-career," he explained. One of these lives makes him appear to be a normal man engaged in an overt job, a business about which he can talk openly and professionally. The other life he lives—and it is the overriding, the primary and principal life—is one in which he is strictly prohibited from talking about his work. He is never able to discuss the work of this second (clandestine) life with his family, or anyone, except fellow clandestine officials who are working on the same target, same operation, or those of his superiors who "have a need to know" about his work.

Having a split personality helped in this kind of life, he noted.

One of the simplest and probably the most used cover for such an officer is that of diplomat, assignment to a diplomatic establishment. Such an official is forced to pretend to be a normal diplomat, performing certain assigned duties; while his real work, the work which counts to him and to his superiors, is that of procuring secret intelligence from a hostile person, installation or group. I believe that a good clandestine intelligence operations officer must have a certain amount of schizoidal tendencies—if he is to be happy while living his cover and working with success in his primary field.

The work of the counterintelligence or counterespionage officer was even more psychologically disturbing, he wrote, because the target was one's own colleagues. "At times, these officers are assigned the task of protecting the security of operations and operations personnel from their own organization; and they can find personnel of their own organization acting as traitors, or, for some less vile reason, breaking security. A less vile reason could be that an operations officer has become tired, worn out and begins to drink to get an extra lift—and perhaps becomes talkative or too lax in some way."

The counterespionage officer, Win said, was even more likely to be schizoidal than the clandestine operations officer. "In the case of a good and active counter-espionage officer, the individual's self-relationship becomes a pseudo-personal one; his true self treats his false self as though his false self were another person."

Win had managed scores of secret agents in his thirteen years in Mexico. He knew the pathology of the profession, and he recognized it in himself. There was the real Win Scott, who had a family and friends, and the false "Willard Curtis," who ran covert operations with and against knaves. He knew from personal experience how the false self of a secret agent could take over. It was the nature of the job.

"Clandestine operations all have the common features of seeking for wanted information or intelligence information," he explained, "of looking for access and access capability, spotting a potential procurer, agent or knave; recruitment, after as careful study and assessment as is possible; protection of the agent and of yourself, the case officer; evaluation of the product obtained; and, always, careful handling of the principal agent."

This manipulation required careful study, he noted. "Clandestine intelligence operations officers must be students and be willing to spend hours, many hours in each detail of each and every operation in which they are involved." They had to deal with people whom he delicately described as "other than normal." He said the spy always "must be on the look-out for indications of deceit, excessive fear or even of a coming break-down in his agents."

"Above all, he must know and realize that almost all agents are knaves, in the worst sense of the word. But, he must treat them as if he thought them gentlemen." Along the way, the counterespionage officer becomes "depersonalized," loses his true self altogether. Success, he observed, was especially corrosive. "The false-self which becomes dominant, could think, 'he (the true self) is too cautious, too frightened, not daring enough.' . . . after a few successes, a counterespionage officer is inclined to believe (or to have his false self [believe]) that his opponents are incapable of beating him."

He described the process of psychological deterioration that he had observed. "The false (counterespionage) self comes to believe: 'I am too smart for my opponents; they can never outwit me.'" And failure follows. "This danger of conceit is something which all chiefs of operations units in clandestine intelligence organizations must watch for. It can destroy—and has destroyed—many of the best clandestine intelligence officers long before they had reached their peaks as officers, and long before their successes warranted even the slightest conceit."

Win named no names, but he might have had some examples in mind. Was he thinking of David Phillips, a brilliant operations officer shocked by the defeat at the Bay of Pigs and the failure of all his psychological warfare schemes to "peel Castro like an onion"?

Win wrote: "Those who become conceited and are not destroyed, ruined for future use, are frequently so shocked by a failure so deeply that they are useless, at least temporarily, as clandestine operations officers. Some such failures are said to have developed microcosms within themselves; and, as a result of such an autistic, private, self-contained life, they cannot be used—since, for a time, they cannot associate themselves with a life of reality, which must be lived with, and to a degree, shared with others."

Was this a reference to his friend Bill Harvey, the once brilliant officer who had descended into alcoholism? At a doctor's recommendation, in 1966 Harvey was recalled to Washington, where he received "special assignments" at which he could work at his own pace and did not have to show his face in public.

Or was Win thinking of Angleton, the leading theorist of counterintelligence in the halls of the CIA, whose intellect proved no match for Kim Philby's guile and whose arcane theories of Soviet deception operations were fast losing credibility? Autistic was not an inappropriate metaphor for Angleton's state of mind in 1970. Obsessed by the possibility of another Philby in the ranks of the agency, the counterintelligence chief had grown ever more reclusive over the years. He drank heavily and lived in the microcosm of what he called the Monster Plot in which a near-omnipotent KGB deployed liberals, socialists, third world revolutionaries, and the Chinese government in a fiendishly effective unified campaign to get America to relax its guard. In this private, self-contained life, Angleton imagined himself as the last line of defense against the impending victory of global communism. In fact, his family life was a shambles, his files a mess. When he was finally forced into retirement in 1975, his successor found his office "a desolate situation." Others might have said it was disturbing.

Angleton had files on the assassinations of John and Robert Kennedy, including autopsy pictures of the remains of RFK, who had been slain by a Palestinian waiter in a Los Angeles hotel in June 1968. Although Angleton's interest in the Soviet defector Yuri Nosenko might explain his files on JFK's assassination, no one could explain his interest in the cause of Bobby Kennedy's death. Both the RFK autopsy photos and the JFK files were destroyed without being made public. Even admirers would later admit that Angleton had outlived his usefulness and should have been removed from his job long before he was forced out in December 1974.

Win was not the type to name names. He just wanted others to know the perils of the profession.

Win was glad to leave his false self behind and wanted to help other officers do the same. He recommended that "a counterespionage officer, particularly, should have a comparatively short period of active field operational work, and in the interim should be given less demanding work, work less demanding of a schizoidal life." He proposed early retirement for any clandestine intelligence officer who had spent five years outside of the United States. Since he had lived outside of the United States for almost three times as long as that, Win must have known something of what he called "the schizoidal life." He spoke from personal experience when he wrote that the intelligence officer inevitably comes to "mistrust almost everyone, to look for the hidden meaning and motives behind even the most sincere statements of friends and loved ones."

Nonetheless, the retired station chief was proud of his service and sacrifice. He wished only that he had more often acted as father, husband, and friend over the years, and less as a spy. "Now that I view [the] years I put into clandestine operations works, I realize that I gave myself far too completely to the work and gave too little time and attention to recreational and normal family life and activities," he said, "and I fully realized that in all those thousands of hours of work as I beavered away, 'I looked for much, and lo, it came to little' for me and for my country."

Win wrote that line on the last page of his manuscript. He sent it off by night mail.

23

A Fall in the Garden

On March 30, 1971, Janet threw a festive surprise party for
Win's sixty-second birthday at 16 Rio Escondido. Sixteen couples
came for a buffet dinner featuring roast beef with mushroom sauce,
tomato aspic, peas and carrots, and spoon bread accompanied by
plenty of Pouilly-Fuissé and Chablis. The Scotts had much to cel-
ebrate. Michael and George were finishing tenth grade at the Taft
School in Connecticut. Diversified Corporate Services was doing
lucrative business, and Win was close to completing the revision of
his manuscript. At John Barron's suggestion he changed the title of
the book from "It Came to Little" to "Foul Foe," to emphasize
communist perfidy. The second draft had been delivered to a typist.
Janet did not care for the book but knew better than to try to talk
Win out of something he desired. He was planning to go to Washington to see Dick Helms himself to discuss his plans to publish. He
knew from John Horton, his successor as station chief, that the director did not like the idea, but he thought that something could be
worked out.

Win, in his innocence, did not know that John Barron had already
shown the first draft to Helms. The CIA director recognized that Win
was not America's answer to Kim Philby. Philby was, no matter what
you thought of his political morality, a skilled writer: observant in
details, witty in asides, erudite in references, and cunning in polem-
ics. Win Scott the author, alas, lacked such finesse. What's more,
Win's narrative strayed into dangerous territory. Philby was a humiliation for the British and a lasting black eye for the agency and for
Angleton more than anyone. Oswald was a closed issue that Win had
been warned not to talk about. Win's account of Oswald's Mexico

City trip, and his speculations about a Soviet conspiracy behind JFK's assassination could only feed the widespread skepticism about the Warren Commission and the growing suspicion of the agency itself. Win was recounting an eventful career that covered the entire existence of the agency at its most senior levels. It could only help the Soviets understand and penetrate U.S. secret operations. What's more, Helms also knew something that Win did not: Dave Phillips, the man in the middle of Oswald's Mexico City odyssey, had just orchestrated a political assassination in Chile for the White House less than six months before.

Helms was fully prepared to go to court to block publication of Win's book—he already had the personal approval of President Richard Nixon to block another book by a former CIA officer—but he hoped it would not come to that. In the spring of 1971 Helms asked John Horton to sound out Win about his publication plans over lunch. When Win made it clear he was not going to be talked out of publishing a book, Horton recommended that Helms send someone whom Win respected to talk to him—someone like Jim Angleton. But even that was a delicate proposition because his friendship with Win had cooled. Win decided he would go to Washington to meet with Helms personally to see if something couldn't be worked out.

One evening he and Janet went out to dinner at Bellingshausen, a favorite restaurant that had started as a German beer hall in the early 1900s. It was located across the street from the original U.S. embassy residence in Mexico City, an ornate nineteenth-century building where President Kennedy had stayed in 1962. After the meal, Win and Janet were standing outside waiting for the valet to bring their car when they noticed that the embassy residence was being torn down. Only one corner of it had been preserved. Astonished at the sight, they went over to the rubble and asked a man working there why the residence had been razed. The land was going to become a parking lot, the man said.

"Why are you saving that corner?" Win asked.

"That's the room where Kennedy slept," was the answer.

At home, Janet went to bed, and Win went out into the backyard of the house to breathe the night air and check on his latest home improvement. New houses were under construction across the field behind 16 Rio Escondido, and Win had decided to replace the wire fence that marked the edge of his property with a high stucco wall. He climbed up a ladder to the top of the wall. The lights of Mexico City were spread out in the distance. A security guard stood watch. He and Win chatted in Spanish for a few minutes. As Win turned around to descend, he missed the step of the ladder and tumbled down into the thicket of the rose garden ten feet below. He got up, scratched and bruised, and gingerly made his way back into the house, where he went to bed. When Janet woke up the next morning, she was startled to see her husband's face was black and blue.

"God what happened to you?" she said.

"I fell off the ladder and crashed into the roses," he said.

He did not feel well, so he spent most of the day in bed. He made a trip to the hospital, where doctors detected no broken bones or serious injuries. He told Gregory the story about the U.S. embassy residence being torn down save for the room where Kennedy slept. On Sunday morning he drank a glass of orange juice and suddenly felt chest pains.

"I can't breathe," he said. "It hurts."

He went back to bed, and a doctor was called. The doctor looked him over and said he was fine. The doctor explained that the pain may have felt like a heart attack, but it was probably just the combination of his bruises and the cold juice, which had simply tightened up Win's chest muscles and hindered his breathing. He advised more rest. So Win stayed in bed reading all day. At one point, Gregory and a friend looked in on him.

"Hi, Mr. Scott, how are you doing?" asked the friend. "Do you think you're going to live?"

"Oh, I'm fine," he waved them off.

The next morning Gregory went off to teach his English student. Win had a meeting at the office with John Barron to talk about the manuscript. Janet's mother came down for breakfast. Janet had gone to the kitchen to check on the eggs when she heard Win cry out in pain. She rushed back to the kitchen table and found Win slumped over in his chair.

"I knew he was gone," she said. "As soon as I looked, I knew."

An ambulance came, and so did doctors, but Win could not be revived. He was dead at age sixty-two. Janet called the embassy and told John Horton that Win had passed away. She realized someone needed to call Michael and George at boarding school and John at college, and someone did. John Leddy, in turn, called his father to tell him that he was going to take Michael and George to Mexico City. "Yes, I heard about Scott," said Ray Leddy. Stoic to the end, he let no more words pass his lips about his former friend's passing.

When Anne Goodpasture heard the news in Washington, she went straight to Jim Angleton's office. The counterintelligence chief had already heard. "I think he's got classified documents at his house," she said. To her way of thinking, Win had no right to have them.

Helms later allowed to congressional investigators that he may have authorized Angleton to go to Mexico City. He said he was worried about the contents of Win's safe. Helms might have guessed that Win had tapes and photos of Oswald. He certainly knew about Win's unpublished memoir and its refutation of the CIA's and the Warren Commission's claims about what the station knew of Oswald's Cuban contacts. He knew how sensitive Angleton and Phillips were about that issue. He himself shared that sensitivity. "There may have been some concern that maybe Scott had something in his safe that might affect the Agency's work," Helms told the investigators with studied casualness. "The Agency just wanted to double check and be sure that there was not anything of that kind there."

Soon, Jim Angleton boarded a plane bound for Mexico City. He, most of all, wanted to bury Win's story forever. In flight, fortified by drink, he recalled his great good friend from their glory days in London and Washington and rehearsed his condolences for the widow.

Afterword

Win Scott ("Willard Curtis"): Scott is buried in the Panteón Americano in Mexico City.

Paula Murray Scott: Win's second wife is buried about fifty yards away.

Kim Philby: The unrepentant communist spy lived in Moscow from 1963 on. He felt neglected by the Soviet government, which he had secretly served for seventeen years. He died on May 11, 1988.

Ray Leddy: Win's former friend went on to serve as a deputy assistant secretary of defense in the late 1960s. He retired to Carlisle, Pennsylvania. He died on March 5, 1976.

Adolfo Lopez Mateos (LITENSOR): The former Mexican president died in Mexico City on September 22, 1969.

Gustavo Díaz Ordaz (LITEMPO-2): The stigma of the Tlatelolco massacre prevented Díaz Ordaz from ever having much of a role in Mexican public life after his retirement in 1970. He died, bitter and disillusioned, on July 15, 1979.

Fernando Gutiérrez Barrios (LITEMPO-4): The chief of the Defensa Federal de Seguridad was promoted to secretary of Gobernacion in the late 1960s. He served until 1985. His control of the Mexican intelligence apparatus gained him a reputation as "the J. Edgar Hoover of Mexico," a man with incriminating secret information on many in the political elite. He died on October 30, 2000.

Luis Echeverría Alvarez (LITEMPO-8): As president of Mexico from 1970 to 1976, his tenure was noted for its leftist foreign policy and lavish domestic spending. In July 2006, he was indicted for genocide in connection with the Tlatelolco massacre of October 1968. The charges were dismissed, reinstated, and dismissed. He lives in Mexico City.

James Angleton: The chief of the Counterintelligence Staff was forced to resign in December 1974 when it was revealed that he had supervised the HTLINGUAL program that opened the mail of hundreds of thousands of American citizens. At that time, he said of President Kennedy's assassination, "A mansion has many rooms and there were many things going on. . . . I am not privy to who struck John." He never explained that remark, prompting author Nina Burleigh to note, "History is left to ponder whether he was simply indulging his taste for metaphor or implying knowledge of a conspiracy." Angleton's unique personality, his deeply thought analysis of the Soviet threat, and his bitter alcoholic decline have generated books, novels, and at least two major motion pictures. He died on May 12, 1987.

David Phillips ("Knight"): After rising to become chief of the CIA's Latin America division in 1974, Phillips retired and founded the Association of Foreign Intelligence Officers to combat critics of the CIA in Congress and the media. He took legal action against authors who alleged or implied that he was involved in Kennedy's assassination but ultimately did not dispute that there had been a conspiracy. As noted earlier, Phillips told a JFK researcher in 1985 that "my final take on the assassination is there was a conspiracy, likely including American intelligence officers." Phillips died of cancer in Washington on July 7, 1988. When his friend and colleague Howard Hunt was asked in 2004 about allegations that Phillips was involved in a JFK conspiracy, Hunt answered, "No comment."

Richard Helms ("Fletcher Knight"): Forced into retirement by President Richard Nixon in January 1973, Helms remained a presence on the Washington social and political scene until his death in October 2002. In his posthumously published autobiography, he wrote, "I have not seen anything, no matter how far-fetched or grossly imagined, that in any way changes my conviction that Lee Harvey Oswald assassinated Kennedy, and that there were no co-conspirators."

George Leddy: Michael's stepbrother is a political activist in Los Angeles. With a Ph.D. in Development Policy and Ecology, George says Win was "a functionary in a system of repression and impunity. He was also a very good father."

Gregory Leddy: Ray Leddy's oldest son is a public relations executive.

Janet Graham Scott: Win's widow lives in Europe.

Allen "Beau" Terry: Win Scott's son from his first marriage is a banker in Birmingham, Alabama.

Michael Scott: A filmmaker who lives in Los Angeles, Michael found his own life story in his father's. He enjoyed learning the routines and methods of men at battle in the complex cloak-and-dagger world of the Cold War, even if it was not always easy to come to terms with the shadowy side of his father's secrets, especially as they involved dirty tricks, personal betrayals, assassins, accused war criminals, and the like. He felt a son's pride at defending his father from the suggestion of one agency official that Win had "gone to seed" at the time of his death. To the contrary, he says his father was a rejuvenated man at the time of the accident that took his life. As for Win's role in the events that led to the assassination of President Kennedy, he concluded that the available records show his father helped cover up some kind of authorized CIA operation involving Lee Harvey Oswald in Mexico City in September 1963, an operation that the agency has never acknowledged. Wherever the ultimate responsibility lay, Michael concluded his father played a central, if unwitting, role in the CIA intelligence failure that culminated in the Dallas tragedy. This conclusion did not diminish his love or admiration for the man who was taken from him too early. "He should be judged," Michael said, "in the context of the times in which he lived."

The Oswald tapes: A CIA officer named Paul Hartman saw them in the mid-1970s. "It was a packet of tapes maybe—I never opened the packet because there was no need for it," Hartman said in secret sworn testimony in 1978. "It must have been a packet three to four inches thick. It looked like several of these reel-to-reel boxes of tapes. These came to me—I'm almost certain, from the Mexico Branch. . . . someone cleaned out a safe and sent it to me to put in the file."

The tapes were probably destroyed in January 1987, a few months after Michael Scott filed his first Freedom of Information Act (FOIA) request for his father's manuscript. Mark Zaid, Michael's attorney in litigation related to his FOIA request, points to a CIA destruction order, dated January 23,

1986, for materials taken from Win Scott's home. The items to be disposed of included material "not generally processed into the central system regarding operational research [including] activities of a sensitive nature or those which were transitory targets of opportunity," according to the order. That indirect language, says attorney Zaid, probably referred to the surveillance tapes that Paul Hartman handled and perhaps to the Oswald photos that CIA officers Stanley Watson and Joe Piccolo said they saw. Tapes and photos were "not generally processed in the CIA's central record keeping" system. They resulted from "operational research." And they related to "sensitive activities" and "transitory targets." In short, the CIA found material evidence related to Kennedy's assassination in Win Scott's home office, hid that evidence from all official investigations over the course of twenty-four years, and then, when Michael Scott started asking for his father's effects, destroyed it.

"It Came to Little" ("Foul Foe"): The only complete copies of Win Scott's 220-page manuscript remain in CIA hands. About 120 pages have been publicly released. Under the terms of a legal settlement reached by Mark Zaid, Michael Scott was allowed to learn more about his father. Thirty-five years after it was written, almost half of Win Scott's life story remains a state secret.

Notes

ABBREVIATIONS USED IN NOTES

AARB: Assassination Records Review Board

GD: Deposition of Anne Goodpasture

HMMW: a CIA dispatch

ICTL: "It Came to Little," Win Scott's unpublished memoir written in 1970

MBOP: Mexico Biography of Power by Enrique Krauze

MCJFK Chronology: Chronological summary of Win Scott's JFK file

MCSHE: Mexico City Station History Excerpts

NSAMP: National Security Archive Mexico Project

PROLOGUE: APRIL 28, 1971

This chapter is based on records in the JFK Assassination Records Collection and interviews. The discussion between Jim Angleton and Janet Scott is based on Angleton's not entirely reliable testimony to congressional investigators, two cables written by John Horton, who was present, and accounts that Janet Scott gave to her children. The re-created dialogue, informed by these sources, relies on the account in Horton's cable, in both its language and exposition.

For example: Horton wrote that Angleton "advised [Janet] against reading the manuscript as it discussed in open way intimate matter of previous marriage."

I re-create the conversation like this:

Angleton: "Janet, you do not want to read what Win wrote."

Janet Scott: "Why not?"

Angleton: "It discusses in an open way intimate matters of his previous marriage."

Another example: John Horton wrote of Janet Scott in his cable: "She seemed appalled at idea of publishing manuscript saying that she realized when [her husband] told her of visit to director [meaning CIA director Dick Helms] something was wrong. She also asked [Angleton] about her husband's motivation in this."

I re-create the exchange as follows:

Janet Scott: "I knew something was wrong when he told me he was going to see Helms. Why do you think he wrote it?"

Angleton recalled that Janet Scott opened the conversation by asking, "Why did it take so long for you to come?" Janet Scott told others about Win's request to ask her to type the manuscript, about her sense of being bullied, if not threatened, by Angleton, and about her dislike of the man. The thought attributed to her, "it would have killed Scottie to see Angleton in his house" is based on a comment she made to me during a telephone interview. It was David Phillips who said Angleton looked like a man whose ectoplasm had run out. See *The Night Watch: 25 Years of Peculiar Service*, 239. The literary license I have taken is faithful to the record.

See House Select Committee on Assassinations Interview of James Angleton, October 5, 1978, 125–129, HSCA/Security Classified Testimony 180-10110-1006. John Horton's cables: Dispatch, DIR to C/WH3, April 29, 1971, 8 pp.; and Dispatch, Eyes Only, to DIR, May 3, 1971. These two cables, written by Horton, Mexico City station chief in 1971, were released by the CIA to Mark Zaid, attorney for Michael Scott. I have also used Michael Scott's notes on a conversation with Janet Scott, October 1, 1995; and my telephone interview with Janet Scott, March 13, 1996. Angleton's testimony is not entirely reliable because he says Win's manuscript was fictional and did not include a chapter on Oswald. The only surviving manuscript is clearly nonfictional and does have a chapter on Oswald.

All quotations from Michael Scott, George Leddy, and Gregory Leddy: Interviews conducted in 2006.

"The agency had taken possession": The Zaid material contains index cards of the contents of the material taken from Scott's home. The material is also described in "Memo from B Hugh Tovar, Chief, Counterintelligence Staff to Chief, Liaison and Oversight Control, PCS: Attachment: Inventory of Mexico City COS Records, May 5, 1977."

"Janet had one urgent request": John Horton gave another account of Angleton's visit to Mexico City. In a memorandum for the record, written on February 25, 1992, Horton stated that he had received a phone call from Mark Zaid asking about Angleton's visit. Horton declined to speak with him but did record some of his memories of the event. Horton sent the memo to the CIA, which later released it to the Assassination Records Review Board (ARRB). Horton's memo is now found in the ARRB material in the JFK Assassination Records Collection.

"pulled a fast one": Horton cable, April 29, 1971.

"some vile knowledge on the part of the agency": Horton memo, February 25, 1992.

Horton was "amazed": Horton memo, February 25, 1992.

Oswald tapes: "HSCA Security Classified Testimony of Melbourne Paul Hartman," October 10, 1978, 29, Records of the House Select Committee on Assassinations, JFK Assassination Records Collection, National Archives (hereafter JFK/HSCA), Record number 180-10110-10003. Hartman testified that he saw boxes of tapes labeled "Oswald" that had been delivered from a safe cleaned out in Mexico City. He said he did not listen to the tapes. Thanks to Gus Russo for calling Hartman's testimony to my attention.

CHAPTER 1. UP FROM ESCATAWPA

This chapter is based on interviews with Michael Scott, Ruth Grammar (Win Scott's sister), and John and Gregory Leddy. It draws on a short memoir that Ruth Grammar wrote of her childhood, as well as Win Scott's unpublished memoir, "It Came to Little," and on his fictionalized account of an Alabama boyhood, *MacGee, MacGill and Me*, written in

1967 under the pen name "Ian Maxwell." The chapter also relies on information found in Michael Warner's *Office of Strategic Services: America's First Intelligence Agency;* Peter Grose's *Gentleman Spy;* Burton Hersh's *The Old Boys: The American Elite and the Origins of the CIA;* and Robin Winks's *Cloak and Gown: Scholars in the Secret War 1939–1961.*

It is informed by the microfilm records of the Office of Strategic Services at the National Archives in College Park, Maryland, particularly the OSS War Diary, X-2 History (hereafter OSS Records and X-2 History).

Declassified portions of Win Scott's FBI file were also consulted, courtesy of Mark Zaid.

Win and Dulles meet a few weeks after the war: The first record of the two men meeting is found in Scott's pocket calendar in June 1945 (hereafter WMS calendar).

Dulles family background: Leonard Mosely, *Dulles: A Biography of Eleanor, Allen and John Foster Dulles and Their Family Network,* 13–38.

On a family trip to Washington: Michael Scott interview, February 9, 2006.

Scott family background: This background comes from "Memories," a nineteen-page memoir written by Ruth Grammar for her children in 1990, and a telephone interview with Grammar, October 27, 2005.

Win's fictional account of Alabama childhood: *MacGee, MacGill and Me.*

"Winston insisted that my father": Grammar interview.

"She had the brightest eyes": *It Came to Little,* unpublished (hereafter *ICTL*), 6.

"fancy pants . . . overeducated failure": *ICTL,* 10–13.

"We were asked to align our chairs carefully": *ICTL,* 17.

"Leddy was a trim, correct man": Interviews with John and Gregory Leddy.

Hemingway story: *ICTL,* 53.

Win retreated to the bar of the Wardman Park Hotel: *ICTL,* 55.

The OSS application: From Personal History Statement, Office of Strategic Services, Winston Mckinley Scott, January 13, 1944, Michael Scott collection.

History of British SIS: Warner, *Office of Strategic Services.*

Winfield Scott in Mexico: Enrique Krauze, *Mexico Biography of Power: A History of Modern Mexico,* 143–146 (hereafter *MBOP*).

Win listened to British and American lectures on the nature of espionage: *ICTL,* 68–70.

In June 1944, Win was off to war: OSS War Diary, X-2 History, OSS London, M1623, Vol. 6 Biographies, Scott, Winston M.

"a small outfit with a big reputation": Warner, *Office of Strategic Services,* 29–30; Hersh, *The Old Boys,* 106–108.

Win meets Winston Churchill: *ICTL,* 67.

CHAPTER 2. THE APPRENTICE PUPPET MASTERS

This chapter is based on *It Came to Little (ICTL);* on his pocket calendars found among his personal effects held by Michael Scott; on Win Scott's correspondence with Paula Murray and others, held by Michael Scott; on the OSS Records and its X-2 History; and on the Norman Holmes Pearson Papers at Beinecke Library, Yale University (hereafter NHP).

The depiction of James Angleton draws on Robin W. Winks, *Cloak and Gown;* Burton Hersh, *The Old Boys;* Tom Mangold, *Cold Warrior: James Jesus Angleton; The CIA's Master Spy Hunter;* Kim Philby, *My Silent War: The Autobiography of a Spy;* and Verne W.

Newton, *The Cambridge Spies: The Untold Story of Maclean, Philby and Burgess in America*. The portrait of Paula Murray comes from the Scott correspondence and a letter written by Paula Murray's sister, Terry Duffy of Dublin, responding to my questions. Details of life in London are drawn from Maureen Waller, *London 1945: Life in the Debris of War*.

"They made a handsome couple": WMS physical description comes from OSS War Diary, X-2 History, OSS London, Microfilm Reel M1623, Vol. 6 Biographies, Scott, Winston M.; Paula Murray's background comes from Terry Duffy interview, and also a letter from Loomis L. Colcord, Child Welfare Worker, to Miss Anne Whinery, Supervisor Adoption Reports Section, Dept. of Welfare and Institutions, City of Alexandria, December 8, 1955, 5 pp.

"I shall never recover": Letter, WMS to PM, September 4, 1945.

"became a spy the next": OSS War Diary, X-2 History, OSS London, M1623, Vol. 6 Biographies, Scott, Winston M.; OSS Records RM 1623, Roll 10, Vol. 2, "July, August, September 1944, London Headquarters," 117–118.

"He had the ULTRA clearance": Cleveland Cram interview, May 1996.

"Here was a field in which OSS": Warner, *Office of Strategic Services*, 29.

"Present and Future Prospects": OSS Records, RM 124, Washington Director's Administrative Files Memorandum: "Present and Future Prospects of Clandestine Resistance Movements in Germany," undated.

A new type of German missile, dubbed the V-2: Waller, *London 1945*, 14.

"Working conditions were wretched": OSS Records, Roll 124, Washington Director's Administrative Files. Memo: To: General William J. Donovan From: James R. Murphy, October 1944.

"Win and his staff worked"; Hadley the "miraculous scavenger": *ITCL*, 65–66.

"Win's job was central": OSS Records, Box 161, Memo, "Recommendation for Award of Bronze Star Medal," July 20, 1945.

Angleton as the star of OSS: Winks, *Cloak and Gown*, 328, 349–350.

Angleton's office and flat: Mangold, *Cold Warrior*, 41; Winks, *Cloak and Gown*, 341.

Angleton identified and targeted: OSS Records, RM 1623, Roll 10, Vol. 2, July, August, September 1944, London Headquarters, 123–125.

Hersh description of Angleton: *The Old Boys*, 178–182.

Pearson as Jimmy Murphy's deputy: Pearson's story is told in detail in *Cloak and Gown*, 247–321.

"These leaflets contained": OSS Records RM 1623, Roll 10, Vol. 2, July, August, September 1944, London Headquarters, 123–125.

Cicely Angleton as "vivacious and bright": The adjectives are Winks's from *Cloak and Gown*, 348.

Cicely wondered about their marriage: Mangold, *Cold Warrior*, 43–44.

"It is my opinion that counter-intelligence": Pearson's thoughts on espionage are found in an undated lecture titled "Counter-Intelligence Double Agents in Neutral Countries," Pearson Papers, Box 1, "OSS materials," NHP.

"Paula came from an accomplished family": Terry Duffy letter.

"I walk alone": Letter, WMS to PM, August 27, 1945.

Difference between U.S. and British SCI units: OSS Records, London X-2 Office, RG 226, Entry 119, Box 20, Folder 142.

The winter of 1945: Waller, *London 1945*, 55–57.

In January 1945, Eisenhower asked: OSS Records, RG 226, Entry 190B, Records Relating to Resistance History, Box 31, File "Winston Scott War Room."

"skillful personal negotiations": OSS Records, 57-102, Box 161, 631/31/63/01, Memo, "Recommendation for Award of Bronze Star Medal, July 20, 1945.

Dulles "played up the possibility of a Nazi retreat": What Win Scott called "the reduit," Burton Hersh calls "the Redoubt." *The Old Boys*, 119–136.

"The Alpine reduit" report: OSS Records, London X-2 Office, RG 226, Entry 119, Box 15, Folder 115, report, "The Alpine Reduit."

"Winston 9 Months Old!!": WMS 1945 pocket calendar.

"giddy rush": Waller, *London 1945*, 69.

Win was formally promoted: OSS Records, London X-2 Office, RG 226, Entry 119, Box 15, Folder 109, Branch Order No. 46, May 7, 1945.

The big news of the day: Waller, *London 1945*, 282, 287.

"God bless you all": Text of Churchill's speech is found on the Web site of the Churchill Society: http://www.churchill-society-london.org.uk/YrVictry.html.

"Pearson clambered up on a stone lion": Winks, *Cloak and Gown*, 251.

CHAPTER 3. HIS FRIEND PHILBY

This chapter is based on the correspondence of Win Scott and Paula Murray, noted as Scott Correspondence (SC); the papers of Norman Holmes Pearson (NHP) in Beinecke Library at Yale University; and the OSS Records in the National Archives, College Park, Maryland. It draws on Philby's autobiography, *My Silent War;* Philip Knightley's *The Master Spy: The Story of Kim Philby;* Anthony Cave Brown's *Treason in the Blood: H. St. John Philby, Kim Philby, and the Spy Case of the Century;* Verne W. Newton's *Cambridge Spies;* and Tom Mangold's *Cold Warrior.*

For the evolution of the OSS into the CIA, I relied on John Ranelagh's *The Agency: The Rise and Decline of the CIA;* and R. Harris Smith's *OSS: The Secret History of America's First Central Intelligence Agency.* For the British perspective, I consulted Richard Aldrich's *The Hidden Hand: British, American and Cold War Secret Intelligence;* Hugh Trevor-Roper's *The Philby Affair;* Nigel West's *The Circus: MI5 Operations 1945–1972;* Tom Bower's *Red Web;* and Maureen Waller's *London, 1945.*

Repeated playing of "I Wish I Knew": Letter, WMS to Paula Murray, August 27, 1945, Michael Scott collection. The lyrics are found on the Lyrics World Web site: http://ntl.matrix.com.br/pfilho/html/top40/index.html.

Win's Bronze Star: Memo, "Recommendation for Awards, Ira H. Parson to Norman H. Pearson," OSS, RG 226/147/New York and London Office records, Box 3, Folder 48.

"the professional equal of its British counterpart": Memorandum, William H. Jackson to Gen. Donovan: "Examination of X-2 Branch," June 21, 1945, OSS Records, Roll 124, Washington Director's Administrative Files.

Donovan's visit and dinner at Claridge's and meeting with Dulles: WMS calendar, June 9, 24, and 28, 1945.

"In early July, Paula Murray told him": Letter, WMS to PM, July 5, 1945.

"Dear Puggy, you must remember": Letter, WMS to PM, August 20, 1945.

"Never have I felt so completely whipped": Letter, WMS to PM, August 21, 1945.

"The time with you was wonderful": Letter, WMS to PM, September 13, 1945.

"the most remarkable spy": Knightley, *The Master Spy*, 1.

Win trudged over to St. James Street: OSS, RG226, Entry 190B, Records Relating to Resistance History, Box 31, File "Winston Scott—War Room," Minutes of a meeting, September 21, 1945, at 3:00 P.M., in the conference room at St. James.

"a notably bewildered group": Philby, *My Silent War*, 74.

"Win stood in line to succeed him [Pearson] as chief": Memorandum, October 24, 1945, OSS Records, Roll 124, Washington Director's Administrative Files.

Win says he wants to take Paula to Latin America: Letter, WMS to PM, November 7, 1945.

"He was so infatuated with Paula": Cleveland Cram interview, May 1996.

Angleton's reunion with wife: Mangold, *Cold Warrior*, 43.

Pearson reports on larger role for Philby's office: Memo, To: SAINT, WASHINGTON, From Saint, London (Puritan), "Changes in British SIS," December 12, 1945.

Win as "demigod": Tom Polgar interview, January 26, 2007.

"a lot of them were refugees from eastern Europe,": Cram interview, May 1996.

"Over lunch, he asked Win": Meals with Philby are noted in WMS pocket calendar on March 28, April 12, and April 16, 1946.

Philby speaks of "certain materials": WMS memo to Colonel William W. Quinn, April 30, 1946; Pearson Papers, Wooden Box No. 1, OSS Materials, "Organization" folder.

"London Station Status": WMS memo to Colonel William W. Quinn, April 30, 1946.

"How can you be so cruel?": Letter, WMS to PM, April 30, 1946.

Pearson's "occasional gossipy letter": WMS letters, passim.

Besse Tate Scott arrives: WMS calendar, July 10, 1946.

"My Darling Pug": Letter, WMS to PM, July 17, 1946.

Win's meetings with Philby grew more frequent: WMS 1946 calendar. In October and November 1946, Win recorded two lunches with Philby, two evening engagements where they were joined by their wives, and a play date at Philby's house for Beau. The nature of U.S.-British collaboration at the time comes from Aldrich, *The Hidden Hand*, 83.

Philby "due for an early change of scenery": Philby, *My Silent War*, 129.

"At a morning meeting with Philby": WMS calendar, December 6, 1946.

"Now that I stop and think": Letter, WMS to PM, December 24, 1946.

"This encounter may have been the point": Anthony Cave Brown, *Treason in the Blood*, 360.

Farewells to Philby: WMS calendar, January 8, 11, 21, 1947; Michael Scott collection, January 19, 1947; Philby recounts the event in *My Silent War*, 129–131.

Leddy letter to Scott: January 31, 1947.

CHAPTER 4. SPIES ON THE RISE

This chapter is based primarily on Win Scott's correspondence and desk calendars and on Kim Philby's *My Silent War*. It also depends on Robin Winks's *Cloak and Gown;* John Early Haynes and Harvey Klehr's *Venona: Decoding Soviet Espionage in America;* Verne W. Newton's *Cambridge Spies;* Christopher Andrew's *The Sword and the Shield: The Mitrokin*

Archive and the Secret History of the KGB; David Martin's *Wilderness of Mirrors: How the Byzantine Intrigues of the Secret War between the CIA and the KGB Seduced and Devoured Key Agents James Jesus Angleton and William King Harvey;* John Ranelagh's *The Agency;* Mark Riebling's *Wedge: The Secret War between the FBI and the CIA;* Edward J. Epstein's *Deception: The Invisible War between the KGB and the CIA;* and Richard Helms's *A Look over My Shoulder: A Life in the Central Intelligence Agency.* I reject the far-fetched analysis in S. J. Hamrick's *Deceiving the Deceivers,* but it has relevant details not found elsewhere. Throughout, the chronology of institutional events relies on Richard Aldrich's *Hidden Hand* and Anne Karalekas's *History of the Central Intelligence Agency.*

Recalled from London station in December 1949: Letter, WMS to PM, December 3, 1949.

Angleton on Staff A: Mangold, *Cold Warrior,* 49.

The OSO-OPC rivalry: *History of the Central Intelligence Agency,* 31–41.

Win helped Dulles on two reports: Cleveland Cram interview; Dulles's reports are described in *History of the Central Intelligence Agency,* 43–44, and Riebling, *Wedge,* 95. One of the studies came about when Secretary of Defense James Forrestal proposed in February 1948 that Dulles write a nonpartisan study of U.S. intelligence needs for publication after the 1948 election; Grose, *Gentleman Spy,* 297. The next month, Dulles met with Win in London. WMS calendar, March 5, 1948.

Ray Leddy joined OPC: Confidential interview.

Besse had left him: Letter, Besse Scott to WMS, February 24, 1949.

"Please tell me you still love me": Letter, WMS to PM, December 3, 1949.

"The Soviet menace was everywhere": Brown, *Treason in the Blood,* 409.

Albanian commandos captured: Bower, *Red Web,* 135.

The CIA's temporary offices on the Mall: Grose, *Gentleman Spy,* 309.

Harvey as frequent lunch companion: WMS calendar, June 10, 11, 20, and 21, 1948.

Harvey as "one hell of a case": Riebling, *Wedge,* 87.

Win mouths greetings to forgotten colleagues: Letter, WMS to PM, January 2, 1950.

"You are, as ever, enormously attractive": Letter, PM to WMS, December 7, 1949.

Win's father dying : Letter, WMS to PM, December 21, 1949.

Besse turned hostile: Letter, WMS to John D. McQueen Jr., March 28, 1953.

Terms of the divorce decree: Letter, William R. Vance to WMS, July 24, 1950.

Win's everlasting regret: Letter, WMS to John D. McQueen Jr., March 28, 1953.

"For better or for worse!": Letter, WMS to PM, December 21, 1949.

Paula's parents think she's "rushing off": Letters, WMS to Paula Murray, January 6–7, 1950.

Win's father died: Letter, WMS to Paula Murray, January 20, 1950.

Win and Paula get married: Application for Marriage License, District of Columbia, February 15, 1950, SC.

Celebrating with Angletons: WMS calendar, February 25, 1950.

"Chief of the most important division": Cram interview.

"Angleton brooded longest": Winks, *Cloak and Gown,* 325–326.

Description of Angleton: Brown, *Treason in the Blood,* 393.

Philby and Angleton in address book: WMS calendar 1950.

Philby on "Anglomania": Philby, *My Silent War*, 150–151.

"There were few restaurants in central Washington": Brown, *Treason in the Blood*, 419.

Jim and Kim spoke on the phone "three or four times a week": Philby, *My Silent War*, 151.

Philby's Thanksgiving at the Angletons': Mangold, *Cold Warrior*, 64.

Hillenkoetter eased out: Hersh, *The Old Boys*, 272.

Win sees Sir Kenneth Strong: WMS calendar, November 7, 1950.

Smith brought in Dulles: Karalekas, *History of the Central Intelligence Agency*, 38; Grose, *Gentleman Spy*, 305; Helms, *A Look over My Shoulder*, 101.

"the genial bluff avuncular figure": Phillips, *Secret Wars Diary*, 118.

Win keeps up with VENONA via old British friends: He boasted of many friends in the General Communications Headquarters in a letter to John Barron, November 25, 1970.

Philby visited Arlington cryptography center: Haynes and Klehr, *Venona*, 51–52.

Philby realizes HOMER is Maclean: Andrew, *The Sword and the Shield*, 157.

Code breakers narrow the list: Newton, *Cambridge Spies*, 318.

On Donald Maclean: See the BBC capsule biography: http://www.bbc.co.uk/history/historic_figures/Maclean_donald.shtm.

Philby's alcohol-fueled party: The incident recurs in the literature of Anglo-American intelligence. The fullest account is Newton, *Cambridge Spies*, 305–310. See also Riebling, *Wedge*, 103–104; Brown, *Treason in the Blood*, 426–427.

Geoff Patterson dined with Win: WMS calendar, Friday, April 13, 1951. For Patterson's role in the Maclean investigation, see Hamrick, *Deceiving the Deceivers*, 51.

Win and Ladd: WMS calendar, April 24, 1951.

Win and Tiltman: WMS calendar, May 2, 1951.

Philby was disturbed: Philby, *My Silent War*, 165.

Flight of Maclean and Burgess: Brown, *Treason in the Blood*, 432; Winks, *Cloak and Gown*, 404.

Philby says "the bird has flown": Philby, *My Silent War*, 172.

Philby's explanation accepted by FBI: Riebling, *Wedge*, 4–5.

Washington Post **story:** *Washington Post*, June 8, 1951, 1.

Harvey investigated Philby: Martin, *Wilderness of Mirrors*, 60–61.

"Whatever Harvey wrote about Philby": Cram interview.

The usually perceptive Angleton: Philby, *My Silent War*, 181.

Win met with Angleton and General Wyman: WMS calendar, June 11, 1951. The men apparently made plans to talk some more because Win made a note in his calendar for another lunch date: "Try to get Jim A. and Gen. Thayer for lunch."

Sillitoe arrived in Washington: Hamrick, *Deceiving the Deceivers*, 127.

Harvey memorandum to Wyman: Martin, *Wilderness of Mirrors*, 56.

Angleton did not submit his memo for another week: Ranelagh, *The Agency*, 153; Martin, *Wilderness of Mirrors*, 56.

Clare Petty on Harvey's and Angleton's assessments of Philby: Mangold, *Cold Warrior*, 65–69.

Cram on Angleton's assessment: Brown, *Treason in the Blood,* 563.

Easton came to Washington: WMS calendar, July 12, 15, 16, and 18, 1951.

"although it was clear that this is what they suspected": Brown, *Treason in the Blood,* 441.

"more than 20,000 pages": Andrew, *The Sword and the Shield,* 160.

MacArthur charged that Philby: Andrew, *The Sword and the Shield,* 160.

Angleton traumatized by Philby: Mangold, *Cold Warrior,* 65–69.

"lodged in the deepest recess of Jim's being": Helms, *A Look over My Shoulder,* 278.

Win on Philby's treachery: Letter, WMS to John Barron, November 25, 1970.

CHAPTER 5. OPERATION SUCCESS

This chapter is based primarily on notes from conversations that Michael had with Morgan Scott, his father's youngest brother; on the recollections of George Leddy; on Win Scott's desk calendar; on correspondence and interviews with friends and family; on material found in the David Atlee Phillips Papers (hereafter DAPP); and on the *Foreign Relations of the United States, 1952–1954, Guatemala* (hereafter *FRUS, Guatemala*), published in 2003, and an earlier, less complete volume in the *FRUS* series, *1952–1954,* vol. 4, *The American Republics* (Guatemala Compilation) (hereafter *FRUS, Vol. 4*).

The story of Operation Success is told most comprehensively by Piero Gleijeses in *Shattered Hope: The Guatemalan Revolution and the United States, 1944–1954.* Also informative are Stephen Schlesinger and Stephen Kinzer, *Bitter Fruit: The Story of the American Coup in Guatemala,* expanded edition; and Richard H. Immerman, *The CIA in Guatemala: The Foreign Policy of Intervention.* The CIA perspective comes from two books by E. Howard Hunt, *Give Us This Day: The Inside Story of the CIA and Bay of Pigs Invasion by One of Its Key Organizers* and *Undercover: Memoirs of an American Secret Agent;* two books by David Phillips, *The Night Watch* and *Secret Wars Diary: My Adventures in Combat, Espionage Operations and Covert Action;* and Richard Helms's posthumous memoir, *A Look over My Shoulder.* Also useful were Evan Thomas's *The Very Best Men, Four Who Dared: The Early Years of the CIA;* and Thomas Powers's *The Man Who Kept the Secrets.*

Ray Leddy's service to the State Department and role in Operation Success are traced in *FRUS, Guatemala* and *FRUS, Vol. 4,* which are available online at http://www.state.gov/r/pa/ho/frus/ike. A vast collection of CIA records on Guatemala is found in the CIA's Electronic Reading Room, Guatemala documents (hereafter CIA ERR Guatemala), online at www.foia.ucia.gov/guatemala.asp. Of special interest is a 238-page report, "Project PBSUCCESS," November 16, 1954, which traces the operation on a daily basis from inception to completion.

Ray Leddy and Win meet: WMS calendar, November 11, 15, 1951.

Leddy role in OPC and move to State: Confidential interview.

Ray and Janet buy a house in Montgomery County: Leddy family interviews.

Scott home "in perfect taste": Letter, Loomis L. Colcord, Child Welfare Worker, to Miss Anne Whinery, Supervisor Adoption Reports Section, Dept. of Welfare and Institutions, City of Alexandria, December 8, 1955, 5 pp.

Parties for Menzies, White, and other Brits: WMS calendar, October 11, 25, 1954; Nigel West interview.

Regulars at the Dulles's house: WMS calendar, May 31, 1951, May 14, 1952, July 17, 1952, May 1, 1954, October 11, 1954. Win recorded cocktails at Frank and Polly Wisner's three times: WMS calendar, June 4, 1952, April 28, 1954, March 15, 1955.

Win at Seaport Inn, Arena Stage: WMS calendar, October 10, 1954, February 14, 1955, June 25, 1955.

"Harvey used his connections": WMS calendar, June 4, 1952.

Poker with Angleton: WMS calendar, August 6, 1954.

Angleton's gambling style: Confidential interview.

Women and children found Angleton delightful: Burleigh, *A Very Private Woman: The Private Life and Unsolved Murder of Presidential Mistress Mary Meyer*, 125–128.

CIA's "halcyon days": Grose, *Gentleman Spy*, 350.

Short of money . . . conditions for seeing Beau: Letter, WMS to John D. McQueen Jr., March 28, 1953.

Besse Tate's threat: Michael Scott collection.

Paula could not stay pregnant: Morgan Scott interview with Michael Scott.

British and French question "rollback"; "The British and American secret services now found themselves increasingly at odds on the ground": Aldrich, *Hidden Hand*, 323.

Dulles buries report on émigrés: Grose, *Gentleman Spy*, 348.

Dulles creates inspector general position; Win becomes IG: WMS calendar, April 1953; Cram interview; Karalekas, *History of the Central Intelligence Agency*, 46.

Poles expose WIN: Bagley, *Spy Wars, Moles, Mysteries and Deadly Games*, 122; Grose, *Gentleman Spy*, 355; *New York Times*, December 20, 1953, 1.

Win writes WIN postmortem for Dulles: WMS calendar, February 2, 18, 20, 24, 1953.

Within hours, the agency's Psychological Strategy Board called a meeting: The State Department was notified of the expropriation via telegram from Guatemala at 6:00 P.M. on August 12. See *FRUS, Guatemala*, Doc. 39, Telegram from Embassy in Guatemala, August 12, 1953. The Psychological Strategy Board issued its authorization at an "informal meeting" on the same day. See *FRUS, Guatemala*, Doc. 40. A note in the memorandum by Frank Wisner spoke of the "extremely high operational priority."

Smith on "no direct dealings": *FRUS, Guatemala*, Doc. 40.

"Czechoslovakia in reverse": *FRUS, Guatemala*, Doc. 40. The full text of the State Department paper is found in *FRUS, Vol. 4*, Doc. 17, Draft Policy Paper Prepared in the Bureau of Inter-American Affairs, August 19, 1953.

Sole supporter was Ray Leddy: *FRUS, Guatemala*, Doc. 49, Memorandum from the Chief of the Western Hemisphere Division to the Deputy Director for Plans of the Central Intelligence Agency (Wisner), September 10, 1953.

"a man who could clam up": Gleijeses, *Shattered Hope*, 245.

"improbable that the Communists will gain direct control": *FRUS, Guatemala*, Doc. 34, Letter from the Ambassador to Guatemala (Schoenfeld) to the Secretary of State's Special Assistant for Intelligence (Armstrong), February 13, 1953.

J. C. King on Arbenz's "substantial popular support": *FRUS, Guatemala*, Doc. 51, "Memorandum for the Record," September 11, 1953.

Operation Success cost $3 million: *FRUS, Guatemala*, Doc. 287.

Dulles on Guatemala as "a top priority operation": FRUS, Guatemala, Doc. 66, Contact Report, November 16, 1953.

Hunt on "theatrically handsome" Phillips: Hunt, *Give Us This Day*, 26.

David Phillips biography: Helen Phillips interview; unpublished manuscript, "Popcorn in the Andes," by David Phillips, DAPP; Phillips, *Night Watch*, 3–29.

Helms pointed out the weak spots or absented himself: Hersh, *The Old Boys*, 344.

Armas had little support: Gleijeses, *Shattered Hope*, 248; Thomas, *Very Best Men*, 109–126.

Win meetings with Tracey Barnes and J. C. King: WMS calendar, March 19, 1953, October 28, 1953. Win met with King, Wisner, and Helms, December 28, 1953.

"trained pistoleros" and "high level State thinking": Memorandum for the Record, March 9, 1954, FRUS, Guatemala, Doc. 113.

"Elimination List": FRUS, Guatemala, Doc. 119, "Memorandum from C/[title not declassified], Central Intelligence Agency, to all Staff officers, March 31, 1954. The agency later claimed that no assassinations were ever carried out. See CIA ERR Guatemala, CIA and Guatemala Assassination Proposals, 1952–1954, CIA History Staff Analysis, by Gerald K. Haynes, June 1995, 6–10. In 1979, the agency informed the White House that it had traced the names of 174 Guatemalan communists included in the various disposal lists. "In no case did it appear that any of them died as a result of the upheaval in Guatemala." See CIA ERR Guatemala, Letter to the Honorable Thomas Farmer (White House) Re: PBSUCCESS Project, October 15, 1979. The independent National Security Archive notes that the agency deleted the names of the targeted individuals from the public version of Haynes's report, "making it impossible to verify that none of them were killed during or in the aftermath of the coup."

Win on "a perfectly workable idea": CIA ERR Guatemala, PBSUCCESS: Daily Notes RE Arms Shipments to Guatemala, 7 April 1954 to 29 June 1954, 11–12, 37–38.

"get rid of this stinker": Robe, *Eisenhower and Latin America: The Foreign Policy of Anti-Communism*, 58.

Phillips and Voice of Liberation: Thomas, *Very Best Men*, 107–126; Phillips, *Night Watch*, 44–47.

"Unrest turned to hysteria": Tim Weiner, *Legacy of Ashes: The History of the CIA*, 99.

Win and Ray met at the Roger Smith Hotel: WMS calendar, June 17, 1954.

Castillo Armas reads Phillips script: Immerman, *CIA in Guatemala*, 164–168; Phillips, *Night Watch*, 48.

"armed groups of our liberation movement are advancing": FRUS, Guatemala, Doc. 202, editorial note.

American secret operatives sought to persuade senior military officers to move against Arbenz: FRUS, Guatemala, Doc. 217, Telegram from the Central Intelligence Agency to the CIA Station in Guatemala, June 21, 1954. See also Michael Warner, "Lessons Unlearned: The CIA's Internal Probe of the Bay of Pigs Affair," *Studies in Intelligence* 42 (Winter 1998–1999).

On execution of Operation Success: FRUS, Guatemala, Doc. 287, Memorandum from William Robertson, July 8, 1954.

"crushed by . . . his limited imagination": Gleijeses, *Shattered Hope*, 325; see also Grose, *Gentleman Spy*, 382; Thomas, *Very Best Men*, 122; Phillips, *Night Watch*, 48; Immerman, *CIA in Guatemala*, 167–168; and Hersh, *The Old Boys*, 351.

Guatemala operation run out of the Leddys' basement: Gregory Leddy interview.

Phillips's Distinguished Intelligence Medal citation: "Recommendation for Honors Award: Phillips David Atlee," undated, CIA/JFK 104-10128-10119.

Win lunches with Angleton: WMS calendar, June 28, 1954.

George Leddy comments: Interview.

CHAPTER 6. A NEW LIFE

This chapter is based on my interviews with Michael Scott and Michael's interview of Morgan Scott, Martha Caldwell, and Michael Caldwell; on interviews with George and Gregory Leddy; and on Win Scott's desk calendar for the years 1954, 1955, and 1956.

Additional perspective came from David M. Barrett, *The CIA and Congress: The Untold Story from Truman to Kennedy.*

Ruth Grammar contacts Michael: Michael Scott interview.

"She had about six of them in a row": Morgan Scott interview.

Eisenhower creates Doolittle and Clark committees: Barrett, *The CIA and Congress,* 195. See also letter, Eisenhower, Dwight D., Secret, to James Harold Doolittle, July 26, 1954, in *The Papers of Dwight David Eisenhower,* ed. L. Galambos, Doc. 993, www.eisenhowermemorial.org/presidential-papers/first-term/documents/993.cfm.

Need to compartmentalize: Riebling, *Wedge,* 60.

Win briefs Doolittle: WMS calendar, July 13, 14, and 26, 1954. He also briefed Doolittle's committee on August 10, 12, and 17, 1954.

Win meets with Clark Committee: November 3, 4, 29; December 4, 9, 1954.

Doolittle's comment on "a vast and sprawling organization": Weiner, *Legacy of Ashes,* 108.

Doolittle on "fair play": Weiner, *Legacy of Ashes,* 109; Martin, *Wilderness of Mirrors,* 60–61.

Lovett-Bruce report: The contents of the Lovett-Bruce report, still classified after fifty years, have been reported in two books: Weiner, *Legacy of Ashes,* 133–135, and Grose, *Gentleman Spy,* 445–448. I have quoted from both.

Trips to Rehoboth: WMS calendar, August 7–8, 21–22, 1954.

Paula returned to Ireland: WMS calendar, November 15, 1954.

Win note to send Paula flowers: WMS calendar, November 15, 1954.

Meeting with Deirdre, Father Moffat: WMS calendar, November 24, 1954.

Drinks and dinner with Harvey: WMS calendar, November 17, 23, 1954.

Angleton promoted to CI chief: Mangold, *Cold Warrior,* 50.

"Intensification of the CIA's counterintelligence efforts": Mangold, *Cold Warrior,* 51.

"Harvey was heeding the call to glory": Martin, *Wilderness of Mirrors,* 63.

Beau's last visit: WMS calendar, June 18–20, 1954; Michael Scott timeline.

The Leddys' visit: WMS calendar, April 28, 1955.

Michael's birth and arrival: Letter, Loomis L. Colcord, Child Welfare Worker, to Miss Anne Whinery, Supervisor Adoption Reports Section, Dept. of Welfare and Institutions, City of Alexandria, December 8, 1955, 5 pp.

Win arranged for thyroid operation: From Michael Scott's declassified notes on his visit to CIA, April 4, 1998.

Win and Paula's sixth anniversary: WMS calendar, February 15, 1956.

Win meets with Dulles: WMS calendar, February 16, 1956. Win wrote, "See Mr. Dulles re: Mex-."

CHAPTER 7. THE AMERICAN PROCONSUL

This chapter is based primarily on declassified portions of the Mexico City Station History written by Anne Goodpasture in the early 1970s; the two-part deposition Goodpasture gave to the Assassination Records Review Board in December 1995 and April 1998; and my interview with Goodpasture on May 2–3, 2005. It also draws on interviews with Michael Scott and with Eugenia Francis, whose mother was a good friend of Paula Scott's. It is informed by Philip Agee's portrait of Win in *Inside the Company: CIA Diary*. I interviewed Mel Proctor, a retired State Department official who served in Mexico City at the time. I also interviewed three other retired State Department officials; two retired CIA officers; and one associate of station officer, George Munro, all of whom knew Win Scott in Mexico City. I have respected their request for anonymity.

The names of the agents in the LITEMPO network are still classified information. However, their identities can be definitively determined two ways: (1) by examining internal evidence and (2) through comparison of contemporaneous documents from different sources. The identification of individual LITEMPO agents is described in more detail in the notes.

Information about the Mexican presidency, society, and security services comes from Enrique Krauze, *Mexico Biography of Power (MBOP)*; Sergio Aguayo Quezada, *La Charola: Una historia de los servicios de inteligencia en Mexico;* Jorge Castaneda, *Companero: The Life and Death of Che Guevara;* and Norman Caulfield, *Mexican Workers and the State: From the Pofiriato to NAFTA.*

Goodpasture's history of the Mexico City station: The declassified portions, entitled "Mexico City Station History, Excerpts" (hereafter MCSHE), are found in the National Archives, JFK Assassination Records Collection, Russ Holmes work file, JFK/CIA RIF 104-10414-10124.

Goodpasture's excellence in "flaps and seals": Fitness Report, Anne L. Goodpasture, November 20, 1958, JFK/CIA RIF 104-10193-10084. In Duty Category number 5, "flaps & seals work," Scott gave her a rating of "6," which denoted that she performed "this duty in an outstanding manner found in very few individuals holding similar jobs." See also Goodpasture deposition to the Assassination Records Review Board, December 16, 1995, 14 (hereafter GD, Part I. The April 1998 deposition is GD, Part II).

Julia McWilliams aka Julia Child: Goodpasture interview, May 2–3, 2005.

Phillips on Angleton as Delphic Oracle: *Night Watch,* 189.

"a chiseled, cadaverous face": Riebling, *Wedge,* 136–137.

Counterintelligence Staff had ninety-six professionals, seventy-five clerical workers: The statistics come from an untitled eleven-volume study of Angleton's tenure as counterintelligence chief, written by Cleveland Cram in the late 1970s. The study has never been declassified, but certain portions, including these statistics, are quoted in a January 15, 1997, memo prepared by the Assassination Records Review Board, which had access to the complete study: "ARRB-CIA issues: Win Scott," 20 pp., JFK/CIA RIF 104-10332-10015.

Angleton had a job for Goodpasture: GD, Part I, 10–11, 37.

"Shortly after I arrived . . . I caught on real quick": GD, Part I, 56.

Goodpasture's memory: Dan Hardway and Edwin Lopez, *Oswald, the CIA and Mexico City: The Lopez-Hardway Report (aka the "Lopez Report")* 2003 release, 49 (hereafter LHR). Win's deputy Alan White is quoted as saying Goodpasture had a "marvelous memory."

Paula's golfing: Eugenia Francis interview; retired CIA officer interview.

Win and Paula smitten with baby: Letter, Richard W. Copeland, Commissioner of Public Welfare, to Hon. Paul E. Brown, undated.

Win insisted the station occupy the eighteenth floor: Mel Proctor interview.

Howard Hunt in Mexico City: MCSHE, 7; Hunt, *Undercover,* 96–97.

Hunt joins Operation Success: Hunt, *Undercover,* 183; Phillips, *Night Watch,* 33–37.

Dulles gave him a pay increase: MCSHE, 24. The station chief job was reclassified as GS-17 on the Civil Service pay schedule, which mandated an increased salary.

Winfield Scott history: Krauze, *MBOP,* 143–144.

Win had enough sense to fib about his name: Michael Scott and Ruth Grammar interviews. Michael said his father collected Winfield Scott memorabilia but had no evidence to suggest a relationship. Win's sister Ruth Grammar said that she recalled an occasion where her mother was asked if she had named her oldest son after Winfield Scott and that she replied no.

On the Mexican public and government in the 1950s: Octavio Paz introduction to Elena Poniatowska, *Massacre in Mexico,* xiv. Paz wrote that "by 1950, the [Mexican] groups holding the reins of power in the economic and political sphere—including the majority of technicians and intellectuals—began to feel a certain sense of self-satisfaction at the progress that had been made since the consolidation of the post-Revolutionary regime: political stability, impressive completed public works projects, the birth of a sizeable middle class. In fact, the revolution had been co-opted by the PRI and by a financial oligarchy with intimate ties to huge American corporations."

Guillermo Gonzalez Camarena, inventor of color TV: Archivo General de Nacion, *Mexico: Un Siglo en Imagenes, 1900–2000,* 233.

Progressive Mexico and the countryside: Krauze, *MBOP,* 604.

Watching U.S. communists in Mexico City: GD, Part I, 23–24.

DFS arrests Fidel Castro: Daniel James, *Che Guevara: A Biography,* 86–87; Casteneda, *Companero,* 90. Casteneda writes, "Although Guevara and Cuban historians referred several times to the possible role of U.S. intelligence services in the arrest and subsequent interrogations, everything points to a strictly Mexican Cuban operation. And a rather lenient one at that." Gutiérrez Barrios, the arresting official, said, "I don't feel that the Americans exerted any pressure at all. . . . The Americans were never present, and I do know that because I was in control, especially at the Ministry of Interior." Another account of Castro's arrest is found in Robert E. Quirk, *Fidel Castro.*

Castro had Leonov's business card: Casteneda, *Companero,* 89; Thomas J. Patterson, *Contesting Castro: The United States and the Triumph of the Cuban Revolution,* 32.

Nikolai Leonov and the KGB: This information comes from a translation of "On the Front Lines in Mexico City," a chapter of Leonov's memoir, published in Russian and translated for this book by Elena Sharpova (hereafter Leonov chapter).

Castro departs for Cuba: Casteneda, *Companero,* 98.

Leonov's role in Soviet embassy, views on Mexico: Leonov chapter.

Dulles wanted a "stepped up program": MCSHE, 24.

Win clashed with Ambassador Robert Hill: Confidential interview with an embassy staffer, MCSHE, 448–449; townhouse purchase, MCSHE, 28.

Win traced visa applicants and party guests: MCSHE, 449. Goodpasture wrote, "There was a marked increase in services performed by the station for all Embassy components after 1956. This included traces of names of visa applicants, persons on the Ambassador's guest lists and employee applicants. The COS [chief of station] took an active part in the Ambassador's staff meetings and he briefed visiting U.S. Congressmen and newspapermen."

Win overhauls station's file room: GD, Part I, 48.

"He read everything": GD, Part I, 56.

Win's handwriting style: GD, Part I, 56.

"You could tell from his office": Confidential interview.

Win ran operations himself: GD, Part I, 13; Goodpasture interview, May 2–3, 2005.

Station as "the most elaborately equipped and effective": Testimony of John Scelso [John Whitten] to the Church Committee, May 7, 1976, 48, JFK/HSCA, Security Classified Testimony, 180-10131-10330.

"Hill never learned two words of Spanish": Confidential interview.

"tremendous amount going on . . . 'the real embassy' ": Confidential interview.

The exact moment that Win arrived: MCSHE, 381–382, 409.

"He was a distinguished-looking man": Confidential interview.

LITEMPO as "a productive and effective relationship": MCSHE, 381–382.

Win chose George Munro: Confidential interview; MCSHE, 420.

Munro biography and relations with Win: Confidential interview.

Díaz Ordaz chose Emilio Bolanos: Confidential interview; MCSHE, 420.

LITEMPO budget: MCSHE, 420.

Lopez Mateos as suave, industrious: Krauze, *MBOP,* 628–630.

"Liberty is fruitful only when it is accompanied by order": "Adolfo Lopez Mateos, President of Mexico from '58 to '64, Dies," *New York Times,* September 23, 1969, 47.

Lopez Mateos's amorous exploits: Krauze, *MBOP,* 628.

Díaz Ordaz as homely, hardworking lawyer: Krauze, *MBOP,* 673.

Story about cars for girlfriends: Agee, *Inside the Company,: CIA Diary,* 275.

LITEMPO "paid too much": Whitten wrote this in Goodpasture's 1964 fitness evaluation, March 4, 1964.

Castro's victory a religious revelation: Krauze, *MBOP,* 651–652.

U.S. officialdom worried about "instability": Caufield, *Mexican Workers and the State,* 107.

Thirty-eight sympathy strikes: Caufield, *Mexican Workers and the State,* 116–117.

Díaz Ordaz pounced: Krauze, *MBOP,* 632–635.

"severity of the challenge explains the harsh punishment": Caufield, *Mexican Workers and the State,* 116–118.

Leddy felt overshadowed by Win: Confidential interview, retired State Department official.

Lopez Mateos wanted a reasonable balance: Krauze, *MBOP*, 652.

"bounty of technology": MCSHE, 34.

Thirty telephone lines tapped: Memo, Anne Goodpasture to John Leader, Background on Mexico Station Support Assets, February 10, 1977.

Wiretapping of Lazaro Cardenas: Dispatch, Win Scott to Chief, WH Division, Monthly Operational Report for Project LIENVOY, August 23, 1963. "The following lines were covered during the month of July . . . 10-29-69 Movimiento de Liberacion Nacional." The MLN was Cardenas's political organization.

Goodpasture delivered transcripts to Win: MCSHE, 34, 410.

Díaz Ordaz as LITEMPO-2: Dispatch, Scott to Chief of WH Division, Operational Report, October 1–31, 1963, November 7, 1963, JFK/CIA RIF 104-10211-10102. Scott wrote, "As of end of October 1963, it was well-known that LITEMPO-2 would be the PRI candidate [in the 1964 presidential election]." Díaz Ordaz was the PRI candidate in 1964; therefore, Díaz Ordaz was LITEMPO-2.

"When there was union, peasant, student or electoral repression": Krauze, *MBOP*, 673–674.

Gutiérrez Barrios as LITEMPO-4: Gutiérrez Barrios's identity as LITEMPO-4 is confirmed by comparison of two documents. In June 1964, Gutiérrez Barrios signed a sworn statement to the U.S. government stating that he had interrogated Sylvia Duran, a Mexican woman who had contact with accused presidential assassin Lee Harvey Oswald in September 1963. Three months later, Win noted in a cable to headquarters that the Mexican official known as LITEMPO-4 interrogated Duran. Therefore, Gutiérrez Barrios and LITEMPO-4 were one and the same person.

The signed statement from Gutiérrez Barrios is found in Warren Commission Exhibit 1154, Note from the Mexican Ministry of Foreign Affairs, June 9, 1964, Annex 7.

Win's cable about LITEMPO-4 is listed on page 83 of a detailed chronology of the Mexico City station files on the JFK assassination that was compiled by Anne Goodpasture, in 1968, at the direction of Win Scott. This comprehensive and reliable document is referred to hereafter as the MCJFK Chronology. Goodpasture's notation reads, "COS checked with LITEMPO-4 who personally participated in interrogation of DURAN re OSWALD." The chronology is found in the JFK/ARRB 1996 Release, 104-10014-10046.

Luis Echeverria as LITEMPO-8: The MCJFK Chronology stated that three members of the Warren Commission visited with a Mexican official identified as LITEMPO-8 at 11:30 on the morning of April 10, 1964, as part of their investigation of the assassination of President Kennedy. The summary noted various points of conversation, such as the need for the Americans to submit their questions in writing to the foreign minister. Another report on that visit, written by one of the Warren investigators, David Slawson, stated they visited with deputy interior minister Luis Echeverría at 11:30 on the morning of April 10. Slawson recorded the same points of conversation noted in the MCJFK Chronology. Therefore, LITEMPO-8 and Echeverría were the same person. See MCJFK Chronology 73, JFK/CIA RIF 104-10013-10004; and "Memorandum for the Record on Trip to Mexico City," from W. David Slawson, April 22, 1964, CIA Segregated Collection, JFK/CIA RIF 104-10086-10254.

"I like this guy. Send him again": Interview with Miguel Nazar Haro, February 2006.

"She had such a great manner"; Paula was sad: Eugenia Francis interview.

Michael crashes car: Michael Scott interview, February 2006.

CHAPTER 8. AMCIGAR

This chapter is based on the declassified excerpts from the Mexico City Station History (MCSHE), written by Anne Goodpasture in 1971. The story of the AMCIGAR program is found in regular dispatches between the Mexico City Station, known as MEXI DISPATCHES, and the communications of the deputy director's office, DIR, that are part of the Win Scott material in the JFK Assassination Records Collection at the National Archives. It also draws on a deposition that David Phillips gave in 1983 in connection with his lawsuit against JFK conspiracy author Donald Freed.

Also useful was the Cuban government perspective provided by retired Cuban counterintelligence chief Fabian Escalante in *The Secret War: CIA Covert Operations against Cuba 1959–62.*

Castro met Nixon; "Dictatorships are a shameful blot": Franklin, *Cuba and the United States,* 20.

Dulles brought Eisenhower a plan to overthrow Castro: Hersh, *The Old Boys,* 428; Phillips, *Night Watch,* 87.

Win was briefed on the concept at a conference of Western Hemisphere station chiefs: MCSHE, 228. The conference was held in Panama, May 23–28, 1960. When Scott returned to Mexico, the Cuban target became the station's top priority, with "every investigative asset" deployed.

The model was Guatemala 1954: Immerman, *The CIA in Guatemala,* 187–197. Dave Phillips called Operation Zapata "the Guatemala scenario"; *Night Watch,* 86.

Arbenz drinking in Mexico City: Thomas, *Very Best Men,* 12.

The cast of Operation Success officers involved in Operation Zapata: Phillips, *Night Watch,* 88; Thomas, *Very Best Men,* 242; Weiner, *Legacy of Ashes,* 156.

Dave Phillips took on the same duties for the Cuban exile cause: Phillips, *Night Watch,* 88.

Ray Leddy report and Senate Internal Security Subcommittee: Hugh Thomas, *The Cuban Revolution,* 453.

Plan called for the Cuban exiles' political leadership to establish itself in San José, Costa Rica: Escalante, *Secret War,* 50.

The Americans decided the AMCIGARs should settle in Mexico City: Cable, Droller to MEXI, July 25, 1961, 104-10171-101224. This and all other cables cited in this chapter are from MEXI DISPATCHES in RG 233, CIA Segregated Collection of the JFK Assassination Records Collection, Box 89, Reel 46, Folder 8.

Win checked with Lopez Mateos and Díaz Ordaz, who said they had no objections as long as the Cubans did not violate any Mexican laws: Win summarized the story of the AMCIGARS in Mexico in a cable, MEXI to Director, September 4, 1960.

Win relayed the word to Washington: Cable, MEXI to Director, September 4, 1960.

Hunt thought Win had promised a welcome mat: Hunt, *Give Us This Day,* 40–50.

Phillips as the most experienced on Zapata team, a lecturer on Latin American affairs: Deposition of David A. Phillips, March 25, 1983, *Phillips v. Freed,* 223.

Phillips on "our unfortunate assumption": A copy of the speech is attached to Memorandum, Chief, Personnel Security Division to Acting Chief, Employment Activity Branch, Subject: Phillips, David Atlee: March 15, 1956.

Phillips in Cuba, 1958–1959: Phillips, *Night Watch,* 76–83.

Cover of a public relations firm on Humboldt Street: Phillips, *Night Watch,* 77. Phillips also published a newsletter for American businessmen, a copy of which is reproduced in Jon Elliston, *Psy-War on Cuba: The Declassified History of U.S. Anti-Castro Propaganda,* 201.

Phillips met Che Guevara in a Havana coffee shop: Phillips, *Night Watch,* 80–81.

Hunt had visited for a conference of station chiefs in 1956: Hunt, *Undercover,* 80–90.

Hunt returned briefly in early 1960: Phillips, *Night Watch,* 88.

Hunt to Phillips on "a few mulatas": Phillips, *Night Watch,* 88.

Hunt on Cuban exile politicians as "shallow thinkers and opportunists": Hunt, *Give Us This Day,* 81.

Dulles told Eisenhower there was "no real leader," called them "prima donnas": Newman, *Oswald and the CIA,* 200.

Carlos Todd, editor of the *Times of Havana,* figured out that Phillips was a CIA man: Cable, Director, To: Habana, Security Review of Phillips, August 31, 1959.

AMCIGARs complain to Hunt about having to go to Mexico City: Cable, Droller to MEXI, July 25, 1961, 104-10171-101224. In the cable, Hunt reported he had met with FRD Executive Committee. "They have agreed to apply for visas and complete move to Mexico by August 15, 1960."

Phillips determined to make the best of things: Phillips's job title was chief of Western Hemisphere 4, a propaganda office identified on cables as C/WH/4/Prop. His thoughts are found in a memo dated August 1960, 104-10171-10223.

Cubans set up a radio link to their allies in Cuba: Cable, MEXI to Director, August 19, 1960, 104-10171-10216.

DFS picked up on the transmitter's signal and took action: In an August 27, 1960, cable, Hunt, identified by the code name TWICKER, wrote that the fact that the purchase plan was known to the DFS had an "unsettling effect" on exile leader Tony Varona. Hunt said he would inform Varona that no U.S. government money could be spent on a "unilateral effort" outside the "AMCIGAR framework." Cable, TWICKER to Director, August 27, 1960, 104-10171-10209.

Cubans complained to Hunt about Mexican interference: Cable, MEXI to Director, September 4, 1960, 104-10171-10169.

Mexicans stepped up the pressure: Hunt, *Give Us This Day,* 55.

"HQ should understand that AMCIGAR members are seizing upon any and all factors": Cable, TWICKER to Director, August 26, 1960, 104-10171-10190.

All requests to enter the country referred to Gobernacion: Cable, MEXI to Director, September 4, 1960, 104-10171-10169.

Win on "long delays and/or extra-legal payments": Win quoted MEXI DIS-PATCHES in RG 233 CIA Segregated Collection Box 89, Reel 46, Folder 8, 2 of 4.

Cubans barred from boarding commercial airline flights: Gobernacion in Mexico told a CIA asset that the Mexican government had terminated all Cuban immigration regardless of whether visas had already been approved. Cable, TWICKER to Director, August 27, 1960, 104-10171-10185.

Hunt impressed by Artime: Hunt, *Give Us This Day*, 27–30.

Artime bombarded his CIA friends: Hunt reported that Artime called four times from Detroit due to lack of a visa. Cable, TWICKER to Director, August 31, 1960.

The president assured Win he wanted to be helpful: MEXI to Director cable, September 4, 1960, 104-10171-10169.

Win enumerated a half dozen security violations: Cable, MEXI to Director, September 4, 1960, 104-10171-10169. Win also wrote, "MEXI concurs with Hqs [on] transfer [of] AMCIGAR [to] Miami area."

"As we flew east across the Gulf": Hunt, *Give Us This Day*, 58.

A certain five-step procedure: From MEXI DISPATCHES, Folder 8, 2 of 4, RG 233 CIA Segregated Collection, Box 89, Reel 46.

Subsecretary Luis Echeverria would handle the details: From MEXI DIS-PATCHES, Folder 8, 2 of 4, RG 233 CIA Segregated Collection Box 89, Reel 46.

"A special channel was set up in November 1960": From MEXI DISPATCHES, Folder 8, 2 of 4, RG 233 CIA Segregated Collection Box 89, Reel 46.

Meeting between Dulles and Lopez Mateos: Memo, [Title Withheld] Meeting, January 14, 1961, JFK-MISC 104-10310-10001, 7 pp.

Operation Zapata proved to be a perfect failure: The literature on the Bay of Pigs is vast. I relied on Haynes Johnson, *The Bay of Pigs;* the CIA inspector general's report of October 1961, as published in *Bay of Pigs Declassified*, edited by Peter Kornbluh; and Don Bohning's *The Castro Obsession,* 31–67. Especially revealing of the internal CIA reaction are Phillips, *The Night Watch,* and Hunt, *Give Us This Day*.

There was no student uprising: Interviews with former DRE leaders, Isidro Borja, Manuel Salvat, and Luis Fernandez Rocha.

Artime acknowledged that the CIA planned and directed the invasion: Franklin, *Cuba and the United States,* 42.

Allen Dulles blamed a failure of nerve in the White House: Phillips, *Secret Wars Diary,* 167.

Bissell blamed "political compromises"; Kirkpatrick stirred anger: Kornbluh, *Bay of Pigs Declassified,* 13.

Helms blamed the limitations of the plan: Helms, *A Look over My Shoulder,* 186.

Phillips was drinking heavily: Phillips tells the story himself in *Night Watch,* 109–110.

"Secret shenanigans couldn't do what armies are supposed to do": Phillips, *Night Watch,* 109–110.

Munro hated Kennedy with a passion: Confidential interview.

"The luscious toll/of all you say and do repays": All poetry cited in this chapter is from *My Love,* by "Ian Maxwell."

JFK told aides he wanted to "splinter the Agency into a thousand pieces": Quoted in Taylor Branch and George Crile, "The Kennedy Vendetta," *Harper's,* August 1975, 50.

Kennedy signed three national security memoranda: John Prados, *The Presidents' Secret Wars: CIA and Pentagon Covert Operations since World War II,* 209.

Kennedy rejected a State Department proposal: Kornbluh, *Bay of Pigs Declassified,* 15.

"a busy interregnum marked with flashes of abrupt change": Helms, *A Look over My Shoulder,* 190.

Win's breakfasts with Lopez Mateos: Fergie Dempster interview; Brian Bell interview; Anne Goodpasture interview.

Bell recalled Mann saying: Brian Bell, letter to the editor, *Washington Post,* March 28, 1996.

Dulles on access to Lopez Mateos: Cable, Director to MEXI "for Scott from Dulles," August 28, 1961, JFK/CIA RIF 104-10183-10106.

Angleton seeks to model counterespionage effort in Mexico: MCSHE, 59.

Win was wary of agents operating independently on his turf: MCSHE, 355.

"They were like two boxers in the ring": Confidential interview.

Establishment of HTLINGUAL; a thousand letters opened per month; "vigorously deny": Extracts from CI History, JFK/CIA RIF 104-10301-1001 (hereafter Extracts from CI History).

Angleton had special files with newspaper stories about intercepted communications of elected officials: Extracts from CI History.

JFK affair with Mary Meyer: Burleigh, *A Very Private Woman,* 195.

Angleton's story about Mary Meyer, JFK, and LSD: Burleigh, *A Very Private Woman,* 212.

Angleton's knowledge of the JFK–Mary Meyer affair: *A Very Private Woman,* 196.

Michael's vivid memory of Paula: Michael Scott interview.

At the suggestion of Win's brother Morgan, Paula flew to Atlanta: Morgan Scott interview; Michael Scott's declassified notes from reading "It Came to Little" manuscript at CIA headquarters, April 4, 1998.

Win "always wore a dark suit": Goodpasture interview, May 2, 2005.

The station was "aggressive and well-managed": MCSHE, 39.

Mann wanted to know Lopez Mateos position on agrarian reform: Memorandum for the file: "Visit with LI [redacted]," 21 November 1961, CIA/JFK 104-10183-10103, and MEXI-DIR, November 21, 1961; "At the request of Ambassador Mann," CIA/JFK, 104-10183-10104.

Castro had just expropriated 70,000 acres of property owned by U.S. sugar companies: Franklin, *Cuba and the United States,* 24.

Win escorted Mann to Los Pinos: MEXI-DIR, "COS took Ambassador Mann to Private Meeting," December 4, 1961.

The ambassador agreed not to tell his superiors: MEXI-DIR, "COS Took Ambassador Mann to Private Meeting," December 4, 1961.

Helms mandate to get something done on Cuba: Helms, *A Look over My Shoulder,* 198.

Janet Leddy leaves her husband: Gregory Leddy interview.

"He faced all of his challenges": John Leddy, telephone and e-mail interview, July 29, 2006.

Mexico abstains in OAS vote on Cuba: Franklin, *Cuba and the United States,* 48.

Kennedy brings in Lansdale to work on Cuba; Helms is skeptical: Helms, *A Look over My Shoulder,* 198–201.

Helms serving Bobby Kennedy: Helms, *A Look over My Shoulder,* 165–185.

LIMOTOR generated a steady stream of reports: Dispatch, Chief of Station Mexico City to Chief, WH Division, LIMOTOR Progress Report January–July 1963, October 30, 1963, JFK/CIA RIF 104-10211-10070.

LIEVICT student group: Dispatch, Chief of Station Mexico City to Chief, WH Division, LIEVICT Status Report for May and June 1963, October 17, 1963, JFK/CIA RIF 104-10092-10089.

LILISP: Dispatch, Chief of Station Mexico City to Chief, WH Division, KUWOLF-LILISP, October 14, 1963, JFK/CIA RIF 104-10092-10069.

LITAINT: Cable to Chief KURIOT, from Chief of Station, Mexico City, Subject "Operational Monthly Report, 1–30 Sept. 1963," CIA/JFK RIF 104-10211-010445. David Phillips wrote about planting stink bombs in the Cuban consulate in the first draft of his memoir, "The Night Watch," which he submitted to the agency for prepublication review. He was asked to remove the passage, and he did. Memo from George T. Kalaris to DDO, Subject: "The Night Watch, by David A. Phillips," June 23, 1976, CIA/JFK RIF 104-10105-10118.

Phillips was guiding thirteen propaganda projects: Phillips Fitness Report, June 5, 1962, JFK/CIA RIF 101-10194-10031.

"He is intelligent, imaginative": Phillips Fitness Report, June 5, 1962, JFK/CIA RIF 101-10194-10031.

"I think he trusted me": Phillips testimony to the House Select Committee on Assassinations, April 25, 1978, 30.

Phillips impressed by Win's memory: Phillips, *Night Watch,* 116–117.

CHAPTER 10. KNIGHT

Rural disorders broke out: *New York Times,* June 10, 1962.

Special National Intelligence Estimate: SNIE, 81-62, "Security Conditions in Mexico," June 13, 1962, 1–4, National Security File, National Intelligence Estimates, Box 8, File 81 Mexico, LBJ Library.

"Diverse forces in Mexican official, economic and religious life": *New York Times,* June 23, 1962.

Kennedy's arrival on June 29: *New York Times,* June 30, 1962, 1.

A huge success for both presidents: *New York Times,* July 1, 1962, 1.

"I never heard him complain about his job": David Groves interview.

"Swift, strong, spirited and philosophic": Phillips, *Secret Wars Diary,* 213. Phillips thought that his colleague Richard Welch, assassinated by a shadowy Greek terrorist group in 1976, embodied these qualities.

"It took him a long time to get over that": Helen Phillips interview.

He spoke of firing guns: See Phillips's novel *The Carlos Contract: A Novel of International Terrorism.*

"Madam, you have no *idea* what I do in my job": I was told this by a woman who requested anonymity.

"a guy with a good imagination": Confidential interview.

Phillips as "Knight": Hunt, *Give Us This Day,* 26; Phillips, *Night Watch,* 88.

Phillips meets JFK: Phillips, *Night Watch,* 122–123; Helen Phillips interviews.

"a particularly useful assignment": Unclassified letter, Tom Mann to Dave Phillips, August 9, 1962.

DRE first came to his attention in February 1960: Phillips, *Night Watch,* 93; Elliston, *Psy-War in Cuba,* 201. Fabian Escalante, retired counterintelligence officer of Cuba's Dirigencia General de Inteligencia, said in a 1995 interview that the DGI had a reliable report that put two DRE founding members, Manuel Salvat and Chilo Borja, in Phillips's office in Havana along with Antonio Veciana in this period. Former DRE members had no recollection of such a meeting but did not dispute that Phillips supported their efforts. See "Transcript of Proceedings between Cuban officials and JFK Historians," Nassau Beach Hotel, December 7–9, 1995, 43–44; interviews with Isidro Borja and Manuel Salvat.

Mikoyan's visit to Havana: Alberto Muller interview.

DRE leaders fled to Miami: The story of the DRE is told in a pamphlet that the group published in the summer of 1962 entitled "Those Who Rebel and Those Who Surrender"; Crozier interview, October 1, 1997; HSCA interview with Ross Crozier, January 13, 1978, 3–5.

DRE leaders impressed Phillips and Hunt: Phillips, *Night Watch,* 93; Hunt, *Give Us This Day,* 85; Howard Hunt interview, November 25, 1996.

Muller in Sierra Maestra: Muller interview.

DRE planted bombs that disrupted a campus speech by Castro: "Not Afraid to Die," *Time,* September 7, 1962.

DRE burned down El Encanto: "Not Afraid to Die," *Time,* September 7, 1962.

DRE show on Radio Swan: "Not Afraid to Die," *Time,* September 7, 1962; Elliston, *Psy-War on Cuba,* 59.

Bay of Pigs fiasco devastated the DRE's network in Cuba: "Those Who Rebel and Those Who Surrender."

CIA "conceived, funded and controlled" the DRE: The quotation comes from a CIA memo, Garrison and the Kennedy assassination, June 1, 1967, as quoted in Newman, *Oswald and the CIA,* 325.

DRE's sizeable following: The agency's "Counter/Revolutionary Handbook," sent to the Kennedy White House on October 10, 1962, estimated the DRE's membership at more than 3,000 people, largest of the seven exile groups profiled.

DRE as "instrument of U.S. policy": Paul D. Bethel, *The Losers: The Definitive Report, by an Eyewitness, of the Communist Conquest of Cuba and the Soviet Penetration in Latin America,* 340.

Phillips visited Miami "quite often": HSCA interview of Doug Gupton, August 22, 1978. "Gupton" was a pseudonym for William Kent, according to Phillips.

Crozier took over the handling of AMSPELL: Crozier interview, September 21, 1997.

"There was a mutuality of interest": HSCA interview of Doug Gupton.

DRE could keep a secret: Crozier interview, September 21, 1997.

"The new generation": Interview with Nestor Sanchez, December 19, 1997.

Bill Harvey was busy: Reeves, *President Kennedy*, 335.

Building the resistance movement was not easy: Helms, *A Look over My Shoulder*, 209–210.

"some of the Attorney General's actions bordered on the traitorous": Martin, *Wilderness of Mirrors*, 137.

Shackley quoting Harvey saying "I need authority": Bayard Stockton, *Flawed Patriot: The Rise and Fall of CIA Legend Bill Harvey*, 127.

Rocha stepped into the breach: Rocha interview.

Few cared to discourage Cuban patriots: Crozier interview; Nestor Sanchez interview; Sam Halpern interview.

The DRE struck: "Havana Suburb Is Shelled in Sea Raid by Exile Group," *New York Times*, August 26, 1962, 1; "Havana Area Is Shelled; Castro's Charge of U.S. Aid in Sortie Rejected," *Washington Post*, August 26, 1962. Also "Students Explain Shelling in Cuba," *New York Times*, August 26, 1962, 28; "Exclusive! How Students Shelled Havana," *New York Journal*, August, 30, 1962; "Not Afraid to Die," *Time*, September 7, 1962; interviews with Manuel Salvat, Jose Basulto, Isidro Borja, and Jose Antonio Lanuza.

CIA uses Lem Jones public relations agency: Phillips, *Night Watch*, 101.

"consulted by telephone with members of his staff in Washington": "Havana Area Is Shelled; Castro's Charge of U.S. Aid in Sortie Rejected," *Washington Post*, August 26, 1962.

"Spur of the moment" attack in which the U.S. government had no involvement or prior knowledge: Quoted in "Havana Suburb Is Shelled in Sea Raid by Exile Group," *New York Times*, August 26, 1962, 1.

CIA giving the DRE $51,000 a month: Memorandum for: Mr. Sterling Cottrell, Financial Payments Made by the Central Intelligence Agency to Cuban Exile Organizations, April 1963, JFK Library, National Security Files, Box 52 "Cuba—Subjects—Intelligence."

Helms chides Bobby Kennedy on Cuba: *Foreign Relations of the United States, 1961–1963*, vol. 11, *Cuban Missile Crisis and Aftermath* (hereafter *FRUS, Vol. 11*), Doc. No. 19, Helms Memorandum for the Record, October 16, 1962.

CHAPTER 11. DARKNESS

This chapter is based on interviews with Michael Scott, Anne Goodpasture, a retired State Department officer who requested confidentiality, and Eugenia Francis. Information about Paula's death comes from the letter written by Paula's sister, Terry Duffy. I also quote from the transcripts of interviews with Cleveland Cram and Clare Petty done by author Dick Russell for his book *The Man Who Knew Too Much*.

"to the right of George Wallace": Goodpasture interview, May 2, 2005.

Deirdre could see that her sister's health was not good: "Paula Scott (nee Murray) A Recollection and Reflection by Her Sister Terry Duffy," December 30, 2006 (hereafter Duffy Letter).

She played golf with Anne Goodpasture: Goodpasture interview.

Michael's seventh birthday party: Scott interview.

Goodpasture hears of Paula's death: Goodpasture interview.

Death certificate: Obtained at the Archivo General de Nacion in Mexico City, February 2006.

"Win was not himself": Confidential interview with retired State Department official.

Clare Petty on Win's story: Petty interview with Dick Russell, July 4, 1992.

Cram on double agent story: Cleveland Cram interview with Dick Russell, June 3, 1992.

Over the years, Michael picked up other bits and pieces from friends of Paula's: Confidential interviews.

"My feeling is that Paula committed suicide": Confidential interview.

Sister informed of Paula's death: Duffy Letter.

CHAPTER 12. WEDDING IN LAS LOMAS

Anne Goodpasture saw a man "in deep distress": Goodpasture interview, May 2, 2005.

"carrying a bulging satchel": Phillips, *Night Watch*, 116.

"he was arrogant": Mel Proctor interview, March 1996.

Tom Mann wanted to know what position Lopez Mateos was going to take: Krauze, *MBOP*, 674.

President Kennedy presided over a team of deeply divided advisers: Aleksandr Fursenko and Timothy Naftali, *"One Hell of a Gamble,"* 216–290; Laurence Chang and Peter Kornbluh, eds., *The Cuban Missile Crisis 1962: A National Security Archive Documents Reader.*

Kennedy said he could not hold out much longer: Fursenko and Naftali, *"One Hell of a Gamble,"* 285; Chang and Kornbluh, *Cuban Missile Crisis 1962*, 378.

Khrushchev's concession letter to Kennedy: *FRUS, Vol. 11,* Doc. 102, "Message from Chairman Khrushchev to President Kennedy," October 28, 1962.

Basulto bought the cannon for $300: Basulto interview.

"Exiles Tell of Missiles Hidden in Cuba Caves": *Washington Star,* November 5, 1962, 1.

"We liked each other and we had dinner together": Phillips deposition in *Phillips v. Donald Freed,* March 25, 1983, 88 and 258–259.

"They were good friends": Telephone interview with Maria O'Leary, September 2006.

The *Star* story angered President Kennedy: *FRUS, Vol. 11,* Doc. 154, Summary Record of the 21st Meeting of the Executive Committee of the National Security Council, November 6, 1962.

Kennedy blew up: *FRUS, Vol. 11,* Doc. 170, Summary Record of the 24th Meeting of the Executive Committee of the National Security Council, November 12, 1962.

Helms grills the DRE leaders: Memorandum for the Record, "Mr Helms' Conversation with Luis Fernandez Rocha and Jose Maria Lasa of the DRE Regarding Their Organization's Relationship with the Agency," November 13, 1962, 7 pp.

"This new man will be able to come to me": Memorandum for the Record, "Mr Helms' Conversation with Luis Fernandez Rocha and Jose Maria Lasa of the DRE Regarding Their Organization's Relationship with the Agency," November 13, 1962.

Joannides was serving as deputy chief of psychological warfare: Fitness Evaluation, George E. Joannides, 1 April 1963–31 March 1964, found in "Five Fitness Reports on Joannides George," CIA/JFK RIF 104-10304-1000 (hereafter Joannides Fitness Reports).

He introduced himself as "Howard": Interviews with Luis Fernandez Rocha, Tony Lanuza, and Juan Manuel Salvat.

Win's wedding plans: Paul Deutz interview, November 2006.

"It hurt Win's reputation": William Pryce interview.

"he was one of the most competent political officers": Brian Bell interview.

"Scavenger of men": Confidential interview.

Leddy hired Eddie Hidalgo: Gregory Leddy interview.

"You can get me out of Mexico easier than you can get Win Scott out of Mexico": Mel Proctor interview.

Mann feared the conflict between Win and Ray would end with an "explosion": Letter, Thomas C. Mann to John Ordway, Chief, Personnel Operations Division, Dept. of State, Sept. 30, 1963, Mann Chronological files (correspondence), Thomas C. Mann papers, Texas Collection, Baylor University.

Mann balked: Bill Pryce interview.

"We had secret service personnel galore": Deutz interview.

"The gathering was relatively small": Deutz interview.

"Enlace de Janet Graham y Winston MacKinley Scott": *Excelsior*, December 24, 1962, section B.

"Remember, the law was on Ray's side": Pryce interview.

Christmas in Cuernavaca: Michael Scott, Gregory Leddy interviews.

CHAPTER 13. *"YOU MIGHT HAVE HAD A SEVEN DAYS IN MAY"*

Win walked into Dave Phillips's office: Phillips, *Night Watch*, 126–134.

Phillips and Scott families: Helen Phillips interview.

"the most outstanding Covert Action officer": Phillips Fitness Report, May 26, 1963, JFK/CIA RIF 101-10194-10030.

"a close friendship": Goodpasture interview, May 2–3, 2005.

JFK on "unleashing" the exiles: "'Unleashing' Exiles Not a Solution to Cuba Problem, Kennedy Says," *Washington Post*, April 25, 1963.

FitzGerald meets with Phillips: Phillips, *Night Watch*, 125.

Silver platter for FitzGerald: Anne Goodpasture interview.

Phillips on McCone's "canny premonition": Phillips, *Night Watch*, 125.

Helms as point man on Cuba: Helms, *A Look over My Shoulder*, 198.

"He thought he was a real James Bond": Helen Phillips interview.

Phillips describes his mission in Mexico: Phillips, *Night Watch*, 125.

Phillips receives LIENVOY transcripts: GD, Part I, 61.

Impersonation operation involving Eldon Hensen: Cable concerning unidentified American phoning Cuba Embassy, July 19, 1963, JFK/CIA RIF 104-10014-10044. See also Newman's discussion in *Oswald and the CIA*, 262–263.

Phillips describes himself as a "consultant" on anti-Castro propaganda operations: Phillips deposition, *Hunt v. Weberman*, September 30, 1980, 40.

Seconda Derrota: Enrique Ros, a Cuban historian sympathetic to the Miami exiles, entitled his book about 1961–1962, *De Giron a la Crisis de los Cohetes: La Segunda Derrota*. In English, the title reads *From the Bay of Pigs to the Missile Crisis: The Second Defeat*.

Operation Northwoods: The key documents are found in "Northwoods," a 197-page compilation of documents from the Joint Chiefs of Staff. JCS/JFK 202-100002-10104. James Bamford quotations come from *Body of Secrets: Anatomy of the Ultra-Secret National Security Agency*, 87–90.

Lemnitzer pressed for consideration of "plans for creating plausible pretext to use force," and JFK replied, "We were not discussing the use of U.S. military force": Memorandum for the Record, Brig. Gen. Edwin Lansdale, Subject; Meeting with the President, March 16, 1962, U.S. Dept. of the Army, Califano Papers, Army, CIA/JFK 198-10004-10020.

"inherently extremely risky in our democratic system": Bamford, *Body of Secrets*, 89.

JFK's Cuba policy took shape: FRUS, Vol. 11, Docs. 333, 334, 335, 346, and 348. Document 346 is a CIA paper, dated June 8, 1963, outlining the new Cuba program. Document 348, a June 19 memo, documents Kennedy's approval of the new policy of "autonomous groups."

Helms's doubts about RFK and Cuba: Helms, *A Look over My Shoulder*, 203.

Helms revived contact with Rolando Cubela: U.S. Senate, *Alleged Assassination Plots Involving Foreign Leaders: An Interim Report of the Select Committee to Study Government Operations with Respect to Intelligence Activities*, 88–89, 174–180; Thomas, *Very Best Men*, 299–301. In his posthumous memoir Helms repeats his less-than-credible claim that AMLASH was not recruited for an assassination plot; *A Look over My Shoulder*, 229–231.

Win's men had pitched Cubela in 1961: Background information on Rolando, April 13, 1966 (Cubela Background Brief), CIA Segregated Collection, JFK/CIA RIF 104-10101-10010.

Helms recontacted Cubela in 1963: Cubela Background Brief. In his memoirs, Helms minimized the agency's relationship with Cubela by stating, inaccurately, that the CIA's interest in Cubela began in "mid-October 1963." In fact, after the agency had first pitched him two years earlier and attempted to recruit him again in August 1962, Helms's aide Nestor Sanchez had met with Cubela in Brazil and France in September 1963. Helms's account obscured a rather more extensive history that he never cared to be candid about.

Cubela was a proven gun: Cubela Background Brief. See also George Crile III, "The Riddle of AMLASH," *Washington Post*, May 2, 1976.

Bobby's Cuban allies: Lamar Waldron, with Thom Hartmann, *Ultimate Sacrifice: John and Robert Kennedy, the Plan for a Coup in Cuba and the Murder of JFK*, 153–173. The argument at the heart of *Ultimate Sacrifice*, that the AMWORLD program amounted to a secret plan for a coup in Cuba in December 1963 involving a top Cuban official, Juan

Almeida and Che Guevera that was preempted by a Mafia assassination conspiracy, is conjecture. The notion that Guevara was involved in CIA machinations against the Castro government is indefensible. The claim of a Mafia assassination conspiracy is unsupported by the evidence that the authors present. Nonetheless, the book includes new and useful information about RFK's Cuban allies and the extent of Pentagon planning in late 1963 for an invasion of Cuba.

AMWORLD: All quotations from Book Dispatch: "AMWORLD—Background of program, operational support, requirements and procedural rules," June 28, 1963.

Phillips handled AMWORLD business in Mexico: Memo to COS, Mexico City, Re: "Safehouse," HMMW12052, October 31, 1963.

Win stepped up surveillance of the Cubans: MCSHE, 42.

Win hired four more secretaries: MCSHE, 42.

LIFIRE picks up on travels of Vincent Lee, head of the pro-Castro Fair Play for Cuba Committee: Mexico City Station JFK Chronology (MCJFK Chronology), 51, JFK/CIA RIF 104-10127-10207.

"the usual great amount" of "personality and operational material": Dispatch HMM23434, from RG 233 CIA Segregated Collection, Box 63, Reel 23, Folder 3.

"Positive intelligence" and "security information": MCSHE, 439.

Top priorities in security intelligence: MCSHE, 439.

DRE sent word to Helms: Cable JMWAVE-DIR, February 22, 1963. The cable reported that a DRE leader "reported present AMSPELL mood favors action ops of Havana raid type. AMSPELL feels strong on necessity action that intends to proceed even if KUBARK were to discontinue [deleted] financial support." The leader said he "intends this alert on raid to constitute compliance gentleman's agreement has with DCI."

Alpha 66 struck a Soviet freighter: "Exiles Described 2 New Cuba Raids," *New York Times,* March 20, 1963, 2. Antonio Veciana, the leader of Alpha 66, later told congressional investigators that his CIA handler, a man whom he knew as "Maurice Bishop," had encouraged the actions. Ross Crozier independently told those same investigators that Dave Phillips had used the cover name "Maurice Bishop." But Phillips denied under oath that he ever used the name Bishop, and Veciana, when he finally met Phillips, said he was not the man he knew as "Maurice Bishop." See Gaeton Fonzi, *The Last Investigation,* 391–396.

Bobby Kennedy cracked down: Statement by the Departments of Justice and State, March 30, 1963. See also "U.S. Curbs Miami Exiles to Prevent Raids on Cuba," *New York Times,* April 1, 1963, 1, which says that eighteen exile leaders would be required to get permission to leave the Miami area. Four top DRE leaders were on the list. The DRE records at the University of Miami Library include letters from the INS granting permission for DRE leaders to travel outside of Dade County.

"abandonment, treachery and broken promises": Quoted in "Russians Pull Out of Cuba," *New York Times,* April 4, 1963, 1.

Shackley moved to cut off AMSPELL funding: Chief of Station JM/Wave to Chief of Special Affairs Staff, April 3, 1963.

Helms overruled him: DIR to JMWAVE, April 4, 1963. Headquarters repeated the point in an April 29 cable, stating, "AMSPELL-KUBARK relationship should not be terminated without prior approval HQS."

"But sometimes you want freewheeling": Nestor Sanchez interview, December 19, 1997.

"Instead of standing firm": Hunt; *Give Us This Day*, 13–14.

Harvey visits Rosselli: Shackley, *Spymaster*, 127.

Angleton and Harvey countenanced the flouting of Kennedy's Cuba policy: Angleton Testimony to the Rockefeller Commission, June 19, 1975, 65–66.

Harvey "not a frivolous man": Angleton testimony to Church Committee, February 6, 1976, 27–28.

"We owed a deep obligation to the men in Miami": Angleton quoted in Dick Russell, "Little Havana's Reign of Terror," *New Times*, October 29, 1976.

"It is inconceivable that a secret intelligence arm of the government": *Senate Select Committee to Study Government Operations with Respect to Intelligence Activities* (hereafter *Church Committee*), Hearings, Vol. II, "Huston Plan," 72–73; Mangold, *Cold Warrior*, 351.

"You don't get involved in covert-type operations": Nestor Sanchez interview.

"You're dealing with two guys in the White House": Sam Halpern interview, December 17, 1997.

Bundy on "busy-ness": FRUS, Vol. 11, Doc. 344, Summary Record of 7th Meeting of the Standing Group of the National Security Council, May 28, 1963.

"you might have had a *Seven Days in May*": Halpern interview.

JFK's interest in promoting a movie version of *Seven Days in May*: David Talbot, *Brothers: The Hidden History of the Kennedy Years*, 148.

"Backstage with Bobby": *Miami News*, July 14, 1963.

Phillips's friendship with Hendrix: Deposition of David A. Phillips, March 25, 1983, *Phillips v. Freed*, 111.

"Development of Hendrix as source": Cable, JMWAVE to DIR, October 29, 1962.

CHAPTER 14. A BLIP NAMED OSWALD
This chapter is based on interviews with Brian Bell, G. Robert Blakey, Isidro Borja, Ross Crozier, David Groves, Dan Hardway, Sam Halpern, Bill Hood, Peter Jessup, Howard Hunt, Tony Lanuza, Ed Lopez, Helen Phillips, Luis Fernandez Rocha, Jane Roman, Manuel Salvat, Nestor Sanchez, Ted Shackley, and Antonio Veciana. Three retired Foreign Service Officers and two retired CIA officers were also interviewed. They requested anonymity.

It also draws on the Oswald chapter of Win Scott's unpublished manuscript, *It Came to Little*, by "Ian Maxwell" (*ICTL*); on Edwin Lopez and Dan Hardway, *Oswald, the CIA and Mexico City: The Lopez-Hardway Report (aka the "Lopez Report")*, introduction by Rex Bradford (*LHR*); on the Report of the House Select Committee on Assassinations, June 1978, and accompanying volumes (hereafter HSCA Report); and on the records of the Directorio Revolucionario Estudiantil in the Cuban Heritage Collection at the University of Miami's Richter Library (hereafter DRE Papers).

Oswald's biography: The life of the accused assassin is one of the most contested stories in American history. I have drawn on accounts that scholars and the reading public have found the most credible, while often disagreeing with their analysis. Norman Mailer, *Oswald's Tale: An American Mystery*, strikes a fine balance between open-mindedness and precision. John Newman's *Oswald and the CIA* is the most detailed examination of the CIA's paper trail on the alleged assassin. Anthony Summers's *Not in Your Lifetime: The Definitive Book on the JFK Assassination* is the most persuasive and well-documented case for a conspiracy. Ray LaFontaine and Mary LaFontaine's *Oswald Talked: New Evidence in the JFK Assassination* has the best portrait of the anti-Castro milieu in Dallas in 1963. Gerald Posner's *Case Closed: Lee Harvey Oswald and the Assassination of JFK* is the best brief for the Warren Commission. Priscilla Johnson McMillan's *Marina and Lee* is outdated but still informative. Gus Russo's *Live by the Sword: The Secret War against Castro and the Death of JFK* is one of the first books to delve into the body of JFK records that has emerged since the late 1990s. Michael L. Kurtz's *The JFK Assassination Debates: Lone Gunman versus Conspiracy* is a useful and up-to-date reference. James P. Hosty Jr.'s *Assignment Oswald*, with Thomas Hosty, provides the perspective of a Dallas FBI agent. Harold Weisberg's *Oswald in New Orleans: Case of Conspiracy with the CIA* is cranky, outdated, and occasionally incomprehensible, but its polemic lays bare the problems posed by Oswald's time in New Orleans. Jean Davison's *Oswald's Game* presents the case for Oswald as disturbed loner. Joan Mellen's *A Farewell to Justice: Jim Garrison, JFK's Assassination and the Case That Should Have Changed History* combines factual permissiveness with some credible new information. Whenever possible, I rely on facts agreed upon by authors of different interpretations of JFK's assassination.

Counterintelligence Staff and U.S. defectors to Soviet Union: Newman, *Oswald and the CIA*, 171–173.

Helms "amazed" at the delay in opening of Oswald file: Deposition of Richard Helms to the House Select Committee on Assassinations, September 28, 1978, 90 HSCA/CIA Segregated Collection, 180-10147-10234.

FBI talks to Oswald upon his return from Russia: Hosty, *Assignment Oswald*, 43–44.

Eyewitnesses saw Oswald in offices of Guy Banister: Summers, *Not in Your Lifetime*, 215–244; Kurtz, *JFK Assassination Debates*, 186–187.

DRE received $51,000 a month: Memorandum for: Mr. Sterling Cottrell, Financial Payments Made by the Central Intelligence Agency to Cuban Exile Organizations, April 1963, JFK Library, National Security Files, Box 52, "Cuba—Subjects—Intelligence."

Joannides's "excellent job in . . . handling" the DRE and promotion to chief of the Psychological Warfare branch in Miami: Joannides Fitness Reports.

Oswald wrote to Vincent Lee, executive director of the FPCC: Mailer, *Oswald's Tale*, 568–569.

Oswald and the DRE in New Orleans: Mailer, *Oswald's Tale*, 550–662; Summers, *Not in Your Lifetime*, 215–244; Russo, *Live by the Sword*, 191–206; Posner, *Case Closed*, 121–169; LaFontaine and LaFontaine, *Oswald Talked*, 139–162; and PBS *Frontline* show, "Who Was Lee Harvey Oswald?" November 16, 1993. Transcript no. 1205, 29–38. The account in *The Warren Commission Report*, 407–408, 419, and 728–729, is notable for its omissions. In its account of Oswald's clashes with Bringuier, the report failed to mention the name of the Cuban Student Directorate or the DRE. Carlos Bringuier's account is found in *Red Friday*. Bringuier also testified to the Warren Commission on April 7–8, 1964 (hereafter Bringuier WC Testimony) and the House Select Committee on Assassinations, May 12, 1978 (hereafter Bringuier HSCA Testimony).

Bringuier approached by Warren DeBrueys: *New York Times*, November 23, 1963; Bringuier HSCA Testimony, 70–77.

Bringuier suspected that Oswald had been sent by the FBI or the CIA: *New York Times,* November 23, 1963.

Three members of the DRE delegation spotted Oswald: According to various documents in the DRE papers, they were Celso Hernandez, Miguel Cruz, and Carlos Quiroga.

Oswald "seemed to have set them up": Martello, Warren Commission, vol. 10, p. 61.

Bringuier wrote to Tony Lanuza: Bringuier shared copies of his original letters. The letters also appear in edited form in a special issue of the DRE's monthly publication, *Trinchera,* "President of USA Assassinated," issued on November 23, 1963, DRE Records.

Lanuza shared the news with Fernandez Rocha: Lanuza, Fernandez Rocha interviews.

Fernandez Rocha's meetings with Joannides: Fernandez Rocha interviews.

Bringuier notified his friend Chilo Borja: DRE Records.

Borja and Bringuier as childhood friends: Borja interview.

"This is one of the Cubans who collaborated with me against the Fair Play for Cuba Committee here in New Orleans": DRE records, Departamento Militar, Seccion de Inteligencia, "Confidencial." This file includes dossiers on more than a dozen DRE members, including Celso Hernandez. The note about the collaboration against the FPCC appears in the margin of Hernandez's dossier.

Bringuier sent Carlos Quiroga to visit Oswald: LaFontaine and LaFontaine, *Oswald Talked,* 156–157; McMillan, *Marina and Lee,* 470–472.

Quiroga delivered a stack of FPCC pamphlets: Newman, *Oswald and the CIA,* 339–341; LaFontaine and LaFontaine, *Oswald Talked,* 167.

Quiroga as FBI informant: FBI, Oswald Headquarters File, 105-82555, Section 221, 77 Airtel To: SAC New Orleans, From: Director FBI, November 14, 1964.

Quiroga reported back to Bringuier: Testimony of Carlos Bringuier Sr. to HSCA, 88–91, HSCA CIA RIF 280-20075-10066; Bringuier, *Red Friday,* 32–35.

Bringuier made inquiries with Ed Butler: Bringuier HSCA Testimony, 92.

The CIA's contacts with INCA: Memorandum for the Record, Possible DRE Animus towards President Kennedy, by Arthur Dooley, April 3, 1967, JFK/CIA RIF 104-10181-10113. See also Mellen, *Farewell to Justice,* 68.

Butler called HUAC: LaFontaine and LaFontaine, *Oswald Talked,* 159; McMillan, *Marina and Lee,* 472–473.

Stuckey made a call to the FBI: Davison, *Oswald's Game,* 170.

Butler talked to Bringuier: Bringuier, *Red Friday,* 35.

A local TV news report on Oswald and Cubans on August 21: Mailer, *Oswald's Tale,* 550–662. The footage can be found in the audiovisual section of the JFK Assassination Records Collection, National Archives, College Park, Maryland.

Charges against the Cubans were dismissed: *New Orleans Times-Picayune,* August 13, 1963.

Stuckey interviewed Oswald for a brief news report: Posner, *Case Closed,* 159; Mailer, *Oswald's Tale,* 550–662.

Stuckey invited Oswald and Bringuier to debate Cuba: LaFontaine and LaFontaine, *Oswald Talked,* 158; Posner, *Case Closed,* 159.

Transcript of the *Latin Listening Post* show: Warren Commission Volumes, Stuckey Exhibit No. 2; Mailer, *Oswald's Tale,* 579–591.

Stuckey made a tape of the show: Mailer, *Oswald's Tale,* 586.

"We Cubans who want to regain our freedom in Cuba": Bringuier press release and *"Open Letter to the People of New Orleans"* are found in the Warren Commission Volumes, Bringuier Exhibits 3 and 4.

Phillips praised the group's leaders: Phillips, *Night Watch,* 93.

Phillips on "a very important group both in Havana and Miami": Phillips HSCA Testimony, April 25, 1978, 76, HSCA Records, Security Classified Testimony, HSCA/JFK RIF180-10131-10327.

Phillips received reports from Crozier and Kent: HSCA Report, Appendix to Hearings, Vol. X *"Anti-Castro Activities and Organizations,"* 48–49; interview of "Doug Gupton," August 22, 1978, HSCA/JFK Security Classified File 180-10110-10124. Phillips acknowledged "Gupton" was William Kent and that he supervised both Kent and Crozier; Phillips HSCA Testimony, April 25, 1978, 73–76.

"Dave Phillips ran that for us": Deposition of E. Howard Hunt, HSCA, November 3, 1978, Part II, 29.

Phillips spent time at a CIA training camp in New Orleans: Memorandum for Chief, CI/R&A Subject Garrison Investigation: Belle Chasse Training Camp, October 26, 1967, JFK/CIA RIF 104-10170-10261.

Phillips on DeBrueys; "I remember having been in touch with him": Phillips said so under oath in a deposition he gave on September 30, 1980, in a lawsuit; *E. Howard Hunt Jr. vs. A. J. Weberman,* 9.

DeBrueys's responsibilities: Hosty, *Assignment Oswald,* 71–76.

"That was what the CIA wanted": Lanuza interview.

"That's what the money was for": Borja interview.

Joannides adjudicates dispute involving DRE's Costa Rica chapter: Memo, August 8, 1963, DRE Records.

AMSPELL mission of "political action, propaganda, intelligence collection and a hemisphere-wide apparatus": The phrase appears in Fitness Report, George Joannides, January 1, 1963–July 31, 1963, in "Five Fitness Reports."

"Lee Harvey Oswald was a totally unknown name": Halpern interview.

June Cobb as Phillips agent: Cobb had been a CIA asset since 1960. She was assigned the cryptonym AMUPAS/1. See Memo, "Pierson, Jean," June 6, 1960, JFK/CIA RIF 104-10174-10024. When Cobb moved to Mexico City in 1961, her cryptonym changed to LICOOKY/1. Cobb gathered intelligence on the Fair Play for Cuba Committee using the name of "Clarinda E. Sharpe." Dispatch, Chief of Station, Mexico City, to Chief WH Division, Subject: Viola June Cobb, August 23, 1962, JFK/CIA RIF 104-10175-10365. In October 1963, Scott approved Cobb for further use; COS Mexico City to Chief, WH Division, LICOOKY/1 Action Requested: Process Operational Approval, October 4, 1963.

Phillips interested in the FPCC: Newman, *Oswald and the CIA,* 241–243.

Phillips spied on FPCC chapter in northern Virginia: Newman, *Oswald and the CIA,* 241.

Phillips asked McCord about informing the FBI: Newman, *Oswald and the CIA,* 243.

Joannides did not talk about AMSPELL to the HSCA: I broke the story of Joannides's role as liaison to the HSCA in Jefferson Morley, "Revelation: 1963," *Miami New Times,* April 21, 2001.

The seventeen-month gap: When the JFK Records Review Board asked the CIA to account for the missing monthly progress reports in January 1998, CIA official Barry Harrelson replied that the agency did not really have a relationship with the DRE in 1963. "During this period in question, major policy difference between the DRE and Agency developed. . . . These differences caused the Agency to reduce the level of funding for the DRE. It also replaced the officer designated to deal with the DRE. Then, about the same time, the monthly reports tailed off. It seems probable these two events are linked and that reporting in the form of monthly reports simply stopped."

This statement was almost entirely inaccurate. The supposed "major policy differences" between the CIA and the DRE did not prevent George Joannides from supplying the group's Miami headquarters $25,000 a month for most of 1963. The reduction in CIA funding for AMSPELL did not occur until November 15, 1963, a week before Kennedy was killed. Yet the monthly reports are missing for all of 1963. Thus the two events—funding cutoff and the end of CIA reporting—were *not* linked, as Harrelson asserted. To the contrary, the DRE/AMSPELL received full CIA funding for almost a year, a period for which no monthly reports are available.

See "Memorandum for T. Jeremy Gunn, ARRB," From: J. Barry Harrelson, Subject; Monthly Operational Reports for the DRE, January 20, 1998.

Joannides as recipient of Career Intelligence Medal: Morley Vaughn Index, 148, submitted by the CIA, November 15, 2005, in *Morley v. CIA,* Federal District Court, Washington, DC, Case 1:03-cv-02545-RJL-DAR, Memorandum re: Career Intelligence Medal for Joannides, March 20, 1981, 102. As of September 2007, the memo on Joannides's medal remains "Denied in Full" by the CIA.

Joannides obituary: *Washington Post,* March 14, 1990, B5.

Oswald spoke of hijacking a plane and toyed with rifle: McMillan, *Marina and Lee,* 443–447.

"The last I heard was that he had left the city": Quoted in "Oswald Tried to Spy On Anti-Castro Exile Group," *Miami Herald,* November 23, 1963, 1.

Oswald arrives in Mexico City: Posner, *Case Closed,* 181; Summers, *Not in Your Lifetime,* 261–263.

Checked into a hotel: MCJFK Chronology, 74–75.

Warren Commission finding that bothered Win: *Warren Report,* 777.

Win on Oswald's visit: *ICTL,* 186.

Photographic surveillance expanded on day of Oswald's arrival: Dispatch: To Chief KURIOT, from Chief of Station Mexico City, Operational Monthly Report, 1–30 Sept. 1963, October 18, 1963, 5 pp., Russ Holmes Work file, CIA/JFK RIF 104-10414-10371 (hereafter September 1963 LIERODE Report).

The device triggered by persons entering and leaving: Dispatch: From Chief of Station to Chief KURIOT: Aquatic/use of VLS-2 Trigger at the LIERODE basehouse, November 7, 1963, HSCA Segregated Collection.

Stanley Watson on Oswald photo: *LHR,* 97.

Piccolo saw photos of Oswald: *LHR,* 102–103.

Oswald "was just another blip": Phillips, *Night Watch,* 139.

"Yes there was a photographic coverage of the Cuban embassy": Phillips, HSCA Testimony, November 28, 1976, 67.

Win told Washington that a second camera with an automatic shutter was installed on the day of Oswald's arrival: September 1963 LIERODE Report.

"The underlying problem," according to CIA general counsel Scott Breckinridge: Memorandum for the Record, "Manuscript of former COS, Mexico City," October 6, 1978, JFK/CIA RIF 104-10126-10012.

Duran's explanation of "in-transit" visa: The transcripts of the intercepted conversations can be found in a Memorandum for the Record, Intercepts from the Soviet and Cuban Embassies in Mexico City, from David W. Slawson, April 21, 1964, JFK/CIA RIF 104-100054-100227 (hereafter Intercepts from the Soviet and Cuban Embassies).

Goodpasture on daily delivery of LIENVOY transcripts: GD, Part I, 94–95.

CIA officials "hot for" Oswald transcript: "CIA Withheld Details on Oswald Report," *Washington Post,* November 26, 1976, A1 (hereafter CIA Withheld Details, WP).

"Is it possible to identify?": *LHR,* 125.

Chronology of Oswald phone calls: Intercepts from the Soviet and Cuban Embassies; *LHR,* 117.

Kostikov activities in Mexico: One CIA document identified Kostikov as a fluent Spanish speaker, born in 1933, who arrived in Mexico City as vice consul in September 1961. Memo, Valeriy Vladimorovich Kostikov, CIA/JFK RIF 104-10050-10151. In December 1963, Deputy Director Dick Helms asked Win for the station's personality file on Kostikov, stating there was "little in HQS file on KOSTIKOV." Cited MCJFK Chronology, 55.

Oswald's call marked "urgent" and delivered within fifteen minutes: *LHR,* 126.

"I am certain that the Oswald call came to our attention from the Soviet line": Memo, "Background on Mexico Station Support Assets," from Anne Goodpasture for John Leader, IG Staff, February 10, 1977, 9–10, JFK/CIA RIF 104-10050-10005.

The duplicate tape, or "dupe," as she called it, went into the files: Goodpasture interview, May 2, 2005.

Tarasoff connected Oswald's October 1 call to the Soviets with September 29 call: *LHR,* 85.

"terrible, hardly recognizable Russian": Intercepts from the Soviet and Cuban Embassies.

Phillips's inconsistent accounts: They are found in *Night Watch,* 139; in "CIA Withheld Details," WP, November 26, 1976; in Phillips HSCA Testimony, November 27, 1976; and Phillips HSCA Testimony, April 25, 1978.

Sprague describes Phillips as slithery: Phillips HSCA Testimony, Nov. 27, 1976, 92.

Phillips said he "exaggerated" his involvement: Phillips HSCA Testimony, April 25, 1978, 59.

Phillips's mea culpa: "After this whole thing was over": Phillips HSCA Testimony, November 27, 1976, 105.

Crozier told the HSCA that Phillips used the name "Maurice Bishop": Memorandum, "Addendum to Memorandum of January 16, 1978 re CROZIER interview," Feb. 4, 1978, HSCA/CIA 180-10077-10021. "When first asked about the names, Crozier said he believed but wasn't certain, that Bishop was the name used by David Phillips." Two days later, the HSCA contacted Crozier again. "At this time Crozier said he was now almost certain that David Phillips had used the name Maurice Bishop."

Antonio Veciana's story: Fonzi, *Last Investigation*, 126–139; Summers, *Not in Your Lifetime*, 250–253; Veciana interview, February 2007.

Oswald's visit to Cubans "escalated the importance": Phillips HSCA Testimony, November 27, 1976, 88–89.

Goodpasture on "the dupe" and how Win squirreled it away: Goodpasture interview, May 2–3, 2005; GD, Part I, 147.

Goodpasture looks for Oswald photo: HSCA interview of Anne Goodpasture, November 20, 1978, Afternoon Session, 4–5.

Phillips on "Craig's" draft of Oswald cable: Phillips, *Night Watch*, 139–140.

Phillips admits he approved the cable: Phillips HSCA Testimony, November 27, 1976, 64. There is some controversy about whether Phillips was actually in Mexico City at the time he signed off on the cable. Two CIA records account for Phillips's whereabouts at this time. Cable DIR-WAVE, "Arrival of David Phillips," October 4, 1963, JFK/CIA RIF 104-10100-10134, informed the Miami Station that Phillips will "arrive 7 October . . . for two days consultation." A cable, DIR-MEXI, Re: Mexi TDY visit, October 9, 1963, JFK/CIA RIF 104-10100-10160, did not pinpoint Phillips's whereabouts but expressed regret that Phillips's "tight schedule at headquarters" had prevented discussion of an unidentified operation. Together these records suggest Phillips was in Mexico City until October 4, then went to headquarters in Langley, then to Miami, and returned to Mexico on October 9, 1963. See also Newman, *Oswald and the CIA,* 373. Thus Phillips could have signed off on a draft of a query about Oswald in Mexico City on October 2, 3, or 4.

October 8, 1963, cable on Oswald: Cable, MEXI to DIR, October 9, 1963, HSCA CIA Segregated Collection, JFK/CIA RIF 104-10052-10062. The cable was sent from Mexico on October 8 but arrived in CIA offices on October 9.

"Do you have any explanation as to why that would be omitted?": Phillips HSCA interview, November 27, 1976, 73.

"a grievous omission": Phillips HSCA interview, November 27, 1976, 97.

"No one else would dare make that decision without Win Scott's knowing about it": Phillips HSCA interview, November 27, 1976, 97–98.

CHAPTER 15. OUT OF THE LOOP

Michael Scott's memories of the fighting dogs: Letter to author, September 25, 2005.

Karamessines biography: Lawrence Stern, *The Wrong Horse: The Politics of Intervention and the Failure of American Diplomacy,* 44. Interview with Elias Demetracopoulous, retired Greek journalist who knew Karamessines.

Win acquainted with Karamessines: They had lunch on April 20, 1950, according to Win's calendar.

Karamessines passed on what the headquarters purported to know about Lee Oswald . . . "had a clearly maturing effect": Cable DIR to MEXI, October 10, 1963, in MEXI DISPATCHES, CIA Segregated Collection, Box 90, Reel 46 (hereafter DIR 74830).

Bustos's role in the drafting of the October 10 cable: LHR, 155, in which Bustos is identified by the pseudonym "Elsie Scaleti."

Mission of SIG: Extracts from CI History.

Birch O'Neal as chief of CI/SIG: Extracts from CI History.

O'Neal as Guatemala station chief: CIA in Guatemala, 134; GD, Part I, 34.

Swenson on role of SAS/CI: HSCA Researcher notes, August 21, 1978, JFK/CIA Segregated Collection, 180-10143-10157.

Karamessines on October 10 cable: Testimony of Thomas Karamessines to Senate Select Committee to Study Governmental Operations with Respect to Intelligence Activities, April 14, 1976, 4–5, JFK-SSCSGO RIF 157-10014-10002.

Whitten on the October 10 cable: Deposition of John Scelso, 40–43, HSCA Security Classified Testimony, May 18, 1978, JFK/CIA RIF 180-10131-10330 (hereafter Whitten HSCA Testimony). "Scelso" was Whitten's pseudonym. Charlotte Bustos suggested that Karamessines was informed because Oswald's unusual biography deserved scrutiny from the top. "This was one way of informing him and getting attention at the higher level," she said. See LHR, 155.

Jane Roman interview: John Newman and I interviewed Jane Roman in her home on November 2, 1995. The two FBI documents discussed were the September 10, 1963, report of Dallas FBI agent James Hosty, who was monitoring Oswald's movements for the bureau and a September 24, 1963, letterhead memorandum from the bureau summarizing Oswald's recent political activities including his arrest in connection with an altercation with the Cuban Student Directorate in New Orleans. The CIA routing slips on the FBI reports are reproduced in Newman, Oswald and the CIA, 501–503. The tape of the Roman interview is available in the JFK Assassination Records Collection, College Park, Maryland. All quotations come from the transcript of the tape prepared by the author.

Hood on October 10, 1963, cable; "I don't find anything smelly": Hood interview, January 2007.

Goodpasture explained "the caller from the Cub[an] Emb[assy] was unidentified": Goodpasture made this observation in her chronological summation of the station's Oswald file. MCJFK Chronology, 88.

Ray Rocca says "there was someone down there who wanted to go to Cuba": Deposition of Raymond G. Rocca, July 18, 1978, 83, JFK/HSCA/Security Classified Testimony, 180-10110-10004.

On October 16, 1963, Win sent a memo: From: Winston Scott to the ambassador, "Lee Oswald/Contact with Soviet Embassy, 10/16/63," JFK/CIA RIF 104-10195-10400. In her 1998 sworn deposition to the Assassination Records Review Board, Goodpasture was asked, "Would it be a reasonable assumption that by the time of the October 16th memorandum, someone had gone back and examined intercepts from the 28th?" She replied, "I should think it would." GD, Part I, 130.

"Information about Oswald that probably should have been reported": When Goodpasture was asked by the ARRB if the information about Oswald's visit to the

Cuban consulate should have been relayed to headquarters, she conceded, "Yes." GD, Part I, 130.

Win asked headquarters to send Oswald photo: Cable, Attempts of Oswald wife to return to U.S., October 16, 1963, MEXI DISPATCHES.

Roman writes, "We will forward them to our representatives": Classified Message, To: Department of the Navy, From CIA, Subject: Lee Henry Oswald, October 23, 1963, JFK/HSCA Segregated Collection 104-10067-10069

"They refused to send us a photograph": GD, Part II, 9–10.

Win on "contact by an English-speaking man with the Soviet Embassy": MEXI DISPATCHES, "Monthly Operational Report for Project LIENVOY," November 7, 1963.

"CI operations were frequently conducted": Karalekas, *History of the Central Intelligence Agency,* 47.

"Angleton viewed himself more as a chief of an operational entity"; Angleton's JFK records destroyed: Extracts from CI History.

"At the very best, it [was] not professional": Phillips HSCA interview, November 27, 1976, 96.

Phillips on JFK conspiracy possibilities: Phillips, *Night Watch,* 142.

Phillips on conspiracy involving American intelligence officers: Summers, *Not in Your Lifetime,* 371–372.

CHAPTER 16. "THE EFFECT WAS ELECTRIC"

Win and the kids piled into the car: Interviews with Michael Scott, George Leddy, Gregory Leddy.

Win read a report on foreign businesses in Cuba: MEXI DISPATCHES, HMMA 22524, November 22, 1963, Folder 9, 2 of 2.

He packed up a military identification card: MEXI DISPATCHES, HMMA 22527, November 22, 1963, Folder 9, 2 of 2.

Phillips waiting to hear from a man named Tony Sforza: Cable concerning maritime exfil, JMWAVE-DIR, JFK/CIA RIF 104-10075-10179.

Sforza as "Henry Sloman": In the December 1982 issue of the *Atlantic,* journalist Seymour Hersh wrote, "His cover was impeccable: he was considered by his associates to be a professional gambler and a high-risk smuggler who was directly linked to the Mafia. When Sloman retired, in 1975, he had been inside CIA headquarters in Washington fewer than a dozen times in his career, occasionally meeting high-level officials there on Sunday to avoid the possibility of chance observation by other CIA operatives. He was a fabled figure inside the Agency: there was repeated talk of his participation in "wet ops"—those involving the shedding of blood. He was well known to Helms, who awarded him at least two CIA medals for his undercover exploits, which included other operations—mostly in Southeast Asia—that, Sloman says, were staged expressly on [Secretary of State Henry] Kissinger's orders." His involvement with David Phillips in the assassination of General Rene Schneider is detailed in Peter Kornbluh, ed., *The Pinochet File: A Declassified Dossier on Atrocity and Accountability,* 21–23, 74–76.

Oswald arrived with a package he said contained curtain rods: Posner, *Case Closed,* 224.

Texas was reputedly an inhospitable place: Russo, *Live by the Sword*, 292–293, captures the undercurrent of hostility beneath the warm reception.

"My God, I am hit," Kennedy cried out: *Warren Report*, 50.

"My God. . . . They're going to kill us all!": "The Witness," *Texas Monthly*, November 2003, 120.

Bullet hits the curb: *Warren Report*, 111–116. Posner, *Case Closed*, 324–325, argues that the wounds of bystander James Teague were caused by shrapnel from a shot that hit the limousine, not a missed shot.

Bill Newman lay on the grass: Interview with Bill Newman, November 2006.

On the reaction of bystanders: On this controversial issue, I rely on the survey of witness statements compiled by Marquette University professor John McAdams, a conspiracy skeptic. He concludes that 53.8 percent of witnesses said the shots came from the Book Depository and 33.7 percent from the parking lot area, the so-called grassy knoll, with 4.8 percent saying the shots came from two different directions and 7.7 percent giving other locations. The compilation, while not definitive, shows just how common was the impression of gunfire from two different directions. The compilation and a useful survey of assassination eyewitness testimony are found on McAdams's Web site, http://mcadams.posc.mu.edu/shots.htm.

A policeman and supervisor see Oswald in second-floor cafeteria: McMillan, *Marina and Lee*, 531–532.

Oswald's flight: Posner, *Case Closed*, 273–285.

"I believe it was around lunchtime": GD, Part I, 26.

"The effect . . . was electric": Report, "Oswald's Stay in Mexico," December 13, 1963, 5, JFK/CIA RIF 104-10004-10199.

Jane Roman had been reading reports on Oswald since 1959: Newman, *Oswald and the CIA*, 20–21. Newman notes that the Counterintelligence Liaison office, known as CI/LI, received the initial reports on Oswald's defection in 1959 and that Roman, the chief of that office, "probably" read them.

Egerter controlled access to the Oswald file: CIA official Paul Hartman said "anyone wanting access to that file would have to first get clearance for such access from Betty Egerter or the person and section who restricted it"; Melbourne Paul Hartman HSCA Testimony, October 10, 1978, 11, Security Classified Testimony, HSCA CIA RIF 180-10110-10003 (hereafter Hartman HSCA Testimony).

"You know, there's a 201 file": Hartman HSCA Testimony, 47.

"My first reaction was": GD, Part I, 98–99; GD, Part II, 26.

"That's the man we sent the cable about": Phillips, *Night Watch*, 40.

"He said he had to consult with Washington": Lanuza interview.

Oswald lived in the home of the Soviet foreign minister: Cable DIR-JMWAVE, November 22, 1963, DIR 66782. An unidentified source reported "AMSPELL delegate had radio debate with Lee H. Oswald of Fair Play for Cuba Committee sometime in August 1963. According AMSPELL files, Oswald former U.S. Marine who had traveled Moscow [in 19]59 and turned passport over to American consulate allegedly lived in home Sov[iet] foreign minister for two months."

"One of your guys did it": Haynes Johnson, "Rendezvous with Ruin at the Bay of Pigs," *Washington Post*, April 17, 1981. Johnson was interviewing Williams in the hotel room at the time. Johnson later gave an account of the conversation that suggested Bobby Kennedy made the remark to him. David Talbot reinterviewed Johnson, who said his first account was correct. See Talbot, *Brothers: The Hidden History of the Kennedy Administration*, 9–11, 412.

"Make sure we had no one in Dallas": Helms interview with CBS News correspondent Richard Schlesinger, February 1992.

"I think I brought a tape in": GD, Part I, 147.

Win called J. C. King in Washington: Letter, Win Scott to J. C. King, "regarding permission to give the legal attaché copies of photographs of a certain person," 22 November 1963 JFK/CIA RIF 104-10015-10310 (hereafter Scott Letter to King).

"I felt that it should not be sent out": Goodpasture interview.

Win cabled Washington with word that he had photos: MEXI DISPATCHES, HMMA 22533, "Lee Oswald."

Win asked headquarters for a photo of Oswald: Scott Letter to King.

Tom Mann decided the photographs were important to send to Dallas right away: Scott Letter to King.

FBI agent leaves Mexico City at 10:00 P.M.: MCJFK Chronology, 4–5. Rudd told the Church Committee that he did not recall being aware of a tape recording of Oswald; Church Committee memo, To: Senators Schweiker and Hart, From: Staff, Re: References to FBI review of Tapes of Oswald's October 1, 1963, Mexico City Conversation, March 5, 1975, JFK/SSCIA 157-10014-10168, 3 (hereafter Memo to Senators Schweiker and Hart).

"Enclosed are photos of a person known to you": Scott Letter to King.

Win cabled to say that photos of the man believed to be Oswald were already on their way to Dallas: Cable, MEXI 7019, November 22, 1963.

Washington was a city in a daze: George Lardner, "People Appear Puzzled, Lost as They Wander in the Rain," *Washington Post*, November 24, 1963.

"Pro-Castro Fort Worth Marxist Charged in Kennedy's Assassination": *Washington Post*, November 23, 1963, A1.

Oswald's appearance on radio program: "Suspect Oswald on Aug. 21 Denied Being a Communist," *Washington Post*, November 23, 1962, 12.

"Castro Foe Details Infiltration Effort": *Washington Post*, November 23, 1963, 12.

Johnson meeting with McCone: Memorandum for the Record: "Discussion with President Johnson," November 25, 1963, John McCone Memoranda, Meetings with the President," Box 1, File 23 Nov. 1963–27 Dec. 1963, LBJ Papers. LBJ spent only fifteen minutes with McCone, according to Max Holland, *The Kennedy Assassination Tapes: The White House Conversations of Lyndon B. Johnson Regarding the Assassination, the Warren Commission and the Aftermath*, 68–69.

LBJ dodging reports about a former aide: Holland, *Kennedy Assassination Tapes*, 56.

LBJ facing the prospect that Kennedy might dump him: Holland, *Kennedy Assassination Tapes*, 55.

"Have you established any more about the visit to the Soviet embassy in Mexico in September?": Holland, *Kennedy Assassination Tapes*, 72.

"Inasmuch as the Dallas agents who listened to the tape of the conversation allegedly of Oswald": Cited in Memo to Senators Schweiker and Hart, 3. On page 4 of the memo, the committee reported that Shanklin could not explain Belmont's remark.

Memo about Oswald's life being in danger: Riebling, *Wedge,* 202.

Soviet Russia division checked its records on Valeriy Kostikov: Memo for the Assist. Deputy Director of Plans; from: Acting Chief SR Division: Contact of Lee Oswald with a member of Soviet KGB assassination department, November 23, 1963.

McCone returned to the White House: McCone told LBJ about "the information received from Mexico City." Memorandum for the Record: "Discussion with President Johnson," November 25, 1963, John McCone Memoranda, Meetings with the President, Box 1, File 23 Nov. 1963–27 Dec. 1963, Document 2, LBJ Papers.

All of Kostikov's travel had been previously reported: Cable, MEXI 7024, Regarding Kostikov Travel Outside of Mexico, November 23, 1963. 2 pp., JFK/CIA RIF 104-10015-10125.

Birch O'Neal weighed suggestion to "review all LIENVOY tapes and transcripts since September 27": The cable itself identifies the Counterintelligence Staff as the source of the query. O'Neal is specified as the author in MCJFK Chronology, 6, citing DIR 84886.

Phillips said tapes had been erased: Memo to Senators Schweiker and Hart, 3.

Win relayed three of the transcripts to Washington: MCJFK Chronology, 6–7.

Station's "substantial interest" in Duran: Phillips HSCA Testimony, November 27, 1976, 8.

Duran's affair with Lechuga: Win Scott mentioned the affair to the Warren Commission staffers who visited him in April 1964. Memorandum for the Record on Trip to Mexico City, from W. David Slawson, April 22, 1964, 22–23, CIA Segregated Collection, JFK/CIA RIF 104-10086-10254 (hereafter Slawson Report). See also Newman, *Oswald and the CIA,* 279–282.

"blonde, blue-eyed American": *LHR,* 199.

Win note to Echeverria: Memo: Sylvia Duran, November 23, 1963, JFK/CIA RIF 104-10195-10358.

Win asked Díaz Ordaz to have Gobernacion officers arrest Sylvia Duran: MCJFK Chronology, 6–7.

Win called Díaz Ordaz: MCJFK Chronology, 8.

Lopez Mateos knew about the September 28 call: Cable, MEXI-DIR "Echeverria told COS Duran completely cooperative," JFK/CIA RIF 104-10195-10318.

Whitten called on a nonsecure phone line: Memo for the Record, C/WH/3, November 23, 1963, JFK/CIA RIF 104-10015-10059 (hereafter Whitten Memo for the Record).

Duran arrest as "EXTREMELY SERIOUS MATTER": Cable, Arrest of Sylvia Duran, DIR 84916, November 23, 1963, JFK/CIA RIF 104-10015-10118.

Karamessines speculated "the Cubans were responsible": U.S. Senate, *Final Report of the Select Committee to Study Government Operations with Respect to Intelligence Activities,* 25.

Whitten objected to Karamessines order: Whitten Memo for the Record.

Whitten to Church Committee on Karamessines and war talk "just in the air": Testimony of "John Scelso" to Church Committee, May 7, 1976, 5, JFK/SSCIA 157-100014-10083 (hereafter Whitten Church Committee Testimony).

"At the time we were not sure that Oswald might not have been a Cuban agent": "John Scelso" interview, Whitten HSCA Testimony, 141–142.

Angleton's "vague recollection": Testimony of James J. Angleton to Senate Select Committee on Intelligence, February 6, 1976, 53, JFK/SSCIA 157-10014-10003.

DRE wanted to pin the responsibility for Kennedy's death on Cuba: Interviews with former DRE leaders.

New York Times quoted Bringuier: Peter Kihss, "Career of Suspect Has Been Bizarre," *New York Times*, November 23, 1963.

Miami News reported: Mary Louise Wilkinson, "Suspect Oswald Is Known Here," *Miami News*, November 23, 1963, 1.

The DRE publication on "The Presumed Assassins": DRE records.

Castro on Kennedy's death as "malo noticias": Jean Daniel, "When Castro Heard the News," *New Republic*, December 7, 1963.

"What is behind the assassination of Kennedy?": Castro asked the question in a speech delivered on November 23. The speech was published in the December 1, 1963, issue of *Politica*, the Mexican weekly, under the title "Cuba Ante el Asesinato de Kennedy." An English version appears in E. Martin Schotz, *History Will Not Absolve Us: Orwellian Control, Public Denial and the Murder of President Kennedy*, 53–86.

"How curious! . . . They say he is a Castroite": Schotz, *History Will Not Absolve Us*, 80.

"He could be a CIA or FBI agent": Schotz, *History Will Not Absolve Us*, 80.

Echeverria reported back to Win. . . . "Interrogate forcefully": MCJFK Chronology, 9.

Win informed Mann, who was "very pleased": MEXI 7046.

Echeverria visited Win's office to report on Duran: MEXI 7046. Duran's statement was sent to Washington in MEXI 7105. It is quoted in *LHR*, 190.

Janet and the five kids were watching TV: Gregory Leddy and Michael Scott interviews.

CHAPTER 17. A TRANSPARENT OPERATION

This chapter relies on records from the LBJ Library; the MCJFK Chronology, a 133-page summary of the contents of the Mexico City station's JFK assassination file; and Max Holland's invaluable *Kennedy Assassination Tapes*.

It also benefits from a telephone interview with retired FBI agent Larry Keenan, who also shared an unpublished memoir of the events of 1963.

Johnson feared war: Holland, *Kennedy Assassination Tapes*, 69.

Johnson spent an hour with McCone: Memorandum for the Record: "Discussion with President Johnson," November 25, 1963, John McCone Memoranda, Meetings with the President, Box 1, File 23 Nov. 1963–27 Dec. 1963, Document 2, LBJ Papers. Also cited in Holland, *Kennedy Assassination Tapes*, 82.

"The search for Oswald data on November 22": From "Summary of Relevant Information on Lee Harvey OSWALD at 0700 24 November 1963," JFK/CIA RIF 104-10015-10359.

Win meets with Mann and Manuel Tello: Cable, MEXI-DIR Oswald ordered Rifle, November 24, 1964, JFK/CIA RIF 104-10015-10081.

Duran denied it: Duran said publicly she was not mistreated. But she told close friends about the bruises on her arms and being shaken violently. For example, on December 2, 1963, a North American friend called Luisa Calderon, an employee in the Cuban embassy. "She is ok," Calderon told him, "just some bruises on her arms when they grabbed her very tight." Cited in MCJFK Chronology, 39.

Win came to believe in Oswald-Duran affair: Cable, MEXI-DIR, Subject: Cuba, the [redacted] operation, June 18, 1967. "The fact that Sylvia Duran had sexual intercourse with Lee Harvey Oswald on several occasions when the latter was in Mexico City is probably new but adds little to the Oswald case," Scott wrote. The documentation of the alleged Oswald-Duran affairs is summarized in Newman, *Oswald and the CIA,* 377–391.

Anderson reported what the FBI had learned about the accused assassin: MCJFK Chronology, 13.

Win ordered a name trace on "Alek Hidell": MCJFK Chronology, 18.

Headquarters did not have to worry about Duran's arrest being attributed to the United States: MCJFK Chronology, 13–14.

"I'm a patsy": Summers, *Not in Your Lifetime,* 44. The anticonspiratorial accounts in Posner's *Cased Closed,* Mailer's *Oswald's Tale,* and McMillan's *Marina and Lee* do not mention Oswald's claim that he was a "patsy."

"It is all a plot": MCJFK Chronology, 11.

Hoover speaks with Walter Jenkins: Church Committee, Book V, 33.

Katzenbach to Moyers memo: HSCA Report, Volume 3, 567.

Phillips wanted to refute "the swarm of skeptics": Phillips, *Night Watch,* 140.

Alvarado calls: MCJFK Chronology, 19.

CIA officers picked up Alvarado: MCJFK Chronology, 36.

Win read LIENVOY transcript of Armas-Dorticos phone call: Cable, DIR 85177 to FBI, WH (McGeorge Bundy) and DOS (U. Alexis Johnson), based on MEXI 7068; MCJFK Chronology, 21.

Mann's mounting suspicions: MCJFK Chronology, 22–23, citing MEXI 7072.

"Amb[assador]'s feeling he is not being fully enough informed": MCJFK Chronology, 23.

Headquarters on Alvarado: CIA-White House, FBI, Dept. of State, "Biographic Information on Gilberto Alvarado," November 26, 1963, DIR 85089, JFK/CIA RIF 104-10015-10157. The CIA reported that Alvarado "is a well-known Nicaraguan communist underground member who is also a regular informant of the Nicaraguan Security Service, an officer of which has provided this agency with his reports for over a year."

Win wanted Phillips to question Alvarado: MCJFK Chronology, 23.

Alvarado was lying, "and not very well": Phillips, *Night Watch,* 142.

Phillips asked Alvarado to look at seventeen surveillance photos: Cable, "Alvarado Interview Further Night 26 Nov," MEXI 7098, Russ Holmes Work File, JFK/CIA RIF 104-10434-10094.

"Partial descriptions such as duties, height, skin coloring": MEXI 7098.

Phillips listened to Alvarado's story: MEXI 7069, Mexico 7098.

Mann wanted to arrest Duran again: Cable, CIA to FBI, White House State, Subject, "Suggestions from Ambassador Mann" (DIR 85195), November 27, 1963, JFK/CIA RIF 104-10015-10162.

Helms replied Alvarado's story needed investigation: MCJFK Chronology, 26, citing DIR 85198. Helms reiterates his doubts the next day, November 28. See MCJFK Chronology, 34, citing DIR 85616.

Echeverria called Win about Duran rearrest: Cable: Attn: Knight and Galbond, MEXI-DIR, "Ambassador Mann's Principal Developments of Past 24 Hours," November 27, 1963 (MEXI 7104), JFK/CIA RIF 104-10247-10410. Also in MCJFK Chronology, 28–29.

Mann demanded action: MCJFK Chronology, 28–29, citing MEXI 7104.

Win was less impressed than Phillips with Alvarado's story: MCJFK Chronology, 29, citing MEXI 7107.

Helms told Mann not to expect an immediate response: MCJFK Chronology, 31–32.

Win wanted to turn over Alvarado to the Mexicans: MCJFK Chronology, 34, citing MEXI 7113.

Helms consulted with Birch O'Neal . . . FBI said Alvarado was an agent "under the control" of the agency: Memo, "Lee Harvey Oswald," November 29, 1963, JFK/CIA RIF 104-10054-10279.

Whitten's request to "keep us filled in": MCJFK Chronology 36, citing DIR 85672.

Johnson meets with top advisers to discuss the latest reports from Mexico City; calls Mansfield: Holland, *Kennedy Assassination Tapes*, 119–122.

Hoover sends Keenan, who meets with Win and Mann: Keenan describes the meeting in an unpublished manuscript, which he shared with me, and in an interview, July 5, 2005.

Mann on "the strangest experience of my life": Tom Mann interview with Dick Russell, July 5, 1992, courtesy of Dick Russell.

Gutiérrez Barrios emerged from the Alvarado interrogation at 11:30 that morning: MCJFK Chronology, 37, citing MEXI 7127.

Hoover says, "This angle in Mexico is giving us a great deal of trouble": Holland, *Kennedy Assassination Tapes*, 138.

Bobby and Jackie Kennedy's message to Soviets about "domestic opponents": Fursenko and Naftali, *"One Hell of a Gamble,"* 344–345.

Johnson persuades Warren to head the investigation; Warren has tears in his eyes: Holland, *Kennedy Assassination Tapes*, 160, citing Warren's memoirs.

Gutiérrez Barrios on Alvarado's "fantastic lie" and the "best liar I have ever talked to": MCJFK Chronology, 38, citing MEXI 7156.

Alvarado's handler from the Nicaraguan intelligence service arrived; Gutiérrez Barrios called Win to say Alvarado had recanted: MCJFK Chronology, 39, citing MEXI 7168.

Alvarado had made clear in his first conversation that he hated Castro: Cable, MEXI-DIR, Interview of Alvarado, November 26, 1963 (MEXI 7069) JFK/CIA RIF 104-10195-10213. The coordinating officer responsible for the cable was "Michael Choaden," one of Phillips's many pseudonyms.

Alvarado reverted to his original story: MCJFK Chronology, 49, citing MEXI 7289.

"I have a theory, almost a conviction . . . a transparent operation": Phillips, *Night Watch,* 142.

Three CIA reports from the spring of 1963 demonstrate that Alvarado was an informant: See Field Information Report, "Revolutionary Activities of the National Liberation Front in Honduras and Nicaragua," February 22, 1963; HSCA CIA Segregated Collection (microfilm), JFK/CIA RIF 104-10162-1289; Report Cover Sheet "Re: Gilberto Alvarado Ugarte," March 18, 1963, HSCA CIA Segregated Collection, JFK/CIA RIF 104-10069-10225. While the FBI attaché in Nicaragua expressed "strong doubts" about Alvarado's reliability, the CIA reported that its agent in the Nicaraguan intelligence service "thinks highly of this source." Two months later, that agent passed along another report from Alvarado. Field Report, Activities of the National Liberation Front in Costa Rica and Nicaragua, May 16, 1963, HSCA CIA Segregated Collection (microfilm), JFK/CIA RIF 104-10162-10287.

CHAPTER 18. "I SHARE THAT GUILT"

J. C. King's commendation of Win: Dispatch: "We would like to take time out . . ."; from C/WH Division To: COS, Mexico City, December 17, 1963, JFK/CIA RIF 104-10127-10172.

Win put the letter in his safe: Memorandum for Chief Liaison and Oversight Control, from B. Hugh Tovar, "Inventory of Mexico City COS Records," May 5, 1977.

Whitten, brilliant if overbearing: For a profile of Whitten, who went on to a successful second career as a choral singer in Europe, see Jefferson Morley, "The Good Spy," *Washington Monthly,* December 2003.

Whitten's staff of thirty: Whitten HSCA Testimony, 132.

"Angleton was not able to influence . . . the investigation": Testimony of John Scelso to the Church Committee, May 7, 1976, 48 (hereafter Whitten Church Committee Testimony). "Scelso" was Whitten's pseudonym.

"For the first time I learned a myriad of vital facts": Whitten Church Committee Testimony, 10. Whitten told the same story to the HSCA in 1978. Whitten HSCA Testimony, 113–114.

Whitten and the Christmas Eve meeting: Memo for Chief/CI, Chief SR Division, Chief, CI/SI subject: "Inaccuracies and errors in draft of GPFLOOR Report," December 24, 1963, CIA/JFK RIF 104-10019-10020.

"Helms wanted someone to conduct the investigation who was in bed with the FBI": Whitten Church Committee Testimony, 65.

"Jim would prefer to wait the commission out": From Rock to Dick, Subject "We have a problem here for your determination," March 5, 1964, HSCA Segregated Collection, JFK/CIA RIF 104-10423-10190. Whitten was no conspiracy theorist. He always said he believed Oswald acted alone. But he also thought Helms's handling of the JFK assassination investigation was "morally reprehensible." He testified that J. C. King had told him Angleton blocked inquiries into Las Vegas money-laundering operations to protect his Mafia sources; Whitten Church Committee Testimony, 40–41.

"I understand you all have been cleared for Top Secret material": Slawson Report, 22–23.

Two months earlier, Helms had told the commission: From Richard Helms to Lee Rankin, Subject, "Information Developed by CIA on the Activity of Lee Harvey OSWALD in Mexico City 28 September–3 October 1963," January 31, 1964, HSCA CIA Segregated Collection, JFK/CIA RIF 104-10087-10166.

Win's remarks "disclosed immediately how incorrect our previous information had been": Slawson Report, 24.

LIERODE report: Dispatch: To Chief KURIOT, from Chief of Station Mexico City, Operational Monthly Report, 1–30 Sept. 1963, October 18, 1963, 5 pp., Russ Holmes Work file, CIA/JFK RIF 104-10414-10371 (hereafter September 1963 LIERODE Report).

"In my professional opinion, there probably was not a foreign conspiracy": Slawson Report, 26.

Win not shown Oswald letter to the Soviet embassy: Slawson Report, 26.

"A Mexican pepper pot": Slawson Report, 19.

Warren Commission staffers meeting with Echeverria: Slawson Report, 35–39.

Slawson made a chronology of Oswald phone calls: Slawson Report, 45.

Phillips responsible for the CIA's translation: In 1978, Goodpasture told congressional investigators, "I think Dave Phillips had someone do the translation." HSCA interview of Anne Goodpasture, November 20, 1978, 12.

Duran's story changed: The English translation provided to the Warren Commission became Commission Exhibit 2120. The difference between the November 27, 1963, Spanish version of Duran's statement and CE2120 is noted in *LHR*, 190. "Ms. Duran's strong statement 'He never called her back'" was changed to "she does not recall whether or not Oswald later telephoned her at the Consulate number that she [had given] him." The *LHR* authors noted that without the change "the Warren Commission's conclusions would not have seemed as strong."

"The AMLASH Legacy": Anthony and Robbyn Summers, "The Ghosts of November," *Vanity Fair*, November 1993. Attorney James Lesar of Washington who represented Summers in litigation with Phillips shared a copy of his notes on "The AMLASH Legacy."

Win's evaluation of Phillips: Fitness Report, David A. Phillips, August 31, 1964, JFK/CIA RIF 104-10194-1002.

CHAPTER 19. AN ANONYMOUS WARNING

Three Warren commissioners unconvinced by single-bullet theory: Kurtz, *JFK Assassination Debates*, 22.

Russell's doubts stricken from the record: Kurtz, *JFK Assassination Debates*, 22.

Win received report about Elena Garro: MCJFK Chronology, 87. The chain of communication was elaborate. Garro told a friend, Eunice Odio, who told an agency asset known in the files as TICHBORN, who passed the story to Jim Flannery, the chief of covert action for the station. Flannery told Win.

Win heard the story from June Cobb: MCJFK Chronology, 94.

Garro de Paz's story: The CIA cable traffic on the subject is summarized in the MCJFK Chronology, 87–94. See also Newman, *Oswald and the CIA*, 377–391.

Angleton obtains Mary Meyers diary: Burleigh, *A Very Private Woman*, 244–251.

Ben Bradlee's account: Bradlee, *A Good Life*, 265–271.

RFK comments on the Warren Report: Memorandum, Direccion Federal de Seguridad, Secretario de Gobernacion, November 16, 1964. In the original Spanish, the passage reads, "Sobre el Informe Warren, dijo que estaba de acuerdo y creia en la veracidad del mismo, hasta donde fue posible realizar la investigacion." This comes from a package of documents provided by Archivo General de Nacion, the Mexican government archive in Mexico City.

Bobby Kennedy's suspicions in 1964: RFK's private doubts about the Warren Report during this time are detailed in Tallbot, *Brothers,* 299–308.

Elena Garro's story: MEXI 5621 cited in MCJFK Chronology, 92. FBI legal attaché Clark Anderson said Garro's allegations were "without substantiation"; MCJFK Chronology, 95. Garro replied that she had been held against her will for a week by a Mexican security official because she had spoken about the Oswald-Duran affair the day after the assassination. She told Anderson to check the registry of the Hotel Vermont, where she said she was held. On October 13, 1967, Anderson informed Scott that Elena Paz, "housewife from San Luis Potosi," was registered at the Hotel Vermont on November 23, 1963, left on November 24, registered again on November 25, left on November 27, registered again on November 28, and left on November 30. MCJFK Chronology, 98. So at least part of her story seemed to be true.

"What an imagination she has": MCJFK Chronology, 92 citing "Note to Stan W. from COS."

Win clipped articles about Kennedy's assassination: The articles are cited throughout the Mexico City Station Chronology. The Buckley article cited in MCJFK Chronology, 98.

Win cabled headquarters about March 3 news story on "still secret CIA report": MCJFK Chronology, 105. Helms concurred with Win that the cable should remain classified. It would not be fully declassified until the late 1990s.

Win had high blood pressure: Declassified notes of Michael Scott's visit to CIA, April 4, 1998.

Oscar Contreras story: Official, informal confidential letter, cited in MCJFK Chronology, 114.

LIRING revelation about Sylvia Duran: MCJFK Chronology, 116, citing HMMA 32243.

"That Sylvia Duran had sexual intercourse on several occasions with Oswald . . . is probably new but adds little to the Oswald case": HMMA 32243, cited in MCJFK Chronology, 116, citing HMMA 32243. For discussion of this episode, see *LHR,* 196; Newman, *Oswald and the CIA,* 379–386.

"We are going to peel Castro like an onion": Tom Polgar interview, February 2006.

Memo about Cuban "animus" toward Kennedy: Memorandum for the Record, "Possible DRE Animus towards President Kennedy," March 8, 1967, JFK/CIA RIF 104-10181-10117. The memo was written by Calvin Thomas, an operations officer who had worked with the DRE in 1963. He stated that Garrison's allegations that anti-Castro exiles were behind Kennedy's assassination brought to mind a concern that he felt in November 1963. The DRE leaders, he wrote, had exhibited "chagrin and embitterment that President Kennedy had not more forcefully pursued a 'liberation' of Cuba. Whether or not this animus, which could be discerned as occasional signs of anger or of contempt or discouragement might have been translated into a wish for revenge may be better known to other officers who deal with this group after the summer of 1963."

Thomas's memo was forwarded to Phillips's Cuba Operations Group. One COG employee checked the office files and found a letter, dated January 1963, informing Attorney General Bobby Kennedy of the agency's support for the DRE's propaganda and intelligence collection activities along with the warning that "the DRE is not a group under complete agency control" and warning its members might "undertake isolated paramilitary operations without prior notification." This reminder that Oswald's antagonists in the DRE had a record of unauthorized violent action was not entirely reassuring in the context of the JFK assassination. When Thomas's memo finally reached Phillips's attention, he dismissed its "inadequate information and bias." Two other officers familiar with CIA operations in New Orleans were called in, and they also dismissed Thomas's concern. In his original memo Thomas had specifically suggested talking to the officer who handled contacts with the DRE "after the summer of 1963." That was George Joannides, Dick Helms's man in Miami. His views of the DRE and Oswald went unrecorded.

Helms's "book dispatch" on Warren Commission critics: "Countering Criticism of the Warren Report," April 1, 1967, Russ Holmes Work File, JFK/CIA RIF 104-10406-10110. The author of the dispatch is identified as "Chief of WOVIEW"; WO/VIEW was the code name for the Western Hemisphere Division. Bill Broe was the division chief, but the sentiments are clearly Helms's.

Win talked to Marty Underwood about the Cuban airliner incident of November 22, 1963: Letter, Marty Underwood to David H. Marwell, JFK Assassination Records Review Board, August 25, 1997, courtesy of Gus Russo.

"Lund" letter: Letter, "Thomas Lund" to "Willard Curtis," June 14, 1967, Michael Scott FOIA files. JFK researcher Mary Ferrell speculated that "Lund" was Karamessines. The familiar tone of the letter, the discretion with which it was addressed, and the access to intelligence about LIOSAGE lend credence to such an informed guess. "Lund" had to be a very senior figure who had known Win for a long time and had access to the most highly sensitive information.

Win suggests an Oswald file review: Letter, From: Thomas W. Lund, To: Willard, "Letter Referencing Material Being Reviewed by Warren Commission on Lee Harvey Oswald," July 5, 1967, HSCA CIA Segregated Collection, JFK/CIA RIF 104-10147-10376.

Win kept a copy: The "Lund" letter turned up in the material Angleton and John Horton removed from Win's house in April 1971. Memorandum for Chief Liaison and Oversight Control, from B. Hugh Tovar, "Inventory of Mexico City COS Records," May 5, 1977.

Goodpasture's 133-page chronology: In a 2005 interview Goodpasture said she did not recall preparing the document. Angleton's deputy Ray Rocca said, under oath, that Goodpasture was the author of the "wonderful" document. Deposition of Raymond G. Rocca, July 17, 1978, HSCA Security Classified Testimony, JFK HSCA 180-10110-10004.

"The Warren Commission did not do an adequate investigative job": MCJFK Chronology, 97.

Juana Castro's defection: MCSHE, 46; confidential interview.

"Win never trusted anyone": Goodpasture interview, May 2–3, 2005.

Freeman sought control of presidential contacts and was rebuffed: According to Goodpasture, Mann summoned Freeman to Washington for "a private conversation," after which the matter was dropped; MCSHE, 451. I heard one story that Win's meetings with Díaz Ordaz ended only when Win Scott received death threats. I could not confirm the story. Despite the dispute, Win and Freeman remained personal as well as professional friends.

Agee heard Freeman's "expectations" collided with the president's preference for dealing with Scott: Agee, *Inside the Company*, 525.

Station regarded as "classic" by the agency's inspectors: MCSHE, 47, 401. Among the comments: "Extensive support capabilities, which concentrated on the Cuban community, including, a wastebasket trash operation, recruitment of staff officers of the Cuban Embassy, a tap on every telephone line from the Cuban Embassy or official residence by LIFEAT or LIENVOY; photographer coverage of the entrances to the Cuban embassy (LIONION [a new name for what had been LIERODE]); complete passenger lists from LIFIRE of all incoming and outgoing flights by the 45 international airlines making daily connection in Mexico City, delivered three times a week packed in suitcases."

"He was a meticulous man, a taskmaster": Confidential interview.

Díaz Ordaz "would act in most cases in the manner requested": Dispatch, "Operational/LITEMPO-2 Request for Data on Terrorists Transiting Mexico," October 25, 1963, JFK/CIA RIF 104-10516-10061.

Win's story about Díaz Ordaz standing up: Family interviews.

Echeverria and Gutiérrez Barrios move up: Aguayo Quezada, *La Charola,* 300.

Goodpasture on Gutiérrez Barrios and DFS: MCSHE, 38.

Win's daily report to the Mexican president: Ferguson Dempster interview with Michael Scott; Agee, *Inside the Company*, 526.

Life was good at home: Interviews with Michael Scott, Gregory Leddy, and George Leddy.

Mexico City modernizing: Paul Kennedy, "Big Build-Up Is the Big News in Mexico City," *New York Times,* June 13, 1965, 51.

Win arranges for Marty Underwood to meet Luis Echeverria: Underwood described Win as "one of the most politically intelligent persons I have ever met." Underwood's account is found in notes dated April 21, 1966, that he gave to the JFK Assassination Records Review Board. Courtesy of Gus Russo.

Johnson received a rousing welcome: Henry Giniger, "Johnson Arrives in Mexico City and Receives Rousing Welcome," *New York Times,* April 15, 1966, 1.

Anti-U.S. demonstrations: Airgram, Fulton Freeman to Dept. of State, April 15, 1966, "Visit of President and Mrs. Johnson and Party to Mexico," National Security File, Special Head of State Correspondence, Mexico, Presidential Correspondence, Box 38, Part II [2 of 2], Document 15, Enclosure 5, p. 1.

Nothing but praise for the station's security arrangements: MCSHE, 443.

Arrest and conviction of Galan: MCSHE, 233; Aguayo Quezada, *La Charola,* 131.

Win regarded Galan as "prolific and ardent" apologist for Castro: MCJFK Chronology, 95.

Galan trying to form a new political party: MCSHE, 233.

The role of Miguel Nazar: In a February 2006 interview, Nazar described his close working relationship and friendship with Win between 1960 and 1971. Nazar was probably the paid agent known as LITEMPO-12 in CIA cables. Nazar was a key figure in a shadowy security unit called C-47, according to Sergio Aguayos's account of Galan's arrest. Aguayo Quezada, *La Charola*, 128. Goodpasture told the story of Galan's arrest and the role of C-47 in her history of the station, with emphasis on the role of a Mexican official known as LITEMPO-12; MCSHE, 422–423, of Goodpasture's Mexico City Station history. The similarity of the two accounts is strong evidence that Nazar was LITEMPO-12.

Of the country's 45 million people, 40 percent were landless peasants: Director of Intelligence report on Mexico: "The Problems of Progress," National Security File, Country File, Mexico, Box 60, Mexico Cable, Vol. III 3/67–11/67, Folder 2, Doc. 37, LBJ Library.

Incident of Guatemalan rifles: CIA Intelligence Information Cable, September 27, 1966, National Security File, Name File Bowdler Memos, Folder 5, Doc. 34.

Inspectors want more high-level reporting on communists: MCSHE, 444.

Six days and nights to destroy all the records: MCSHE, 56–56.

Dulles visits Mexico in March 1968: Letter, WMS to Allen Dulles, March 14, 1968, Department of Rare Books and Special Collections, Princeton University Library. The dinner arrangements are found in a party log kept by Janet Scott.

"It was 'Mr. Director, yes sir, no sir, Mr. Director' ": Gregory Leddy interview.

Dulles's letter of recommendation for Win: Letter, Allen Dulles to Win Scott, April 21, 1968, and Department of Rare Books and Special Collections, Princeton University Library.

CHAPTER 21. NIGHT OF TLATELOLCO

This chapter relies on U.S. government documents obtained by the National Security Archive's Mexico Project. The documents are available on the archive's Web site: http://www.gwu.edu/~nsarchiv/mexico/ (hereafter NSAMP).

Win singing song about Castro and coming to police station: Gregory Leddy interview.

Freeman calls a meeting on student protest and reports on "diverse means of gauging and influencing student opinion": NSAMP: U.S. Embassy in Mexico, confidential telegram, June 14, 1968, National Archives, RG 59, 1967–69, Pol 13-2 Mex, Box 2341.

Freeman on "very little possibility that [the student protest] will take on critical proportions": Aguayo Quezada, *La Charola*, 133, citing Freeman cable, State 186094, July 23, Pol 13-2 Mex. National Archives.

Demonstration in the Zocalo as "a classic example of the Communists' ability to divert a peaceful demonstration into a major riot": Secret intelligence summary, "Students Stage Major Disorders in Mexico," August 2, 1968, NSAMP.

The diversity of the student movement: Krauze, *MBOP*, 700–705.

Embassy study of forty incidents of student unrest: Airgram, "Review of Student Disturbances in Mexico in Recent Years," August 23, 1968, U.S. Embassy in Mexico, limited official use, National Archives, Record Group 59, 1967–69 Pol 13-2 Mex, Box 2340.

Win says "Office of the Presidency is in a state of considerable agitation": CIA, confidential intelligence information cable, August 8, 1968, NSAMP.

Win on "the present impasse": CIA top secret intelligence review, Mexican Government in Quandary over Student Crisis, August 23, 1968, NSAMP.

"continued agitation would be suppressed": Secret telegram, "After the Presidential Informe," September 1, 1968, U.S. Embassy in Mexico, National Archives, RG 59, 1967–69 Pol 13-2 Mex, Box 2340; secret intelligence summary, "Mexican Government Stalls Student Movement," CIA, September 6, 1968, NSAMP.

"It seemed as though we were trampling all the politicians' torrent of words underfoot": Poniatowska, *Massacre in Mexico,* 53–54.

"Time of infinite hope and delusion": Krauze, *MBOP,* 735.

Troops move into the universities: Rostow memo to the President, September 19, 1968, National Security File, Country File, Mexico, Box 60, Mexico, Memos and Misc. Vol. IV 1/68–10/68, Folder 7, Docs. 65 and 66, LBJ Library. Also Aguayo Quezada, *La Charola,* 135.

Government "not seeking compromise solution": Secret telegram, "Mexican Government Continues Crack Down," September 27, 1968, U.S. Embassy in Mexico, National Archives, RG 59, 1967–69 Pol 13-2 Mex, Box 2340.

"Any estimate, such as this one . . . must take into account the presence of radicals and extremists": Confidential intelligence information cable, "Situation Appraisal: Student Capability to Cause Disruption to the Olympics," CIA Station in Mexico, October 2, 1968, NSAMP.

The rally in Plaza de Las Tres Culturas: Poniatowska, *Massacre in Mexico,* 202–208; Aguayo Quezada, *La Charola,* 135–148.

Luis Gutiérrez Oropeza . . . had posted ten men with guns on the upper floor of the Chihuahua building and given them orders to shoot: Krauze, *MBOP,* 719–720.

Oropeza was the link between Díaz Ordaz and Echeverria: Jorge Casteneda, *Perpetuating Power: How Mexican Presidents Were Chosen,* 17.

"No one could say precisely where the first shots came from": Poniatowska, *Massacre in Mexico,* 203.

Krauze on a "terror operation": Krauze, *MBOP,* 719–720.

The firing went on for more than hour: Krauze, *MBOP,* 719–720.

"The hail of bullets fired at the Chihuahua building": Poniatowska, *Massacre in Mexico,* 235.

"The dead bodies were lying on the pavement": Poniatowska, *Massacre in Mexico,* 209.

Newspaper accounts: Poniatowska, *Massacre in Mexico,* 200–201.

Win filed his first report around midnight: CIA cable to White House Situation Room, October 3, 1968, received 10:04 A.M., "Mexico City Sitrep as of 0000 local time," National Security File, Country File, Mexico, Box 60, Mexico, Memos and Misc. Vol. IV 1/68–10/68, Folder 7, Docs. 69 and 70, LBJ Library.

Win cites "trained observers": Confidential intelligence information cable, Mexico City Sitrep, CIA Station in Mexico, October 4, 1968, NSAMP.

FBI report on Trotskyite students: FBI cable to the President, "Procommunist Student Activities in Mexico," October 5, 1968, 16:58, National Security File, Country File, Mexico, Box 60, Mexico, Memos and Misc. Vol. IV 1/68–10/68, Folder 7, Doc. 71d, LBJ Library.

Díaz Ordaz said the disturbance had been "carefully planned": FBI cable to the President, "Procommunist Student Activities in Mexico," October 5, 1968, 16:58, National Security File, Country File, Mexico, Box 60, Mexico, Memos and Misc. Vol. IV 1/68–10/68, Folder 7, Doc. 71d, LBJ Library.

Diaz Ordaz and Echeverria had tacitly worked together: Casteneda, *Perpetuating Power,* 11.

Rostow's questions for Win: Sam Lewis memo for Walt Rostow, "Mexican Riots," October 9, 1968, National Security File, Country File, Mexico, Box 60, Mexico, Memos and Misc. Vol. IV 1/68–10/68, Folder 7, Docs. 74 and 74a, LBJ Library.

Wallace Stuart on differing accounts of what happened at Tlatelolco: Confidential Letter, "Embassy Reporting during Student Riots," October 18, 1968, U.S. Embassy in Mexico, NSAMP.

Tlatelolco "accented the turbulence of those years": Aguayo Quezada, *La Charola,* 132.

Win note to Echeverria: Letter, Win Scott to Luis Echeverria, Archivo General de Nacion, Galeria 2, Box 2928.

CHAPTER 22. "THE SLUDGE OF SPIES AND KNAVES"

Attendees at the ceremony: Anne Goodpasture interview.

"Win's retirement didn't have anything to do with the events of October 1968": Broe interview. September 6, 2005.

Helms read the citation: Broe interview.

"In the formative years of our Agency": Report of Honor and Merit Awards Board, May 6, 1969.

"I came away . . . happy and with a feeling of freedom": *ICTL,* 221.

"I was happy to get out of the sludge of spies and knaves": *ICTL,* 220.

He recruited Fergie Dempster: Dempster interview with Michael Scott, May 5, 1987.

"Win was loved and admired": Dempster interview with Dick Russell, July 5, 1992.

Tom Mann thought Win was running "his own personal intelligence organization": Mann interview with Dick Russell, June 1990.

DiCoSe took in $60,000 in commissions: Dempster interview with Michael Scott, May 5, 1987.

Dinner party for Gutiérrez Barrios: January 20, 1970, Dinner arrangement book, Scott family memorabilia.

"You could tell he was excited about the business": Gregory Leddy interview.

"It was my first job, and I got paid fifty pesos a week": Michael Scott interview.

Win brooded accountants had taken over the CIA: *ICTL,* 213.

"I have taken a time of illness to try to put together items from my career": Letter, WMS to John Barron, November 25, 1970, Michael Scott collection.

"If a conservative or a member of a conservative group had shot President Kennedy": *ICTL*, 192.

"The good clandestine intelligence officer should live two lives": This and all subsequent quotations come from *ICTL*, 207–212.

Harvey's alcoholism and "special assignments": Stockton, *Flawed Patriot*, 241.

Or was Win thinking of Angleton: Angleton, who claimed to have read Win's manuscript "pretty thoroughly," told congressional investigators that Win "was making a lot of observations about the world of espionage and me in particular." House Select Committee on Assassinations Interview of James Angleton, October 5, 1978, 117, HSCA/ Security Classified Testimony 180-10110-1006. Angleton's name does not appear in the declassified portions of the manuscript.

"Desolate situation" in Angleton's office; Angleton possessed JFK files and RFK autopsy photographs: Extracts from CI History.

Angleton's admirers thought he had outlived his usefulness: Dick Helms said so in *A Look over My Shoulder*, 284. So did Ted Shackley in *Spymaster: My Life in the CIA*, 36.

Sending the manuscript: Letter, Carta Nocturna, December 9, 1970, WMS to John Barron, Scott legal files.

CHAPTER 23. A FALL IN THE GARDEN

Janet threw a party for Win's sixty-second birthday: Scott family dinner log.

Win planned to see Helms to talk about his plans to publish: Notes from Michael Scott's conversation with his mother, April 13, 1995.

Helms prepared to go to court: In his memoirs, President Richard Nixon says that Helms told him in 1971 that he planned a legal challenge against two CIA officers who were writing a book. Nixon said he would support such action. Helms could not have been referring to Win, both because Win did not have a coauthor and because Nixon dated the conversation sometime after June 1971, at which time Win was dead. But if Helms planned such action against the authors, it is reasonable to conclude he would have taken the same course with Win. See Richard Nixon, *RN: The Memoirs of Richard Nixon*, 640.

Barron gave a draft to the CIA: John Horton said this in correspondence with the Assassination Records Review Board in 1994, now found in the JFK Assassination Records Collection. "Barron, the popularizer of intelligence subjects, turned over to headquarters a manuscript Scott had given him. . . . Scott had said nothing of this to the agency."

Phillips had just orchestrated a political assassination: David Phillips's leading role in the assassination of General Rene Schneider in October 1970 is detailed in Peter Kornbluh's *Pinochet File*, 1–78. Kornbluh's account definitively punctures the cover story offered by Phillips and the agency that the White House had "turned off" the idea of kidnapping Schneider a week before the event and that the CIA was shocked and surprised when their local allies had gone ahead with the hit which they hoped would lead to a military coup. The newly declassified records show that within a few weeks of Schneider's murder, top CIA officials expressed worry that one Chilean involved in the murder had a "detailed record of his activities" with the agency. "The CIA did, in fact, pay 'hush' money to those directly responsible for the Schneider assassination—and then covered up that secret payment for thirty years," wrote Kornbluh. To be sure, Phillips told investigators that he thought the suggestion that Schneider be killed was "a bum idea" (Phillips Testimony, July 31, 1975, 34, JFK SSCIA RIF 157-1002-10165). Nonetheless, he assembled a team of "false flaggers" (Phillips Testimony, 43) who, in turn, approached Chilean military officers known to oppose Schneider's determination to let leftist president-elect, Salvatore Allende, take office (Phillips Testimony, 29). Phillips explained that his team "entertained all possibilities, talked to people, said what can you do and looked for people to support. . . . " Phillips offered one group of conspirators $50,000 and "clean" guns to carry out a plot to kidnap Schneider (Phillips Testimony, 30). With the approval of Karamessines, Phillips's agents delivered the guns to the plotters (Phillips Testimony, 41). Schneider's car was ambushed and he was killed (Kornbluh, *Pinochet File,* 28). Helms soon arranged delivery of $35,000 to the CIA's henchmen. Phillips praised his team for "an excellent job of guiding the Chileans to a point today where a military solution is at least an option for them." No military coup took place and Allende took office without incident (Kornbluh, *Pinochet File,* 34–35).

Win's fall in the garden: Gregory Leddy interview.

Ray Leddy's reaction: John Leddy interview.

"I think he's got classified documents at his house" . . . no right to have them: HSCA interview of Anne Goodpasture, 23–24.

"Maybe Scott had something in his safe that might affect the Agency's work": HSCA interview of Richard McGarrah Helms, August 9, 1978, 45–46.

AFTERWORD

Kim Philby: *The Master Spy,* 248–256.

Ray Leddy: *Washington Post,* March 10, 1976.

Lopez Mateos: "Adolfo Lopez Mateos, President of Mexico from '58 to '64, Dies," *New York Times,* September 23, 1969, 47.

Díaz Ordaz: "Díaz Ordaz, Ex-Mexican President Who Put Down Student Riots, Dies," *New York Times,* July 16, 1979, D7; John C. Fredriksen, "Díaz Ordaz, Gustavo," *Biographical Dictionary of Modern World Leaders: 1992 to the Present* (New York: Facts on File, 2003).

Gutiérrez Barrios: "Fernando Gutiérrez, 73, Head of the Secret Police in Mexico," *New York Times,* November 1, 2000, B14.

Luis Echeverria charges dismissed and reinstated: "Mexico Court Restores Warrant for Ex-President," *Washington Post,* November 30, 2006, A15.

Angleton on JFK: Burleigh, *A Very Private Woman,* 296.

Angleton in retirement: Mangold, *Cold Warrior,* 317.

Phillips founded the Association of Foreign Intelligence Officers: Phillips, *Night Watch,* 285.

Phillips comment to Kevin Walsh: Summers, *Not in Your Lifetime,* 372.

Phillips death: "David Atlee Phillips Dead at 65; Ex-Agency Was Advocate of CIA," *New York Times,* July 10, 1988, 24.

Hunt's comment on Phillips and JFK: A. L. Bardach, "E. Howard Hunt Talks," Slate, October 6, 2004, http://www.slate.com/id/2107718/.

Helms forced into retirement in January 1973: Helms tells his version in *A Look over My Shoulder,* 412–413.

"I have not seen anything . . . that in any way changes my conviction that Lee Harvey Oswald assassinated Kennedy": Helms, *A Look over My Shoulder,* 229.

Hartman on Oswald tapes: HSCA Security Classified Testimony of Melbourne Paul Hartman, October 10, 1978, 29.

Destruction order: "ARRB-CIA issues: Win Scott," Mark Zaid interview, July 2007.

Bibliography

ARCHIVAL SOURCES

Achivo General de Nacion (AGN), Mexico, D.F. Galerias 2, 7.

Department of Rare Books and Special Collections, Princeton University Library.

JFK Assassination Records Collection (JFK), National Archives, College Park, Maryland.

Lyndon Baines Johnson Library (LBJ), University of Texas, Austin.

Thomas C. Mann papers, Texas Collection, Baylor University.

MaryFerrell Foundation: www. Maryferrell.org.

Norman Holmes Pearson Papers (NHP), Yale Collection of American Literature, Beinecke Rare Book and Manuscript Library, Yale University.

David Atlee Phillips Papers (DAPP), Library of Congress.

Records of the Directorio Revolucionario Estudiantil (DRE), Cuban Heritage Collection, Richter Library, University of Miami.

Records of the Office of Strategic Services (OSS), National Archives, College Park, Maryland.

Michael Scott Collection (SC).

GOVERNMENT REPORTS

Report of the President's Commission on the Assassination of President Kennedy (Warren Report).

U.S. House of Representatives. *Report of the Select Committee on Assassinations.* 95th Cong., 2nd sess. Report No. 95-1828 (HSCA Report). Washington, DC: Government Printing Office, 1979.

U.S. Senate. *Final Report of the Select Committee to Study Government Operations with Respect to Intelligence Activities.* 94th Cong., 2nd sess. Report No. 94-755 (Church Committee). Washington, DC: Government Printing Office, 1976.

BOOKS

Agee, Philip. *Inside the Company: CIA Diary.* New York: Stone Hill Publishing, 1975.

Aguayo Quezada, Sergio. *La Charola: Una historia de los servicios de inteligencia en Mexico.* Mexico City: Editorial Grijalbo, 2001.

Aldrich, Richard. *The Hidden Hand: British, American and Cold War Secret Intelligence.* London: Overlook Press, 2002.

Andrew, Christopher. *The Sword and the Shield: The Mitrokin Archive and the Secret History of the KGB*. New York: Basic Books, 1999.

Archivo General de Nacion. *Mexico: Un Siglo en Imagenes, 1900–2000*. Mexico City: Direcciones publicaciones y de Difusion, 1999.

Bagley, Tennent H. *Spy Wars: Moles, Mysteries and Deadly Games*. New Haven, CT: Yale University Press, 2007.

Bamford, James. *Body of Secrets: Anatomy of the Ultra-Secret National Security Agency*. New York: Doubleday, 2001.

Barrett, David M. *The CIA and Congress: The Untold Story from Truman to Kennedy*. Lawrence: University Press of Kansas, 2005.

Bethel, Paul D. *The Losers: The Definitive Report, by an Eyewitness, of the Communist Conquest of Cuba and the Soviet Penetration in Latin America*. New Rochelle, NY: Arlington House, 1969.

Bohning, Don. *The Castro Obsession: U.S. Covert Operations against Cuba 1959–1965*. Washington, DC: Potomac Books, 2005.

Bower, Tom. *Red Web*. London: Arrow Books, 1993.

Bringuier, Carlos. *Red Friday*. Chicago: Chas. Hallbert and Company, 1969.

Brown, Anthony Cave. *Treason in the Blood: H. St. John Philby, Kim Philby, and the Spy Case of the Century*. Boston: Houghton Mifflin, 1994.

Burleigh, Nina. *A Very Private Woman: The Life and Unsolved Murder of Presidential Mistress Mary Meyer*. New York: Bantam Books, 1998.

Casteneda, Jorge. *Companero: The Life and Death of Che Guevara*. New York: Knopf, 1997.

———. *Perpetuating Power: How Mexican Presidents Were Chosen*. New York: New Press, 2000.

Caufield, Norman. *Mexican Workers and the State: From the Pofiriato to NAFTA*. Fort Worth: Texas Christian University Press, 1998.

Chang, Laurence, and Peter Kornbluh, eds. *The Cuban Missile Crisis 1962: A National Security Archive Documents Reader*. New York: New Press, 1992.

Corn, David. *Blond Ghost: Ted Shackley and the CIA's Crusades*. New York: Simon and Schuster, 1994.

Davison, Jean. *Oswald's Game*. New York: Norton, 1983.

Elliston, Jon, ed. *Psy-War on Cuba: The Declassified History of U.S. Anti-Castro Propaganda*. Melbourne: Ocean Press, 1999.

Epstein, Edward Jay. *Deception: The Invisible War between the KGB and the CIA*. New York: Simon and Schuster, 1989.

Escalante, Fabian. *The Secret War: CIA Covert Operations against Cuba 1959–62*. Melbourne: Ocean Press, 1995.

Fonzi, Gaeton. *The Last Investigation*. New York: Thunder's Mouth Press, 1993.

Foreign Relations of the United States of America, 1952–1954, Guatemala. Edited by Susan Holly. Washington, DC: Government Printing Office, 2003.

Foreign Relations of the United States of America, 1961–1963. Vol. 11, *Cuban Missile Crisis and Aftermath*. Edited by Edward C. Keefer, Charles S. Sampson, and Louis J. Smith. Washington, DC: Government Printing Office, 1996.

Franklin, Jane. *Cuba and the United States*. Melbourne: Ocean Press, 1997.

Fursenko, Aleksandr, and Timothy Naftali. *"One Hell of a Gamble": Khrushchev, Castro and Kennedy, 1958–1964.* New York: Norton, 1999.

Gleijeses, Piero. *Shattered Hope: The Guatemalan Revolution and the United States, 1944–1954.* Princeton, NJ: Princeton University Press, 1992.

Grose, Peter. *Gentleman Spy.* Boston: Houghton Mifflin, 1994.

Hamrick, S. J. *Deceiving the Deceivers.* New Haven, CT: Yale University Press, 2004.

Hardway, Dan, and Edwin Lopez. *Oswald, the CIA and Mexico City: The Lopez-Hardway Report (aka the "Lopez Report") 2003 release.* Introduction by Rex Bradford. Ipswich, MA: Mary Ferrell Foundation Press, 2006.

Haynes, John Early, and Harvey Klehr. *Venona: Decoding Soviet Espionage in America.* New Haven, CT: Yale University Press, 1999.

Helms, Richard, with William Hood. *A Look over My Shoulder: A Life in the Central Intelligence Agency.* New York: Random House, 2003.

Hersh, Burton. *The Old Boys: The American Elite and the Origins of the CIA.* New York: Scribner's, 1992.

Holland, Max. *The Kennedy Assassination Tapes: The White House Conversations of Lyndon B. Johnson Regarding the Assassination, the Warren Commission and the Aftermath.* New York: Knopf, 2004.

Hosty, James P. with Thomas Hosty. *Assignment Oswald.* New York: Arcade, 1996.

Hunt, E. Howard. *Give Us This Day: The Inside Story of the CIA and Bay of Pigs Invasion by One of Its Key Organizers.* New Rochelle, NY: Arlington House, 1973.

———. *Undercover: Memoirs of an American Secret Agent.* New York: Putnam's, 1978.

Immerman, Richard H. *The CIA in Guatemala: The Foreign Policy of Intervention.* Austin: University of Texas Press, 1982.

James, Daniel. *Che Guevara: A Biography.* New York: Stein and Day, 1969.

Karalekas, Anne. *The History of the Central Intelligence Agency.* Laguna Park, CA: Aegean Park Press, 1977.

Knightley, Philip. *The Master Spy: The Story of Kim Philby.* New York: Knopf, 1989.

Kornbluh, Peter. *Bay of Pigs Declassified: The Secret CIA Report on the Invasion of Cuba.* New York: New Press, 1998.

———. *The Pinochet File: A Declassified Dossier on Atrocity and Accountability.* New York: New Press, 2003.

Krauze, Enrique. *Mexico Biography of Power: A History of Modern Mexico 1810–1996.* Translated by Hank Heifetz. New York: Harper Perennial, 1998.

Kurtz, Michael L. *The JFK Assassination Debates: Lone Gunman versus Conspiracy.* Lawrence, KS: University Press of Kansas, 2006.

LaFontaine, Ray, and Mary LaFontaine. *Oswald Talked: New Evidence in the JFK Assassination.* Gretna, LA: Pelican, 1995.

Mailer, Norman. *Oswald's Tale: An American Mystery.* New York: Random House, 1995.

Mangold, Tom. *Cold Warrior: James Jesus Angleton; The CIA's Master Spy Hunter.* New York: Simon and Schuster, 1991.

Martin, David. *Wilderness of Mirrors: How the Byzantine Intrigues of the Secret War between the CIA and the KGB Seduced and Devoured Key Agents James Jesus Angleton and William King Harvey.* New York: Harper and Row, 1980.

Maxwell, Ian. *MacGee, MacGill and Me.* Philadelphia: Dorrance, 1968.

———. *My Love*. Philadelphia: Dorrance, 1962.

McMillan, Priscilla Johnson. *Marina and Lee*. New York: Harper and Row, 1977.

Mellen, Joan. *A Farewell to Justice: Jim Garrison, JFK's Assassination and the Case That Should Have Changed History*. Washington, DC: Potomac Books, 2005.

Mosley, Leonard. *Dulles: A Biography of Eleanor, Allen and John Foster Dulles and Their Family Network*. New York: Dial Press, 1978.

Newman, John. *Oswald and the CIA*. New York: Carrol and Graf, 1995.

Newton, Verne W. *The Cambridge Spies: The Untold Story of Maclean, Philby and Burgess in America*. New York: Madison Books, 1991.

Nixon, Richard. *RN: The Memoirs of Richard Nixon*. New York: Touchstone, 1990.

Patterson, Thomas J. *Contesting Castro: The United States and the Triumph of the Cuban Revolution*. New York: Oxford University Press, 1994.

Philby, Kim. *My Silent War: The Autobiography of a Spy*. New York: Modern Library, 2002.

Phillips, David Atlee. *The Carlos Contract: A Novel of International Terrorism*. New York: Macmillan, 1978.

———. *The Night Watch: 25 Years of Peculiar Service*. New York: Atheneum, 1977.

———. *Secret Wars Diary: My Adventures in Combat, Espionage Operations and Covert Action*. Bethesda, MD: Stone Trail Press, 1989.

Poniatowska, Elena. *Massacre in Mexico*. Translated by Helen R. Lane. Introduction by Octavio Paz. Columbia: University of Missouri Press, 1992.

Posner, Gerald. *Case Closed: Lee Harvey Oswald and the Assassination of JFK*. New York: Random House, 1993.

Powers, Thomas. *The Man Who Kept the Secrets*. New York: Pocket Books, 1979.

Prados, John. *The Presidents' Secret Wars: CIA and Pentagon Covert Operations since World War II*. New York: Morrow, 1986.

Quirk, Robert. *Fidel Castro*. New York: Norton, 1993.

Ranelagh, John. *The Agency: The Rise and Decline of the CIA*. New York: Simon and Schuster, 1986.

Reeves, Richard. *President Kennedy: Profile of Power*. New York: Touchstone, 1993.

Riebling, Mark. *Wedge: The Secret War between the FBI and the CIA*. New York: Knopf, 1994.

Robe, Stephen G. *Eisenhower and Latin America: The Foreign Policy of Anti-Communism*. Raleigh: University of North Carolina Press, 1998.

Ros, Enrique. *De Giron a la Crisis de los Cohetes: La Seconda Derrota*. Miami: Universal Editions, 1997.

Russo, Gus. *Live by the Sword: The Secret War against Castro and the Death of JFK*. Baltimore: Bancroft Press, 1998.

Schlesinger, Arthur. *Robert Kennedy and His Times*. New York: Ballantine Books, 1978.

Schlesinger, Stephen, and Stephen Kinzer. *Bitter Fruit: The Story of the American Coup in Guatemala*. Expanded edition. Cambridge, MA: Harvard University, David Rockefeller Center for Latin American Studies, 1999.

Schotz, E. Martin. *History Will Not Absolve Us: Orwellian Control, Public Denial and the Murder of President Kennedy*. Brookline, MA: Kurtz, Ulmer and DeLucia, 1996.

Shackley, Ted. *Spymaster: My Life in the CIA*. Dulles, VA: Potomac Books, 2005.

Smith, Joseph B. *Portrait of a Cold Warrior: Second Thoughts of a Top CIA Spy*. New York: Putnam's, 1976.

Smith, R. Harris. *OSS: The Secret History of America's First Central Intelligence Agency*. Berkeley: University of California Press, 1972.

Stern, Laurence. *The Wrong Horse: The Politics of Intervention and the Failure of American Diplomacy*. New York: Times Books, 1977.

Stockton, Bayard. *Flawed Patriot: The Rise and Fall of CIA Legend Bill Harvey*. Dulles, VA: Potomac Books, 2006.

Suarez, Andres. *Cuba: Castroism and Communism 1959–1966*. Cambridge, MA: MIT Press, 1967.

Summers, Anthony. *Not in Your Lifetime: The Definitive Book on the JFK Assassination*. New York: Marlowe, 1998.

Thomas, Evan. *The Very Best Men, Four Who Dared: The Early Years of the CIA*. New York: Simon and Schuster, 1995.

Thomas, Hugh. *The Cuban Revolution*. New York: Da Capo Press, 1998.

Trevor-Roper, Hugh. *The Philby Affair*. London: William Kimber, 1968.

Waldron, Lamar, with Thom Hartmann. *Ultimate Sacrifice: John and Robert Kennedy, the Plan for a Coup in Cuba and the Murder of JFK*. Updated paperback edition. New York: Carroll and Graf, 2006.

Waller, Maureen. *London 1945: Life in the Debris of War*. New York: St. Martin's Press, 2005.

Warner, Michael. *Office of Strategic Services: America's First Intelligence Agency*. Washington, DC: Government Printing Office, n.d.

Weiner, Tim. *Legacy of Ashes: The History of the CIA*. New York: Doubleday, 2007.

Weisberg, Harold. *Oswald in New Orleans: Case of Conspiracy with the CIA*. New York: Canyon Books, 1967.

West, Nigel. *The Circus: MI5 Operations 1945–1972*. New York: Stein and Day, 1984.

Winks, Robin W. *Cloak and Gown: Scholars in the Secret War 1939–1961*. New York: Morrow, 1987.

Index

surveillance, 161, 162, 181, 182
  photographic, 179
Swenson, Harold, 193

Taft School, Michael at, 3, 7, 276, 284
Tarasoff, Boris, 182, 183, 184, 186, 199, 237
Taylor, Maxwell, 120
Technical Services Division (CIA), 93
Terry, Allen "Beau" (Winston Scott, Jr.),
    8, 28, 52, 60, 78, 277, 291, 298
  visit from, 42–43, 50
Texas School Book Depository, 203,
    204, 240
Thayer, Charles, 58
Thirteenth Department (KGB),
    Kostikov and, 208
TICHBORN, 337
Tiltman, John H., 56
Times of Havana, 104
"Time to Kill, A" (Scott), 7, 135, 136
Tlatelolco housing project, 260
  massacre at, 269, 270, 271, 290
  photo of, 251
  student demonstrations at, 268
Today Show, Fernandez Rocha on, 143
Todd, Carlos, 104
Tolson, Clyde, 54
Trafalgar Square, photo of, 254
Trinchera, on Oswald/Castro, 212
Trouyet, Carlos, 147, 148, 260
Trujillo (Dominican dictator), 68
Truman, Harry S., 38, 54, 59
Tunheim, John, 168

Ukrainian anticommunist forces,
    decimation of, 50
Ulmer, Al, 274
ULTRA program, 25
UNAM. *See* Universidad Nacional
    Autonoma de Mexico
Underwood, Marty, 244, 261, 339
United Fruit Company, 65, 117
Universidad Nacional Autonoma de
    Mexico (UNAM), 88, 121
  anti-Castro students at, 128–129
  protests at, 261

University of Havana, 104, 109, 159
Unsolved Mysteries, Michael and, 14, 73
U.S. Army, OSS and, 25
U.S. Embassy (Mexico City), photo of,
    251
U.S. Information Agency, 113, 121
U.S. Navy, 20, 25

Vance, William, 52
Veciana, Antonio, 185, 314, 319, 320
VENONA, 55, 56
Voice of Liberation, 69

Walker, Edwin, 233
Wallace, George, 133, 234
Walsh, Kevin, 202
Walton, William, 227, 228
War Department, Donovan and, 22
Warren, Earl, 228–229
Warren Commission, 219, 232, 254, 277,
    279, 280, 331, 336
  Angleton and, 233
  conspiracy theories and, 220
  criticism of, 242, 243, 246, 285
  Dulles and, 234
  Duran and, 236
  Helms and, 243
  Mexico City station and, 278, 287
  Oswald travel plans and, 185, 186, 245
  report by, 178, 240, 241, 243, 337
  Win and, 234
War Room, 31, 36, 38, 55, 274
Washington Post, 63, 182, 184, 233
  on Burgess/Maclean, 58
  on Havana shelling, 131
  on Joannides, 177
  on Oswald/assassination, 207
Washington Star, on Cuban missile crisis,
    142, 143
Watson, Stanley, 235, 242, 292
  LIENVOY and, 189
  Oswald photos and, 179–180
werewolf, prospects for, 26, 32, 33
White, Alan, 156, 217, 221
  Alvarado and, 220
  on Goodpasture, 306